CAST OF CHARACTERS

EDITED BY THOMAS VINCIGUERRA

Conversations with Elie Wiesel

Backward Ran Sentences:
The Best of Wolcott Gibbs from The New Yorker

CAST OF CHARACTERS

Wolcott Gibbs, E. B. White, James Thurber,
and the Golden Age of *The New Yorker*

THOMAS VINCIGUERRA

W. W. NORTON & COMPANY
Independent Publishers Since 1923
NEW YORK   LONDON

For Robert Collins Christopher and Judith Crist

CONTENTS

CONTENTS

A CHRISTMAS GREETING
TO THE NEW YORKERS

A cat may look at a king, I'm told,
So perhaps a poet may make so bold
As to send a greeting, on Evergreen,
To the staff of her favorite magazine
And hearty as bells in a country steeple
Say "Glad Noel" to the following people:

To Mr. Ross whom of course I'm able
To feature only as myth, as fable,
As an awesome figure I'll never see,
An editorial deity;
To Mr. Gibbs who with consternation
Surveys my various punctuation;
To Mr. Mosher whom I have yet to
Pay a cherished and certain debt to,
Since he was the first to assure me, sighing,
I might write verse if I kept on trying;
To E. B. White who was one time haughty
Because I envied the Literati,

And would have kept me, I greatly fear,
With "Ivanhoe" and the Young Idear;
To Mr. Thurber, another myth
But one I'm better acquainted with;
And of course to the Lady of my Delight,
The small, superlative Mrs. White.
To them and anyone else I've missed
From a somewhat extemporaneous list,
I send my greetings (as note above)
And my ardent, but perfectly proper, love.

May the New Year bring you a lot of things,
Like pictures funny as Little Kings,
And writers writing hilarious stories
And scribes acquainted with Gotham mores,
For Talk of the Town a thousand thoughts
And never a one about Clever Tots,
(And not too many about their mammas);
Light verse poets who know their commas,
Millions and millions of new subscribers,
A host a fans and a dearth of gibers,
No libel actions with which to cope,
Printers infallible as the Pope;
And for Shouts and Murmurs (oh precious store)
One joke that's never been heard before.

Ladies, gentlemen, all the staff,
Of my Christmas wishes that's only half.
For you all blessings and none sent thinly
Is the holiday hope of

PHYLLIS McGINLEY (SIGNED)
(1934)

CAST OF CHARACTERS

INTRODUCTION

"EITHER COMPETENT OR HORRIBLE"

Τhe tensions of the summer of 1958 were in many ways typical of the ostensible peace that had followed the worst war in human history. In July a bloody coup killed the king, crown prince, and premier of Iraq's pro-Western government, prompting the United States to send troops to Lebanon and Great Britain to do the same in Jordan. Hungary executed its former premier, Imre Nagy, two years after he had been kidnapped during the 1956 revolution. In Cuba, Fidel Castro continued to make inroads against the military government of Fulgencio Batista; within a few months, he would triumph completely and establish the first Communist foothold in the Americas. The space race was well under way, with *Sputnik 3* and *Explorer 1* whirling about just beyond the atmosphere, raising the terrifying specter of orbiting H-bombs.

If there was refuge from these and myriad other concerns, foreign and domestic, it could be found on Fire Island. Local vacationers had tentatively established the first permanent communities on this narrow, fragile barrier beach just south of Long Island in the late 1800s. Now the rhythms of the place were as reliable as the calendar. For nine months of the year, Fire Island was home to a mere handful of hardy souls. During the winter, they might subsist only on fish and potatoes; periodically they were cut off from the rest of the world by the ice that would choke the waters of the Great South Bay. But from Memorial Day to Labor Day, the population swelled to thousands of summer people in search of respite from hot apartments, torpor, and for the men anyway, their workaday routine. For those with money and inclination, it was a temporary semblance of heaven on earth. One writer would rhapsodize,

> I guess I really like it here better than any place in the world, he thought, and for the moment his delight in Fire Island, in this one place where life could be slowed to the almost forgotten tempo of childhood, seemed as much as he could bear. The distance from New York, by train and boat, was only fifty terrestrial miles, but in spirit it was enormous. You ate and slept in the dark, untidy little houses that lay along the dunes between the sea and the bay, but most of your life was spent on the loveliest beach in the East, a narrow, sunny shelf that ran thirty miles along the Atlantic, from Babylon to Quogue, and here you just lay in the sun, and all the staggering complexity of your relations with others, the endless, hopeless bookkeeping of your personal morality with too many people, could be put aside for a little while. It was a state of wonderful irresponsibility, a time in which you belonged to nobody but yourself, on which there were no immediate claims from the world.

The author of this deeply felt passage, Oliver Wolcott Gibbs, was at first glance hardly the rusticating type. Most of his professional life had been spent on the staff of *The New Yorker*, which for much of the literate reading public was the last word in smart, urbane journalism. Founded by Harold Ross thirty-three years before, the weekly magazine, filled with rollicking prose and humorous drawings, quickly came to epitomize cynical, bustling Manhattan. Its writers, artists, and editors had thumbed their noses at Prohibition and roared their way through the last half of the 1920s. Then the existential challenges of the Depression, World War II, and ultimately the Cold War deepened and broadened the magazine's outlook. As worldly as Fire Island was sleepy, *The New Yorker* was now a national and international forum for masterful fiction, factual reporting, penetrating poetry, and astute criticism. Its contributors were university professors and Pulitzer Prize winners, their work setting ever-higher standards for American letters.

Gibbs had been a major part of that effort almost from the beginning. Joining the magazine as a copyreader in 1927, he quickly graduated to writing short comic sketches and line editing. Soon he was dashing off deft short stories and proving so good an editor that he came to specialize in spoofing the work of others. A contributor to the magazine's lead section of humorous true-life vignettes and anecdotes, "The Talk of the Town," he had for some years written "Notes and Comment," the closest thing it had to formal editorials. His Profiles were sly, stilettolike dissections of their unfortunate subjects. So were many of the theater reviews he had composed since inheriting the job of first-string drama critic from Robert Benchley just before the war.

On this particular August night at "The Studio," his Fire Island home, this thin, mustachioed, bespectacled man held before him a palpable reminder of that broad range—an advance copy of a collection of his best pieces, sent to him by his publisher, Henry Holt. The title, *More in Sorrow,* was a curious choice; it had been the headline of Gibbs's review of an obscure 1942 production called *Janie.* But his critique had been as forgettable as its subject ("It is the kind of play about adolescence that, if it recalls your own youth at all, is apt to bring on only a dim embarrassment and perhaps a certain relief that the average man is young just once"), and Gibbs hadn't included it here.

The cover, though, was ideal—a caricature of the worried-looking author drawn by his buddy Charles Addams, whose deliciously ghoulish cartoons were one of *The New Yorker*'s most popular features. Addams had appropriately sketched Gibbs as a lord high executioner in black cape and gloves, surrounded by a medieval-looking crowd that had presumably gathered to watch him cut down his literary victims. In that regard, the contents did not disappoint. Here, for instance, was "Death in the Rumble Seat," a spot-on parody of Ernest Hemingway. ("If you don't know anything about driving cars you are apt to think a driver is good just because he goes fast. This may be very exciting at first, but afterward there is a bad taste in the mouth and the feeling of dishonesty.") Among the Profiles was one of former New York governor Thomas Dewey, twice-defeated Republican nominee for the presidency. As U.S. Attorney for the Southern District of New York, Dewey had shown as much capacity for headline grabbing as for crime busting; Gibbs conveyed his disdain for the man by dwelling on his strange physical features. "His face, on the whole, has a compressed appearance, as though someone had squeezed his head in a vise," he wrote. "Altogether—smallish, neat, and dark—he looks like a Wall Street clerk on his way to work; unlike the late and magnificent Harding, he is a hard man to imagine in a toga."

The pièce de résistance of the new book was "Time . . . Fortune . . . Life . . . Luce," a maliciously gleeful evisceration of Henry R. Luce and his Time Inc. empire. Gibbs's special stroke of wicked editorial genius had been to fold the details of Luce's life and business operations into an over-the-top lampoon of *Time* magazine's bizarre prose style. In pointing up *Time*'s appetite for rumor, bias, and outright sensationalism, Gibbs expertly limned the magazine's patented neologisms and fractured syntax ("Timen have come to bulge to bursting six floors of spiked, shiny Chrysler Building, occupy 150 rooms"), its obsession with trivia ("eat daily, many at famed Cloud Club, over 1,000 eggs, 500 cups of coffee"), and especially its bafflingly inverted narrative form, using a phrase with which he would forever be associated: "Backward ran sentences until reeled the mind." The result was so uproarious that even before it had hit the newsstands, Luce had hit the roof, seething over his public pillorying as an "ambitious, gimlet-eyed, Baby Tycoon." That Luce issue had set a seasonal record, selling three thousand copies more than the one preceding it and making its author a temporary celebrity. "Everyone who read this parody will have echoes of it ringing in his mind when hereafter he sees *Time* doing one of its jobs," crowed Bernard DeVoto. More than that, DeVoto said, Gibbs had performed admirably by taking some of the air out of the self-important, even dangerous Luce brand of journalism: "The sheet has been magnificently laughed at, and in a democracy ridicule is more effective than censorship."

The imminent publication of the new book had cheered Gibbs. He had recently sworn off smoking and drinking, and the change seemed to do him good. And as was true every summer, Fire Island was a source of joy to him. It had furnished material for two of his proudest achievements. (He dismissed the *Time* parody as "a competently executed trick.") The first of these was a series of nine short stories about the island's colorful denizens and doings that had originally appeared under the heading "Season in the Sun" and had formed the basis of an eponymous hit Broadway comedy in 1950. The second was *The Fire Islander,* a weekly newspaper he had founded four years later to chronicle this most precious of locales. Though he had relinquished control a couple of years back, the paper continued to convey local information and intelligence to a grateful community readership.

Nonetheless, in the summer of 1958, the fifty-six-year-old Wolcott Gibbs was not looking forward. He was an alcoholic who had always tended toward depression, and *More in Sorrow* was a poignant reminder of the passage of time. The Luce Profile had come out in 1936, more than twenty years before. All the other pieces in the book similarly dated back a ways. As the author had noted with perverse pride, the collection contained "no references to juvenile delinquency, the atomic bomb, supersonic flight, Miss Marilyn Monroe, or any of the other phenomena peculiar to our times." That was no accident: much to Gibbs's regret, the wisecracking attitude that had driven so much of his work at *The New Yorker* was now largely consigned to the past.

Gibbs hadn't been in *The New Yorker* for three months. The proximate reason was that the theater was dead in the summer. But his current lack of output went beyond seasonal cycles. Save for three stories and a poem, the magazine had published nothing of Gibbs's for the past four years outside of his theater column. He had publicly mused that he might step down even from that. Small wonder that he observed in his introduction to *More in Sorrow*,

> It occurs to me that writers don't change much from the time they are thirty or thereabouts until they are laid away—permanently, I trust. As they grow older, they are apt to perform at somewhat greater length, age being garrulous, and their prose is perhaps a little more ornate, conceivably because they have so much time for the superfluous decoration on their hands; but the essence remains the same. An author is either competent or horrible in the beginning, and he stays that way to the end of his days, unless certain pressures force him into other and shadier occupations, like alcohol or television.

The August 23 issue of *The New Yorker*, now on the stands, was notable for the absence not only of Gibbs but of some of the major voices of its heyday. Harold Ross, the magazine's guiding light—not to mention the nearest thing Gibbs had ever had to a father—was dead almost seven years. The insouciant Robert Benchley had barely outlived the war, dying in November 1945; when he passed on, Gibbs had affectionately observed, "He took up so much room in so many lives." Gibbs's good friend, the temperamental John O'Hara, author of trenchant fiction that was practically synonymous with the magazine, was still very much alive and spent summers near Gibbs at his place in Quogue. But still burning from a *New Yorker* drubbing of his novel *A Rage to Live*, he hadn't published a short story in the magazine since late 1949.

There were other keenly felt lacunae. Nowhere in this issue—glimpsed only once so far this year in the magazine, in fact—was the eternally restless, maniacally funny, incessantly chatty James Thurber. His neuroses and insecurities, much like those of Gibbs, had found expression in innumerable short pieces about hopelessly harried persons menaced by a world with which they could barely cope—persons like his creation Walter Mitty, who had entered the vernacular as shorthand for an archetypal daydreamer. "I wish to Christ I had your grasp of confusion," Gibbs had told him. But Thurber's oeuvre was rather different from Gibbs's. For one thing, he was a cartoonist as well. True, his crude, misshapen draftsmanship conformed to no accepted aesthetic; Dorothy Parker once said that his characters had the "semblance of unbaked cookies." Yet their quirky truth telling held undeniable, almost universal appeal.

"The War Between Men and Women," the title of one of his ongoing series, this one about the battle of the sexes, resonated wherever couples bickered. No one but Thurber could have conjured up a cartoon of a seal peering over a bed's headboard, overlooking an annoyed wife telling her befuddled husband, "All right, have it your way—you heard a seal bark!"

Thurber was a fantasist extraordinaire. His various "Fables for Our Time" imbued their animal subjects with a sharp twentieth-century sensibility and turned the received truths of Aesop and his ilk on their head by demonstrating that nothing in life is certain. His morals were shaggy dog lessons in unconventional wisdom, like "He who hesitates is sometimes saved" or "Early to rise and early to bed makes a male healthy wealthy and dead." Wordplay was his specialty. In a typical entry, "What Do You Mean It *Was* Brillig?" the narrator had to deal with a maid who mispronounces so badly that her references to "cretonnes for the soup" and a relative who passes his "silver-service eliminations" provided him with "the most satisfying flight from reality I have ever known." The year before, Thurber had published *The Wonderful O,* wherein a pirate takes over an island and banishes the letter *O* along with, naturally, such things as love and hope.

Such charm was becoming rare for him. Totally blind for some years,

Thurber had drawn his last cartoon, a self-portrait for the cover of *Time*, back in 1951. (By most accounts, that gesture and the accompanying story about him had buried the Lucean hatchet with *The New Yorker*.) His lack of vision now combined with a natural irascibility and a thyroid condition to make his writing and persona alike just plain ornery, even malicious. More than once, echoing Gibbs, Thurber had complained aloud about *The New Yorker*'s declining acceptance of humor. But then, he had long ago quit the staff of the magazine and transcended its pages, as triumphs like his smash Broadway show *The Male Animal* and the *Time* cover had shown. At the moment he was in London, where a few weeks prior he had been the first American since Mark Twain to sit down to lunch—to be "called to table"—with the editors of *Punch*. Still, Thurber could not escape *The New Yorker*. At the moment, in fact, he was writing a book about Ross, and Gibbs had just fired off a response to one of his several requests for memories and anecdotes.

Also not in the current magazine was E. B. White. Like Thurber, he had done much to set the tone of *The New Yorker*. "It would not be unfair to say that if Ross created the body," declared a former colleague, "Thurber and White are the soul." Like Thurber, he hadn't been on the staff in years. And like Thurber, he had developed a style uniquely his own, one simultaneously simple and elegant that expressed itself in what one admirer called "some of the most moral, living prose produced by hand in the country." White had started innocently enough; his first pieces were bits of light poetry and whimsical, slice-of-life encounters and musings. But soon the quiet young man's supple way with words was finding a regular home in "Notes and Comment" and defining its very form. "I think of White as the conscience of the magazine," Ross said.

White's material melded an understated strength, a deceptively off-hand wryness and an utter lack of pretense that became a model for the rest of *The New Yorker*. When FDR took action at the very start of his administration to stem a bank panic, White didn't weigh in with ponderous thoughts about presidential power or the climate of economic fear.

Instead, he observed, "The town was strangely quiet the first morning of the bank holiday. Every time a liner in the river blew its whistle, people jumped. We had a feeling that if anybody had broken rank and started down the street at a fast trot, the whole town would have followed him, thinking he knew where to go."

"White's prose had almost nothing in common with the kind I had been instructed to turn out by the various men who had been in charge of my early education," said Gibbs, "but I had sense enough to realize it was superior." And perhaps because he was at heart not primarily a jester or satirist but rather an essayist and belletrist, White seemed to have little trouble adjusting his bailiwick to shifting social landscapes. His scope was considerable, his output correspondingly diverse. At various points he had pleaded for world government and against McCarthyism. As opposed to Gibbs, who relied on Fire Island as a genuine escape from his work, White had long used his farm at Allen Cove, Maine, as a sanctuary that freed him to traverse larger issues in the guise of homely wisdom. "Death of a Pig," for instance, while ostensibly about its title subject, was really a poignant reflection on the eternal human condition. He was still doing "Comment" in his own inimitable way; reacting recently to the prospect of the Soviet canine cosmonaut Laika, White wrote, "The Russians, we understand, are planning to send a dog into outer space. The reason is plain enough: The little moon is incomplete without a dog to bay [at] it."

His real passions were to be found in the pieces that he was now infrequently dispatching as "Letter from the East," "Letter from Maine," or "Letter from the North." Here White would ruminate about the state of his affairs or those of the world, often simultaneously. The previous summer, in the course of a single column, he had crafted some two dozen paragraphs that encompassed the persistence of mosquitoes, the evils of nuclear waste and testing, and the grammar and usage lessons taught by his old Cornell English professor William Strunk—these last shortly to form much of a new edition of the soon-to-be-classic writing primer

The Elements of Style. To top things off, White was a beloved author of children's books. By this time, *Charlotte's Web* and *Stuart Little* were as much a part of the juvenile canon as anything by Laura Ingalls Wilder or A. A. Milne. As he closed in on his sixtieth birthday, White was an American literary original. If Thurber had been the first Yankee since Sam Clemens to be called to the *Punch* table, it was because White had declined the honor, out of "panic," some years before.

Gibbs, Thurber, White, and their compatriots had come a long way from their start during what Corey Ford—who had bestowed the moniker "Eustace Tilley" on *The New Yorker*'s top-hatted, Beau Brummell-esque cover mascot—called "the time of laughter." Precisely when that laughter had stopped, or had at best softened to a chuckle, was anyone's guess. The moment might have come with the passing of Benchley; when O'Hara got the news, he said he felt like "the party was over." Perhaps the turning point was the "noiseless flash" that the *New Yorker* writer John Hersey had found in a city called Hiroshima. For Gibbs, it may well have been with the final performance of a quintessential torch singer he had celebrated in "Comment" less than two months before Pearl Harbor:

> Helen Morgan's singing belonged in a speakeasy. The sad, boozy, rakish little songs she sang just fitted the peculiar temper of the period, providing synthetic tears for the synthetic gin. Her death brought back to us all the dark, illicit rooms we used to sit in, full of love for our fellow-lawbreakers, full of large theories about nothing, full of juniper berries and glycerine. We're going to miss "My Bill" and "Can't Help Lovin' That Man of Mine," just as we have long missed all the other things that went with them—the chained and mysterious door, the proprietor reputed to be a celebrated gunman, the beautiful young women so determined not to go home with the men who brought them, the whole sense, in short, of being mixed up in a novel by F. Scott Fitzgerald, another singer of the day, who also died before his time.

Whenever the end might have come for Gibbs's laughter, it came for the rest of him on the Saturday night of August 16, 1958, when he climbed the stairs of The Studio to his bedroom, his copy of *More in Sorrow* close at hand.

———————

"The New Yorker, like New York itself, is always better in the past," wrote the critic Joseph Epstein. "Did the magazine, founded in 1925, have a true heyday? People differ about when this might be. *The New Yorker's* heyday, it frequently turns out, was often their own."

True enough, but few would deny that a certain golden age of the magazine flourished between the two world wars. Much of it was attributable to the three men whom Ross described as his staff "geniuses"—Gibbs, Thurber, and White. Their tripartite editorial unity extended to their personal relationship with Ross, as he had discovered in the summer of 1947 when he took them to dinner. White was so dizzy from the heat that he thought the sidewalk was rising up to attack him. Gibbs found himself in a whirl after a car whizzed past him the wrong way on a one-way street. As for Thurber, he could barely navigate with his impaired vision. When the editor got back to the office, he proudly called out, "I've just been to dinner with three grown men who wouldn't have been able to get back here without me." Thurber agreed. As far as Ross was concerned, they were a "trio about whom he fretted and fussed continually."

By all rights, that trio was really a quartet. Historians of *The New Yorker* point out that more than anyone else it was White's wife, Katharine, one of Ross's earliest hires, who transformed the magazine's poise, especially insofar as its fiction was concerned, from glib, easy, and even smug into deep, revealing, and memorable. Ross probably did not lump her with his other geniuses because as a man's man, he always treated women as a breed apart. Moreover, the self-assured and self-possessed Katharine did not require continual fretting and fussing. Quite the contrary: she was so organized and visionary, said White, "I can't imagine what would have happened to the magazine if she hadn't turned up."

But whatever the exact number and composition of this inner circle—and it included, in addition to those aforementioned, names either famous or obscure like Peter Arno, St. Clair McKelway, Russell Maloney, Alexander Woollcott, Hobart Weekes, and Gustave Lobrano—its members and their associates would go down in magazine history. Rarely has such a group of literary and artistic talent been assembled at a single place at a single time. Rarely would it leave so enduring a mark.

CHAPTER 1

"A LUDICROUS PASTIME"

When, late in his life, James Thurber gathered in book form a series of pieces he had published about Ross and *The New Yorker* in *The Atlantic Monthly,* he titled one chapter "Who Was Harold, What Was He?" He actually spent the entire book trying to answer that question. Like many others, he found his boss so elusive a target that he couldn't quite pin him down. "There were so many different Rosses, conflicting and contradictory," Thurber wrote, "that the task of drawing him in words sometimes appears impossible."

Thurber was right, as the testimony of those who worked with and knew Ross shows. Was he "warm and personal" (Harpo Marx) or possessed of "a general tenor of irritable stupidity alternated with capricious acts of cruelty" (Edmund Wilson)? Was he "a kind person" (Harriet Walden) or someone who "found it hard to be entirely kind to others" (A. J. Liebling)? Was he "a vitally intelligent man" (Janet Flanner) or "the most uncompromising lout, hick, clod and boor I think I have ever met" (David Cort)?

At least a few things about Ross's unlikely swath through the literary establishment are certain. "I am frequently regarded as ignorant, I guess, because I haven't a conventional college education," he told John O'Hara. He acknowledged, too, that his magazine had succeeded against most odds. "*The New Yorker* is pure accident from start to finish," he confided to George Jean Nathan. "I was the luckiest son of a bitch alive when I started it."

And there is ample evidence from a constellation of parties that Ross's more outrageous mannerisms and habits, the ones that have entered the realm of popular anecdote, were bona fide and pervasive. Ross did indeed discourage people from talking to him in the halls, lope through them scowling and preoccupied, exclaim *"Jee-sus!"* in frustration, complain aloud "I am sorely pressed," swear like a sailor, pound out memos with such rapidity that entire sentences had to be X'd out, type "Who he?" or "Bushwah" upon encountering a previously unmentioned name or piece of nonsense, run his fingers through his hair in exasperation, resort to underlings to do the firing for him, and take his leave by muttering, "God bless you."

But in recent years, a more nuanced view of Ross has emerged. Ultimately more revealing than any aspect of his makeup or the role that fate may have played in his success is an understanding of what he set out to do as an editor, and how he did it.

Harold Wallace Ross was born on November 6, 1892, in Aspen, Colorado. From his father, George, who had been a grocer, carpenter, contractor, scrap dealer, and especially, silver miner, he inherited a determined entrepreneurial streak. From his mother, Ida, a former teacher, he received a high regard, even a reverence, for the English language. When the young Harold came home from the classroom, Ida gave him additional books to read and lessons to learn. The instruction made its mark. Decades later, when confronted with copy he regarded as confusing, mangled, or just plain sloppy, he would cry, "God damn it, all I know about English is what I learned in a little red grammar and Jesus Christ, this ain't it!"

Ross was tall, rangy, and rawboned, with a majestic pompadour, a pendulous lower lip and a noticeable gap between his front teeth. More important than his physiognomy was his verbal finickiness, a trait that struck some people, even the punctilious Edmund Wilson, as "annoying or comic." He insisted on direct prose leavened not by adjectives or figures of speech but by the strength of simple structure and composition. "Ross had an unquenchable thirst for clarity," said E. J. Kahn, Jr., "and to slake it one simply had to learn to write better."

That was because Ross was a reporter to his core. By the time he was twenty-five, he was the veteran of a fistful of newspapers—the *Marysville Appeal*, the *Salt Lake Telegram and Tribune*, the *New Orleans Item*, and the *Denver Post* among them. ("If I stayed anywhere more than two weeks, I thought I was in a rut.") He also put in time at the *Atlanta Journal*, where he distinguished himself with his coverage of the Leo Frank case. Though a perfectly respectable practitioner of his trade, Ross was a "tramp"—a working stiff who went from town to town as the jobs became available. If his prose was no better than workmanlike, it had the virtue of being accurate and straightforward and concerned with facts above all.

"I have never been sure just what Ross really thought about facts. All I know is that he loved them," said his successor as editor of *The New Yorker*, William Shawn. "Facts steadied him and comforted him. Facts also amused him. They didn't need to be funny facts—just facts."

When he was in his early twenties, Ross found that his appetite for facts was being ever more whetted both by the rigors of big-time journalism and by the culture of the cities that fostered it. When he joined the *Call & Post* of San Francisco around 1915, the metropolis had largely rebuilt itself from the devastation of the 1906 earthquake. It glittered with business and life, as embodied by the Panama-Pacific International Exposition, the world's fair that opened in the City by the Bay just as he was arriving. Ross's appreciation of the wider world was enhanced when he enlisted in the army's Eighteenth Engineers regiment in World War I. Before long he had joined the staff of *Stars and Stripes* and would eventually become its editor. When not in the fields of France or at the office, he spent what time he could in the cafés and byways of Paris. There he was often joined by several comrades, including Alexander Woollcott—on hiatus from his job as drama critic of *The New York Times*—who with him made up the *S&S* ad hoc editorial board. Sometimes they would discuss what they would do after the war. Ross apparently "liked the idea of a high-class tabloid. Occasionally there was talk of a magazine that would report a city in somewhat the manner they were trying to report the war. There would be humor and personalities and straight descriptive writing, all aimed at an intelligent audience."

It would be a while before Ross reached that goal. Upon his arrival in the United States in the spring of 1919, he began work on the veterans-oriented publications *The Home Sector* and the *American Legion Weekly*. He was now in New York City, the center of the country's cultural and business universe. He had made previous tentative forays into the area's journalism, just as the tinderbox of Europe was about to explode; he had worked briefly at the Hoboken, New Jersey–based *Hudson Observer* and the *Brooklyn Eagle*. Now he and the city alike had grown up. Ross had become a seasoned reporter, writer, and editor, while Gotham was undergoing an unprecedented boom in theater, finance, building, nightlife, and publishing.

The time was right for *The New Yorker*. A magazine that would, as he put it in his prospectus, "be a reflection in word and picture of metropolitan life," with the emphasis on "gaiety, wit and satire," was in line with popular titles like *Vanity Fair, Life,* and *College Humor.* Ross, however, set his sights not on a national audience, as those periodicals did, but on a more concentrated local one. Knowing that advertising is the lifeblood of any magazine, he realized that it made little sense for a New York retailer to try to appeal to readers far outside the metropolitan area. Thus *The New Yorker* (a name coined with apparent effortlessness by a Broadway press agent named John Peter Toohey after much sweating by others) would draw on the commerce, as well as the creative talent and raw material, of the immediate vicinity.

Focusing on New York had another advantage. By deliberately not casting a wide readership net, Ross could eschew the tired, corny, middle-brow tone that infected ostensibly humorous entries like *Judge*—which, by an odd coincidence, he had reluctantly edited for five months in 1924 prior to finally committing to *The New Yorker*. And he sidestepped a tendency toward sameness that often colored even the best national magazines. As Groucho Marx punned in *The Cocoanuts,* which opened on Broadway less than a year after *The New Yorker* debuted, "Remember, there's nothing like Liberty—except *Collier's* and *Saturday Evening Post!*" Ross started *The New Yorker,* White said, "more *in contempt* of what was being published rather than with any notion of how to improve it."

Finally, the content of *The New Yorker* would eschew certain areas in which some of its potential competitors had come to specialize. Ross's new magazine would not delve into muckraking like *Collier's*. It would not engage in outright advocacy and activism like *The Nation*. It would not dwell on political analysis like *The New Republic*. Instead it would play up personalities, light humor, poetry, fiction, and cultural criticism.

Many other magazines offered these features. But *The New Yorker* would, after some experimentation, put them together in one uniquely assembled package. Readers would first be able to answer the question "What shall we do this evening?" by skimming the listings in "Goings On About Town." This would be followed by a more general appraisal of their environs through the collection of musings and random intelligence that Ross called "Notes and Comment." Referred to in shorthand as "Comment," it fell under the rubric of "The Talk of the Town," the balance of which was devoted to largely anecdotal matter. Casual contributions, interspersed as the years went by with serious short stories, solid reportage, and bona fide criticism, would eventually constitute a singular formula.

The New Yorker's main benefactor was Raoul Fleischmann, of the wealthy yeast-making family. Initially convinced to pledge half of the estimated $50,000 start-up—Ross and his wife, Jane Grant, contributed roughly the other half—Fleischmann would over the first three years of the magazine's life spend some $700,000. Even for this exorbitant amount, he would receive ample payback. Reportedly, within just a couple of years of the magazine's founding, he was offered three million dollars for his shares of stock, an offer he turned down.

Ross had met Fleischmann through the poker games of the Algonquin Round Table. The two were never more than ancillary members of that fabled and frequently overestimated group of writers, critics, artists, and all-around literary bons vivants. Still, Ross had a personal connection to the assemblage. He had met Jane during the war via Woollcott, her colleague at *The New York Times*. In 1922—along with Hawley Truax, Woollcott's Hamilton College friend and classmate—the three moved into a cooperative apartment arrangement at 412 and 414 West 47th Street. The quasi-salon quickly became the site of many alcohol-infused revels, card games, and other forms of horseplay. Woollcott, of course, was a mainstay (and in his own mind, grand panjandrum) of the Algonquin set, and into the Rossian orbit he drew its marquee names—Franklin P. Adams, Marc Connelly, George S. Kaufman, Heywood Broun, Robert Benchley, and Dorothy Parker, who dubbed the 412-414 setup "Wit's End."

Accounts of the quips and antics of the Algonquin crowd long ago passed into threadbare legend. Their actual contributions to *The New Yorker* varied in quality and quantity. But their brand of humor proved crucial in giving Ross an example to emulate. And several of them lent their names to an "advisory board" of editors that ran prominently as a masthead of sorts in the front of the new magazine, giving it some badly needed credibility. One was the Barnard College graduate Alice Duer Miller. Best remembered today for *The White Cliffs*, her best-selling wartime love letter to England, Miller was known not only for her books and magazine pieces for *The Saturday Evening Post* but for her determined feminism. A series of satirical poems that she published in the *New-*

York Tribune was collected in 1916 under the title *Are Women People?*, a rallying cry for the suffrage movement. With the passage in 1920 of the Nineteenth Amendment, granting women the right to vote, Miller was in her prime. So Ross agreed to consider her request for an editorial position for her cousin, a young and diffident newspaperman named Oliver Wolcott Gibbs.

Gibbs's extended family was, he admitted, a model of "undeniable respectability, as represented by some three hundred years of comparative solvency, freedom from jail, and legitimacy of descent from one generation to the next." But the clan held no hint of a literary future for him. What it did possess was an undercurrent of diminished fortunes and even tragedy.

He was descended from three remarkable branches. His great-great-great-grandfather, Oliver Wolcott, from whom he inherited his first and middle names, signed the Declaration of Independence and was governor of Connecticut.* Wolcott's son, Oliver Wolcott, Jr.—also a Connecticut governor—served as John Adams's secretary of the treasury and became wealthy by speculating on the early republic's fledgling currency. Gibbs blood entered this political dynasty when George Gibbs III, a powerful shipping magnate, married Oliver Jr.'s daughter Laura. Among their seven children was Francis Sarason Gibbs, whose failed grain exporting business heralded a long family decline. "The Gibbses were always boys for thin chances," observed their most literary-minded scion. "Grandfather Gibbs bought something like 1,000 acres of land out in New Jersey. He was wrong. They are kind of under water."

---

* Gibbs hated his first name so much that he never used it. As for his middle name, he complained that it had been misspelled so often—"Woolcott," "Walcott," "Wooloot," "Wollcott," and "Wilcot" were among the variants—that he wished "the signer for whom I was named had been called Button Gwinnett."

Gibbs's mother, Angelica Singleton Duer, was born in 1878 to a family that had been leaders of New York State since before the Revolution; her maternal grandfather was none other than Martin Van Buren. In 1901 she married Francis's son, a Cornell-educated mechanical and electrical engineer named Lucius Tuckerman Gibbs. At various times Lucius worked for Otis Elevators, American Rheostat, and several mass-transit systems; he also patented heating systems, motors, and running gears. His son, Oliver Wolcott, arrived in 1902, on the Ides of March. Gibbs was born in Manhattan at a time when his father Lucius was moving all over the Northeast.

"I spent considerable segments of my childhood in the states of New York, Vermont, Maine, Pennsylvania, Maryland, Wisconsin, New Jersey, Connecticut, Rhode Island, and Massachusetts, not necessarily in that order," he said. "The reason for all this gadding about was that my father was an inventor, always under the impression that the climate for invention would be a little more favorable in another town."

Lucius's passion was attempting to perfect the electric automobile; at one point he formed a namesake company to manufacture their motors. But amid increasing signs that gasoline, not electricity, would power the horseless carriage, the firm was petitioned into involuntary bankruptcy in 1904. Not long afterward Lucius packed up with Angelica and young Wolcott to take a position with the B&O Railroad in Baltimore. It was there that Gibbs's sister, Angelica, was born in 1908. And it was there that Lucius died of lobar pneumonia on January 22, 1909, at the age of thirty-nine.

A second devastating blow developed: Angelica the mother was an alcoholic. The family whispered that she "went bad," entertaining gentleman callers and otherwise acting in a way unbecoming a widow. And so her brother John and his wife, Aline, took the slender, blond Wolcott and his sister into their home in Altoona, Pennsylvania, a city so heavy with industry that young Angelica would always remember the curtains being filthy from the smoke. Gibbs was so scarred by his dislocation that he was rarely able to bring himself to talk about those painful days. When he attended the opening of Eugene O'Neill's wrenching marathon drama *Long Day's Journey into Night,* he twisted in his aisle seat and tried to face the back of the auditorium. He left abruptly during the second of the play's four acts, curtly explaining later that O'Neill's merciless examination of a family destroyed by a mother's drug addiction and madness had "cut too close."

The alienation that marked Gibbs's childhood increased when, after attending New York City's Horace Mann School and Riverdale Country Day School, he was shunted off to the Hill School in Pottstown, Pennsylvania. The idea was that he would become an engineer like Lucius and his uncle George Gibbs V, a planner and builder of major portions of Grand Central Terminal, Pennsylvania Station, and the New York City subway system. But a regimen of plane and solid geometry, trigonometry, and other loathsome forms of mathematics tormented him. His teachers found him "not industrious" and "erratic" and criticized his "tendency to dream."

His grades ranged from good to dismal; with perverse pride, Gibbs claimed he once got 17½ out of a possible 100 on a geography test because he had mistakenly studied a text on geology. "It proved substantially impossible to teach me anything whatever," he admitted. "As nearly as I can put it, I held strong and wayward opinions on practically every subject in the world, and when I found that they seldom coincided with those forced upon me by my instructors, I simply stopped listening."

He responded with pranks and was eventually caught. "His particular activities," read his 1919 expulsion letter, "consisted of smoking in Alumni Chapel, smoking in a near by [sic] cemetery, where very unworthy behavior was indulged in by his friends and himself, and his complicity in the persecution of younger and less quick-witted boys in his Form." Still, George Gibbs refused to give up on his nephew and in 1920 enrolled him in the Roxbury School (today the Cheshire Academy) in Connecticut. It was, Gibbs said sourly, "beyond question the most efficient of the New England tutoring schools, the ultimate hothouse for forcing talents elsewhere abandoned as dead on the vine." But Gibbs didn't ripen. "I got fed up," he admitted, "and didn't pass those college board [sic] exams."

At the age of eighteen, Gibbs had few prospects. He plugged away at a series of dead-end positions including timekeeper, chauffeur to an eighty-seven-year-old actor, and draftsman "morosely designing plumbing fixtures for the rich." Realizing his aimlessness, his family put him to work on the bottom rung of the Long Island Rail Road, a division of the Pennsylvania ("Pennsy"), to which Uncle George and other relatives had ties.

Based at the Bay Ridge Interchange Yard in southern Brooklyn, Gibbs helped route freight carried on huge barges called car floats across the Upper Bay of New York Harbor, to and from the Pennsy complex at Greenville in southern Jersey City. With the title of brakeman, he worked with the engineers and train crews in coordinating the movement of the rolling stock. By night, they did so with the semaphorelike patterns of swinging lanterns. By day, they used hand signals to cover every possible movement and instruction. Gibbs might indicate "pull" by holding his arms straight out in front of his body. Two taps of his fingertips on each shoulder specified track four. To get someone to drop a load, Gibbs would pat the top of his head twice. So elaborate was all the maneuvering that the brakemen would sometimes put their whole bodies into it, practically jigging in place. Onlookers in adjacent Owl's Head Park would watch these mysterious dances in fascination, occasionally applauding the performers as they went through their motions. Workers from other LIRR yards called Bay Ridge "The Nuthouse."

It was repetitive, dirty work with periodic diversions—like the time a dead cow was found in a boxcar and the crew, unable to get anyone to take responsibility, disposed of it in the harbor. On another occasion, Gibbs was sent to demolish an unused siding, a low-speed section of a main line used for loading and unloading, the storage of rolling stock, and similar nontransportation purposes. It adjoined the property of a local millionaire who kept a pond well stocked with trout. The road gang decided they were in a mood for fresh fish, so they lit a couple of blasting caps, tossed them in, and brought up their lunch. But all together, after four years on the job, Gibbs came to regard the LIRR as "a pretty comic kind of railroad" and the time he spent on it as "utterly wasted."

Alice Duer Miller agreed. "It seemed to her," Gibbs said, "that a member of our family, which is unquestionably one of the most extensive on the Eastern Seaboard, should certainly be more respectably employed than pushing freightcars around." So on "one black afternoon" in 1925, she asked him, "How would you like to be a writer?"

"Not particularly," he replied. After all, he was making a perfectly adequate seventy dollars a week. And except for a few short stories and poems in the Hill literary magazine, he had never published anything in his life. Gibbs thought that "writing was a ludicrous pastime, when I had either the time or energy to think about anything." But Miller insisted and set him up with their wealthy cousin by marriage, Lloyd Carpenter Griscom. A former diplomat, Griscom had bought a couple of Long Island newspapers (why would "always be a secret between himself and his God") and made Gibbs associate editor of one of them, the *East Norwich Enterprise*. "I had simply become a writer," Gibbs realized, "very much against my saner judgment."

The *Enterprise* was a dull, staid weekly that covered the 29,600 dull, staid inhabitants of the villages that made up the town of Oyster Bay on Long Island's North Shore. It was "dedicated to the social activities of the community, which were repetitious, and the interests of the Republican party, which were corrupt beyond belief," said its new associate editor. But Gibbs did well enough in reporting on the usual suburban mélange of minor politics, zoning meetings, accidents, social events, and break-ins that after a year or so, Griscom made him coeditor of the *North Hempstead Record*, responsible for Great Neck and Manhasset. Here he had greater power to print what he wanted, expressing his growing confidence in editorials that were often set off by pointed headlines like "If This Be Bias—" and "Oh, Nonsense!" Gibbs also introduced a new editorial-page feature that was literally entitled "Anybody Can Write a Column." Though it was ostensibly open to any and all readers, it usually fell to Gibbs to fill the space himself. After a bout of appendicitis, he penned this observation:

A LITTLE MURDER NOW AND THEN

A week in bed and we have come to fancy ourselves as something of a connoisseur of detective stories. It is our perverse habit always to identify ourselves with the murderer and in a week we have done away with quite an imposing array of wealthy old ladies, retired majors and beautiful heiresses. There are of course one or two crimes that stand out pleasantly in our memory. There was the time we removed grandfather from any further participation in this troubled adventure by the rather unique device of spreading his razor with anthrax germs. Grandfather had been something of a gay dog, it appeared, and his hand was notoriously unsteady. And, of course, the time we disposed of our invalid wife by cleverly inserting a silenced .44 in our daughter's camera and blandly snapping her into eternity. We utilized, we believe, practically everything except government alcohol.

Of course, we always get caught due to an unfortunate habit of leaving our fingerprints on things. Just the same it was lots of fun while it lasted.

The "we" locution of this and other columns that Gibbs wrote for the *Record* may well have been inspired by the collective voice of "Talk of the Town." At the very least, he became aware of Ross some months hence when he conducted an interview with him (sans byline), undoubtedly at Miller's behest. Describing his subject as "one of America's distinguished literary lights," he affected a tongue-in-cheek attitude:

And what excitement did you have as editor of the *Stars and Stripes* during the war?

He began with a merry twinkle in his eye which goes far to explain why these magazines have been so successful as witty warriors of human existence:

"In the Battle of Soissons, Alexander Wolcott [*sic*], now the play critic of the world, and I were forced to sleep in the back seat of an old Ford while the battle raged. Owing to the amount of space occupied by Mr. Wolcott, I was obliged to hang my legs over the side of the car. In the early dawn I was awakened by the sound of a clicking typewriter, (which seemed strange amid the roar of guns) and looking up I saw an officer's automobile drawn up alongside our bus.

"An officer, evidently of high rank, was busily engaged in writing on a little Corona typewriter which rested on his knees. I immediately jumped up and saluted violently. He finally acknowledged my salute with a nod, and from an officer nearby I learned that this was the famous General Harbored, commander of the Second Division, writing his daily letter to his wife."

Five days later, in Griscom's newest newspaper, the *Nassau Daily Star,* Gibbs ran a front-page account of a huge Ku Klux Klan rally, complete with a hundred-foot-high burning cross, in the South Shore town of Freeport. Gibbs made sure to mention that a process server was present to confront Imperial Wizard Hiram Wesley Evans, who failed to show. It was around this time that Ross agreed to Miller's suggestion that he be given a position. According to Gibbs, she "told Ross he better hire me if he wanted to get to any more parties at her house. So he did."

The job interview was unconventional, to say the least. Following their desultory conversation, Ross agreed to take Gibbs on, "to superimpose grammar as far as possible on genius." Then as they were finishing up, Ross told him, "I don't give a damn what else you do, but for God's sake don't fuck the contributors."

———————

Gibbs's arrival at *The New Yorker* completed the first major phase of Ross's largely gut-driven search for talent and ensured that the magazine would survive. It had been a near thing. *The New Yorker,* White said much later, was "lousy the first year or two," filled with uninspired, warmed-over humor and offering little to differentiate it from the competition that Ross had set out to best. Even toward the end of his life, Ross would cringe at his early, awkward efforts. "You don't want to read that stuff," he told an assistant, Dan Pinck, when he found him browsing through the issues of 1925. "That stuff gives me the shakes whenever I even think about it." Fleischmann was so unhappy with the magazine's lack of subscriptions and overwhelmingly indifferent reception that he came within a hair's breadth of pulling out.

By most accounts, matters began to turn around nine months after the magazine first hit the stands, with the publication in the November 28 issue of "Why We Go to Cabarets: A Post-Debutante Explains." The piece (and its sequel, published two weeks later) was no masterpiece; it was a flip, sassy repudiation of boring debutante balls and their pimply, stiff Social Register escorts, in favor of the forbidden pleasures of speak-easies and night spots. What really brought the article, and *The New Yorker,* to public attention was its author: Ellin Mackay, the daughter of the socially prominent multimillionaire Clarence Mackay (as well as the niece of Alice Duer Miller). In an unforgivable repudiation of her father's station, she had been seen publicly succumbing to the charms of Irving Berlin, whose songwriting fame could not disguise his Jewish origins as Israel Beilin from tsarist Russia. For Mackay to not only be linked to

Berlin, but to proclaim her rejection of her background in the pages of an upstart magazine, proved to be delicious front-page fodder.

In the wake of this cause célèbre, it didn't take long for Ross to acquire a mass of warm bodies who could provide the magazine with its necessary supply of weekly material. Morris Markey, a graceful writer late of the *Daily News* and the *World,* established the "Reporter at Large" genre, publishing in rapid succession a series of deft pieces about such quintessentially New York subjects as Earl Carroll's bathtub scandal, Tammany Hall politics, and the Tombs. A striking Vassar graduate named Lois Long wrote two columns that captured the smart but not smart-alecky tone that Ross envisioned. "On and Off the Avenue" constituted the first serious fashion criticism in the magazine industry, while "Tables for Two," cheekily signed "Lipstick," was a flapper's-eye take on the myriad speakeasies and nightclubs that defined Prohibition-era Manhattan. Robert Benchley's nonsense stories and Dorothy Parker's savage book reviews and toxic poetry helped attract an audience. So did Alexander Woollcott's "Shouts and Murmurs" page of racy gossip and anecdotage.

Still, something was missing. What Ross wanted most fundamentally to pull *The New Yorker* together was an all-encompassing voice that would be informed yet curious, searching yet self-assured, tapping into the heart of the metropolis and, as need be, the wider world. He found that voice with Elwyn Brooks White, his "great path-finder."

White's father, Samuel, was a sometime songwriter and the eventual president of Horace Waters & Co., a Harlem-based piano factory. His mother, Jessie, was concerned mainly with the rearing of her six children in the comfortable Westchester suburb of Mount Vernon. It was there that Elwyn, the youngest, was born on July 11, 1899. "If an unhappy childhood is indispensable for a writer, I am ill-equipped," he wrote. "I missed out on all that and was neither deprived nor unloved." Still, he confessed to "the normal fears and worries of every child"—schoolwork, dark corners, and so on. As the baby of a large family, too, "I was usually in a crowd but often felt lonely and removed." Therefore, "I took to writing early, to assuage my uneasiness and collect my thoughts, and I was a busy writer long before I went into long pants." At the age of eight, young Elwyn began keeping a journal. By the time he was fourteen, he had won one literary prize from the *Woman's Home Companion* and two from *St. Nicholas* magazine. At Mount Vernon High School he was editor of the literary magazine *The Oracle*.

Then came four formative years at Cornell University in upstate Ithaca, New York. Apart from earning the nickname "Andy"—traditionally bestowed upon any student with the surname White, in honor of Cornell's first president, Andrew D. White—he gained a measure of confidence through extracurricular activities. President of Phi Gamma Delta and editor-in-chief of the campus newspaper, the *Cornell Daily Sun*, he was also a member of the Manuscript Club, founded for students and faculty who "wrote for the sake of writing" and read their work aloud to one another.

Another profound influence was William Strunk's course in advanced writing, English 8, and the "little book" the professor wrote to accompany it, *The Elements of Style*. The thin volume was "Strunk's *parvum opus,* his attempt to cut the vast triangle of English rhetoric down to size and write its rules and principles on the head of a pin." Strunk lived by its precepts. "When he delivered his oration on brevity to the class, he leaned forward over his desk, grasped his great coat lapels in his hands, and in a husky, conspiratorial voice said, 'Rule Seventeen. Omit needless words! Omit needless words! Omit needless words!' "

White figured he would be a newspaperman, but circumstances and his own temperament conspired against him. Almost immediately upon graduating from Cornell, he got a job with the United Press but quit after taking the wrong train to cover Senator Philander C. Knox's funeral. He lasted only a few weeks writing press releases for a silk mill. He found a similar publicity job for the American Legion News Service (working, unbeknownst to him, in the same building where Ross also toiled) that was both painful and boring. A stint as a layout man for the Frank Seaman advertising agency proved no better.

What White really wanted to be was not a journalist ("When three or more facts have to be marshaled, I get upset") but a *writer*, with all its romantic notions. "Writing is a secret vice, like self abuse," he admitted. Like many similarly situated aspirants, he kept hope alive by submitting verses and squibs to Christopher Morley's "The Bowling Green" column in the *New York Evening Post* and Franklin P. Adams's "The Conning Tower" in the New York *World*, occasionally being rewarded with their publication. A 1922 cross-country trip he took with a friend in his Model T roadster, affectionately dubbed "Hotspur," offered much to see and describe, generally in colorfully concrete terms. ("Success seems to be imminent. Newspapers are rotten to the core. Filling stations look like hotel lobbies. The air is free.") And a job that he got at the *Seattle Times* when he reached the West Coast yielded, as it did for Gibbs in a quite different situation, a regular column that allowed him to write as he pleased—by turns humorously, musingly, and lyrically. In a bit of free verse, he revealed much about his struggles to put exactly the right words onto paper:

> *Capturing a thought*
> *And hoping to display it in words*
> *Is like capturing a sea gull*
> *And hoping to show its velvet flight*
> *By stuffing it—wings outstretched—*
> *And hanging it in a window*
> *By a thread.*

White first picked up *The New Yorker* in Grand Central Terminal and figured it might be the sort of publication where his thoughts could find a home. His first piece, published in the magazine's tenth issue, was not especially noteworthy; he merely wondered what would happen if a copywriter were assigned to tout the coming of spring. The result, "The Vernal Account," consisted of six squibs, e.g. "Mrs. Vander Regibilt Gives Her Nose This Exquisite Treat: 'I smelled the new 1925 daffodil to-day. It is surely the pot of gold at the end of the rainbow. Now I wouldn't smell anything else.'"

He followed this slim effort three weeks later with a wry casual essay titled "Defense of the Bronx River." A deceptively deprecating homage to the waterway of the title, it ended with what would become his personal trademark of a tiny surprise: "Here is one commuter who wouldn't trade this elegant little river, with its ducks and rapids and pipes and commissions and willows, for the Amazon or the Snohomish or La Platte or the Danube, or the Mississippi, even though the latter does rise in Lake Itaska and flows south to the Gulf of Mexico and is wider." He ended the year with "Child's Play." Its subtitle, "In Which the Author Turns a Glass of Buttermilk into a Personal Triumph," pretty much tells the story. When a waitress in a bustling Childs' restaurant spills some buttermilk onto the narrator's blue serge suit, he turns her mortification into a self-awarded accolade by not only paying the bill but by nobly leaving a twenty-five-cent tip. White later told his brother:

> I discovered a long time ago that writing of the small things of the day, the trivial matters of the heart, the inconsequential but near things of this living, was the only kind of creative work which [sic] I could accomplish with any sincerity or grace. As a reporter, I was a flop, because I always came back laden not with facts about the case, but with a mind full of the little difficulties and amusements I had encountered in my travels. Not till the New Yorker came along did I ever find any means of expressing those impertinences and irrelevancies.

Normally, Ross would have had little patience with a self-confessed flop of a reporter. But one of his editors saw merit in White's prose.

Sometime early in 1926, at this editor's suggestion, Ross invited White to drop by *The New Yorker*'s office at 25 West 45th Street. Awaiting him was Katharine Sergeant Angell.

Hired the previous August as a part-time reader at twenty-five dollars a week, this small, dowdy woman of finely tuned literary tastes quickly proved to be so indispensable that a couple of weeks later she was taken on full time at double the salary. The investment was a bargain. "More than any other editor except Harold Ross himself," said William Shawn, "Katharine White gave *The New Yorker* its shape, and set it on its course." No appreciation of her value to the magazine and its founder could be more vivid than this one, offered by her second husband:

> Ross, though something of a genius, had serious gaps. In Katharine, he found someone who filled them in. No two people were ever more different than Mr. Ross and Mrs. Angell; what he lacked, she had; what she lacked, he had. She complemented him in a way that, in retrospect, seems to me to have been indispensable to the survival of the magazine. . . . She had a natural refinement of manner and speech; Ross mumbled and bellowed and swore. She quickly discovered, in this fumbling and impoverished new weekly, something that fascinated her: its quest for humor, its search for excellence, its involvement with young writers and artists. She enjoyed contact with people; Ross, with certain exceptions, despised it—especially during hours. She was patient and quiet; he was impatient and noisy. Katharine was soon sitting in on art sessions and planning sessions, editing fiction and poetry, cheering and steering authors and artists along the paths they were eager to follow, learning makeup, learning pencil editing, heading the Fiction Department, sharing the personal woes and dilemmas of innumerable contributors and staff people who were in trouble or despair, and, in short, accepting the whole unruly

business of a tottering magazine with the warmth and dedication of a broody hen.

Her antecedents were pillars of the old colonial establishment. The Sergeants had arrived in Branford, Connecticut, not long after the Pilgrims disembarked from the *Mayflower*. Several proved crucial in the formation of what became Princeton University and one helped write the New Jersey state constitution. Rev. John Sergeant, a Yale scholar, was a founder of Stockbridge, Massachusetts; his son Erastus fought in the Battle of Ticonderoga and Shays's Rebellion. Katharine's father, Charles, was an executive of the Boston Elevated Railway.

Born on September 17, 1892, Katharine grew up in "the rich men's town" of Brookline. Many years later she would render this charmed period as "a series of Victorian postcards. A small girl carefully snips a backyard rosebud for the breakfast table; with her sister, trims their Boston schoolgirls' hats with flowers from the shrubbery; paddles in a canoe, in the glorious early-morning light, to pick water lilies on the lake at the foot of Mont Chocorua."

She was not destined to be a Mackay-type debutante. The Sergeant house set great store by the life of the mind. "I was the youngest in a family that read aloud," Katharine recalled. "I was continually listening to books that were 'too old' for me—or, at any rate, ones that would be called too old by today's educators." Katharine wrote, too; like Andy, she received a silver badge for her contributions to *St. Nicholas*. Her education at the proper Miss Winsor's School—where she earned the sobriquet "Goody" for her bright, upright behavior—prepared her for Bryn Mawr. Here she flourished, as Andy would at Cornell. She rose to become editor of both the biweekly magazine *Tipyn O'Bob* (Welsh for "a bit of everything") and the literary annual *The Lantern*, finishing fourth in the seventy-nine-member class of 1914.

Katharine had been engaged throughout her college career to Ernest Angell, a Harvard-educated lawyer, and married him the year after she graduated. Thus began a decade-long search for herself. It was understood that young Bryn Mawr alumnae of that era would become wives and mothers but would also make solid contributions to the professions and establish themselves in a world were traditional gender roles were being upended. The intelligent, determined Katharine was initially stifled in her attempts. She and Ernest moved to Cleveland; while he practiced law, she busied herself with the activities of the Cleveland Playhouse. She also held a couple of jobs, taking a door-to-door survey of the local crippled and handicapped and inspecting factory conditions. These were not steps toward a career, however, especially after Ernest enlisted as a lieutenant to fight in World War I in 1917 and she found herself bringing up their baby daughter, Nancy. Home life became even more central after Ernest returned from France and the couple moved to New York City, the birthplace of their son Roger, a future *New Yorker* star.

"I have and always have had, a personal need for the opportunity to follow my own heart," she said. "One hesitates to use that much overworked and now somewhat ludicrous term 'self-expression'—but if honest, I must admit to a distinct personal ambition that is thwarted and an underlying cause for unhappiness when I cannot do the work of mind, not hands, for which I am best fitted." She found a bit of salvation in 1922, when Ernest represented citizens of Haiti and the Dominican Republic during a Senate investigation of the U.S. occupation of those countries. Dispatched to Hispaniola, he took along Katharine. She put the occasion to good use, filing two perceptive, colorful dispatches for *The New Republic*. But only three years later, after her writer friend Fillmore Hyde said that a new magazine called *The New Yorker*, where he was then working, might be able to use her, did she find her métier—and, as it turned out, White.

Working in concert, Katharine and Ross persuaded the young writer to join the staff on a part-time basis. His first regular contributions were "Newsbreaks," those sharp, bottom-of-the-page rejoinders to flubs and confusing prose found in other publications. White honed them to a fine sparkle. Confronted, for instance, with an advertisement in a Pittsburgh newspaper that declared, "GENT's laundry taken home. Or serve at parties at night," White responded sourly, "Oh, take it home." Over time he grouped these squibs under such enduring headings as "Letters We Never Finished Reading," "Neatest Trick of the Week," and the "Uh Huh Department." And almost immediately he was doing "Talk of the Town" stories and especially "Notes and Comment." White's very first "Comment," from early in 1927, typified his ability to merge whimsy and minor profundity with a bit of poetry:

> Quite well aware that most persons, in their earthly glee, are too forgetful of the heavenly bodies, we are greatly pleased to hear that plans are under way for a star-gazing wing at the Museum of Natural History. There is talk of installing a planetarium, where moon and stars would pursue their course with marvelous intimacy. Nothing, really, is more exciting—and surely New York is the city nearest the sky.

White's contributions, said Thurber, "struck the shining note that Ross had dreamed of striking." They made a deep impression on Thurber: "Until I learned discipline in writing from studying Andy White's stuff, I was a careless, nervous, headlong writer. . . . The precision and clarity of White's writing helped me a lot, slowed me down from the dogtrot of newspaper writing tempo and made me realize a writer turns on his mind, not a faucet."

Thurber was literally in a good position to watch White work that kind of magic. For the first several years of the magazine, as White wrote in "Comment," Thurber wrote and rewrote much of "Talk." They toiled closely together in an office "the size of a hall bedroom," White remembered. "There was just room enough for two men, two typewriters, and a stack of copy paper." Their admiration was mutual.

"His mind was never at rest," said White, "and his pencil was connected to his mind by the best conductive tissue I have ever seen in action. The whole world knows what a funny man he was, but you had to sit next to him day after day to understand the extravagance of his clowning, the wildness and subtlety of his thinking, and the intensity of his interest in others and his sympathy for their dilemmas."

This extraordinary man entered the world on December 8, 1894, in Columbus, Ohio. James was the second of three brothers, and in his literary productivity and originality, he was a classic middle child, always striving to be noticed in that precarious position between eldest hero and youngest dotee. If the family was far from poor, it was decidedly lower middle class. Thurber's father, Charles, was a self-made political operative who kept failing in his runs for elective office. Still, he managed to serve in a series of minor posts, including as a staff member to two Ohio governors and secretary to the mayor of Columbus.

"My father was not a machine man," Thurber said. "He wasn't even a politician, and it's kind of hard to explain why he stayed in politics, but, as they say in the theatre of a bad play, it was a job." It was Thurber's mother, Mary, who truly helped mold him. "I owe practically everything to her, because she was one of the finest comic talents I think I've ever known," he said. "Mame" Fisher was a high-strung and often erratic woman, a frustrated actress who contented herself with mimicry and practical jokes—activities in which her middle son would later engage in abundance.

Thurber's life changed irrevocably in 1901 when, while playing a version of William Tell, his older brother William shot an arrow into his middle brother's eye. Through a series of delays and misunderstandings, the eye was lost and "sympathetic ophthalmia"—effectively a spreading of the attendant infection—attacked the healthy eye. Despite an agonizing series of operations, Thurber would become increasingly blind, finally losing his sight altogether. His degenerative condition would in large part define him for both ill and good, closing him off from much of the world but also bringing out the best of his rich interior existence.

That interior life quickly found creative outlets. Thurber was typing by the time he was seven, the same age at which he began to draw. He was, a classmate at East High School recalled, "a studious and sometimes withdrawn type, a kind of loner. But he wrote much better than the rest of us, and that made the teachers love him. He was, without a doubt, their favorite." Elected president in his senior year, Thurber graduated with honors and enrolled at nearby Ohio State University. There, on the vast fraternity-and-football-conscious campus, the gangly, shy teenager felt overwhelmed. During the 1914–15 academic year, he didn't pass a single course. Botany was a particular bugbear, his semiblindness wreaking havoc in the lab. ("I would put my eye to the microscope and see nothing at all except now and again a nebulous milky substance—a phenomenon of maladjustment.") His compulsory course in military science and tactics was similarly bedeviling. "You are the main trouble with this university," the commandant of the cadet corps would yell at him on the drill field. "Either you're a foot ahead or a foot behind the company."

But eventually, encouraged by his athletic, outgoing friend Elliott Nugent, he blossomed. He was a reporter for the *Ohio State Lantern,* editor of the humor magazine *Sundial,* and a member of the campus theatrical troupe The Strollers. In the classroom, he threw himself into English courses, where he learned a genuine appreciation of fine literature, above all the work of the "great God" Henry James.

Yet in June 1918 he quit Ohio State, having accumulated little more than two-thirds of the credits he needed to graduate and eager to make some contribution to the war effort. His glass eye and flat feet rendered him incapable of soldiering. So he wangled a position as a code clerk for the State Department, joining a training class that included Stephen Vincent Benét. Thurber ended up spending more than a year at the U.S. Embassy in Paris, where the charms of that metropolis captured him just as they had Ross. Paris was, Thurber said, the "City of Light and occasional Darkness, sometimes in the winter rain seeming wrought of monolithic stones, and then, in the days of its wondrous and special pearly light, appearing to float in mid-air like a mirage city in the Empire of the Imagination."

His return to the States in the spring of 1920 began a nearly seven-year period of frustrating journalism and attempts to define himself as a writer. A reporting job at the *Columbus Dispatch* revealed to him the dispiriting experience of covering city hall and similar civic grist. "My anxiety dreams," he said much later, "are still about the *Dispatch,* where I'm with no paper, no pencils, a typewriter that won't work, [editor] Gus [Kuehner] glaring over my shoulder, and the clock frozen at one—with one o'clock the deadline."

For most of 1923, he had a half-page Sunday column, "Credos and Curios," a hodgepodge of anecdotes, observations, and literary allusions. But after the column was canceled, he became so discouraged that he quit to write unpublished short stories and an equally unsuccessful musical. In 1925 he retreated to Paris and jumped ahead of some twenty-five applicants for a job at that city's edition of the *Chicago Tribune* by answering the interview question "By the way, what are you—a poet, a painter, or a novelist?" with the disarming response, "I'm a newspaperman." Thurber filed some fine dispatches about the expatriate life and managed to connect with Isadora Duncan and Rudolph Valentino. But he lived beyond his means, especially when he joined the slim Riviera edition of the *Trib.*

He came back to the United States in June 1926; nearly penniless, he moved into a basement flat in Horatio Street and got a job with the *New-York Evening Post.* He made a bad start: just as White botched his assignment to cover Senator Knox's funeral, so Thurber screwed up covering a fire in Brooklyn by repeatedly taking the wrong subway, elevated trains, and streetcars to get there. Finally, "I stopped off for a minute and bought a *Post* and the story about the fire was all over the front page." Switched from breaking news to features, he did somewhat better, scoring memorable interviews with Thomas Edison and Harry Houdini's widow.

By that time he had become aware of *The New Yorker.* He fired off pieces to the fledgling magazine that came back so quickly that he began to think that the place "must have a rejection machine." He managed to place two short pieces of doggerel—"Street Song" and "Villanelle of Horatio Street, Manhattan"—in the issue of February 26, 1927. But these unremarkable jottings were hardly indicative of his strengths. His wife, Althea, suspecting he was spending too much time on his efforts, urged him to spend no more than forty-five minutes composing his pieces. Thurber did so and found his voice with "An American Romance," about a nondescript man whose entrapment in the revolving door of a department store makes him an overnight sensation, in the pole-sitting and goldfish-swallowing mode of the day. Ross hired him not long afterward, thanks in large part to his passing acquaintance with White. By an extraordinary coincidence, Thurber had met White's sister, Lillian, on his second passage to France. She had mentioned the early, tentative success of her brother with *The New Yorker,* and when Thurber later came calling at Ross's ramshackle offices, it was White for whom he inquired. "I knew Ross was looking for new talent on the small staff," White remembered. "Thurber was looking for another job, and so I arranged for him to meet Ross."

The impulsive editor hired Thurber on the spot, but as an editor, not a writer, a species he regarded as "a dime a dozen." However—at least according to Thurber—it did not take Ross long to downgrade him to a writing position, after he determined where Thurber's interests and strengths lay. "You've been writing," Ross told him. "I don't know how in hell you found time to write. I admit I didn't want you to. I could hit a dozen writers from here with this ash tray. They're undependable, no system, no self-discipline." He finally declared, "All right then, if you're a writer, write! Maybe you've got something to say."

He did indeed. So did Gibbs and White. And under the tutelage of Ross and Katharine, both of whom shared their "visceral abhorrence of anything that suggested the reflexively modish, the cornball or the cliché," they came to constitute the essence of *The New Yorker.*

CHAPTER 2

"INFATUATION WITH PINHEADS"

"Ross gave us all a curious sense of destination," White recalled of the start of *The New Yorker.* "The magazine seemed in motion and headed toward a place worth getting to." Thurber, by contrast, said that Ross "was by no means absolutely sure where he was going in his tremulous flying machine." In the interests of efficiency, the eccentric editor would order, then just as peremptorily scrap, the construction of partitions and phone systems, chains of command and paper flow. He tinkered endlessly with his format and formula, striving for just the right combination of casuals, factual pieces, criticism, and art, all somehow united in their tone and attitude.

Ross similarly tinkered with his charges. "The cast of characters in those early days," White recalled, "was as shifty as the characters in a floating poker game. People drifted in and drifted out." Considering the editor's obsession with clarity, accuracy, and other cardinal tenets of journalism, he was a model of caprice and intuition when it came to assembling a staff. As the examples of Gibbs and Thurber in particular had shown, Ross's approach was haphazard at best. "Hell, I hire *any-body!*" he was often heard to exclaim.

Gibbs agreed. For a while, he said, Ross had an "absolute infatuation with pinheads." The very first "Talk of the Town" writer/editor, an Irish-born sportswriter named James Kevin McGuinness, lasted only a few months before lighting out for Hollywood, to end up in relative obscurity except for such infrequent triumphs as co-writing *Rio Grande* and providing the scenario for *A Night at the Opera*. Ross's first de facto managing editor, Joseph Moncure March, seems to have been brought on board more by virtue of being the son of General John Pershing's chief of staff than for his qualifications—which in any event consisted only of having edited the New York Telephone Company's house organ. One of March's successors, Scudder Middleton, eventually stopped coming to the office after lunch, phoning in from the Players on Gramercy Park with such nonsensical explanations as "I won't be back this afternoon because I have to buy my little boy a chemistry set." His tenure ended when, in his cups at the club with Ross, he suddenly announced, "You can't fire me"—whereupon Ross did. Ross ended up going through so many disappointing underlings that he learned to refine his dismissal succinctly: "I am firing you because you are not a genius." Sometimes he would not go even that far. Murdock Pemberton, the magazine's first art critic, recalled, "I got a sad letter saying that he thought writing about art was no career and good-bye. He wouldn't explain."*

Such techniques may have been ruthless. But through them, Ross

---

* Pemberton said he later found out that Ross had fired him because he had published an unenthusiastic review of a gallery show by the wife of the magazine's informal art director, Rea Irvin. The reason was more likely Pemberton's own incompetence. Katharine White reported that he delivered "the worst copy we get so far as accuracy and diction go. His facts are unreliable, nearly all names are misspelled, and a good many dates are wrong. He appears quite unable to be accurate. He writes very ambiguously." Gibbs also had low regard for Pemberton: "[H]e used to write the messiest copy we ever got. He used to blame all the mistakes, including the factual ones, on the fact that he used an electric typewriter, which sort of got going on its own."

got the qualified stable he wanted. A number of them would remain with and define the magazine for the rest of their careers.

There was Hobart Godfrey "Hobie" Weekes, a grammar fetishist and eventual chief of copy, known as "Comma King" for his command of punctuation. Later he would become A-issue editor, reading the entire magazine before it went to press to check for glaring inconsistencies. The wealthy son of a prominent architect, Weekes attended the Hill School (where he loaned Gibbs copies of the works of the droll Canadian humorist Stephen Leacock), Princeton, and Oxford but refused to succumb to any Social Register tendencies. Instead, he became "an incandescent liberal." In his person he was rubicund and jolly-faced; upon meeting you in the corridors of the magazine, he would raise his eyebrows and form his mouth into a surprised O. Weekes was an anglophile and exceptionally well tailored; four years after graduating the Hill, he would design its blue-and-gray-striped tie. Naturally he was a clubman, a member of the Century and the University but especially the Coffee House. There, upon his death, it turned out that he had made arrangements for his friends to have a drink on his posthumous dime in lieu of a memorial service. He was so affected in his deportment that some suspected him of being gay. Actually, it was generally understood that he was a habitué of prostitutes.

There was the makeup chief, Rogers E. M. Whitaker, known because of his prematurely gray hair as "Popsy" and, in "Talk" columns, as "The Old Curmudgeon." Like Weekes, he was a grammarian. Like Weekes, he took care with his dress, wearing expensively tailored trousers that rose almost to his armpits. Unlike Weekes, he was sharp and abrasive; colleagues who felt his tongue-lashing called him "The Assassin." Physically and sartorially he looked "like a cross between Winston Churchill and W. C. Fields." His particular affectation was railroads. In his eighty-one years, he traveled more than two and a half million miles by train, writing of his journeys under the strange pseudonym "E. M. Frimbo." So much did he hate automobiles that he called them "a rolling sneeze" and "a little slice of selfishness." And so much did he love the iron horse that he stuffed his warrenlike *New Yorker* office with railroading magazines, to the point that they threatened to immure him.

There was a "gentle, venomous, red-eyed" editor named Clifford "Kip" Orr, whose horn-rimmed glasses accentuated his owlish countenance. Educated at Dartmouth, he was almost as full of acid as was Gibbs. Assigned the task of answering readers' letters, he would sometimes respond, "If you don't like us, read something else." He would creep about the corridors on crepe-soled shoes, imparting gossip into the ears of unsuspecting passersby. "One Easter, when I thought I was alone in the office," recalled the journalist Margaret Parton, "I heard soft footsteps outside the door. In a moment, Kip's deadpan face peered in at me. 'Christ has risen and seen his shadow,' he whispered. 'We'll have forty more days of rain.'" Orr, a hopeless alcoholic, himself endured only fifty-one years of life.

There was also Frederick Packard, another Hill cohort of Gibbs's and the head of the magazine's storied fact-checking department for more than a quarter of a century. Hired in 1929, Packard had a bushy black mustache that somehow made him look like "a beef-eating Englishman," and his authority matched his appearance. "Facts were sacred to him," said a colleague, "and woe betide the writer who chose to be approximate rather than precise!" To his job Packard brought not only exactitude but a keen literary sensibility, having been a member of Philolexian, the eminent Columbia University speaking and dramatic society. He would contribute an abundance of pieces to *The New Yorker,* many of them concerned with the finer and more obscure points of language and letters. He reveled in nominative absurdities, larding the "Incidental Intelligence" section of "Talk" with gems like "The Penna Wine Company puts out a California Chianti bottled in New York" and "Solar pawnbrokers, at Fifty-Sixth Street and Eighth Avenue, has changed its name to 116th Street Pawnbrokers." He loved poring over reference works, especially when he could catch them in error. "If for any reason, you look up 'table d'hôte' in 'The Reader's Encyclopedia,' you are advised to find out about it under 'à la carte,'" he cautioned, only to discover that "[t]here is no entry for 'à la carte.'"

That particular example was near his heart. Packard was a francophile whose love of the French extended to his disdain for Americans who dropped their words indiscriminately and snootily into everyday conversation. To that end he composed a mock letter describing a visit to a resort on the Bay of Biscay:

> The *pavés* were very *étroits*, and one had to keep stepping off them and risking *écrasement* by the *autos*. To sit at a *terrasse* was to have one's *pieds* stepped *on tout le temps*. To go bathing was to share the surfless and shallow water with the same *bébès, viellairds,* and *mamans*, plus *maîtres, nageurs, canots, pédalos,* rubber rafts, balls, and small Coast Guard *bateaux*. It was not *agréable*. We finally found the nicest *café* in the *ville*, far away from *la plage*, and though *parfait* in every *façon*, it had almost no customer except *nous autres, ma femme et moi.*

"He wasn't funny at all—he came *out* funny," said assistant art director Frank Modell. "Everybody said, 'Whenever you see Freddie Packard, don't use the cliché "How are you, Freddie?" because he'll keep you there for 30 minutes.'" One day Modell encountered Packard vigorously scratching himself. "And, I, the non-listening person that I am, said, 'How are you doing, Freddie?' And he said, 'I've got this terrible itch and the doctor says if I don't stop scratching it, it's going to get infected.' So I said, 'Well, you shouldn't be scratching it now!'" Gesturing desperately, Packard responded, "No, it's not here, it's back *here!*" The routine, as Modell had been warned, went on for some time.

And there was a moon-faced misanthrope named John Chapin Mosher whose many duties included being first reader of unsolicited manuscripts. This "delightful deviant" once summed up his career before joining *The New Yorker* thusly: "Newspaper man—cook—dishwasher—pleasure seeker—

idler—zealot—martyr—victim—wage earner—addressing employees—explorer—literary man—bohemian—artist—hack writer—invalid—nervous wreck—tourist—salesman (nails my specialty)."

Hailing from Albany, Mosher graduated from Williams College in 1914 and worked first at *Every Week* magazine under Bruce Barton, then briefly at *Leslie's Weekly*. He had the distinction of having two of his one-act plays—*Sauce for the Emperor* and *Bored*—staged during the first New York season of the Provincetown Players in late 1916 and early 1917, sharing the bill with works by Floyd Dell and Eugene O'Neill. Enlisting in World War I ("By help of 'pull' became Private First Class! Summary court martial—but considered generally inoffensive and good tempered"), he served in the shell shock ward of a U.S. hospital in Portsmouth, England. When the conflict was over, he had what he called "some years of general confusion" and became part of Hemingway's Lost Generation, ending up in Paris in 1922. There he fell in with Virgil Thomson, who found him so fascinating that the composer painted his musical portrait in a series of namesake waltzes.

Mosher returned stateside in 1923 to teach English for two years at Northwestern University and joined *The New Yorker* a year after it was founded. Thurber regarded him as "an editor whose prejudices were a mile high and who had only a few enthusiasms." One of those enthusiasms was turning down other people's work. Often he would declare, following lunch, "I must get back to the office and reject." In the space of a morning, "working in complete silence save for an occasional ejaculation of disgust when he found himself reading an exceptionally bad manuscript," he could get through as many as one hundred submissions.

When not busy breaking would-be contributors' hearts, he had by 1928 become the magazine's first regular film critic. His aesthetic tastes were so refined, and his demand for excellence so exacting, that he once prompted Howard Dietz, the head of MGM publicity, to explode, "Jesus, what a review. Do your technical considerations always outweigh the emotional impact of a film? . . . [T]he office vote was overwhelmingly against your sanity. It was something you ate no doubt." The producer Walter Wanger called Mosher "that God damned old woman" for reasons that probably had as much to do with Mosher's personal life as with his critical eye. Mosher was unreservedly gay (improbably, a 1940 collection of his pieces was titled *Celibate at Twilight*), and even in a creative environment that usually shrugged off such predilections, his behavior made some people uncomfortable. At one point Katharine White told him that she and Ross would much prefer if he could somehow be less obvious. The tip-off, Gibbs said, was a Mosher review of *Mädchen in Uniform*, "in which he explained that it was high time Americans realized that there was more than one kind of sexual love. This piece was blown up to about eight feet by three and displayed in front of the theatre and it caused Ross acute embarrassment."

In nominal control of these and other fabled oddballs was Ross, perhaps the biggest oddball of them all. Among the most arresting portraits captured of him was this, by one of his innumerable office boys, Dan Pinck:

> Mr. Ross usually showed up in the office around eleven. Often he would call just before he left his apartment on Park Avenue, and I would go across the street to a drug-store and purchase a half-pint of cream [for Ross's ulcers] and a five-cent package of cheese crackers. I would time my entrance with the food to coincide with his arrival. As soon as he took off his battered old hat and hung up his battered old coat, he would sit down at his desk and open his briefcase. Then I would pour his cream into a glass. "I wish I were running a newspaper," he would moan, gruffly rhetorical. "Out West." Then he would drink the cream and make a face of utter disgust. "Goddam." I would take a look at his pencils. "Why did I

ever start this magazine?" I would open the cheese crackers and put them on a plate on his desk. "At least somebody does something around here. Son, you sharpen pencils good." He was all set.

As is often the case in large organizations, it was a small cog that kept day-to-day operations running. At *The New Yorker,* this indispensable person was office manager Daise E. Terry, a native Kansan who had left her home state in 1918 to join the International Red Cross, serving as a stenographer in Italy after World War I. Though no more than five feet tall, she conveyed authority with her "piercing blue eyes" and determined demeanor. Her standard incantation to new typists was, "We want ladylike clothing and ladylike behavior at all times." To this "short, fierce, dignified woman who always wore a hat" fell myriad minor but essential tasks, everything from ordering supplies to adjusting the temperature in individual cubicles.

"Her job was to hire and subsequently tyrannize the half-dozen young women who constituted the typing pool," remembered the cartoonist James Stevenson. "Inevitably, the pressure would become too great—a legal document would be misspelled—and the typist would fly from the room in tears."

In retrospect Terry comes across as a frustrated spinster with a soft side. "She was not popular among the secretaries because she was a hard taskmaster and did not approve of romance or marriage, and was very upset when they went out with editors for lunch or anything of the sort," said Katharine White. "I remember a girl coming in once to me just after she had been hired. She was in tears, and asked me 'What shall I do? Miss Terry has just called me "a silly ass."' I consoled the girl and assured her that Miss Terry's bark was worse than her bite—and it sure was."

Among many other affectations, Terry would sternly warn uninitiated staff members, "Never say hello to Mr. Ross." Stevenson took this advice a little too seriously. "I didn't know what Mr. Ross looked like, so I selected the most important-looking man I could find, and avoided speaking to him." E. J. Kahn did so as well; in his case, he thought Packard was Ross and didn't realize his mistake for three days.

Terry made up for her foibles by toiling sixty to seventy-five hours a week, frequently on trivial tasks that no other administrator would have taken on. Just before Christmas 1939, White (who called her a "maid-of-all-work") sent her fifteen dollars to buy a Brooks Brothers sweater for Katharine's daughter Nancy and sheepishly inquired by way of thanks, "I have asked a man who makes pears, in Oregon, to send you a box for Christmas, with my love and greetings. Do you like pears?" Thurber instructed her before he took an extended leave, "God only knows who will use my typewriter while I am gone. But I don't want no blue ribbin [sic] in it. If they dont [sic] want black, let em [sic] eat cake. I want it kept covered too. Will you kind of ask people to be kind to this old machine, which is now in excellent shape." When the publisher John Farrar sent Gibbs a long and breathless request that he contribute to a volume called *The Bedroom Companion,* about "the hazards of man's life among womankind," Gibbs gave Terry the letter with a cover note that read simply, "Please lose this."

Her efficiency could be grating. "Miss Terry perhaps would be a little trying to a man of more spirit than I have," Gibbs complained to Katharine. "She is in and out of here all the time, jogging my memory about things I ought to have done. I think it is something they teach them in secretarial school: 'He may try to put things off, but keep everlastingly at him. Be tactful!' She is also always monkeying around with the papers in my baskets and I wish there was something in there that would bite her but there isn't." Even that would not necessarily have chastened her; she once divested a couple of tough office boys of a length of pipe and a blackjack. So complete was her control of office protocol that the staff once sent her this collective memo, with innumerable strikeouts and insertions:

PETITION TO MISS TERRY

We, the undersigned, object to the new paperclips—the ones that look like waterbugs [sic]. In elaborate tests shown that it takes just f ur [sic] times as long to attach them as it did the old paperclips—the ones that look like worms. It was also shown that it is impossible for a nervous man to attach one to a thin sheet of paper without everything wrinkling up, including the operator. The whole thing of course boils down into whether it is important to tear editors or manuscripts [.]

Terry may have been a consummate office manager, but Ross found himself for the first decade or so of *The New Yorker*'s existence in dire need of an all-powerful, all-efficient managing editor. This "dehumanized figure, disguised as a man," as Thurber described him, was the "Jesus"—a corruption of "genius" and/or a nod to Ross's tendency to spout "Jesus!" in exasperation over trouble of any sort. Approximately two dozen Jesuses populated the magazine's first six years alone. None of them ever met Ross's lofty expectations.

The pattern was set with the very first jobholder, Ralph McAllister Ingersoll, who would go on to a storied career at Time Inc. and create the newspaper *PM*. If nothing else, he left *The New Yorker* with one indisputable legacy:

It was I who invented—literally—the *form* of the Talk Department. Not the style, God forbid, nor the polish—but the form: of alternating short essays with anecdotes; inventing the several different essay forms . . . consisting of "visit pieces," miniature Profiles, dope stories (background pieces to newspapermen) etc.; the whole anecdotal warp and short essay woof to be woven into a disguised but discernible pattern to cover those fields of Metropolitan interest which were our special province: each of the arts, Park Avenue and a touch of Wall Street, the beginnings of what's known as Café Society, etc.

But in his five years at the magazine, Ingersoll may have been better remembered for clashing regularly with his boss. "Ingersoll was a great man for system," Ross said. "If I gave him a thousand dollars a week just to sit in an empty room, before you know it he'd have six people helping him." Ingersoll suffered a nervous breakdown after working sixteen-hour days for Ross and staunchly defended his record. If Ross was the father of *The New Yorker,* he insisted, then "I was the mother. It came out of my loins, with all the pain and agony of childbirth and it was my child by an exasperating unholy ghost whose materialization looked like a gargoyle with crew-cut hair."

By late 1926 Ingersoll had eased himself into a slot as a senior editor or "Jesus emeritus," as he called it. It was around this time that Ross hired Thurber to take his place—that is, if Thurber can be believed. A chronic exaggerator, he spun yarns generally designed to elevate his profile or embellish his misfortunes. In subsequent retellings, Thurber would play up his centrality and duration as the Jesus. He might well not have held the job at all; he was likelier Sunday editor, charged with getting late reviews into print and making sure that last-minute snafus were rectified.

But Gibbs, while admitting that the stories about Thurber's office conduct were "manifold, peculiar, and perhaps as much as fifty percent true," distinctly remembered him in the Jesus slot. "I know that he was employed as managing editor in 1926, a job for which he was about as adequately equipped as he would have been for dentistry," he wrote. "This was because Harold Ross felt that he needed an editor, having far too many writers around as it was." Whatever Thurber's exact title, Gibbs admired his peculiar ideas about administrative procedure: "Every evening on his way across the street for a drink at the Algonquin, he would take the day's accumulated memoranda, telling him what to do tomorrow, out of his pocket, tear them up, and drop them in the gutter. It is a commentary on the rather casual methods of the magazine that this worked very nicely for quite a while."

Such future eminences as Ogden Nash and James M. Cain occupied the slot for varying durations. The brief tenure of the latter proved memorable. "It was a lively, stormy time," said Katharine White. "Cain was not an administrator and therefore tried to set up all sorts of crazy devices, such as tagging the boards of cards of fiction, memoirs, humorous essays, poetry and verse bought and in our 'bank' of manuscript and proof to be scheduled. He did it by color—red for very timely, Green for 'Soon,' and Yellow for any time. The joke was that Raymond Holden, who was to watch over administering this timeliness matter, was color-blind and could not tell red from green."

Nor did Cain take to Ross personally. "In this otherwise courteous man, so easy in conversation, there lurked something peculiar, a streak of self-consciousness, or shyness, or social kinkiness, that was anything but easy, and was in fact downright wacky," Cain recalled. That wackiness, Cain found, infected the entire operation. It was in "a chronic state of paralysis," filled with "incompetent secretaries, girls with poor gifts to start with, little training and less experience, whom The New Yorker had loaded up with by a policy of paying too little." When Cain suggested that Ross simply hire better secretaries, Ross—who somehow regarded them as less than human by definition—refused. "If I told him I had leprosy," Cain remembered, "I couldn't have gotten a more hostile reaction."

It was typical of Ross. Cain considered him "a problem child in the office [,] perpetually creating the chaos he wanted to cure." The last straw came when Ross promised John O'Hara a thousand-dollar advance without telling Cain about it. Cain exploded and, in an agonized conversation with himself that evening at home, he asked, "What in the hell are you doing this goddamn job for anyway?" He later admitted, "[On] my last days on *The New Yorker* I was going somewhat mental."

Cain was also vexed by the talented writer Geoffrey T. Hellman, who would briefly quit *The New Yorker* to work for *Fortune* in the early 1930s. The proximate issue was Hellman's apparent dismissal following some personnel-related misunderstandings. More generally, the brouhaha reflected the frenetic goings-on within Ross's budding shop. The Hellman-Cain correspondence reflects a confounding mutual tenacity and animosity. Cain drew first blood:

> You seem to be under the impression that you are the victim of injustice, or something, and I don't think that is true. You were not fired in the ordinary sense, but declined to do the only work that was here for you. . . .

Hellman returned fire the next day with a detailed response that included:

> To sum up this whole dreary business: I am still under the impression that I was quite definitely fired without cause; that some time later I was, out of charity or whatnot, offered the job I had when I first came to The New Yorker, involving work less congenial and less well paid than that which I had been doing for the last five or six months; work, in short, which I undertook two years ago in the encouraged expectation that, well done, it would lead to an editorial job; and that naturally I refused it. There was no question of my "preferring to quit," as you say; at the time of my dismissal I had no choice, Ross's only offer having been one to do free lance work—meaningless, as you know; I merely declined a later offer to take an inferior job, designed as a method of letting me out easily.

To which Cain volleyed back:

> Let us get this thing clear: Within a day or so my coming to The New Yorker you came into Ross's office, and you and Ross and I had a talk. Ross explained to you that my coming meant a readjust-

ment of the Talk department. I was going to handle it, he told you, and he asked you whether you wanted to be a reporter. Salary, so far as I recall, was not mentioned as we didn't get that far. You said you didn't want to be a reporter. You wanted to be an executive at $150 a week. . . .

You were not fired at all. You were offered a kind of work you were able to do at the salary you would be drawing. You would not take it. That is the whole story. . . .

This correspondence becomes more and more absurd. I write you this detailed letter chiefly for the sake of a record.

This particular poison pen correspondence would eventually be resolved by Hellman's quick return to *The New Yorker*. Though he would annoy Ross as much about issues of pay and reimbursement as he did Cain about his actual employment, he would become among the magazine's most loyal and prolific employees. Cain, by contrast, undertook no such peacemaking. Years after he left the magazine and achieved fame with *The Postman Always Rings Twice*, Gibbs solicited him to contribute to the magazine. With memories of his editorial purgatory still fresh, Cain refused:

On the whole, I would rather be dead. You see, by the time I thought up a list of ideas and submitted them and found out the one I liked Ross didn't like, and then wrote one up and sent it on and then got it back again with 32 numbered objections from Mrs. White, and then rewrote it and sent it back, then considered the proposal to buy the facts from me for $50 and have Andy White rewrite it, and finally it came out as a "Reporter" piece by Markey—I would probably be dead anyway.

By far the most important Jesus came via Joel Sayre, an old friend of Thurber's. "Honest to Jesus, Kay, I do wish you'd take him under your wing," he wrote to Katharine White. "He's the best un-magazine-published writer I know, a great guy, and needs money terribly."

Sayre's friend was a tall, broad-shouldered charmer of a newspaper-man named St. Clair McKelway. Joining the staff in 1933, he began contributing "Talk" items, Profiles, and "Reporter at Large" stories. His subjects were equally famous (the dancer Bill "Bojangles" Robinson) and undistinguished (a local woman who had abandoned her twin baby girls, one in a subway lavatory and one in a church vestibule). Almost from the start, he demonstrated editing prowess as well. When Katharine White asked him to fix up a piece, she found he did so "exactly as it should have been done." Thus informed that McKelway could turn other people's copy around, Ross told the young reporter, "If you can, it's God-damned unusual!"

Toward the end of 1936, McKelway agreed to Ross's request that he take on the "Jesus" slot, provided he was paid fifteen thousand dollars annually and hold the job for only three years. Most important, McKelway also insisted that the blurry administrative border between the magazine's departments of fiction and fact be clearly established, with himself responsible only for the latter. Secure in his fiefdom, McKelway set about recruiting and training some of *The New Yorker*'s most prolific and familiar names, including Joseph Mitchell, Philip Hamburger, Brendan Gill, and E. J. Kahn, Jr. It was McKelway who helped A. J. Liebling transform his first major *New Yorker* effort, a hopelessly disorganized Profile of the messianic preacher Father Divine, into a masterful two-part article, meriting a joint byline. It was McKelway, too, who installed two highly qualified assistants, Sanderson Vanderbilt and William Shawn.

Handsome, with trim facial hair, McKelway was a dapper dresser and debonair to a fault. "He was Mr. Congeniality," said the writer and editor Gardner Botsford, "giving out assignments apologetically, like a man forced to bring up business affairs at a cocktail party." He might also have been the most soft-spoken member of the staff. "An awful lot of speech was lost in that sandy moustache!" said the short-story writer Edward Newhouse.

It may have been inevitable that McKelway enter journalism. His namesake great-uncle had been editor of the *Brooklyn Eagle,* and his brother Benjamin would go on to be editor of the *Washington Star* and the Associated Press. His father, Rev. Alexander Jeffrey McKelway, one of a number of Presbyterian ministers on both sides of his family, had been editor of both the *North Carolina Presbyterian* and the *Charlotte News.* Using these platforms, he became an early and tireless opponent of child labor. By the time his fifth and youngest child, St. Clair, was born in 1905 in Charlotte, North Carolina, he had largely given up the pulpit to become the southern secretary of the National Child Labor Committee. In that capacity, he helped push through some of the nation's earliest anti–child labor legislation. This struck the young McKelway as "rankly paradoxical," given that his upright relatives expected him to chop wood, dry dishes, and perform other household chores from an early age.

"The general idea was that a child would be given small doses of work when he was still in rompers so that he would eventually become a helpless work addict like Old Testament laborers," he recalled. "Like most children, I enjoyed daydreaming, and this delightful pastime was continually being interrupted by some grown Presbyterian."

Like Gibbs, McKelway lost his father early on. Rev. McKelway was only fifty-two, and St. Clair only thirteen, when he died of a heart attack in 1918. The death was especially haunting because at the time the family home in Washington, D.C., was under a six-week quarantine, with St. Clair suffering from scarlet fever. The place was practically deserted, all of his siblings being either in the army or having been sent away for the duration. When mother gently informed son, "God has taken him," he didn't cry. Nor did he weep at the funeral or the interment. But when the family pet, a Boston terrier named Bessie, greeted him joyfully after having not seen him during his illness, he broke down.

The academic indifference that Gibbs experienced as an adolescent similarly took hold of McKelway. He began cutting classes at Western High School and, with money earned through some pretty thefts, ran away to Florida when he was just fourteen. There he supported himself for a few months working as a stevedore on the Jacksonville docks and working as an all-night counterman at a restaurant in St. Augustine, which he thought "a great place to study human nature." Returning to Washington, he told his mother flat out that he was tired of school and was ready to earn a living. Surprisingly, she acceded.

Working through a series of minor jobs at the *Washington Herald*, the teenaged McKelway itched to become a reporter. He got his chance in the summer of 1922 when his managing editor told him to dig up a feature story at the zoo. He quickly found that Jack, a white male cockatoo from Malaya, had just died of old age, and that he and his mate, Jill, had been in the habit of pecking at each other, "their wings outspread and flapping." The editor seized on this angle, and the next day on page three there appeared McKelway's first professional effort under the headline COCKATOO AT ZOO KILLS MATE; KEEPER PUTS HER IN SOLITARY.

Just seventeen, McKelway embarked on a vagabond journalistic course somewhat like the one undertaken by Ross. Within the next few years, he would be either a reporter or editor on the *Chicago Tribune*, the *Philadelphia Daily News*, the *New York World* and the *New York Herald Tribune*. Ultimately he commenced an around-the-world trip that came to a stop in 1930 in Siam, where he became editor-in-chief of the *Bangkok Daily Mail*, a late-afternoon publication geared toward the resident British and American colonies. It was the personal property of King Prajadhipok, and McKelway was paid his salary in gold. When not engaged in "graceful muckraking" he gave frequent dinner parties for both the international and the American communities and played a variety of sports, including polo with his own pony.

While McKelway was in Bangkok the Siamese revolution of 1932 erupted on June 24, ending nearly seven hundred years of absolute monarchical rule. In the *Mail*, McKelway praised the cleanliness of the coup in prose that could be read as either gushing or, more likely, bemused: "Not a single measure that would ensure the preventions of bloodshed, violence or disorder was overlooked in the meticulous plan that was carried out. The soldiers were trained to a fine point of discipline so that not only did they act with marvelous precision and dispatch but they refrained from a too-exuberant enthusiasm even when they saw that their long dreamed of plan was at last a success." On the afternoon of the takeover, he was the first foreigner admitted to the provisional government headquarters. In dispatches to the *Herald Tribune*, McKelway extolled the revolutionaries as reform-minded, idealistic, and incorruptible: "The leaders of the movement ride to the Throne Hall on their own motorbicycles [*sic*] or in their own motor cars, though each prince in custody has dozens of fine cars which might have been seized." These subtleties were lost on the populace; when the country's first permanent constitution was adopted that December, they asked, "Who is this Mr. Constitution?"

After three years at the *Mail,* McKelway returned to New York and the *Herald Tribune.* He wrote a number of crime stories, including one about the murder of Joseph "Spot" Leahey, a "valued gorilla" who was reportedly on Dutch Schultz's payroll.

At the Broadway Towers, where Leahey was registered as James S. Boyer, he had managed to keep his rowdy manner under subjection. He used his $50 a month room only for sleeping, according to attendants, and always came in alone.

In his room detectives found only his wardrobe, consisting of several expensive suits, many white shirts and a few blue ones, all with collars attached, and other clothing.

Leahey's appearance was peculiarly suited to such a dual role. His countenance, puffy and fairly pink, was bland; he could maintain an immobility of expression even while enacting feats of cruelty. Speakeasy bartenders, who considered him one of the messiest men who ever stood at a bar, will never forget the terrifying[,] quiet way in which he would say "Oh, yeah?"—drawing out the syllables while he reached for a bottle and broke off the neck to a rhythmical motion that would end as the jagged edge was ground into the face of some luckless bar-fly who had insulted him.

Such prose made him a natural for Ross's shop, and after six months at the *Herald Tribune,* he transitioned to *The New Yorker* easily. "In a very short time," he said, "I felt at home." By this time as well, *The New Yorker* itself was wholly established. Its personnel no longer resembled White's "floating poker game" but were, rather, a fully functioning team.

CHAPTER 3

"BOY, DO I LIKE TO
HANDLE AUTHORS!"

A high school student named Merritt Nelson once wrote to *The New Yorker* to ask, apropos of a homework assignment, "What is the purpose of your magazine?" He received a curt response: "We haven't any purpose."

This, of course, was nonsense, as Ross's original editorial manifesto had made abundantly clear. In fact, *The New Yorker*'s identity would become so well established that one of its periodic statements of editorial policy and purpose offered the following all-encompassing definition of self:

> In the minds of Harold Ross and his associates back in 1924, there existed a clear comprehension of one very basic fact. They recognized that a civilization had grown up in and around New York and other large cities which differed from that of a mass of the people.
>
> They recognized that there was a group of intelligent, discriminating, unprejudiced, cultured people whose outlook on life was broader and more tolerant, whose minds had greater understand-

ing, whose desires and interests were more varied, and whose standard of living was much higher than that of other people. This group was limited in number but it was steadily increasing in size and importance. No magazine had ever before been edited solely for such people.

It was believed that these people possessed an inner craving for finer things: that they were not content with the commonplace, the stereotyped, tinted reporting, comic strip humor, the Boy Meets Girl story, and the like: that they had matured in broadmindedness and discernment to the point where they would not be offended by, but would enjoy a publication which sometimes satirized and ridiculed the foibles, the superstitions, and the stuffiness of our times.

As John Crosby, television critic of the *New York Herald Tribune* observed upon the death of Ross, "An awful lot of malarkey disappeared from journalism in the twenty-five year history of *The New Yorker.*"

It was clear pretty much from the start that it was E. B. White who most singularly achieved this effect, with his offhand, slightly superior approach in "Comment." His paragraphs might occasionally be frivolous. More often they would bring a smile and an understanding nod of recognition. "I can't remember a piece by anyone but E. B. White that Ross ever really thought just right," said Ingersoll. "White was the exception to prove his lack of faith in everyone else." As Thurber put it, he offered "silver and crystal sentences which have a ring—like the ring of nobody else's sentences in the world." No matter how serious the subject, White could be relied on to bring it down to earth, as he did in this entry from the first days of the New Deal:

We notice that the minute government entered into partnership with business, President Roosevelt put right to sea. As yet we haven't discovered just what the government's part will be in the business of getting out this magazine, but we hope for great things. We hope for more than a merely regulatory function: we want sympathetic advice and actual assistance. Let's get this partnership idea started off on the right foot—we could use an article right now (about 1,500 words) by Mr. Roosevelt himself called "Rolling Down to Campobello," or "Amberjack and No Work Makes What?," or "Amberjackstraws in the Wind," or "Two Weeks before the Mast." And next month, when we will be cruising down in Maine ourself, we would appreciate it if Washington would assign one of its undersecretaries to write our stuff for a couple of weeks. *That* would be our idea of government working with industry.

While White was dominating "Comment," Thurber was focusing on its counterpart, "Talk," not only writing original pieces but also running the work of many others through his typewriter to achieve an all-important consistency of tone. (This prompted White's quip that most "Talk" pieces represented the labor of two contributors, the reporter and the rewrite man, "each as guilty as the other.") Thurber was a natural at rewrite, said Gibbs, "since his mind worked on a queer secondary level, and while the facts were usually there, they had a way of suggesting something a little dramatic and deranged or supernatural about his subjects."

"I'm sure that Andy White would agree that it was Thurber, more than anyone else, who reached out, captured, and molded into reality Ross's inchoate dream of what Talk should be," said the art critic and short-story writer Robert M. Coates. "It wasn't an easy task, I realize now. A good, crisp writing style, mingling the essayistic deceptively with the reportorial, was required, first of all. Jim had that."

From the start, Thurber made an even greater impression with his casuals and short stories. Pieces like "If Grant Had Been Drinking at Appomattox" reflected his ability to plausibly spin out wildly absurd scenarios. But inspired by authors ranging from Henry James to Lewis

Carroll, he also brought an unexpected literary and psychological depth to much of what he wrote. A good example was "A Box to Hide In," from 1931. On the surface, it was little more than a yarn about a beleaguered man's quest for the object of the title. But the neurotic subtext (" 'It's a form of escape,' I told him, 'hiding in a box. It circumscribes your worries and the range of your anguish. You don't see people, either' ") was such that it made an immediate impression. According to Joel Sayre, the piece "brought mail in from dozens of psychiatrists who offered to feel Thurber's noggin free of charge. He turned them all down."

As for Gibbs, he initially punctured "the foibles, the superstitions, and the stuffiness" of those days by pouring forth an abundance of casuals, many of them drawn and exaggerated from his own life. "Mars" was about his brief time in the Student Army Training Corps at the Hill School, laden with memories of his commanding officer ("a small red man, brisk as a fox terrier, with a loud voice and a simple vision of paradise as a boundless parade ground with all the cherubim in step") and hand-grenade practice ("I can't forget my horror, after I had pulled the pin, standing there with that deadly [and possibly defective] mechanism, waiting for the premature crash which would be my last memory this side of the grave"). He made light of his fiendish cigarette consumption in "Wit's End," wherein his character awakes in his hotel room to find himself surrounded by smoke and flames. While making numerous, unsuccessful attempts to complain to the management via telephone, he catches a chill—the first hint of the pneumonia that will ultimately kill him.

The merit of these and myriad other kinds of pieces (Profiles, "Reporter at Large" articles, "Letters" from around the country and the world, serious short stories, criticism of all sorts) by a welter of contributors (S. J. Perelman, Janet Flanner, John Cheever, Lewis Mumford, Rebecca West, and Joseph Mitchell, to name a few) was not achieved by accident. It was the result of endless consideration and reconsideration by authors and editors alike. The *Saturday Review* critic John Mason Brown, a good friend of Gibbs's, commented that the magazine's "touch is so light that you are not aware of how much thought, effort and real brain sweat has gone into the sentence that comes out." As it developed, that effort was not just a matter of producing a superior periodical. It turned out to be an essential factor in forming lasting friendships, occasional romances, and not infrequent enmities.

The "brain sweat" of which Brown spoke started at the top, with Ross. His oversight was total. "Ross is usually in a towering rage before passing the third paragraph," *Harper's* noted. "He pencils such outbursts as 'What mean?' and 'Oh, my God' furiously in the margins, and upon coming across a piece of slang with which he is not familiar he is likely to accuse the writer of making it up. If a piece of pertinent information, such as the subject's birth date, is omitted, his indignation is boundless." Ross's "query sheets," wherein he attacked imprecision, missing facts, or what he regarded as just plain nonsense, became infamous for their length and irascibility alike.

Ross was by no means infallible. He had blind spots and hang-ups. When one writer proposed a series about reptiles, Katharine White cautioned that her boss had "a prejudice against writing about snakes. He thinks that so many people find snakes entirely repulsive that it is dubious to write about them. If anyone mentions snakes to him he always says 'Talking about snakes gives women miscarriages!' " But more often than not, Ross's editorial calls were on target. Moreover, his example was inspiring. As time went on, his staff became as critical as he was, eyeing manuscripts as if they were guilty before being presumed innocent.

The fiercest reader of all was Mosher. His letters to aspiring authors were peppered with terse comments like "Not these," "This just isn't for us," "Slight," "Not this time," "I'm afraid this won't do," and so forth. His disdain for much of what crossed his desk was immortalized in an in-house mock rejection slip:

Sorry, this isn't quite right for us,
We find that it's rather slight for us,
A shade—just a shade—too light for us,
And, of course, just a trifle thin,

Although you sound like a jerk to us,
And reading your stuff is an irk to us,
Please send more of your work to us,
We like to have oodles come in

"One of the most dangerous things in our dangerous history was the selection of the great and wonderful John Mosher as first reader," Thurber told White. "God knows what gems of purest ray serene we lost because of his unique and forever evident taste." His ruthless efficiency had its drawbacks; Katharine White recalled that Sally Benson, author of the stories that later became *Meet Me in St. Louis,* had to be enlisted to second-guess his discards, "just to catch any love stories etc." that he had too readily dismissed.

Gibbs was no slouch in the rejection department himself. After serving briefly as a copyreader, he was installed as Katharine White's right-hand man, a position in which a flood of submissions flowed through his hands. Many were subpar at best, and he made no bones about saying so. He once offered this critique of a Profile of Janet Lord Roper, the Seaman Church Institute's house mother, by Djuna Barnes. Barnes had a solid reputation in bohemian literary circles but to Gibbs, she came across as a "lunatic":

I have never seen so many facts so insanely assembled, I guess. (I have always thought Miss Barnes was cracked, though Mosher loves her.) Anyway, I don't see how on earth you're going to bring anything out of all this confusion. It would have to be completely rearranged—the series of flash-backs [*sic*] in the first half is enough to drive you crazy—the romantic and literary note would have to be removed; almost every sentence fixed for clarity or just foolishness. Principally I doubt whether there is a story under all this hysteria.

"Bad writing was an affront to him," recalled Gardner Botsford, "and he could be cruel, almost vindictive, in his reaction to it." Gibbs even corrected his son's letters sent home from prep school. But he was as hard on himself as on any of his writers. He would revise his own pieces several times in an Eagle number-one pencil until they were nearly indecipherable.

Assuming that an author could get a manuscript past the front door, the hard work had just begun. "An average Profile-writer gets from twenty to thirty editors' queries," remembered Margaret Case Harriman, the daughter of Frank Case, the owner of the Algonquin and herself a quite skilled practitioner of the form. "Practically perfect writers like Wolcott Gibbs and St. Clair McKelway seldom get more than five or six." Harriman recalled with considerable humiliation that a twelve-page Profile she submitted was returned "with six pages of editors' queries—sixty-one queries in all, meaning that the editors had found it obscure or intolerable about every forty-nine words. This was before the checkers had even had wind of it." Similarly, when Geoffrey T. Hellman got back his first proofs on a three-part series about the Metropolitan Museum, there were 147 numbered queries, and even Hellman didn't think that was a record.

Gibbs was probably second only to Ross in his ability to massage a piece to its fullest realization. His 1935 query sheet regarding a Profile of an investigator for the American Society of Composers, Authors, and Publishers reads uncannily like any of Ross's many no-nonsense, even crabby, written demands for clarity and basic information:

Good enough subject, but a pretty dispirited treatment generally. Routine approach, flat anecdotes, and I'm still curious legitimately about a lot of details that he doesn't explain. They're covered in my notes. Also another piece that I take to be a composite, and Malloy a made-up name, but I don't know and that bothers me too. I think on the whole subject would get by, if author could be persuaded to go over it meekly with somebody, and then if it were edited pretty severely here.

1. Well, what are the terms? What do these places pay on an average? Does it mean you get the right to play all music controlled by ASPAC [sic] or do the contracts vary? He must fill this out.
2. Where is up here? The indirect approach. He tells later, but it stops you here.
3. Also something about the mechanism of this somewhere.
4. To be divided among how many? And how divided? Berlin for instance get [sic] same as author of one song? How is all this figured out? All part of the story, I think.
5. Thought he worked out of town. And not so damn memorable. Typical example of how his anecdotes let you down.
6. The high whine of a reporter at large.
7. In what percentage of cases do they sue? How many suits on an average? How many places subject to ASPAC [sic]. Vaguest piece I've read in years.
8. Can they collect at both ends of the radio? Also how manufacturer of a victrola or pano [sic] liable for what's played on it? Manufacturers of records and rolls perhaps, I don't know/ [sic]
9. But it seems he didn't find Washington Hollow. See below.
10. It has not been a matter of volition in my life.
11. Sounds like a demotion.
12. Gets Ny in what capacity. Might also go into the organization

of this thing, too. Needs half again as many facts before we're going to get anywhere, I think.

If a piece was particularly long and convoluted, Gibbs would book a hotel suite, lay out the article page by page on the floor, cut it into paragraphs with a scissors, rearrange them, write transitions, and then line-edit the result from beginning to end. A single word, not quite properly used, would raise eyebrows. "Being slow in paying debts doesn't really imply dishonesty, does it?" Gibbs wrote to one contributor. "In this case more like poverty, I think." Among Harriman's most tortuous experiences was a Profile of Helen Hayes; she made the mistake of offhandedly describing the actress as "not beautiful in the classic sense." Ross, who admired Hayes as much as Harriman did, roared, "Helen Hayes is a beautiful woman, and any reporter who says she isn't is a goddam bad reporter." It took a solid week and three separate conferences with three separate editors—McKelway, Gibbs, and Sanderson Vanderbilt—"before Ross and I could be brought to a meeting of minds about Miss Hayes's looks," Harriman said. As printed, the compromise locution was, "She is not strikingly beautiful."

Such fights were waged over matters of opinion. Altogether different was the exhaustive process of fighting to confirm certain facts. An ex-newspaperman, Ross was consumed with their veracity. Reportedly, he was inspired to create the magazine's fact-checking department after a 1927 Profile of Edna St. Vincent Millay appeared that was so filled with errors—for example, that her father was not in fact a stevedore—that he was forced to run a two-column letter from the poet's mother in a subsequent issue. This mortification apparently registered so profoundly with Ross that all manuscripts eventually went through the verification process—with Freddie Packard in sure command and a battery of checkers under him.

In their pursuit of accuracy, the checkers ran down newspaper clippings, hunted up dusty reference works, grilled the authors, and frequently contacted the subjects of the articles themselves. There seemed to be no limit to the obscurity of the facts that Packard in particular was called upon to establish. "Mr. Ross says that he has heard that there is an error in the title of the Spanish movie marked on the attached tearsheet," Ross's assistant Louis Forster informed him. "Somebody says that 'padre' should be 'patria', or some such. Would you please let me know about it, and may I have a translation of the title." Packard once wrote to the Justice Department to determine if the position of "Executive Assistant to the Administrative Assistant to the Assistant Attorney General" did in fact exist. The staid reply was that although there was no such title, the department did have "an Executive Assistant to the Attorney General, an Administrative Assistant to the Attorney General, and the Assistant to the Attorney General." For a listing of purveyors of homemade foods, he seized on a vendor who had informed him, "I regret that we cannot ship our Xmas cookies as they are too fragile. We sell them for $1.25 per lb. plus carrying charges." Packard responded, appropriately, "Dear Mrs. Jones: Thank you for your note. We don't understand, however, what you mean by 'carrying charges,' since you say you cannot ship your Christmas cookies. We would be grateful if you would explain how you mail your boxes."

Not that mistakes didn't slip through. One evening while riding the bus home, Packard found himself flipping through a typically thoroughly checked issue of the magazine and found to his horror that the name of world heavyweight champion Joe Louis had been misspelled "Joe Lewis." Packard dropped the magazine and, as his astonished fellow passengers looked on, began sobbing.

Assuming that a manuscript cohered enough to make it past macroscopic line editing, it was then subjected to the microscopic nitpicking of copyediting. Punctuation, grammar, usage, and style were as of much concern to Ross as storytelling and tone. "Ross has two gods," said the writer John McNulty. "Upper Case and lower case." No detail was too small; a particular fetish was the deployment of commas. "Commas in *The New Yorker* fall with the precision of knives in a circus act, outlining the victim," said White. As if in confirmation, someone once scrawled on Gibbs's office wall, "Wolcott ('Comma') Gibbs." He accepted the rebuke. "Since I'm one of the oldest people around here in point of service," he was later able to claim, "they aren't supposed to change me around much in the copy room. They make up for it by punctuating the hell out of me." Thurber, particularly protective of his copy, once burst out to Ross, "[I]f youse guys want to go around sticking in commas you know where you can stick them."

The copy desk's rules and guidelines could be maddening. "Did you know," White asked Thurber, "that Weekes was compiling a New Yorker style book which is longer than Gone With the Wind and more complete than Mencken's American Language?" This exhaustiveness was matched only by its capriciousness. The editor Ik Shuman once came up with a list of words and phrases that he said should be "blacklisted, or, at least, queried until further notice," among them "turn of the century," "oddly enough" and "audition (as verb)." With the utmost solemnity, Whitaker once determined the conditions under which the term "prefabricated" could be used. "It seems that all refrigerators are prefabricated, i.e. all ready to be plugged in when they come," Gibbs told White. "Bathtubs are not prefabricated because they have to be painted and soldered to do the plumbing. This seems to me a fine and foolish distinction, and I wouldn't bother with it. Boy, do I like to handle authors!"

Astute contributors realized that for all its difficulties, the editing process served them well. "The editors I had at The New Yorker quietly helped me in peculiar, small ways," recalled Irwin Shaw. "One thing they taught me was the value of cutting out the last paragraph of stories, something I pass down as a tip to all writers. The last paragraph in which you tell what the story is about is almost always best left out."

"I wish editors were always right about everything, or else always wrong," wrote Clarence Day, author of the beloved "Life with Father" series, to Katharine White. "I wish Ross and you and the copy room never caught me with my pants down. Sometimes when Ross opens his box of little grammatical rules and disallows my best blasts of music and punctures my bag-pipes [*sic*] I wish to God I could exchange places with him for a minute. At other times however I'm obliged to him damn it. And I'm often grateful to *you*."

These attitudes tended to be the exception. "Since I never write, for publication, a single word or phrase that I have not consciously examined, sometimes numerous times," Thurber informed Ross, "I should like to have the queriers on my pieces realize that there is no possibility of catching me up on an overlooked sloppiness. I think I can say this, without smugness, but with some fire." Gibbs himself threw up his hands to Ross at one point: "I wish you and your associates would let up on the 'indirection' theme for a while. There are crises in English composition when pronouns have to precede their nouns and even when the first mention of a person, place, or thing is not necessarily definitive. See Genesis 31:1."*

In fact, by the time he began stepping down as Katharine White's assistant in late 1936, Gibbs had become so appalled—and yet so amused and even impressed—by the magazine's editorial quirks, any number of which he had ruthlessly enforced himself, that he composed an in-house memo entitled "Theory and Practice of Editing New Yorker Articles." He began by declaring, "The average contributor to this magazine is semiliterate; that is, he is ornate to no purpose, full of senseless and elegant variations, and can be relied on to use three sentences where a word would do." Gibbs then proceeded to lay down some rules and observations designed "for bringing order out of this underbrush." Among them:

1. Writers always use too damn many adverbs. On one page recently I found eleven modifying the verb "said." "He said morosely, violently, eloquently, so on." Editorial theory should probably be that a writer who can't make his context indicate

---

* "And he heard the words of Laban's sons, saying, Jacob has taken away all that was our father's; and of that which was our father's has he gotten all this glory."

the way his character is talking ought to be in another line of work. Anyway, it is impossible for a character to go through all these emotional states one after the other. Lon Chaney might be able to do it, but he is dead.

3. Our writers are full of clichés, just as old barns are full of bats. There is obviously no rule about this, except that anything that you suspect of being a cliché, undoubtedly is one and had better be removed.

7. The repetition of exposition in quotes went out with the Stanley Steamer:

Marion gave me a pain in the neck.

"You give me a pain in the neck, Marion," I said.

This turns up more often than you'd expect.

13. Mr. Weekes said the other night, in a moment of desperation, that he didn't believe he could stand any more triple adjectives. "A tall, florid, and overbearing man called Jaeckel." Sometimes they're necessary, but when every noun has three adjectives connected with it, Mr. Weekes suffers and quite rightly.

14. I suffer myself very seriously from writers who divide quotes for some kind of ladies' club rhythm.

"I am going," he said, "downtown" is a horror, and unless a quote is pretty long I think it ought to stay on one side of the verb. Anyway, it ought to be divided logically, where there would be a pause or something in the sentence.

15. Mr. Weekes has got a long list of banned words beginning with "gadget." Ask him. It's not actually a ban, there being circumstances when they're necessary, but good words to avoid.

19. The more "As a matter of facts," "howevers," "for instances," etc. etc. you can cut out, the nearer you are to the Kingdom of Heaven.

23. Writers also have an affection for the tricky or vaguely cosmic last line. "Suddenly Mr. Holtzmann felt tired" has appeared on far too many pieces in the last ten years. It is always a good idea to consider whether the last sentence of a piece is legitimate and necessary, or whether it is just an author showing off.

30. Try to preserve an author's style if he is an author and has a style.

"How many of these changes can be made in copy depends, of course, to a large extent on the writer being edited," Gibbs said as he neared his conclusion. "By going over the list, I can give a general idea of how much nonsense each artist will stand for."

There is no record that he ever actually did. But Katharine White took up the challenge. Following a series of public slams against *New Yorker* fiction—including a review stating that the stories Irwin Shaw did *not* publish in the magazine were better than the ones he actually did—she wrote an anguished memo to Ross. "I rather think that if we polled all our contributors, we'd find more dissatisfied than happy ones on this matter of editing," she said. "I feel that too often we have to ask for changes to meet preconceived standards of our own that may be good standards but that, if insisted upon, make our fiction less individual than it would be if edited less and even if it was far less perfect and precise."

She ticked off a list of dissatisfied contributors, among them Kay Boyle, Mary McCarthy, John Hersey, A. J. Liebling, Irwin Shaw, and Clarence Day. "Many of them write so badly that they haven't a leg to stand on," she acknowledged, "but some write well and even the foreigners like to feel their individual style can be kept." She pleaded, "We've always been purists and I do not suggest that we give up editing. I only suggest that unless we soon make a considerable revision in our habits in handling the work of professional writers, we won't have any good fiction at all to publish."

This kind of consideration toward authors was typical of Katharine White. "'Maternal' is the word that best describes her concern for the work and lives of writers and artists," said William Maxwell, a trusted adjutant in her department for decades. "They found themselves confiding to her. When they turned work in, they felt she was on their side, and in fact she was." She once sent a five-and-one-half-page letter to Jean Stafford filled with ideas about how to salvage her short story "The Children's Game."

She held fiercely to her standards. "I believe in all of us expressing our ideas in loud clear tones and don't believe in our being polite or sparing feelings," she told Maxwell, and she practiced what she preached. Thinking that she might approach P. G. Wodehouse to write for the magazine, she read hundreds of pages of his Jeeves stories to get their flavor. She did so "without one smile," she told Ross, finding the stories not only formulaic but "boring and feebleminded." She dismissed their former colleague Raymond Holden's novel *Chance Has a Whip* as "the g-d-est trash I ever read," composed by an author who "never could write prose." She once agonized over whether to encourage her own sister, Elizabeth, to embark on a Profile; the best she could muster up about her sibling's literary ability was "She can write English."

Gibbs considered Katharine White "the most ravishing creature he ever knew." His was a minority opinion. In her person, she was—in a word that almost everyone who met her used at one time or another—formidable. "I was intimidated by her," said Ross's private secretary, William Walden. Gordon Cotler, a contributor and staff member, referred to her as "the terrible Katharine White." He recalled, "When she stomped down the hall, everyone trembled." Austere, proper, and not particularly humorous (one writer called her "a cold-blooded proposition"), she was known to everyone who worked with her as "Mrs. White." In all the time that Gibbs was her deputy, he was never able to bring himself to call her by her first name. When asked why, he replied, "I always had a feeling it would [be] like taking your finger out of the dike." Even Clarence Day, one of her more welcome contributors—as well as a bona fide friend—cowered before her. He once sketched himself on hands and knees outside her door, identifying himself as a "worried caller trying to see if you're mad at him." In another drawing he depicted himself reproaching a dinosaurlike creature perched above a prostrate figure labeled "KSW": "That'll do, Fido. Don't kill her—She didn't mean to hurt me I guess."

Katharine commanded such authority because Ross had utter faith in her. "I regard Mrs. White as essential to the magazine, along with White, more essential than the entire business organization put together, and most of the editorial," he told Raoul Fleischmann. "She is irreplaceable, which very few other people are." So complete was his trust, said the humorist Frank Sullivan, that in the event of disaster, "He didn't want anyone to run the magazine except Mrs. White."

It must be said that if one got to know her as a friend, and won her respect as a writer, there would be revealed a woman of considerable sensitivity—"a velvet hand in an iron glove," as the catchphrase went. Sullivan went so far as to call her "sainted." Her letters to her favorite authors were filled with compliments and praise, "way beyond the call of ordinary niceness," said one contributor. "If you are too cross with me I shall weep, so don't be," she wrote Clarence Day when rejecting one of his "Father" stories. When she told Will Cuppy, "It is many ages since you have sent us anything and we hope that you will have some humorous material for us before long," the paranoid humorist responded with his thanks but also his suspicions: "I'll surely try something else if I can recover from my delusions of persecution and [a] bad cold. I hate to think that there is a Hate Cuppy Movement in full swing, but I've checked up on it and it seems to exist. I have never really had any fun in life except when I had stuff in the New Yorker, so you can see that I'm in earnest about trying." Katharine's response was both reassuring and firm: "I think the 'Hate Cuppy Movement' must be purely a figment of your imagination, so you'd better quickly get over your delusions of persecution, as well as your bad cold."

In the course of working so closely with Gibbs, she appears to have had a civilizing influence on him. As caustic as he could be in his internal memoranda, he was generally polite when dealing with authors either via mail or in person, urging them to keep trying their best. One day over cocktails, Jerome Weidman was bewailing the agonizing life of a writer, fraught as it was with contradictory, often counterintuitive, standards of acceptance and rejection. Taking a sip of his drink, Gibbs responded with an inspiring soliloquy:

> There is abroad in the land a lamentable tendency to confuse failure with quality. The notion that because nobody will buy it, it must be great, is as foolish as the belief that a rookie who can't find the plate is obviously major league material. I'm sure the history of publishing is full of stories about great manuscripts that editors are too stupid to buy. I'm equally sure the word "full" is an outrageous exaggeration. Human beings make mistakes, and editors are human beings. It's been my experience that, by and large, material that merits publication manages somehow to get published. The boys in the ivory towers are probably doing worthwhile work, but I think it's worthwhile only to themselves, the way an aspirin is worthwhile to a man with a headache. It isn't really art. It's therapy. Therapy for the man in the ivory tower, I mean. It's foolish, even inhuman, to be against that kind of therapy, but it's equally foolish, and to me even more inhuman, to try to foist the treatment on the healthy. What the man up there in the ivory tower produces is worthwhile only when it has value to the man down in the street. . . . Always write as well as you can, without ever forgetting how important it is to keep trying to write better than you can, but never forget that writing is a form of communication, probably the noblest form ever invented by the human animal, and for God's sake don't ever stop battling us to pay you higher prices for what you write.

"Few of the people who were fortunate enough to know him better than I did realized, I find, how thoughtful a man he was," Weidman concluded.

Weidman got advice of a rather different sort from a fellow short-story writer who was also a friend of Gibbs. "Once a writer has finished a story to his own satisfaction," this man said, "there's only one thing he can do to improve it, and that's tell the editor to go fuck himself." It was the sort of thing one could expect from John O'Hara, a doctor's son from Pottsville, Pennsylvania, who exerted as profound an influence on *The New Yorker*'s content as anyone ever did.

O'Hara first appeared in the May 5, 1928, issue of the magazine with "The Alumnae Bulletin," a two-hundred-word monologue of a woman reading her college magazine's class notes. For this he received fifteen dollars from the irascible John Mosher, who had previously rejected O'Hara's contributions as too "elliptical." He began publishing casuals with astonishing rapidity, making his early reputation with fourteen sketches about the "Orange County Afternoon Delphian Society" and an equal number of arch pieces devoted to the "Hargedorn & Brown-miller Paint and Varnish Co." But these were mere "finger exercises," Gibbs said. Before long O'Hara would become, by popular and critical acclaim, a master of the short story and especially the kind of short story that Katharine White would frequently favor—largely devoid of narrative momentum, heavy on dialogue and suggestive anecdote, concerned less with plot than with establishing mood and character. Although she encouraged O'Hara's ambition in that direction, it was Gibbs who truly brought out the best in his work. "He carried O'Hara along with me," Mrs. White acknowledged—so much so that the writer dubbed his fictionalized version of his hometown "Gibbsville."

O'Hara's ability to capture the mores and attitudes of places as different as Hollywood, Broadway, Long Island's South Shore, Beekman Place, and Riverside Drive registered strongly with Gibbs. "The particular virtue of Mr. O'Hara," Gibbs wrote, "may be that he is equally at home in all these worlds, understanding the idiom and moral climate and even the clothes and house-furnishings of each one as if he'd lived there all his life." He regarded O'Hara not simply as a keen social observer but also as a skilled practitioner of the demanding genre of serious short fiction. In a blurb for "Over the River and Through the Wood," Gibbs applauded O'Hara's "rigid economy, accomplished without any sense of strain, that excludes all irrelevancies and still leaves nothing out. Each sentence, that is, has its clear purpose, carrying its full legitimate weight of information, and no more. This kind of writing is, of course, an editor's delight. It is also the kind that leaves no doubt in the reader's mind that he is being offered the truth."

J. D. Salinger, among many others, agreed; he told Gibbs that Julian English, the central character in O'Hara's *Appointment in Samarra*, represented a hundred-fold improvement on Jake Barnes, the tragic hero of Hemingway's *The Sun Also Rises*. Joel Sayre was impressed not only with O'Hara's craftsmanship but also with his discipline. "No matter how bad things were, how broke, sick, sad or overhung he was, he kept turning those pieces out," he said. "He was like a peasant having chores to do and doing them. Why, O'Hara got so that he could write when he was loaded. Countless times he rolled home late from some party, put paper in the typewriter, spit on his hands and stuck with it till he had a finished piece that went off to the magazine that very day—often without a word changed—and it was soon in print."

Ross, however, had terrible ambivalence about him. On the one hand, he recognized O'Hara's value to the magazine. As early as 1934, the editor said, "At his best he is one of the foremost writers in the country" and indeed "has written more words for us than any other non-departmental writer." On the other hand, Ross often had trouble with his subject matter, especially his apparent fixation on sex. Ross was delighted to run his "Pal Joey" stories about the venal yet raffish nightclub entertainer Joey Evans. But when Rodgers and Hart began working with the author to adapt the material for the stage, Ross confided in Gibbs, "How the hell is O'Hara going to make a musical comedy out of *that* character?"

Nor did the literal-minded editor care for O'Hara's artistry in its subtler moments. A good example of his befuddlement can be found in his response to "Fifteen Dollars," which Gibbs, running interference for *The New Yorker,* conveyed to O'Hara verbatim:

> The ending must be clear, of course. I don't know what it means and think you and Gibbs are guessing. I know in general, but I don't get the significance of the blotting of the first check. Why? Why didn't he just make out a $15 check [*sic*]. Also the Communism thing may be misleading, although it didn't throw me off. I think the ending should clinch definitely the question of whether the boy is telling the truth. From earlier references, I suspected (and still suspect) that the boy is building up this girl to capitalize a weakness of his father's for tosh-tosh people. O'Hara says earlier he was preparing to make a touch. Was he going out with such a girl or a little cutie with no automobiles and no wealth?

In that same letter, Gibbs said he was rejecting another story, "Pretty Little Mrs. Harper," because, similarly, "nobody at all knows what we're supposed to deduce from the end."

"On the whole John needed very little editing," said Katharine White. She estimated that Ross seldom made more than half a dozen inquiries on any of his manuscripts. But every one of those inquiries counted (Ross once spent more than a hundred words asking O'Hara if he was quite sure of his use of the word "starlet"), and Gibbs told the temperamental writer that he was simply trying to make "a very earnest attempt to reconcile your point of view and The New Yorker's." Katharine found him "unfailingly polite" when it came time for revision, yet suspected that it was "mostly because I was a woman but also perhaps because he knew I was head of the Department."

The men O'Hara dealt with, mainly Ross and Gibbs, were not as fortunate. Gibbs recalled that O'Hara entered his life "with some of the accumulating violence of a hurricane." Once, the two were going over a manuscript, and as the process continued, their two voices began rising. Finally, O'Hara exploded, "Gibbs, you're *fucking* my story!" and stormed out. He did not take well to having his stories turned down ("I have decided to reject your rejection," he once told Ross), in part because stories tailored for *The New Yorker*'s particular requirements were often unsellable elsewhere.

He had an extraordinary capacity for throwing his presumed weight around. "I am very discontented," he fumed from Los Angeles in 1936. "I want more money and a lot of it. I also want Fleischmann fired and Fadiman transferred to As To Men and the signature, The New Yorkers, restored to Talk,* I also want The New Yorker to send for me, paying all expenses, to talk things over." His cover letters were filled with self-aggrandizement and occasional self-abasement. "These pieces, and a slice of raw onion, will bring tears to your eyes," he told Maxwell. He once sent Katharine White a one-sentence letter: "My pieces don't run second." Katharine, who found O'Hara "a lovable man" in many ways, also called him "the greatest egotist I have ever known."

"Somebody told me that O'Hara's new book is the best thing he ever did," Gibbs wrote. "Possibly O'Hara."

In fairness to his excesses, Katharine observed, "He started out with many handicaps. To begin with he was not attractive to look at generally, although his Irish blue eyes and broad face and even his acne-scarred skin were not unattractive when he was not in a rage. He knew he was a small town boy and at first he had a terrible inferiority complex in New York because of this." O'Hara was equally ashamed of what he regarded as his lower-middle-class Irish background and, invariably, the

---

* Clifton Fadiman was the magazine's book reviewer at the time. "As To Men" was a short-lived column devoted to masculine fashion and style that was written by George F. T. Ryall, aka "Audax Minor," who wrote the horseracing column for the magazine for more than fifty years. "The New Yorkers" was the collective authorship for "Talk" during a certain portion of the 1920s.

fact that he had not gone to Yale, which he regarded as the entrée to class and respectability. Consequently, he set obsessive store by associations with and memberships in clubs and exclusive circles, and *The New Yorker* was literary cachet defined. "My little pieces in The New Yorker, unimportant though they are, are the only things that make the difference between my being dead and alive," he confessed during his lean years of the early 1930s. "I don't mean only that the money keeps me alive. I mean that I do nothing else, and except for them I might as well be dead."

In trying to puzzle out what the magazine wanted, O'Hara once put together a few rough thoughts. He shared them with his brother Tom, who was aspiring to write stories for the magazine:

> You probably won't sell many—maybe not any—but they will criticize what you *do* send in a way that will enable you to discover, ultimately, what they like and don't like. Don't hesitate to use my name in writing to Gibbs, but don't bother sending them anything that mentions the name of a celebrity, like F.P.A. [Franklin P. Adams]; don't send them anything pertaining to journalism or advertising, no puns, no Greenwich Village stuff, nothing with a trick ending. . . . Be careful not to send them stuff that is too long, and don't send them too many pieces. Write every day if you can, and send The New Yorker your best. (I'm a swell one to talk, who just got back two pieces.)

It was sound enough advice. And yet an author could follow every piece of editorial guidance, could observe every absurd in-house rule, could even be published in the magazine regularly, and still feel ill treated. O'Hara's insistence that his stories not run second found parallels in the complaints of the temperamental poet Louise Bogan, who objected to her serious, experimental verse being juxtaposed with what she regarded as "silly, vulgar drawings." Gibbs, who himself was skeptical about "advanced and intellectual verse," felt obliged to call Ross out on the matter when Bogan swore to resign "from all further contact with the New Yorker," especially as resident poetry critic:

> She says that she has no delusions of persecution, though she admits she has other delusions, and that it is a known fact that there are several people in the makeup department who dislike her extremely, and would go to any lengths to embarrass her, even to the extreme of ornamenting her verse with a drawing by Carl Rose which as far as she can tell is the damn silliest drawing she ever saw anywhere. She did not say that she thinks Carl Rose was asked to draw this picture for the sole purpose of insulting and degrading her, but that's what she thinks. "Here comes an especially beautiful Bogan" she imagines them saying, "get out that damn Rose." Just as somebody once willfully transposed the lines in a verse of hers so that it meant nothing and her freinds [sic] thought she'd gone bats.

Gibbs did his best to placate Bogan; he protested to Ross personally about "the juxtaposition of the lovely and the obscene." He acknowledged, "I guess there's no question about her position in the poetry world. She is one of the most distinguished members of the 'poetry gang' and probably the most authoritative critic of their work." But he also admitted he was "just buttering her up" in attempting to woo her back. Bogan saw through his flattery immediately:

> I meant what I said about resigning. —I need the money and the job, God knows, but under the circumstance, I would rather char. . . .
>
> You might intimate to Whitaker, Weeks [sic], and the other great human beings who are capable of these tricks, that it is terribly easy to hound a woman. With a man it is different. Even

men with pasts are capable of giving people socks in jaws. But a woman can't do this.

And some women wouldn't do anything. But they picked the wrong woman, in me.*

Yet in the end, Bogan served as the magazine's poetry editor for forty years. Over roughly the same period, O'Hara became synonymous with the magazine. Such was the complicated, love-hate nature of the editor-author relationship at *The New Yorker*. Whether the issue was a semicolon, typography, placement among pages, or an entire theme, the tension was ever present. As Janet Flanner remarked, "Writers are uterine egotists [;] a good piece when finished feels like a baby and one wants it born and thought handsome at once."

---

* Relations between Bogan and Gibbs had not always been this fractious. A few years before this exchange, she had written Gibbs, "[Y]ou probably use grammar more wittily than any man alive—with the possible exception of Max Beerbohm."

CHAPTER 4

———

"MOST INSANELY MISCAST"

"*The New Yorker* expects to be distinguished for its illustrations," Ross wrote in his original prospectus for the magazine, "which will include caricatures, sketches, cartoons and humorous and satirical drawings in keeping with its purpose."

Considering that Ross was a prose man, he succeeded beyond his expectations. Ninety years after he put down those words, it is still received wisdom that the first thing a casual reader of *The New Yorker* will do is flip through and have a chuckle over the cartoons. The graphic legacy that Ross left is as significant as its journalistic counterpart: *New Yorker* art set so lasting a standard that the magazine is now the only general-interest periodical left in the nation that still fills its pages with the sight gags that were once a staple of the industry.

Such durability and quality were evident almost from the beginning. As early as October 1925, when the magazine was still scrambling to find its audience, Ross noted, "Everybody talks of the *New Yorker*'s art, that is its illustrations, and it has been described as the best magazine in the world for a person who can not [sic] read." Philip Wylie, one of Ross's first permanent hires, recalled, "The one thing Ross had demanded till all heads rang with it—from early 1925 until it began to become fact, a year or so later, was this: 'Get the prose in the magazine like the art!'"

Ross eventually had plenty of worthy art to work with; before its tenth anniversary, the magazine was getting as many as a thousand drawings every week.

Following World War II, the figure was up to 2,500.

Part of the reason for this avalanche was the magazine's ability to accommodate wildly different voices and styles. For many years at *The New Yorker,* its editors insisted that there was no such thing as a "typical *New Yorker* short story." Assuming the assertion was true—and there are still many critics who would dispute it—the same could be said about its cartoons. The simple and charming "Little King" illustrations of Otto Soglow had as little in common with the stuffy clubmen and devilish rakes of Peter Arno as the abstract musings of Saul Steinberg had with the affected suburbanites of Whitney Darrow, Jr. True, some of the magazine's staple subjects and situations proved more durable than others. Today *The New Yorker*'s illustrated spoofing of cocktail parties, breakfast table conversations, precocious children, psychiatrists' offices, corporate boardrooms, and all other manner of middle-class neuroses is taken for granted.

It shouldn't be. What Ross had in mind for the magazine, and what he accomplished, marked a radical departure from what had been appearing in *Life, Judge,* and similar titles, as Thomas Craven noted in his 1943 volume *Cartoon Cavalcade:*

> Conceived in the spirit of the boulevards, The New Yorker departed from the old tradition of American humor, the tall tales and outlandish fables, which survive in the comic strips, and developed the funny idea with a witty, one-line caption to clinch the joke. The one-line caption had been used before, but sparingly and never with such originality and intelligence.
>
> The most pointed drawings of The New Yorker present an idea

or predicament that screams for clarification. The drawing alone, more often than not, is enigmatical, but in conjunction with the surprising title beneath it becomes explosively funny. And the fun is clean. Though far from squeamish, this clever magazine has never played upon seductiveness or trafficked in nudity.

Even the manner in which *New Yorker* cartoons were conceived and executed was different, Ross told the artist Alice Harvey:

[B]efore the *New Yorker* came into existence, the humorous magazines of the country weren't very funny, or meritorious in any way. The reason was that the editors bought jokes, or gags, or whatever you want to call them, for five dollars or ten dollars, mailed these out to artists, the artists drew them up, mailed them back and were paid. The result was completely wooden art. The artists' attitude toward a joke was exactly that of a short story illustrator's toward a short story. They illustrated the joke and got their money for the drawing. Now this practice led to all humorous drawings being "illustrations." It also resulted in their being wooden, run of the mill products. The artists never thought for themselves and never learned to think. They weren't humorous artists; they were dull witted illustrators. A humorous artist is a creative person, an illustrator isn't.

Much of the credit for this revolution in attitude goes to Rea Irvin, the magazine's first de facto art editor. Large and good living, eleven years older than Ross, he was a worldly and charismatic figure. A one-time actor and member of the Players, the private theatrical and literary club on Gramercy Park, Irvin wore a fedora with a brim so wide that it resembled a ten-gallon hat. At his affluent peak, he stocked his home in Newtown, Connecticut, with an assortment of animals, including some horses that he called his "models." But behind his genial eccentricities lay the sure eye of a former art editor of *Life*. In *The New Yorker*'s early, parlous days, Irvin provided necessary graphic gravitas. It was he who drew Eustace Tilley for the cover of the very first issue, modeling him on a caricature of the Count D'Orsay striking a pose with a walking stick. The caricature dated from the December 1834 issue of *Fraser's Magazine* and was hardly representative of the smart, jazzy image that Ross wanted to project for his new magazine. But by adding the touch of having the fop look disinterestedly through a monocle at a butterfly, Irvin conveyed the essence of *The New Yorker*—a slightly condescending but consummately tasteful arbiter of the larger world.

"At the very beginning, of course, Ross was fussing with the format of the magazine and here Rea Irvin was endlessly helpful. He drew all the small department headings and the big ones," recalled Katharine White. "Rea was especially good on covers and on color, and was himself one of the great cover artists. The Eustace Tilley anniversary cover is one of the least beautiful of those that he did. He had studied Chinese art and many of his covers had a kind of Chinese look to them."

Thurber agreed. "The invaluable Irvin, artist, ex-actor, wit, and sophisticate about town and country, did more to develop the style and excellence of *New Yorker* drawings and covers than anyone else, and was the main and shining reason that the magazine's comic art in the first two years was far superior to its humorous prose," he said.

The process gelled in *The New Yorker*'s famous art meetings that took place at two p.m. on Tuesday, the only day of the week that Irvin, who had other irons in his various fires, would actually appear in the office. In the beginning, the routine was simple: "Wylie would hold up the drawings and covers, and Irvin would explain to Ross what was good about them, or wrong, or old, or promising."

But as *The New Yorker* caught on, and Ross began bringing to these meetings the same eagle eye he brought to bear on the magazine's written material, things became more complicated, with the proceedings dragging on for three hours or more. Hundreds of specimens had to be examined, discussed, criticized, accepted, and rejected. Ross would pounce at faulty draftsmanship, missing details, insufficient clarity, and other shortcomings, literally pointing out the problems with a knitting needle and asking, "Where am I in this picture?" "Who's talking?" and even "Is it funny?" Frequently he didn't get that far. When he would snort, as he often did, "Goddam awful," "Get it out of here!" or "Cut your throat!" that would be the signal for Wylie or whoever was displaying the art to quickly bring up the next specimen.

Always he was consumed with believability. Once, after scrutinizing for two minutes a possible cover of a Model T wending its way along a dusty back road, he insisted that the artist draw "better dust." During World War II he was so concerned about the details of the torpedo tubes and the windshield in a drawing of a PT boat that he insisted that the manufacturers approve of the rendering. It took him a long time to run Arno's rendering of a man drowning in a shower and desperately signaling to his wife to open the door. A man *couldn't* drown that way, Ross reasoned, because even if (a) he couldn't turn the faucets off or (b) the drain was hopelessly clogged or (c) the door was sealed utterly tight, then surely (d) the water would spill over the open space at the top of the shower itself. The editorial assistant Dan Pinck would never forget his art-meeting encounter with Ross that hinged on a drawing of golfers that Ross insisted had "too many goddam clubs" in it:

> The cartoon showed two caddies standing on the green, one holding the pin in back of the cup. They each had a bag of clubs slung over their shoulders.
>
> I started to take the cartoon away, and put another in its place, but Mr. Ross said, "Bring it back, son."
>
> I replaced it on the drawing board.
>
> "Is the caddy allowed to go on the green with a golf-bag?" he asked.

Nobody answered him.

Then I did. "No, sir," I said, to everyone's surprise. "A caddy is definitely not supposed to carry his bag on the green. At any time." Then I added, "I'm pretty certain of that."

"Have you caddied?" Mr. Ross asked me.

"Yes, sir," I said. "I used to caddy for a former National Open Champion. Lew Worsham. I'm from Bethesda, Maryland, near the Burning Tree Country Club, where Worsham used to be the pro, before he won the championship."

"Did you ever caddy for him in tournaments?" Mr. Ross asked.

"No," I said.

"Well, this needs checking," he said. He waved his baton at me, and I put another drawing on the board.

His attention to detail extended across issues. Upon being informed that from 1936 to 1947 the magazine had published twenty cartoons on the theme of counting sheep—including five in 1947 alone, with two in the art bank—Ross wrote to Weekes, "Drawings of sheep jumping fences are not to be run oftener than once in six months. (We had two in successive issues recently, which was certainly very bad.)"

Just as Ross was obsessed with risqué themes in the work of Woollcott and O'Hara, he would ask of the art, "Is it dirty?" He didn't always get the right answer. In 1930 he printed a full-page Garrett Price drawing of an astonished young woman on an operating table exclaiming to an entering surgeon, "Why, Henry Whipple, I thought you were still in medical college!" without realizing that one of the instruments on the nurse's tray was a double-spoon curette, used in abortions. On the other hand, he knew exactly what he was doing by running an Arno of a motorcycle cop being approached by a young woman and a harried-looking man holding a car seat saying, "We want to report a stolen car." It has been widely reported that the editor was so ignorant that he didn't realize why it was only the seat, as opposed to some other part of the car, which was left behind. Not so, he told O'Hara: "I wouldn't have bought it if I hadn't known what it meant. It was not one of those pictures that could be interpreted two ways."

For a while, Ross tried dealing with artists one on one. With rough sketches spread in front of him, he would stride up and down, shoulders hunched, his head sunk, and growl, "Not a bad idea . . . think it up yourself? . . . You can make a better drawing . . . this drawing stinks . . . the guy looks like a peddler . . . ought to look like banker . . . haven't found yourself . . . an artist's best friend is his editor."

But that process was hopeless. There was simply too much art to consider, and the editor needed to rely on more than just his own opinion. Then too, said the artist Carl Rose, "The strain of looking into the stricken eyes of cartoonists who had been asked to redraw something for the umpteenth time may have been too much for Ross."

So in addition to Ross and Irvin, the meetings would come to include Katharine White and at least one other editor. All would participate in the cross-examination, punctuating their comments and questions with their own knitting needles. Daise Terry acted as secretary. Sometimes her notes on a particular specimen would simply read, "Try," meaning that the contributor should develop it more fully, or "Get idea," meaning that the material should be purchased but given to an artist better suited to convey the point. More often her reminders reflected the many ways that a piece of art could go wrong and need improvement. Here are some of Terry's excerpts from the art memo of August 29, 1933, at which forty cartoons were deemed to have at least some merit that could be developed:

SOGLOW King dressing in cowboy costume to receive a delegation from Texas or Oklahoma. In fourth picture have the attendant hanging robe up and show king's heel leaving picture. Make it Oklahoma instead of Texas.

HILTON	Man leaning over parapet speaking to girl down below. "Hello Mrs. Pennyfeather. I'm pouring hot oil on you." Better picture.
SORETSKY	Girls reclining in chairs. "Were you ever kissed and kissed and kissed and kissed?" Do in coherent style.
ANTON	Patent attorney's office. Eager inventor "Do you think I can get a basic patent on it?" Another gadget.
PRICE, GEORGE	Colored mammy. Man sitting in lap. "Beggin' yo' pardon Mars' Dan'l, but ain't it 'bout time yo' all outgrew this habit?" Make man southern colonel, black tie, and goatee.
STEIG, WM.	Woman and newsboy. "I thought you said he was found dead!" Caption vague. Why is <u>he</u>?
HOKINSON	Woman in department store dressing room. "This isn't exactly what I had in mind!" Not a corset. Strange costume.
ALAIN	Tourist asking way of flashily dressed woman. "Pardon me, Madame, is Cook's this way?" Tone down and put clothes on woman in doorway. Take out numbers.

And here are the summations and comments on the all-important cover ideas that were taken up at that same meeting:

DECKER	INFORMATION DESK in department store with girl smiling in midst of confusion and Bewilderment on part of public. Make fewer heads and bigger faces.
BARLOW	Couple in bed asleep. Child and toys. Try from another slant.
HARVEY	Thanksgiving over. Couple entertaining in crowded room with some guests having to sit in hall. Make it definitely an interior; more people, no monocle on man, and host and hostess should be young and poor.
OTMAR	Picnic and thunderstorm. Make strap plain black.
BARLOW	Woman finding large queer-shaped package under Christmas tree. Try again.

REA   Man in club being served tiny bit of turkey. Man ought to be farther removed to show that its [*sic*] a club. Should be alone.

REA   Pumpkin sketch. Pumpkins should be stacked on lawn not on stands.

For several years, the actual conveying of such criticisms to the artists fell to Gibbs. There was a certain logic to this assignment. He had a good aesthetic sense and enjoyed sketching offbeat subjects, especially dinosaurs, self-caricatures, and faces in general, many of them distinguished by their grotesque features and fierce teeth. As a sketchbook he sometimes used a copy of an obscure novel called *The Crime in Car Thirteen*, which, thanks to a bookbinder's error, was filled with nothing but blank pages.

Gibbs may also have unwittingly ensured his place at the art table by publishing a brief essay called "The Cartoon Situation" in the December 28, 1929, issue. He observed that in the past year, "American newspapers and magazines published something like three hundred thousand topical cartoons" on such diverse and contentious issues as Prohibition, crime, censorship, birth control, and big business. In all cases, the point was the same: "some person or principle is to be abandoned or demolished in favor or some other person or principle." He protested, though, that the welter of symbols, labels, and other methods of visual shorthand the cartoonists employed to make this identical point was overwhelming and disconcerting.

To avoid any confusion, Gibbs suggested supplanting all future cartoons with "a sort of Master Cartoon, an abridged editorial commentary on all crises, all campaigns, all crusades." His candidate was "Dropping the Pilot," which had appeared in *Punch* back in 1890 following Bismarck's forced resignation as chancellor of Germany. It depicted a haughty Kaiser Wilhelm II, complete with crown, regarding Bismarck as he stolidly descended the gangplank of the ship of state, preparing to enter a tiny launch. Here, Gibbs said, was the ideal editorial cartoon template:

> The ship in every case can represent the American People; Bismarck, whatever person or principle it is believed desirable to eliminate; and the Kaiser, the individual or organization responsible for its downfall. In treating the Eighteenth Amendment, for example, we might label the ship, the American People; the Kaiser, Public Opinion; and Bismarck either Liquor or Prohibition, depending on our personal convictions. It would be as simple as that.

There was one final, important reason that Ross wanted Gibbs at the art meetings. Consistent with his peculiar ideas about chains of command and production systems, Ross specifically preferred that a non-artist deliver the bad news, feeling that contributors would resent one of their own passing judgment.

Yet for all his qualifications, Gibbs was a curious choice. "A great deal of what was put before the art meeting was extremely unfunny," said William Maxwell. "Gibbs was repelled by the whole idea of grown men using their minds in this way and seldom said anything." This lack of enthusiasm was apparent to the artists he dealt with. Gibbs, recalled Syd Hoff, "always seemed uncomfortable at this chore, and impatient for me to leave." At the opposite extreme, he could be exasperatingly exacting. Michael Berry, an émigré from Nazi Germany, recalled that both Gibbs and Ross "would make you redraw cartoons five or six times with minor changes. Weeks passed each time before you were able to see the editors again. That made me very nervous and I soon gave up."

Some sense of the tortuous process of refining the inchoate thoughts and drawings that crowded the art meeting until they were finely honed comic gems can be gleaned from this letter to Arno:

Arno:

There's so much here that I guess a note is simpler.

On the cover, I'm afraid that the meeting wasn't as favorably disposed as I was. They all feel it isn't up to your standard, and isn't a cover you yourself would like to see on The New Yorker. Ross thinks that there are possibilities for a lot more humor in both figures and for a more colorful or interesting background. He also complained that the little man looked more like a street-cleaner than a janitor. I'm afraid I started all the trouble when I sent you Hall's sketch, lending you to follow too closely the layout of a not very inspired artist. I hope you'll be willing to try the thing again because everybody likes the idea, and I'm sure you can work it out.

On your own cover idea, the hunt dinner, we think the idea certainly merits a sketch.

"Dammit, I said julep": they liked this idea, but think it would be clearer if the jap [*sic*] had brought the tulip in a little vase instead of this glass. As it is, there is some confusion, a couple of people getting the idea that the jap [*sic*] had just brought a rose in a julep glass, missing the tulip idea altogether.

"My God, what happened to LaGuardia?": We weren't quite sure what your idea here was. Is it still supposed to be LaGuardia's car with LaGuardia missing, or another car altogether [*sic*]. I'm sure it's the latter, and in that case, I imagine it could be a lot clearer, and perhaps funnier, if the cops suddenly found themselves escorting a little guy in a model T Ford. If it's clear, it's good, Ross says.

"Frankly, Mr. Digby . . .": the meeting decided that quadruplets were a little excessive, and would prefer triplets. They'd also like the father to be an older man, "less nondescript." A normal-looking man, but getting along, that's all.

I'm afraid it was no on the others.

Gibbs

Reportedly, only two artists were immune from constant requests for revision: Gluyas Williams, whose clean, graceful renderings of comically cluttered situations had a delicacy that belied their strength, and Helen Hokinson, who poked fun at the foibles of clubwomen and matrons with an eye that was never malicious. As for the rest, they simply had to accept whatever recommendations were made. The system didn't always work. Once a drawing by Alice Harvey was accepted but languished in the art "bank" because no one could devise a satisfactory caption for it. As weeks went by, letters flew back and forth between Harvey and *The New Yorker*, with Harvey becoming increasingly impatient for payment. After yet another disgruntled letter from her, an exasperated Gibbs wrote to Ross, "Want me to run up to Westport and bump off this girl?"

Gibbs could have avoided making that offer simply by turning Harvey's work over to White, *The New Yorker*'s caption whiz. Confronted in 1928 with a Carl Rose sketch of a mother and a tot at a dinner table, he came up with the archetypal exchange "It's broccoli, dear." "I say it's spinach, and I say the hell with it." When it came to art, though, White gave the magazine far more than captions. He gave it an utterly original contributor in the form of Thurber himself.

It is startling to consider that Thurber, whose *New Yorker* pictures would become as well known as his *New Yorker* prose, published none of the former for his first few years on the staff. But to hear him tell it, he was more of a doodler than an artist: "For years I had been scrawling drawings on pieces of yellow copy paper and throwing them on the floor or leaving them on my desk. I began drawing at seven, mostly what seemed to be dogs, and carried the practice into the years of so-called maturity, getting a lot of good, clean, childish fun out of filling up all the pages of memo pads on the office desks of busy friends of mine, seeking to drive them crazy." Thurber succeeded; Gibbs observed that those busy friends regarded this manic activity "as a hell of a way to waste good copy-paper, since his usual output at a sitting was twenty or more."

In drawing up a storm, even famously doing so on office walls—portions of which were preserved for posterity—Thurber was not simply working off nervous energy. Forever seeking to be the center of attention, he was practically begging to be noticed. Eventually he was. "It was White who got the mad impetuous idea that my scrawls should be published," he recalled, "and, what is more, paid for with money."

"I don't remember just when I began to take Thurber's drawing seriously," White said. "I didn't really know art, or draftsmanship, but the drawings seemed funny, above anything else."

It took White a while to get others to feel similarly; his first attempts to have Thurber's drawings published met with firm rejection from Rea Irvin. Then in 1929 the two collaborated on *Is Sex Necessary? or Why You Feel the Way You Do,* a lighthearted look at the eternal male/ female divide, couched in part in mock-clinical terms. Among the highlights were Thurber's fifty-two illustrations. When they met with their editor, Eugene Saxton, at Harper & Bros. and White spread the drawings on the floor, Saxton beheld the flaccid, misshapen, sexless images and said, "These, I take it, are the rough sketches from which the drawings will be produced?"

"No," White replied, "these are the drawings themselves." As he explained in closing the volume,

[I]t was I who, during those trying months when the book was in the making, picked up the drawings night after night from the floor under Thurber's desk by gaining the confidence of the char-women, nightly redeemed countless other thousands of unfinished sketches from the huge waste baskets; and finally, it was my incredible willingness to go through with the business of "inking-in" the drawings (necessitated by the fact that they were done in such faint strokes of a broken pencil as to be almost invisible to the naked eye) that at last brought them to the point where they could be engraved and reproduced.

Is Sex Necessary? sold fifty thousand copies in its first year, an extraordinary figure considering that it appeared just as the stock market was collapsing. Ross was not exactly enchanted. "How the hell did you get the idea you could *draw?*" he asked Thurber after seeing a copy. The editor was annoyed; he distrusted publishers in general and didn't like that two of his top people had sold some of their best work elsewhere.

Still, he knew he had a new artist of sorts on his hands. Thurber's first drawing in *The New Yorker* appeared in its 1930 anniversary issue, part of a series called "Our Pet Department" that spoofed newspaper pet columns. In setting down such outlandish creatures as a moose that is actually a horse with antlers strapped to its head, and a fish with ears, Thurber was not only expressing his rich whimsy. He was beginning to break new ground in what kind of nonsense could be put on paper and accepted by an appreciative public. As the years went on, Thurber's flights of fancy became ever more exotic. A perfect example of how his infectious wordplay combined with ingenious artistry was his "New Natural History," depicting words as they might appear in animal form. "The Chintz" is an especially prim, precious chinchillalike critter; "The Upstart" is a close relative of a gull just beginning to take flight. Thurber's prehistoric animal "The Stereopticon" naturally has two enormous eyes, while "The Hexameter" appropriately has six legs and might pass for a strange hamster.

His best-known animals, of course, were not his mythical concoctions but his dogs—endlessly climbing, crouching, pouncing, drooping, sniffing, and snooping. What for other people were companions or pets were for Thurber perhaps the most admirable, maintenance-free beings in the universe. Dogs "would in all probability have averted the Depression, for they can go through lots tougher things than we and still think it's boom time," he observed. "They demand very little of their heyday;

a kind word is more to them than fame, a soup bone than gold; they are perfectly contented with a warm fire and a good book to chew (preferably an autographed first edition lent by a friend); wine and song they can completely forgo; and they can almost completely forgo women."

The importance of this last trait, insofar as it informed his artistic output, cannot be overstated. Thurber's complex relationship with virtually all women ran the gamut from adoration to terror. His entire approach to the female of the species jibed with H. L. Mencken's memorable assessment: "The allurement that women hold out to men is precisely the allurement that Cape Hatteras holds out to sailors: they are enormously dangerous and hence enormously fascinating." Thurber's friend Joel Sayre thought Thurber's feelings about the fair sex rather less ambivalent. "He hated their goddam guts!" Sayre said.

Thurber's high-water mark as an artist may have been reached with seventeen dialogue-free panels that began appearing in *The New Yorker* on January 20, 1934, and ended on April 28. "The War Between Men and Women" depicted a literal campaign of aggression between the sexes, starting with a Thurber man tossing a drink in a Thurber woman's face and concluding with a wholesale surrender by the men. "The War Between Men and Women" was not merely the title of a series but became shorthand for an entire Thurber view of the world, set forth and refined over the course of his drawing life, in which men are harried and haunted and the women demanding and predatory.

Frequently, Thurber combined his fantasy and sex-against-sex worlds. A woman in a restaurant, announcing the baffling appearance of a couple of semitransparent owls by exclaiming "Look out! Here they come again!" doesn't scream in fright. Instead, she cries in devilish delight; her male companion, by contrast, merely scowls. A scoffing man tells his female companion, "You and your premonitions!" with neither of them seeing that a Nosferatu-like demon with bared teeth is roaring down at them from the sky. The quintessential expression of this otherworldly theme was "Home," wherein a Thurber man tentatively approaches a house whose back portion has taken on the form of a huge, menacing Thurber woman.

His art was sui generis. Yet he outwardly dismissed this entire aspect of his *New Yorker* life. "My drawing?" he once said to an interviewer. "I've never taken it very seriously." This nonchalance is hard to believe, given the efforts he put into his work. As his blindness worsened, drawing became much harder, made possible only with brighter lights and larger magnifying loupes.

Irrespective of his physical infirmity, he labored mightily and let the staff know it. He once called for an "outside opinion" on a certain cartoon he had drawn, insisting that because he had such high standards for himself, he should be exempt from the art meeting's capricious procedures. "I very much resent being lumped in with the *New Yorker* artists," he wrote to Daise Terry. "I send in about two drawings every week, not fifty-two. I do fifty-two, and make my selections, with at least as much understanding of what is funny as the Art Conference has. Then, zam, I am lumped together with Zilch and all the other artists, although I am not an artist at all, in their sense, and dont [sic] belong with them." Thurber vented his frustration by sketching himself slumping over his drawing table and looking dejected while one observer remarks to another, "He's trying to think of something that would amuse the Art Conference, but there isn't anything." Another sketch along these lines was captioned "5.45 P.M. The Art Conference reaches the Thurber drawings." The facial expressions of the editors in response to one of Thurber's submissions are utterly blank.

Gibbs, too, was frustrated by the persnickety protocol of the conferences—the endless criticisms, the requests for revisions, and so on. But even though he felt he was "most insanely miscast" in these marathon sessions, he was called upon to defend the results. This he did in a preface to *The Seventh New Yorker Album,* published in 1935. It was actually the second of two prefaces in the volume. The first, by the magazine's architecture critic, Lewis Mumford, was a curiously lukewarm appraisal of the contents. Mumford baldly said that he found the volume's cartoon humor "a little too pure for my taste"—that is, too genteel and not sufficiently "tainted with dust and carbon monoxide." He summed up, "The comedy has that special kind of temporary madness that springs out of a tough day at the office and three rapid Martinis. It is titillating but a little frothy; it tickles me but it remains peripheral; it has flavor but it lacks salt."

In his response, Gibbs acknowledged that his job as editorial liaison was a "perplexing lot" and that "any attempt to reconcile the warring aspirations of four editors and fifty artists is, of course, a matter of considerable confusion and embarrassment to everybody concerned." He concluded on a maddeningly indecisive note: if Mumford was dissatisfied, he wrote, "it is the fault of the editors, who in ten years have done little or nothing toward formulating a coherent political philosophy (beyond the negative one of suspecting all such philosophies), and have, I'm afraid, practically no intention of beginning now."

It would take time, but Gibbs would come to better appreciate *The New Yorker*'s artists, doing so in part in the introductions that he wrote to some of their collections. Gibbs declared George Price, creator of squalid households populated by equally unfortunate and oddly angled denizens, to be "one of the most alarming and hilarious artists in the business." He praised Alan Dunn's "economy of means (he is matchless at the extremely difficult feat of drawing pictures that get along hilariously without captions) and highly intelligent topical comment." Gibbs also had high regard for the "intensely emotional atmosphere" that the fanciful William Steig created around his characters. "In the best of his pictures (or the ones I happen to like best)," Gibbs wrote, "there is the queer, distorted, absolutely faithful definition of character available to most of us only in alcohol or a dream, when an old friend is apt to appear fantastic but recognizable, as the essence of what he is rather than what he looks like." Steig, he said, possessed "a rare and happy combination of honest observation and of a technique by no means as simple as it seems." One of his other few favorites was Al Frueh, who, from Manhattan and his place in West Cornwall, Connecticut—which he nicknamed "Belly Acres"—drew for the theater page what Gibbs called "the best caricatures in the country."

By far the most personal introduction Gibbs wrote was for a compilation by an outsize, jovial fellow with a taste for the macabre:

> I can only report that he seems to me very little different from my other friends—a little larger and more casually assembled perhaps, and, of course, somewhat set apart from them by his mysterious dealings in ancient crossbows, articulated bones, and costly, buglike foreign cars. Of the morbid eccentricities that you have undoubtedly been led to expect, however, I'm sorry to say that there is scarcely any trace. It is true that once he gave my ten-year-old son a gleaming human skull, but this, I should say, was merely an example of his generous and perceptive spirit (it was clear that the child needed a skull beyond anything else at the moment in the world), and I doubt if he can be charged with any desire to add one more budding monster to his black domain.

The very first piece of art that a young Charles Addams of Westfield, New Jersey, sold to *The New Yorker* was a February 6, 1932 "spot" of a window washer high atop a building. It took him almost another year before his first full-fledged cartoon appeared, a simple line illustration of a stocking-footed hockey player on the ice sheepishly confessing to his teammates, "I forgot my skates." Neither offered any hint of the unique contribution he would make to the magazine for more than half a century.

No *New Yorker* artist ever generated as much curiosity about his personal life as did Addams, and none ever offered a greater contrast between his private and public self. Virtually everyone who ever met the man agreed that he was gentle, cheerful, and companionable. "He had a sweetness that someone who was less of a man would be afraid to show," said Walter Matthau's wife, Carol.

Those who didn't know him never quite believed it. No one who drew a two-headed woman blocking the view of an ordinary one-headed man in a movie theater, they figured, or who depicted a snowman as dead by toppling it on its side, impaled by its own broomstick, could be quite normal. And so devoted readers bombarded Addams with ideas, most of them too grisly for consideration. "That's really not the sort of thing we do at *The New Yorker*," he would tell would-be gagsters in social situations before slipping away. Protests notwithstanding, Addams had his eccentricities. He picnicked in graveyards and visited freak shows and lunatic wards in search of raw material. Rumors to the contrary, he didn't sleep in a coffin or keep a full-sized guillotine around the house. But his midtown Manhattan apartment was indeed filled with medieval arms and armor, a sewing basket made from an armadillo, and a table formerly used for human embalming. He relished playing the part of the devilish cherub, presenting acquaintances with bizarre tokens—like the black rubber spider and assorted toy lizards he gave to Burgess Meredith's two-year-old son, Jonathan.

"Charley is this kind of a guy," Meredith told a reporter. "No sooner are you settled down, the kids are put to bed, and the first drink is coming around, when he says, with that quiet grin of his, 'Lot of ticks out here this time of year. If they bite you, you know, there's no cure.'"

Actually, much of Addams's humor wasn't mordant; witness his cartoon of one bear asking another after hibernating, "What in the world was the matter? You tossed and turned all winter." Invariably, though, readers responded most enthusiastically to his blackest images, like the one of an annoyed woman in a jungle bungalow snapping, "Oh, speak up, George! Stop mumbling!" unaware that George has been devoured by a giant snake. Addams generally resisted the urge to examine the source of his demons too closely. "I don't think much about why I do what I do," he said. "Probably better not to. If I found out why, I might lose it." Pressed, he would reply, "Oh, I suppose it represents a kind of separate life, a dream thing."

Perhaps it was for that reason that the shy, gloomy Gibbs especially took to the ebullient, ever-smiling Addams. In his dark art, Addams offered Gibbs a twinkling spin on his natural pessimism. Addams's universe, said Gibbs, reflected life's "dominant strain . . . as if God had shrugged His shoulders and given up the world, natural selection has reversed itself and presently our civilization will once again belong to the misshapen, the moonstruck, and the damned."

For all his negativity, Gibbs the art conference appraiser responded to a job well done, and in Addams he saw a true craftsman. So deeply did he admire Addams's work that when, like Thurber, he impetuously dashed off a cartoon on a corridor wall, it was an Addams parody. Situated near the water cooler, it depicted a nurse outside a maternity ward handing a baby to a monstrous-looking father and asking, "Will you take it with you or will you eat it here?"

Gibbs was especially taken with Addams's most famous creation, his clan of creepy eccentrics known first colloquially and later formally as "The Addams Family." He may have glommed onto them because their brittle, dysfunctional father-mother-son-daughter arrangement offered some parallels to his own household. The father figure held particular interest for Gibbs, resembling as he did a squat, evil-looking Thomas E. Dewey, whom Gibbs loathed with particular gusto. Whatever the reason, Gibbs yearned to collaborate with Addams on a project involving the brood, as he suggested in 1947:

[S]omething really ought to be done about that haunted house bunch, and if you haven't made any other arrangements, I'd love to try a play with you. As I see it, you've really got most of the lines already, since, surprisingly, about half the lines and situations from the other pictures could just as well be part of that series and could certainly be borrowed for it. There's never been material so rich in sight gags, characters, atmosphere, and perfect curtain lines. The trouble, again as we said, is to avoid that old, foolish scream-and-trap-door note, and the problem is to get a soundplot [sic] to offset too much fantasy, but I think it can be done. You'd probably be better off with sombody [sic] like [Lindsay] Crouse, who knows his business though otherwise a pinhead, but if my version didn't work out, you could always get him or somebody like him in the end.

Although that proposal came to nothing, the following year he tried collaborating with Addams on a very different venture—a slim effort he called "The Christmas Caller." Subtitled "A Gothic Gift Book for a Bad Child" and taking place at Addams's haunted house ("Holocaust Hall"), it opens with the Addams children whiling away their Christmas Eve boredom by conjuring up phantoms and threatening to put curses on each other. There is much talk of presents: "six cases of weed killer," "one blunt instrument," "some more of those little pills that make me see in the dark," and so on. There are also suitably unsettling details (rooms identified as "Jeopardy" and "Doom"; a cryptic entry in a notebook that reads "Joseph Force Crater. August 6th, 1930"). Considerable excitement ensues when a certain Mr. Smith, actually Santa Claus in disguise, pays a call. But when he bestows upon the children such disappointingly conventional gifts as baseball equipment, a teddy bear, and worst of all, a doll that wets its pants but doesn't bleed, he is left to the tender mercies of "an old lady upstairs."*

---

* The book was never published because Addams, after reading Gibbs's manuscript, decided against illustrating it. "I ended up feeling that it would be detrimental to the series and that it might end it for good," he wrote. "I think that perhaps the house should be pictured but not written about." Upset, Gibbs asked Ross for a second opinion. Ross, who admitted that he didn't understand the text very well, agreed with the cartoonist. "I'm convinced that getting any more definite with the Addams haunted house characters that we have gone [sic] would destroy their romance and illustration, and mystery," he told Gibbs. "This [is] the only piece of yours I've ever been stuch [sic] on, that I recall."

For all his fascination with "the haunted house bunch," Gibbs never actually passed judgment on them for *The New Yorker*. The cartoonist placed his first Addams Family drawing in the magazine in August 1938, more than a year after Gibbs managed to abandon his place at the art conference by fobbing it off on new arrival William Maxwell. Maxwell turned out to be no more enthusiastic about his art meeting duties than Gibbs was and so began looking for someone who could replace *him*. His choice was James L. Geraghty, the magazine's very first formal art editor.

One of eleven children of an Irish immigrant, Geraghty was a lapsed Catholic who had gone to Gonzaga Prep and, subsequently, Gonzaga University in Spokane, Washington. He was expelled from the latter in 1927 for writing an essay that compared its Jesuit teachers unfavorably with the Harvard professoriat. (A notation on his transcript stated that he had "started to develop Bolshevik tendencies.") For a time, Geraghty drove a beer truck in Seattle while pretending to go to school. Eventually he drifted to New York, where he oversaw secretaries at McGraw-Hill. But with an eye on his brother, John, a graphic artist, he yearned to enter a more exciting aspect of the media. "So quit your job!" said his wife, Eve. "I've been waiting for you to say that!" Geraghty replied.

Somehow he wangled a writing gig for Tim and Irene Ryan's radio show, crafting exchanges in the vein of Burns and Allen. After three years of work in the depths of the Depression, he earned just five hundred dollars. He contemplated moving to New Hampshire and the potentially welcoming arms of Eve's family. Then one day she brought home a copy of *The Writer* magazine containing an article that described how cartoonists paid for ideas. Not an artist himself, Geraghty threw himself into this new possibility, rising at five a.m. every day to brainstorm. One of his markets was, naturally, *The New Yorker*. Soon he was coming up with gags for such regulars as Barney Tobey, Richard Decker, Perry Barlow, and Peter Arno, averaging about eighteen dollars per notion.

Maxwell hired him in 1939, largely on the strength of Geraghty's ability to persuade the stubborn Arno to straighten out a drawing that looked nothing like what he, Geraghty, had conceived. Told by Maxwell to come in three days a week, he made a habit of coming in four. Inevitably he met Ross in the hall. "What are you doing here?" the editor snapped. "What does it matter," the art editor shot back, "so long as I get my job done?"

Geraghty would get that job done at *The New Yorker* for thirty-four years. He was a man of quiet economy; quite often his only advice to the artists was "Make them funny" or "Make it beautiful." Frequently he would not even say that much. With twitches, vague gestures, and other nonverbal communication, he would somehow get his criticisms and suggestions across. He butted heads with Ross frequently, occasionally forging the editor's signature of approval to get a piece of art into the magazine. Once when Geraghty protested that a certain drawing was good enough for publication, Ross offered a memorable retort: "Nothing, Geraghty, *nothing* is ever good enough." Left unsaid, Geraghty felt, was a corollary: "And don't you forget it."

With Geraghty at the helm, *The New Yorker*'s art, already famous, would become world renowned. No one was more pleased with the final arrangement than Maxwell's predecessor. "Gibbs was delighted not to screen the incoming work," Geraghty recalled. "He said after looking at it for an hour or so he felt he should wash his hands with a strong soap."

As his various cartoon-book introductions indicated, Gibbs did admire certain contributors. But Geraghty was largely right about Gibbs's disdain for the art process. "I got very sick of transmitting notes to the artists, which always read 'Better pix,' 'Who's talking?', or just 'Make funnier,'" Gibbs said. He recalled what finally drove him to sign off: "It always meant that the meeting had no real intention of buying the picture, but sometimes the poor bastard would do things over six or seven times. The big mystic problem was which artists were permitted to leave out the wires leading to lamps and the rugs on the floor."

CHAPTER 5

———

"SOME VERY FUNNY PEOPLE"

ecause the prime movers of *The New Yorker* were so creative and productive, their raw energy created a superabundance of drama and comedy. Ordinary problems became magnified and fragile egos threatened to implode.

The pattern was set during the heady 1920s when the young staff, under Ross's relentless direction, by necessity drove itself to extremes. "We thought nothing of working from early morning until nine or ten at night, with a sandwich for lunch at our desks," wrote the author Marcia Davenport, daughter of the opera singer Alma Gluck. "Then after dinner break the proofs would start coming in. They had to be corrected and rewritten in whole or in part after Ross got his hooks into them, so it was the rule rather than the exception to work from eleven or twelve at night until dawn. Three or four hours' sleep and we were at it again."

Some of the frenetic atmosphere was engendered by the haphazard arrangement of the early *New Yorker* offices at 25 West 45th Street. (The headquarters moved to 25 West 43rd Street in 1935.) Their disarray was compounded by Ross's ceaseless quest for an efficient layout. Lois Long would later satirize the physical setup of the place:

There was always the little game of trying to find your desk, for instance. The offices, such as they were, were distributed all over the unrented sections of the building and the greatest delight of our editor (he still retains this lovable characteristic) was to move the desks about prankishly in the dead of night. The result was that you could easily spend an entire morning which you might have spent—God forbid—in honest labor, running up and downstairs in the elevators looking for your office.

The crap game started at four-thirty, at which time it was the particular delight of the Talk of the Town editor, the Art editor, and your correspondent to send our movie critic home to the wife and kiddies without his weekly pay check [*sic*]. This being accomplished with astounding regularity, everybody went out arm in arm to dinner.

Long contributed to the informal tenor by working in her slip in hot weather and frequently misplacing the key to her cubbyhole. When that happened, "she used the doorknob as a footrest and propelled herself gracefully over the partitions." As for the crap games she referenced, they were eventually supplanted by poker games. Don Mankiewicz, briefly on the staff, remembered different-colored routing slips being used as betting chips.

Chaos reigned, too, when it came to the material itself. Robert Benchley, for instance, refused to double-space his copy. "The single-spaced stuff drove the proof and checking departments crazy because they couldn't write between the lines, which I'm sure was his object," said Gibbs. "And the fact that it was not only single-spaced but also crowded off to one side of the page made it almost impossible to get a word count without actually counting the words. It always came out shorter than I thought it was going to, and it was hell working out last minute fillers."

At least Benchley could be relied on to file. Not so the erratic Dorothy Parker. "[She] would tell me on Friday that her piece was all finished," Gibbs said, "except for the final paragraph, and stall me along that way until late Sunday evening when she'd say she just tore the whole thing up because it was so terrible." Once he dispatched her a telegram that read, SWELL JAM I'M IN STOP COMMITTING SUICIDE IF NO COPY FROM YOU TODAY.

Gradually, as the Depression set in and *The New Yorker* settled down to the serious business of staying afloat, the irresponsibility and horse-play tended to diminish. But befitting a magazine of metropolitan gaiety, its corridors still rocked with nonsense, never more so than when its personnel were simply endeavoring to carry on. In a poker-faced vein, Ross once asked Fleischmann to set up a new room for the art conference, which at that time was being "held very clumsily in Mrs. White's outer office with the juggling of a lot of tables, doors, etc." Ross rejected the idea of holding the meeting in the reception room: "Every word spoken in the corridor outside of Gibbs', McKelway's and Mrs. White's offices can be heard over the partition. The other day Mr. Winney* was telling someone I was out when I was heard talking four feet away. This is terrifying to several of us down here."

Indeed, that reception room—the holding pen of the asylum, as it were—spawned its special brand of bedlam, as Gibbs recalled:

> I saw some very funny people in the old reception room in the days when I was an editor of some kind: DeWitt Wallace whom I gave permission to print Talk in Reader's Digest free, just because he struck me as such a pathetic hick; Maxwell Bodengiem, who came up with a bunch of poems but finally settled for a loan of fifty cents; a Mr. Zogbaum, who was Baird Leonard's husband, and delivered her copy when she was reviewing books. It was usually just a drunken scrawl on the backs of a lot of bills and

---

* Harold Winney, who eventually became Ross's personal secretary, ended up embezzling more than $70,000 from him and committing suicide.

envelopes, and for quite a while I wrote Miss Leonard's books [*sic*] reviews, as I did those signed by Nancy Hoyt and, once, one by Sally Benson's sister, Agnes. In many ways, the Nyer's [*sic*] debt to me is enormous.

Past the reception room was *The New Yorker*'s unique in-house web of intrigue—what White memorably called "a cesspool of loyalties." He might well have added "disloyalties." In its loves, hates, feuds, alliances, and similar dynamics, the cesspool was practically a culture unto itself.

And as was the case with editorial policy, Ross set the tone from the top down. The editor had many troubled relationships over his life, and the one he had with his publisher, Fleischmann, was as poisonous as any of them. The two were forever wrangling over expenses, equity, ownership, stock options, advertisements, promotions, and the like. More than once Ross threatened to quit. The famed *New Yorker* separation of church and state was as much a function of the two men's mutual antipathy as it was Ross's way of keeping the magazine's content free from corrupting business influences. Ross, never particularly sensitive to the feelings of others, came to regard the gentlemanly Raoul Fleischmann as a meddling bankroller. In return, Fleischmann would regard Ross as impractically single-minded. Sometimes when the publisher would pass the editor in the corridors, he would sneer, "Pest." And the editor would snarl, referring to the source of the family fortune, "Yeast."

At the other extreme was the way Ross dealt with writers. He wanted to reward them as best he could, but for a long time, he couldn't. Thurber was almost certainly exaggerating when he said, "*The New Yorker* did not begin paying its contributors real dough until it was nearly twenty years old." Still, Ross acknowledged in the late 1930s that he was paying some of his top contributors "a ribbon clerk's salary." The lack of pay was the main reason such figures as Fitzgerald and Hemingway barely published anything in the magazine. As late as 1934, after they had more than proved their worth to Ross, White and Thurber were each receiving seventeen cents a word. Two years later Gibbs was getting half a penny less— hardly a windfall, even during the Depression.

If Ross could not make his people rich, he could at least make them feel they were needed. His letters to his favorites would be just as supportive as those of Katharine White, albeit more direct, such as WRITE SOME PIECES, DAMMIT! When not hard at work at his desk, he gregariously roamed the halls to drop by cubicles to jaw, wanting to be kept informed of progress and encouraging activity. Towering above the pack was White, the man he felt could do no wrong, the possessor of his own unique moral editorial compass. "There is only one White," Ross confided in him.

"Harold's relationship with Andy was special in a way no one else's was," said Katharine. "Nine times out of ten when he arrived at the office and got out of the elevator on the 19th floor he would turn left, to look in on Andy if only to be sure he was there or discuss a newsbreak line or tell him a joke or kick things around, instead of turning right to his own office. It was the way he started the day. . . . Ross trusted a few of us implicitly and Andy was one in whom he had complete faith."

By contrast, it took White a while to acquire faith in others, including his colleagues. After all, it had taken all of Ross's and Katharine's combined powers of persuasion to get him to join the staff. He was very much a loner. "White's customary practice in those days," said Thurber, "if he couldn't place a caller's name, was to slip moodily out of the building by way of the fire escape and hide in the coolness of Schrafft's until the visitor went away." The two may have shared an office at the beginning, but when Thurber first asked him to lunch, White replied curtly, "I always eat alone." Before long, though, the two were friends, spurring each other on. "We got on fine together," said White. Early in 1929, when White found himself despondent enough to consider quitting his job and leaving town, the mere thought of a funny Thurber drawing revived him sufficiently that he determined to stick around. But there was more to Thurber's tonic than his art. "[O]ne of the persons I like best in the world is Thurber," White said. "Just being around him is something." At the end of his life, White had on his bookshelf a ceramic rendering of a comic Thurber scene.

Still, the White-Thurber axis was troublesome. "To know Thurber and have him as a friend was a pleasure, but it was also a challenge—sometimes almost a full-time job," White told Lillian Hellman long after Thurber died. "I discovered this early on, and I'm still at it. . . . I had to give up Thurber, after a few years, the way you give up coffee or cigarettes or whiskey. He became too strong for my constitution."

Thurber's force of will was frequently on display when, fortified by drink, he began acting up. "With Thurber, the scene was always in the offing," said one witness. "He'd soften you up and then spring like a rattlesnake, but without the warning. He attacked both men and women; your sex was no protection. He could pick on you in a feline, catty kind of way." Katharine White agreed. "We Whites were in such a difficult position about him because we loved him dearly up to a certain point—the point where he began to attack all women, including me." As Maxwell put it, he had "a talent for the unforgivable."

Beneath Thurber's friendship with White ran an undercurrent of jealousy and envy. He was beholden to White as a writer, a pose that White found baffling. "I've never known, and will never know, how much Jim was influenced by my stuff," he confessed. "It has always seemed to me that the whole thing was exaggerated. Jim himself exaggerated it, as he exaggerated other matters and events. . . . My memory of those early days was that Jim was writing very well indeed and needed no help from me or anyone else." Yet in his insecurity he couldn't help measuring himself against White. The self-imagined competition was often absurd. Early on, White told Katharine, Thurber began "discussing his bowels and comparing them to mine, claiming that his are better than mine, adding that of course he is older and taller than I am."

Gibbs, a standoffish figure in the White mold, albeit more misanthropic, did his best to avoid friendships and rivalries alike. Much of his time in the office was spent kept to himself. "He had the semi-hangdog air of someone who drank a lot," said the "Talk" reporter Jim Munves. By contrast, the assistant art editor Frank Modell remembered Gibbs as so dapper that he reminded him of Fred Astaire. Modell vividly recalled Gibbs pacing in the hallway, apparently composing a piece in his head. "I can almost hear his leather heels clicking on the floor and see the intensity on his face. It was a very impressive act."

Gibbs did not make for mixing. In the *New Yorker* corridors, Edmund Wilson recalled, he "glided past like a ghost. His eyes always seemed to be closed." Truman Capote went so far as to call him a "sourpuss." "I never saw him smile," said Modell. "The few times I saw him in the hall, I could just tell from his attitude that he didn't want to be talked to," said Ross's private secretary, William Walden.

But try though he might, Gibbs could not avoid entanglements. Some were salutary. He set great store, for instance, by his closeness with Benchley. Benchley was not merely, as White said, a man whose "high spirits are those of a retired reformer, who got all his good deeds behind him safely in his twenties." At his core was considerable kindness and sensitivity; he had a knack for setting the neurotic Gibbs's mind and soul at ease. "When you were with him," Gibbs recalled, "in the wonderful junk shop he operated at the Royalton in '21,' or in less fashionable saloons which had the simple merit of staying open all night, you had a very warm and encouraging feeling that the things you said sounded quite a lot better than they really were and, such was the miracle of his sympathy and courteous hope, they often actually *were* pretty good. He wanted his guests to feel that they were succeeding socially and he did the best he could to make it easy for them."

Gibbs was also devoted to the self-confident, frequently womanizing Addams, who could draw him out of his shell. In the 1930s they would make the rounds of the local watering holes, sometimes with Thurber, riding in a car down Third Avenue with "Gilbert Seldes hanging on the running board." Addams "was a really dependable, almost miraculously dependable, friend," said Gibbs's son, Tony. "If there was a crisis, Addams would suddenly appear."

But such confidences, for Gibbs, were rare. More often he retreated from emotional contact. He tooled down Third Avenue with Thurber, but as time went by, he relished such experiences with the high-strung humorist less and less. "They were not pals," said Katharine White. In fact, Thurber would periodically and gratuitously tell Gibbs, "You think you can be as good a writer as Andy White but you never will be."

Rather more vexing and problematic was the Gibbs-O'Hara connection. "Don't think I am any less misanthropic than Gibbs is," O'Hara confessed. "It's just that I sputter and Gibbs is beautifully articulate." By the same token, Gibbs had high regard for O'Hara as a writer; he once compared *Appointment in Samarra* to *The Great Gatsby*. (Gibbs, in turn, personally reminded O'Hara of Fitzgerald.) "If," Gibbs predicted early on, "he can contrive to write about the things he authentically hates— waste and hypocrisy and the sadness of potentially valuable lives failing, but not without some dignity, because they were not born quite strong enough for the circumstances they had to meet—and if he can write about them with the honesty and understanding which he possesses in as great a measure as anyone writing today, then he will certainly be one of our most important novelists."

For his part, O'Hara characterized Gibbs as "a kindly man whose days as an employe [sic] of the Long Island Rail Road have left him intolerant of cruelty." Gibbs, he thought, was possessed of his own brand of worldliness, one that he came to appreciate as the years went by. "The conversation was animated, brilliant, and as might be expected of two men who have known each other for twenty-six years, classified material," O'Hara wrote following one of their many lunches in the early 1950s. "I may say, however, that following our custom, we re-examined certain human frailties, such as the nocturnal, the fiscal and so on. After one of these lunches, a kind of euphoria takes hold—at least in my case—

because in all the world there are only two men who are so free of pomposity, gallant but not silly in their relations with the opposite sex, gifted writers but not competitors, figures of consequence in Upper Middle Bohemia, men of experience without being dwellers in the past." He once sent Gibbs a case of whiskey at Christmastime, with Gibbs reportedly returning it because he could not accept so extravagant a gift. "Gibbs and John were real intimates," said Katharine White.

Still, O'Hara could be utterly exasperating. Egotistical and insecure, famously known as the master of the fancied slight, he was forever picking fights, especially when he had been drinking. "I have no arguments with anything said about John O'Hara as a gifted, and subsequently mistakenly overlooked American author," said Peter Kriendler, the operator of "21," where O'Hara enjoyed being seen. "But as a man I remember him as a pain in the ass." Once, for reasons now unknown, O'Hara ordered a glass of brandy for the express purpose of tossing it in Gibbs's face. When asked why he would do such a thing, he pouted, "But it was the *best* brandy."

Another time, when O'Hara was "putting wrestling holds on ladies and otherwise acting churlish," Benchley tried to put a stop to it. O'Hara responded by knocking Benchley's cigar out of his mouth. The next morning he called to apologize.

"Look, John, please don't apologize to *me*," Benchley told him. "You're a shit and everyone knows you're a shit, and people ask you out in spite of it. It's nothing to apologize about."

"Do you mean that?" asked an astonished O'Hara.

"Of course I mean it, John. You were born a shit just as some people were born with blue eyes, but that's no reason to go around apologizing for it. People take you for what you are." Benchley's bracing honesty and acceptance, spoken with the utmost gentility, reduced O'Hara to tears.

"I know him better than anybody," Gibbs told Katharine White, "but that's handicap more than anything else, I'm afraid."

Gibbs and O'Hara could be afforded their complicated mixture of admiration and animosity because they were genuine intimates. A different instance altogether was the tragic case of Russell Maloney. Gibbs barely knew him, and yet he ended up as Maloney's sworn enemy. So did a few others.

In addition to many stories, familiar essays, and casuals, Maloney published *New Yorker* Profiles of figures like Orson Welles, Leonard Lyons, and Alfred Hitchcock. His most famous fictional concoction was the wildly imaginative "Inflexible Logic," about a hapless fellow who disastrously tests the old notion that six monkeys pounding on six typewriters for a million years will eventually type out every book in the British Museum. "Talk" was his special forte. In taking over the rewriting of the section largely from Thurber, Maloney turned out reams of copy; he boasted that he ultimately wrote more than two million words for the magazine, including "something like 2,600 perfect anecdotes." He was, Geraghty said, "a cranky genius who could do anything around the place that could be done with a typewriter."

And yet he left the staff, embittered, in 1945, after only about a decade. Two years later he published a piece about *The New Yorker* in *The Saturday Review* that his former colleagues derided as inaccurate and mean-spirited. By Maloney's sights, both Thurber and White had been "very bad reporters" before joining the magazine; he said that for Ross, "Perfection is not a goal or an ideal, but something that belongs to him, like his watch or his hat." In response, Ross denounced him as "totally incompetent," "never a good fact man," someone who "wouldn't know a reporter if he saw one," and "a social suicide" to boot. Referring blithely to his "psychosis," Katharine White said that Maloney had made his post–*New Yorker* living "mostly by abusing us."

The reasons for Maloney's downfall were complex. Like his Profile subject Welles, he peaked early. Growing up in Newton Centre, Massachusetts, he was only about nine when his domineering mother insisted that he be issued an adult library card because he had already read all the books in the children's section. Despite the prejudices of its Brahmin establishment against the Irish, Harvard admitted him; there he won the George B. Sohier Prize for the best thesis written by a student of English or modern literature. He began contributing cartoon ideas to *The New Yorker* for Peter Arno, Helen Hokinson, Thurber, Carl Rose, Mary Petty, Whitney Darrow, and others before he graduated in 1932; two years later Mrs. White invited him to join the staff.

It was a rapid rise, but to Maloney's mind, it led nowhere. After a few years of "Talk" rewrite and other comedic duties, he found himself bored. It didn't help that like all "Talk" contributors, he toiled in anonymity. He was sensitive, too, and thus ill equipped for an office where prankish insults and put-downs were routine. Arguably underappreciated and certainly overworked, especially during the war, he felt himself capable of better things. In 1943, when Clifton Fadiman quit as the magazine's chief book reviewer, Maloney lobbied for the job. When it went to Edmund Wilson, Maloney "went stomping in to Ross and told him that this time, positively, he had gone too far."

In short, Maloney felt that professional growth had eluded him. "As far as I can tell, I have managed to stand completely still," he complained. "My first piece might have been my last, and my last my first, as far as any merit is concerned." During the first half of the 1940s, he tried variously to wrest from Ross a substantial raise, an exclusive service contract, and more responsibility on his terms. He got nowhere.

Ross valued Maloney, so much so that when the latter became convinced that the bottles in the office water coolers were being "filled by a Greek from a faucet in a mop closet" and were thus unsanitary, Ross wrote a two-page memo on the subject and paid a local chemist ten dollars to test the stuff. (It displayed "no evidence of bacterial pollution.") But the extraordinary effort of getting out a magazine starved for both personnel and resources during wartime didn't allow him to indulge the temperamental writer. He had his own explanation for why Maloney quit.

"He was frustrated in his desire to be a critic," Ross told O'Hara, "which I would never let him be, because I didn't think he had the balance, the judgment, and the character to be a critic. He's influenced almost exclusively by personalities, as nearly as I can see, is a disgruntled soul, and a critic has got to have objectivity." Certainly Maloney's forays into criticism could be unfortunate, never more so than in 1939 when he slammed *The Wizard of Oz* as having "no trace of imagination, good taste, or ingenuity." He called it a "stinkeroo."

Unable to accept that criticism was perhaps not his strong suit, he began to see conspiracies. One day he announced, "The Giants have come down from the hills!" Actually, it was only the Whites. "They were giants all right but no [sic] benign ones," Geraghty mused. "Not to Maloney. To him they were ogres out to get him."

His greatest jealousy and hatred was of Gibbs. White vividly remembered Maloney during the war "in his gas mask and helmet, ready to save everybody in New York except Gibbs." When Gibbs temporarily couldn't continue as the main "Comment" writer because he had fallen down and broken two fingers, Maloney was elated. During contract negotiations with Ross, he pressed for such outlandish concessions as "a bonus of twice the difference between Gibbs' yearly income and mine, if mine is smaller" and "a definite offer of the Theatre column when Gibbs goes too crazy to write it any more." Dismissing Gibbs as "the current Eustace Tilley" shortly before Pearl Harbor, Maloney wrote the Whites that his nemesis was "trying to spit on the theatre and on current events at the same time, and he hasn't enough spit."

Whence came this enmity? Gibbs suspected he had driven his colleague crazy through an act of "mistaken kindness"—namely, introducing Maloney to his future wife, Miriam Battista. "One night, when he first came to town," Gibbs said, "he told me he didn't know any girls, so I said 'There is nothing easier' and called up Miriam who was working in a show called *Mulatto*. I'm afraid I told him in effect that she was a sure lay. . . . A month or so later, I remembered to ask him how he made out and, of course, he never spoke to me again because they were married."

Gibbs personified everything Maloney wished to be: a witty man about town, a wearer of many editorial hats, an arbiter of taste. Actually, Maloney was already well established in that persona and, with a few more years of seasoning, might have achieved it entirely. But stymied in his early thirties, Maloney became convinced that Gibbs "was out to do away with me." And so he determined to destroy him:

I started reading Comment very carefully, every week. Whenever I found an error in judgment or grammar, a phrase or an idea that Gibbs was using too often, or something that was inconsistent with something he'd said before, I'd write duplicate memos to Ross and Shawn. . . . I did this for about a year. Then, one week, Gibbs had an ill-made little sentence about somebody or other being in his "customary dilemma." I wrote a little memo that Fowler would have been proud of, pointing out that a dilemma is something you don't get into voluntarily, and that Gibbs must have been trying to say "usual dilemma." I remember I had several sentences illustrating proper uses of the different words, like "Gibbs had his customary dinner of eight Martinis, and next morning had his usual hangover," and "Gibbs took his customary crack at Jed Harris's latest play, because Harris once rejected a play he had written." And I said that, even if I wasn't considered enough of a stylist to write really important things, at least I'd never used words I didn't understand. Two weeks later, Shawn was put in charge of Comment and I was asked to contribute, and, after about six months of my doing it in competition with Gibbs, he announced that he was sick and tired of doing that boresome [*sic*] drivel, and wanted to be an editor again.

I wish I could put into words the satisfaction it gives me to think about this. It's like lying on a feather bed and being massaged by angels.

If Gibbs truly did want to get rid of Maloney, or if Maloney really did undermine Gibbs, the evidence is elusive. Gibbs himself said that he gave up "Comment" in the early 1940s because "getting out a weekly collection of trivia about Armageddon was absurdly beyond my talent or inclination." But even if Maloney actually could have sabotaged Gibbs, surely no amount of revenge would have satisfied his need for self-realization. When Maloney quit *The New Yorker,* he did so ostensibly because at thirty-five he was too old to maintain his pace. Actually, he said, it was "to broaden my scope."

And broaden it he did, both before and after leaving. He published in *Life, Collier's, The Atlantic Monthly,* and *The New York Times Book Review.* He doctored plays, did a new version of the book of *Die Fledermaus* for the Philadelphia Opera Company, and wrote for Orson Welles, Billie Burke, and Fred Allen. Though he never succeeded Fadiman, he reviewed books for the *Chicago Sun* and on Thursday nights hosted a CBS radio program called *Of Men and Books.*

What should have been his crowning triumph was his original musical comedy *Sleepy Hollow,* based on the legend of Ichabod Crane, which opened on Broadway in June 1948 and starred Miriam. Unfortunately, it ran for only twelve performances.* The show's collapse destroyed what was left of Maloney's already precarious finances. (His last *New Yorker* casual, printed in 1944, had been a darkly humorous take on bankruptcy.) Less than three months after *Sleepy Hollow* closed, its author succumbed to a stroke at age thirty-eight; he had suffered from severe

---

* In his review, titled "Washington Irving Slipped Here," Gibbs dismissed the musical without particular rancor or invective. He called it "pretty" and "melodious" but mainly "dull." He did say that the songs and dances, for which Maloney was not responsible, were "often first-rate."

idiopathic hypertension all his life and had long predicted he would die young. In addition to Miriam, Maloney left a three-year-old daughter, Amelia, and more than ten thousand dollars in debts. Many years later, invoking the considerable contributions that her late husband had made to *The New Yorker,* Miriam would appeal to the magazine for financial assistance, in vain.

———————

In its youthful heyday, the *New Yorker* crowd was a rowdy bunch. At the magazine's tenth anniversary party in 1935, when Morris Markey saw McKelway accompanied by Stanley Walker, the former city editor of the *Herald Tribune,* he quipped, "Ah, here's Mac, surrounded by beauty as usual." McKelway flailed but failed to connect; Markey hit his opponent in the chest, sending him backward over a table. The very next day at Gibbs's apartment, when Thurber beheld Elinor Gibbs quite pregnant with Tony, he sneered, "You ungainly creature, you." This so infuriated Gibbs that he bloodied Thurber's nose and mouth.

From the beginning of his enterprise, Ross was determined to circumvent at least one form of internal mingling and mangling. "I am going to keep sex out of this office," he vowed. He was not always successful. Early on, in fact, he undermined himself by setting up a salon in a Fleischmann-owned property on 45th Street. "He thought if the magazine had its own speakeasy it would be safer for us and that the same general decorum could be kept that Mrs. White inspired at the office," said Lois Long. "Then Ingersoll came in one morning and found Arno and me stretched out on the sofa nude and Ross closed the place down. I think he was afraid Mrs. White would hear about it. Arno and I may have been married to one another by then; I can't remember. Maybe we began drinking and forgot that we were married and had an apartment to go to."

Long and Arno would likely have gotten into trouble on their own even without Ross's inadvertent assistance. In fact, they were *The New Yorker*'s poster children for intramural love gone sour. Their marriage in 1927 was perhaps as inevitable as their divorce three years later. Both of them—Long, comely and flirtatious; Arno, well built and square-jawed—were after-hours embodiments of the Jazz Age. Arno, slightly younger than Long, had been born Curtis Arnoux Peters, the son of a New York State Supreme Court justice. A graduate of the Hotchkiss School, he played the banjo in a band at Yale and was later in a group whose members included Rudy Vallee. He changed his name to Arno, he told friends, because he wanted to separate his identity from that of his respectable family. He was right to do so; his first drawings in *The New Yorker*, which appeared shortly after its 1925 debut, were defined by their sardonic take on Manhattan's booze-laden, libidinous speakeasy culture.

"I've always rebelled against the social order, if you get what I mean," he griped. "At least, some aspects of it. As I grew up I became dissatisfied with the life around me." He was determined to expose the "fatuous" crowd he himself ran with. "I had a really hot impulse to go and exaggerate their ridiculous aspects. That anger, if you like, gave my stuff punch and made it live. I mean, I don't know anything better to call it than anger." Arno especially despised "vain little girls with more alcohol in their brains than sense."

Lois Long had more sense than alcohol in her brains. But Arno, who was convinced that "at no time in the history of the world have there been so many damned morons gathered together in one place as here in New York right now," somehow saw in her an embodiment of the social whirl he enjoyed attacking. When he spoke of his anger, he was not exaggerating; Long was sometimes his target. "Occasionally she would come into the office with a bruise or black eye and reply if sympathetically asked what had happened, 'Oh, I ran into a door in the dark,' or 'I was in a taxi accident,'" said Marcia Davenport. Years after her divorce from Arno, their acrimony continued unabated, with Arno failing to provide agreed-upon alimony and child support payments. At one point, he owed her over fourteen thousand dollars yet lived in a ten-room penthouse and "was busy buying champagne and brandy all over the place."

It was typical behavior for Arno, who often lived as if Prohibition had never been repealed. Outwardly a cheerful soul, singing as he drew and painted, he had a mean and arrogant streak. He paid the artist Arthur Getz fifty dollars for a cover design and then, after minor revisions, pretty much passed it off as his own, losing the original rough in the process. Another time, when two of his cartoon captions were changed without his permission, he insisted that if anything like that ever happened again, the magazine would have to pay him five hundred dollars. His love life was the stuff of comic books: Cornelius Vanderbilt, Jr., once chased him down the street, brandishing a revolver, after Arno had embraced Mrs. Vanderbilt. He carried on a well-publicized affair with the debutante Brenda Diana Duff Frazier and, during a late-night row, gave her a shiner.

And yet, as Arno had accurately assessed, his anger provided important fuel for his artistry. At one point he telephoned Geraghty to announce, after three years of psychoanalysis: "Jim, congratulate me. I've lost my arrogance." Geraghty replied, "Peter you should lose your drawing arm first." Arno eventually became something of a gun nut, with "quite an armament, licensed and otherwise," and although he remarried and continued cartooning for *The New Yorker* up to his death in 1968, he eventually settled into a "seething reclusivity."

Other *New Yorker* unions were more successful. One was that of William Walden and his wife, Harriet, aka "Tippy"; she succeeded him as Ross's private secretary when he joined the army during the war. Another was that of Freddie Packard and Eleanor Gould; her microscopic dissection of syntax, vocabulary, punctuation, and similar myriad details for fifty-four years perfectly mirrored her husband's obsession with facts. She would often write in the margins of passages that baffled her, "Have we completely lost our mind?"

But for the sheer communion of souls, no *New Yorker* marriage could surpass the long and happy merging of E. B. White and Katharine Angell. At first glance, their joining was unlikely. White was a relative novice in the romance department; he had had a couple of girlfriends, most notably a Cornell compatriot named Alice Burchfield. But he was awkward and chaste; his letters to her from the early 1920s were never signed "fondly" or "affectionately," let alone "love," but "sincerely" or with nothing other than his name. Early on at *The New Yorker*, White also had a brief dalliance with one of its young secretaries, Rosanne Magdol. Although he considered marrying her, she remembered that they mainly went for walks.

Katharine, meanwhile, was in the last throes of her marriage to Ernest. The first seven years, she said, had been happy. But by 1922 it was clear that the union was untenable. Ernest had a terrible temper; awful arguments became commonplace. Perhaps worst of all, he was a philanderer. As Katharine remembered it, at one point he even lived with "a much older woman all his working week" and returned to his family only on weekends.

Finding kinship in their gentility, their appreciation of fine prose, and their close working relationship, White and Katharine were drawn together. But the process was neither easy nor straightforward. Katharine, almost seven years older than White and technically higher on the masthead, was still married. White was both shy and conflicted. However their mutual interest began, it was in full swing by June 1928. By that time, when Katharine, Ernest, and the children went for a month to Paris, she and White contrived to meet each other there on the sly. They even managed to slip away to St. Tropez and Corsica. However, upon their return to New York, both Katharine (blocked by her devotion to her children) and White (reluctant as always to be tied down personally or professionally) decided to end the affair. For some months they maintained a miserably inconclusive friendship. Then, in February 1929, possibly having learned of the affair, Ernest knocked Katharine to the floor. In May she took up residence in Nevada preparatory to obtaining a divorce. "I went to Reno with no idea that Andy and I would be married," she wrote later. "I had been hurt too much & saw no future in a marriage with a man nearly 7 years younger than I. He felt the same reservations."

Nonetheless, she wrote him scores of letters both longing ("I do want to see *you*") and humorous ("This attractive thing is a chart of my sunburned nose—It's peeling all over"), filled with details about her daily routine, which included horseback riding, and about her fellow denizens of the Circle S Ranch. Once she sent him a sage blossom. But White did not venture west to visit her. On the contrary: his nerves frayed by his involvement with Katharine, and beset by internal doubts, he decided to take an indefinite leave of absence from *The New Yorker* and lit out for Camp Otter, in Ontario, where he had once served as a counselor.

Come the fall, though, once Katharine's divorce came through and both she and White returned to New York, it was all but obvious that they were destined to be together. On November 13 they slipped away to Bedford Village, fifty miles north of the city, and were quietly married, telling no one. Walter Winchell soon broke the news in his column, leaving their co-workers and relations agog. White acknowledged, "This marriage is a terrible challenge: everyone wishing us well, and with all their tongues in their cheeks." But once committed, he had no doubts, as he told Katharine shortly after their wedding:

I have had moments of despair during the last week which have added years to my life and put many new thoughts in my head. Always, however, I have ended on a cheerful note of hope, based on the realization that you are the person to whom I return and that you are the recurrent phrase in my life. I realized that so strongly one day a couple of weeks ago when, after being away among people I wasn't sure of and in circumstances I had doubts about, I came back and walked into your office and saw how real and incontrovertible you seemed. I don't know whether you know just what I mean or whether you experience, ever, the same feeling, but what I mean is, that being with you is like walking on a very clear morning—definitely the sensation of being there.

Their happiness needed no further emotional cementing. But the birth of their son, Joel, the following year, made it complete.

———————

Ross may have been bent on keeping sex out of the office, but there was little he could do to guide his people through their private romantic entanglements, especially when they came into contact in some way with *The New Yorker* itself. In fact, he was a test case. His first wife, Jane Grant, was instrumental in the success of his enterprise; they had pooled their life savings to establish *The New Yorker,* and Jane had played an early and invaluable role in getting its feet on the ground. By Ross's admission, "She is the one who got Fleischmann interested in promoting the magazine. There would be no *New Yorker* today if it were not for her."

But Grant's strident feminism, coupled with Ross's single-minded devotion to his creation, led them to divorce in 1929 after nine years as husband and wife. Ross remarried twice, and both unions ended unhappily. From Grant, he went first to a "beautiful and mysterious Frenchwoman half his age," a divorcée named Marie Françoise Elie. But they had almost nothing in common and split in 1939—not, however, before they conceived Ross's beloved daughter, and his only child, Patricia. Ross's third wife was Ariane Allen, an alumna of Barnard and the University of Texas, a charming and flirtatious minor actress and model; they married in 1940. But her show business way of life simply did not wear well with the fun-loving but rather more literary-minded Ross. *The New Yorker,* said Thurber, "was the deadly and victorious rival of each of his three wives."

Thurber's involvement with women never interfered, at least not seriously, with his life at the magazine. But he did manage to intertwine his personal and professional worlds, generally in an awkward fashion.

At parties with staff members and friends, he could often be counted on to make drunken and clumsy passes—a "grabber," in short.* Much of this behavior was a consequence of his unhappy first marriage to Althea Adams, an associate from his Ohio State crowd who hung about Columbus following their graduation. The large-boned Althea stood five feet nine inches tall, with a personality to match her stature. "She was the domineering type, bossy and pushy, always wanting her own way," said Thurber's brother Robert. "Why Jamie married her, I'll never know."

Thurber owed Althea his first professional success at *The New Yorker*—specifically, his casual "An American Romance." But she was simply too much the archetype of the Thurber woman for their marriage to endure, and they divorced amid considerable press attention in 1935. That same year Thurber married Helen Wismer, a smart, confident Mount Holyoke graduate who would provide him with the succor and support he needed as he became both increasingly famous and progressively infirm. He proposed to her immediately following his divorce. "When we finally found each other in the Algonquin lobby that day and sat down to have a drink," Helen remembered, "he just turned towards me and said, 'Will you marry me?' I said, 'Wait a minute,' went to the ladies' room to recover, and when I came back, I said, 'Yes.'"

But before Thurber married Helen, he became enmeshed with and was periodically overwhelmed by Ann Honeycutt, a blond, somewhat plump Louisiana expatriate known as "Honey." A radio producer for WOR and CBS, Honey was a bona fide free spirit, living in digs that were painted in shades of pea green and eggplant. She wrote only a handful of pieces for the magazine. But because she ran with its regulars so often, and Ross saw so much of her, he concluded that she was a member of his staff. At one point he remarked, "That was a good piece you did on the Philippines," when in fact she had written no such thing. (She thanked

---

* Helen Stark, the magazine's longtime librarian, never recalled seeing Thurber in the company of any woman except his mother.

the confused editor anyway.) She was the magazine's darling, with an extraordinary ability to bewitch gentlemen without meaning to. Edward Newhouse recalled that if any man between sixteen and ninety was in the same room with her for an hour, he was a lost cause: "You were in love!" For a few years she was the third of McKelway's five wives.*

For all her flirtations and affairs with others on the *New Yorker* staff, Honey and Thurber became each other's particular fascination. "I'd been thwarted by much of life, and Jim opened doors for me," she said. "He claimed to suffer from inferiority feelings and said it was why he needed to be seen with attractive women." Improbably, Honey insisted that she and Thurber never had intercourse. Nonetheless, she said, "for a half-dozen years I had more fun with Jim Thurber than I'd ever had with anyone in my whole life."

"He always carried a torch for her," said Thurber's colleague "Jap" Gude. "She was something special, perhaps unattainable, for him." Many years after his initial intoxication with her had worn off, he told White that he realized that at heart he didn't particularly like her. "Our love," he explained, "never ripened into friendship."

The spell that Honey cast on the men at the magazine enveloped Gibbs as well. He dated her on and off, even though he was decidedly ambivalent. He called her "Miss Honeyclutch, who makes me think of walking up two flights into the smell of cabbage." Yet he once sent her a telegram that read IN BED A BROKEN MAN AFTER CALLING YOU FOUR THOUSAND TIMES. They shared an unlikely love of baseball and, even more unusually, boxing; he once took her to a bout between Primo Carnera and Jack Sharkey. For a while, in the early 1940s, Gibbs and Honeycutt even constituted a third of the owner-management of the decidedly second-rate heavyweight fighter Melvin "Eddie" Edge.

---

* McKelway married his first wife, Lois Little, the sister of the United Press correspondent Herbert Little, in 1925. His second wife was Estelle Cassidy, whom he married in 1929. His fourth and fifth marriages will be discussed presently.

Honeycutt was not the only *New Yorker* woman with whom Gibbs found himself involved; among those he squired was the exotic correspondent Emily Hahn. As was the case with Thurber, his romantic encounters began with the erosion of his first marriage. When it came to affairs of the heart, the young Gibbs had been hopelessly inexperienced. What with his prep school upbringing, summers sequestered with relatives in the town of Merrick on Long Island's South Shore, and the all-male company of Long Island Rail Road crews, females had never really been part of his world.

As he entered his early twenties, spurred in part by his fragmented home life, Gibbs found himself searching for someone to love, only to get nowhere. Poems to two of his would-be conquests, their identities lost to history, reflected that frustration:

Paula

You made your pose a lack of pose,
Suave seeker after paradox;
Shunned worldliness and rather chose
To mock this callow soul that mocks.
Not cynicism would you sing,
Enthusiasm's quite the thing,
Agnosticism's on the wing
It's sweller to be orthodox.

Babette

She wears a white star in her hair
And holds herself aloof from "mushing."
Today when children lisp of Freud
She's disinterred the art of blushing.
The rose that glows in Babette's cheek

Proclaims the child an early riser.
Babette is pure and good and sweet.
And so I'm going out with Liza.

But on July 24, 1926, while still a cub reporter at the *East Norwich Enterprise,* Gibbs married Helen Marguerite Galpin, the daughter of William Galpin, an English-born butler and all-around jobs boss for Mortimer Schiff, the immensely wealthy head of the financial firm Kuhn, Loeb. Gibbs apparently met her through his publisher cousin, Lloyd Griscom. At that time, Griscom was chairing a drive to raise money to build a local Boy Scout camp; the project had the full blessing of Schiff, the Scouts' international commissioner. Somewhere along the way, Gibbs encountered his butler's daughter. A twenty-year-old student at Elmira College, Helen had demure looks, wavy, bobbed blond hair, and an aristocratic voice. She was something of a flapper, loving jazz and venturing from her Oyster Bay home whenever possible to take advantage of Manhattan nightlife. For the perpetually insecure Gibbs, she would have been an exotic creature.

Unfortunately, the union was impulsive and calamitous. In a short story called "Love, Love, Love," composed some twenty years later, Gibbs would write that he had married Helen following an all-night revel with several other couples. Because she was "a respectable girl with a family to whom it would be impossible to explain an overnight absence," she became hysterical the following morning. Gibbs was able to alleviate her "climax of despair" only by promising her to drive them as soon as he could to the nearest justice of the peace. This he proceeded to do; one of his fellow *Enterprise* reporters, Louis Stancourt, and his wife, Evelyn, served as witnesses. When he awoke the following morning, he found himself staring blankly for about half an hour at his coat, in which was contained his marriage license. "I thought there might be some way I could just ignore the whole thing."

He couldn't, of course. Even if the marriage had taken place under better circumstances, Gibbs and Helen were still a bad fit. In real life, Helen was sassy and outspoken; in columns he published in the *North Hempstead Record*, Gibbs would disguise her as a dangerous harpy named "Hilda." He wrote of her becoming so enraged at a Long Island Rail Road conductor who demanded her ticket, even though she couldn't get a seat, that she attacked him with an ax and tossed his body out the train window. He imagined himself throwing her into Camann's Pond in Merrick: "She looked perfectly absurd rooting down there in the eelgrass and we had a good hearty laugh as we hauled her out and thumped some of the water out of her."

The marriage ended in divorce around the time Gibbs came to work at *The New Yorker*.* Then, in August 1929, he married Elizabeth Ada Crawford, a native of Detroit who worked as a writer in the magazine's promotion department. It was as impulsive a joining as the one with Helen; the two were wed at a "Gretna Green"—a locale where they could escape tiresome premarriage legal procedures—in Connecticut. Still, by all accounts the young couple flourished, and Elizabeth was one of the most popular members of the *New Yorker* staff. After a sojourn in Bermuda, they settled down to what appeared to be a secure domestic life.

That all ended, tragically, on March 31, 1930, when Elizabeth committed suicide by jumping out of a window of the couple's seventeenth-floor apartment in Tudor City. Some accounts state that Elizabeth leaped when Gibbs was talking with O'Hara and the men would not let her join in the conversation. Others believe she was driven to kill herself after Gibbs cruelly and repeatedly mocked her attempts to be a writer.

---

* Details of the breakup, including its exact date, are elusive; neither Gibbs nor Helen discussed the subject. Indeed, their children from their subsequent unions were unaware of the names of their parents' first spouses until this author informed them. Helen subsequently married Howard Powers, the manager of a Cadillac dealership in Brooklyn; together they had two sons. One of them, after providing critical biographical information about his mother, resisted further contact. Helen died in 1985.

As best as can be determined—and the details still seem improbable—Gibbs and Elizabeth had attended a performance of *Death Takes a Holiday* the week before at the Ethel Barrymore Theatre. In this memorable work, a beautiful young girl falls in love with Death (played on Broadway by Philip Merivale), who is masquerading as a handsome young man. When Death returns from a three-day holiday on Earth, he takes the young girl back with him as his bride. Gibbs informed the police that Elizabeth had told him, "One of these days, I am going to jump out of the window"—an indication that she somehow wanted to join Death on a permanent holiday. "I never, of course, took her seriously, and her remark had slipped my mind, almost immediately after she said it."

Katharine White said that Gibbs and Elizabeth had been up all night prior to her suicide and that when she pretended to be asleep that morning, she had jumped out the bathroom window. But all press and police accounts contradict her recollections: Gibbs's sister, Angelica, who was about to graduate from Vassar, had been lunching with them at their apartment. At one point, Elizabeth excused herself to the bedroom. When she failed to return after a few minutes, Gibbs looked out the window and saw her on the pavement, a crowd rapidly gathering around her.

The fallout was appalling. Gibbs phoned Katharine at the office and exclaimed, "Could you come right over—Elizabeth has killed herself!" Katharine dashed from her desk and arrived to find Gibbs moaning, "I never should have left the room." He was in hysterics. "He was already threatening to kill himself and he kept emphasizing what bad publicity this was for *The New Yorker* and said he could never return to the magazine again," Katharine remembered. Somehow she got Gibbs into a hospital, where he was sedated. The death was shocking enough to make tabloid headlines and rattle even the case-hardened detectives of the East 51st Street Station. "If I were God," said one of them, "I would bring her back to life again." So concerned was O'Hara about Gibbs's sanity that he stayed with him following the nightmare.

After Elizabeth's death, Gibbs managed some semblance of a home life with his newly college-graduated sister, moving into an apartment with her at 21 East Tenth Street. Like her brother, Angelica was finding her way in the literary world. Having co-edited an anthology of poetry at Vassar, she would go on to be an editor at *McCall's* and publish some fine Profiles and fiction in *The New Yorker*. Her short story "The Test"—a subtle, sensitive glimpse of racism in action—was anthologized in one of the magazine's prestigious fiction collections. Life with Wolcott, by contrast, was not as pleasant. Gibbs dubbed Angelica, not known for her housekeeping, "Miss Dirty Dishes of 1931" and called their joint quarters an "orange and green seraglio."

When Angelica left to get married and settle in suburban Port Washington, Long Island, Gibbs took in the future Broadway producer Leonard Sillman for seven months. The room that Sillman rented from him had its own entrance from the hallway and a connecting doorway with Gibbs's room; Sillman would slip his ten-dollar rent under the door between them. They rarely met; Silllman was generally out at night and Gibbs all day. But they did occasionally encounter each other, after a fashion, as Sillman recalled:

When I got back to the apartment I heard my landlord in the adjoining room bidding goodnight to some guests. I heard him say his goodnights and I heard him close the door and then I heard him close the door and then I heard a ghostly sort of a "plop!" Alarmed, I unlocked the door that separated us and entered Mr. Gibbs' apartment. My landlord lay in a heap by the door.

I picked him up, carried him to his bed, undid his tie, took off his shoes and laid his blankets over him. I tiptoed back to my room, got my overcoat, and hell-footed it up to Harlem.

That scene was repeated several times.

Gibbs's view of life, already dark, became even more desperate. The perplexing personalities of women in general became toxic for him. In his own way, he was as much a misogynist as Thurber. After the death of his second wife, he held forth at grisly length on the "new girl" of the era:

> Hats in this unfortunate year sit far back on their wearer's heads, disclosing foreheads curiously like white and bulbous tombstones. Scarlet lips and great fringed eyes stare out of faces as pallid as plumbing fixtures. Long red fingernails seem to threaten the startled young man's throat as they reach across the table for another of his cigarettes. Altogether the effect is unpleasantly mortuary and, hard as it is to believe, probably intentionally so.

Around that time, though, Gibbs met the apparent love of his life. Nancy Hale, a writer at *Vogue,* began contributing to *The New Yorker* in 1929. The granddaughter of Edward Everett Hale and the great-niece of Harriet Beecher Stowe, she would eventually become well known for novels and short stories about New England and the complex lives of fashionable women. Hale was elegant, distinguished, frank, and beautiful, and Gibbs was her editor. It was not long before they became romantically involved.

Their affair apparently began in either the latter half of 1930 or the first half of 1931. From the start he was besotted, and for the better part of two years he maintained a uniquely barbed tone of infatuation:

> It seems very likely to me that I am going to die at about four o'clock this afternoon unless you telephone me or something.

> I love you because you're smarter and better looking than anyone I know, and have the most appalling character.

> I miss you terribly already and I'm beginning to get some fine morbid ideas. I can see you sitting on the nice clean sand and

making up your mind that I'm a sort of mushroom growth, urban and sickly, and not practical at all.

Christ, a year ago I didn't give a God damn whether I could write, or how I looked, or what people thought about me, and now I want to be swell at everything so that you'll think of me as a bargain.

When you're away I equip you with a beauty and wisdom and nobility of character that would be quite impossible in a human being—like the girls who were always kicking off with t.b. in old poems. I wouldn't like it at all if you were really like that, but there's a gloomy satisfaction at the moment. Darling, I wish loving you didn't make me talk silly.

There was only one problem: Hale was married to one Taylor Scott Hardin, and the couple had a child, a baby boy named Mark. The marriage was admittedly rocky, and Gibbs spilled much ink trying to persuade Hale to leave her husband for him. Hale and Hardin did eventually divorce, in 1936; she would marry again, to the Time Inc. writer and editor Charles Wertenbaker, then to the University of Virginia English professor Fredson Thayer Bowers.

But she did not wed Gibbs. Sometime in the spring of 1933, Hale determined that she would try to make her union with Hardin work. She seems to have insisted that she and Gibbs separate for a year, making no promises about what would happen when the twelve months were up. The news devastated him:

Darling, I've spent two days now just on the edge of putting my head down and howling like a dog. Everything seems to be in some damn kind of conspiracy to make it worse. The telephone has been ringing every ten minutes and I always answer it just as hopefully, and every book or paper I pick up has something in it that brings me right back to you again. . . . I just sat here and made up lists of the things that aren't going to be any more— no more having you walk into speakeasies, mostly legs, to meet me for lunch, no more little bed that falls apart in the night (there ought to be an Indian word for that), no more taxi-rides when I could kiss you. . . . Oh darling whatever happens, I'm so damn glad that you have slept with me, and I have something to remember.

Not long after Hale parted with Gibbs, O'Hara introduced the heart-broken writer to the last of his three wives. Elinor Mead Sherwin was born on May 15, 1904. Her lineage, if not as quite glitteringly Social Register as Gibbs's, was nonetheless distinguished. She was distantly related to the Sherwins of Sherwin-Williams paint fame and had been given her middle name after William Rutherford Mead, of the architectural giants McKim, Mead & White, to whom her family was also dimly tied. Her father, Harold, was an architect himself, specializing in woodworking. (Elinor would quaintly refer to him as being "in trade.") After attending Rye Seminary and graduating from the Brearley School, she entered Wellesley in 1922. There she spent little more than a year, dropping out because she hated the food and was uninterested in such offerings as the required course in Biblical History 101. For a while she made a living as an actress in silent films. Thin, pretty, and slightly toothy, she was so captivating that a Hollywood producer reportedly named a seventy-foot schooner for her. Returning to Manhattan, she worked as a model, being paid in clothes.

In her off-hours she milled with a shifting group of bored socialites, dissipated literati, and assorted hangers-on. One was Alec Waugh, the older brother of Evelyn Waugh and already a prolific and respected author in his own right. In the grim winter of 1930–31, he found himself entertaining "honorable intentions" toward Elinor—intentions he claims she did not reciprocate because she was "unsatisfactorily entangled with a married man. I did not reach second base."* Still, during their elusive courtship he wrote a slim volume of barely disguised reminiscences, one chapter of which he devoted to his fascination with her:

> A love story, to be typical of New York, would not so much have to show the impact on a foreign mentality of a girl who typified the city's life, as [of] the city itself that would direct the course of a man's love for her.
>
> In its way, it would probably be a conventional enough story; there would be the conventional chance meeting in a friend's house; the start in the man's side as there walked into the room in a green dress, a girl in the early twenties, very slim, and slight and townlike and the thought that came to him: "That's some one terribly pretty," he says. "I must talk to her."
>
> Her voice is low pitched and to an English ear difficult to follow. They are discussing the theatre, and he tells her that no, he has never seen *Hamlet*. She smiles at that and her smile is friendly.
>
> "Now what do you think I was asking you," she said.
>
> "What I thought about John Barrymore."
>
> She laughed, "I was asking you if you didn't think one saw plays better from the balcony."
>
> "I suppose that you've heard as much of my conversation as I've heard of yours."
>
> "Haven't you heard much of mine?"
>
> "About one sentence in every four."
>
> And they laugh together and the laugh is a bond between them. And they talk easily and lightly, conscious of kinship and attraction, as though they had been friends for years. "She's nice,"

---

* Waugh's great-nephew, Alexander, disputes this: "My great-uncle Alec was a sex maniac so I have no doubt that he performed some injustice upon poor Mrs. Gibbs."

he thinks, "and sweet and real." And he looks across the room at her as she stands beside the man who has brought her to the party, and a queer feeling of jealousy twitches him.

It was this sort of innate, effortless charm that led Gibbs to meet and wed her within a matter of a few months. For the third and last time, he married on impulse, scurrying up to Stamford for the occasion on October 14, 1933, once again before a justice of the peace.

For twenty-five years, Gibbs and Elinor remained devoted to each other. His world-weary cynicism perfectly matched her natural irreverence, which was so saucy that her nickname was "Flip." On one occasion when a friend was admiring sea gulls, Elinor replied, "Yes, the little darlings will peck your eye out." When Gibbs's niece, Sarah, had her first child, Elinor insisted that the baby not be proffered to her: "Don't hand her to me—I'm always afraid their heads will fall off!" They had two children, Wolcott, Jr. (known as "Tony" because he resembled the nephew of a nurse of his at New York Hospital), in 1935, and Janet in 1939.

The marriage was far from perfect. There were whispers of mutual infidelity. When he became the magazine's theater critic, Gibbs would sometimes go to opening nights with actresses when Elinor couldn't accompany him; he was particularly devoted to one Susan Douglas, a tiny woman who had been born Zuzka Zenta Bursteinová in Vienna. By the same token, O'Hara asserted that Elinor was the mistress of Gibbs's good friend, the playwright and New Yorker contributor Sam Behrman. When Benchley died, Elinor's grief was so great that it was thought they must have been romantically involved.

As the years went by, the union cooled. "They lived in the same house," recalled a childhood friend of Janet, "but beyond that it wasn't much." An adult acquaintance went so far as to call their relationship "quite strange." But at its base was a genuinely sustaining love of a kind Gibbs had never known. Once when he was left in New York without

Elinor, he dispatched to her a poignant mixture of domestic detail and heartfelt longing:

> I think I've done everything you told me, too. Herta [the maid] has taken the money to your mother, and is giving kitty the pills, and will take her up to the doctors Wednesday. The money envelopes look a little peculiar, sort of running over and mixed up, but I haven't investigated them very carefully. There is nothing serious though, except the state of mind, which is what they call booze-gloom. This passes. I miss you and love you more than anything in the world, darling. What an enormous bed!

CHAPTER 6

"AN OFFENSE TO THE EAR"

O ne of the most important pronouncements that Ross wrote in his original prospectus for *The New Yorker* was "It will hate bunk." That last word was one that Gibbs would frequently use in his own copy. Reviewing William Saroyan's *The Beautiful People,* he summed up by calling it a play "which I strongly suspect of being largely the bunk." For Ross and his crew, any sort of soft-pedaling of the truth as an informed author saw it was anathema to honest journalism.

The attitude was most clearly expressed in the magazine's reviews. Edmund Wilson was a case in point. He came to *The New Yorker* after a stellar career at *The New Republic* and with a reputation for producing such solidly reported, solidly written book-length sociological and historical works as *The American Jitters* and *To the Finland Station.* Failing to persuade Ross to establish a purely literary journal with himself, Wilson, as editor, he was instead offered the post of book critic, replacing Clifton Fadiman. Wilson got an office, a secretary, $10,000 a year, and $3,000 for expenses; in return, *The New Yorker* could boast some of the best literary cachet in the country.

Wilson's work was perceptive, deeply intelligent, authoritative, and exceptionally well crafted. It could also be devastating. He hated hack-work; he dismissed the novel *The Turquoise* by Anya Seton as being "as arbitrary, as basically cold and dead, as a scenario for a film" and "arid rubbish, which has not even the rankness of the juicier trash." Frequently, the object of his venom didn't even have to be incompetent. "It has happened to me from time to time to run into some person of taste who tells me that I ought to take Somerset Maugham seriously," he wrote, "yet I have never been able to convince myself that he was anything but second-rate." He considered the breathless reception of Maugham's presentation of the original *Of Human Bondage* manuscript to the Library of Congress "a conspicuous sign of the general decline of our standards."

Another leading practitioner of the critical put-down was Lois Long. Her "On and Off the Avenue" column covered not only fashion and style but all manner of related subjects with assessments that were often scathing. She dismissed a certain Coty hand lotion as "nothing but rose water and glycerin with a little milk." When a promoter sent her a tchotchke called "Pair o' Lipstick," she told Ross, "It's lousy and silly, just one of those stunt ideas. Seeing as how I get about twenty-five bottles and jars and junk a week, I have gotten used to trying them out in my own good time."

Occasionally, Long went too far. She once angered Elizabeth Arden with an impending item about how the cosmetician ostensibly served grapefruit juice to her patrons as a beauty aid. Arden's attorneys insisted that she did no such thing and threatened to bring action if the paragraphs were published. Ross, who had privately warned Long, "Your emotions must not destroy your conscience and your conscientiousness," turned the item over to White. He recast it in a more innocuous form in "Comment."

It was an appropriate move. As White and Thurber had demonstrated amply in "Comment" and "Talk," *The New Yorker* derived much of its form from its special brand of elegant arrogance. In time, this poise would permeate the entire magazine. A typical example was a two-part Profile by Matthew Josephson of the banker Leon Fraser. The opening paragraph set the tone:

> Leon Fraser is one of New York's few cases of successful reincarnation. Today president of the classically conservative First National Bank of Wall Street, he began his adult life, while a student and a member of the faculty at Columbia University, as what is now called a liberal and in those days was called, usually within quotation marks, a radical. Along with other members of the Morningside Heights intelligentsia, he used to think that bankers were vulgar. His own ambitions were vaguely literary; he wrote a number of highly unmarketable short stories and did occasional book reviews for the *World*. In addition, he was strenuously interested in political theory including the theory that something might be the matter with capitalism. As a young political-science instructor, he belonged to the impractical, somewhat threadbare element which was intent on making the world over. His companions were men like the progressive Professor Charles A. Beard; Professor Carlton J. Hayes, who was then practically a Socialist; and Joseph Freeman, who was warming up to become editor of the *New Masses*. Late in the fall of 1916, several months before the United States entered the first World War, Fraser acquired the reputation of being one of Columbia's more vocal pacifists, and as a result was eventually eased off the faculty.

This sort of approach—simultaneously impressed, bemused, patronizing, and informed—was unique. As an anonymous *New Yorker* editor told an annoyed reader, "We seldom make idols of our subjects."

That operating philosophy was bound to rankle. Even some contributors were not entirely comfortable with the magazine's posture. Frank Sullivan once confided to White:

I think I may have bothered Ross and Gibbs today. I hope so. This is strictly between ourselves, but I saw them both at Muriel King's [the] night before last, and listened to them talk for an hour or so, and believe it or not, my dears, they didn't approve of one single g.d. thing that was mentioned. Really, I wish they could have got a perspective on themselves, and how they sounded. Not unlike a ladies sewing circle composed mainly of virgins, elderly and involuntary virgins. . . . I asked them to try not to be so god damn [sic] supercilious, for the sake of their own mental health, and suggested that theirs was the attitude of a couple of callow sub-editors from the Harvard Lampoon.

In putting down everything within sight, Ross may not have exactly been endearing. Nor might he be considered wholly objective. Still, he hated bunk as he saw it, and he tried to combat it through trenchant writing. His bullheaded bluntness would lead him and his crew into innumerable conflicts.

One of these arose with the publication of a Profile of the *New York Mirror* gossip columnist and radio fixture Walter Winchell. Written by St. Clair McKelway, it ran in a staggering six parts from June 15 through July 20, 1940. Winchell, an admirer of *The New Yorker*, had had no idea that what Ross and McKelway had in mind was not merely a Profile of a colorful personality but a condemnation of the whole gossip industry, as evidenced by the man who was arguably its most prominent practitioner. He had therefore agreed to be interviewed. "I had an unexpectedly long and free talk with Winchell last night," McKelway told his legman on the Profile, John Bainbridge, late in 1939. "He is all for the piece, and apparently is prepared to talk his head off as soon as I am prepared to listen."

Winchell did indeed talk his head off to McKelway over the ensuing months. In the meantime, Bainbridge dug into the tiresome task of determining the accuracy of his reportage. Aided by his wife, he did so through semiscientific means, taking as a sampling Winchell's five Monday columns for the month of April. There were 239 items, separated by Winchell's trademark three-period ellipses. Of these, 108 were "blind"—that is, no names were mentioned—and were therefore uncheckable. Bainbridge made every attempt to reach the subjects of the remaining 131. Among those he queried were Jimmy Durante, Al Smith, U.S. Senate Rules Committee chairman M. M. Neely, Rudy Vallee, Attorney General Robert Jackson, Beatrice Straight, Franz Boas, Louis Armstrong, Erich von Stroheim, French ambassador René Doynel de Saint-Quentin, George Raft, Martha Raye, Franchot Tone, and the chief of the Miami police. Responses poured back. Bainbridge found that sometimes Winchell got his facts straight. "The statement 'Ethel Merman has purchased a beer baron's yacht,' made by Mr. Winchell in his column, is quite correct," the diva informed him.

But others refuted Winchell's sloppy reporting. In one column he announced, "The real reason [Leopold] Stokowski is feuding with The Theatre Authority is that its agent shouted at him: 'How do you know? Some day they may have to run a benefit for you, and then you will need us!'" The conductor replied,

> The statement of which you write is completely untrue. I have never had any "feud" with Theatre Authority. I have never had any dealings with them of any kind. No agent from them has ever "shouted" anything at me. There never has been any question of my conducting a benefit for the Theatre Authority. I belong to the American Federation of Musicians but I do not belong to the Theatre Authority because I am not an actor but a musician.

Claudette Colbert's publicity people told Bainbridge that "the item regarding separation rumors on the actress and her physician-husband falls into your classification 'c'—that is, completely inaccurate." The secretary to the Japanese ambassador told Bainbridge that a Winchell item about his boss was "completely inaccurate and groundless."

Bainbridge did the math on the 131 checkable items. It turned out that 53 were accurate, 24 were partially inaccurate, and devastatingly, 54 were completely inaccurate. "A large number of the flat statements Winchell makes in his column and on the radio are impossible to prove or disprove," McKelway acknowledged. Nonetheless, he wrote, based on the sampling, "Winchell was not quite half right in the month of April."

Armed with interviews, supporting material, and raw data, McKelway retreated to the Foundation Inn in Stockbridge, Massachusetts, a sanitarium, to dry out and write his series. "This is a good place," he told Ross. "It would have benefited Winchell in his youth, I think." He emerged with a triumph. "There's no use taking up your time with an encomium," Shawn told Ross after reading McKelway's results. "A magnificent piece, and that's all there is to it." He knew, though, that there would be a backlash: "God help McK and The New Yorker after publication." Ross was uncharacteristically ambivalent about the tenor of the investigation. "My instinct is for blood, and more blood," he told Shawn. "But I think McK's alalytical [sic] tone here is the treatment. Probably far more effective than serious bitterness."

Even in the first part, which gave a duly respectful nod to Winchell's reach and power, there were hints of the shredding that was to come:

> When Winchell is talking about himself, he demands the unwavering attention of his listeners. James Cannon, a former sportswriter and one of his closest friends, was in a restaurant one night with his girl and was joined by Winchell. Winchell started to talk about himself. He talked for ten minutes without interruption. Cannon began to wonder if his girl would enjoy the evening more if she had another drink. Keeping his eyes fastened on Winchell's face so as to appear to be attentive, he said to his girl rapidly, "Honey, you want something?" Winchell stopped in the middle of a sentence and grabbed Cannon's arm. "Jimmy!" he said reproachfully. "You're not listening!"

Winchell read this and the succeeding installments with growing rage. By the fifth installment, McKelway—having tackled everything from Winchell's impoverished childhood to his "continued friendship with gangsters"—reached the heart of his thesis: Winchell's newspaper and radio items were often wildly erroneous, even "dreamy." He cited instance after instance. Contrary to the columnist's radio dispatch that "Buron Fitts, district attorney of Los Angeles County, is reported to have boarded a ship for an unknown destination," McKelway found that Fitts "was sitting at the home of a friend with nine Los Angeles judges listening to Winchell's news broadcast." Without comment, McKelway recalled a 1937 Winchell item that stated that Hitler and Mussolini were no longer allies. He shot down Winchell's wild story that E. B. White was the brother of the poet Elinor Wylie.

Ross himself might have written McKelway's summation of Winchell's approach:

> Intrusiveness is the nature of journalism; it is its sharpest and most necessary instrument and it is also its most agonizing responsibility for journalists who choose to accept any responsibility at all. Intrusiveness is journalism's power and its curse. Only taste and a sincere respect for accuracy can govern the power and remove the curse. Journalism is as complicated and as difficult as that. Winchell has no taste and he has no sincere respect for accuracy. If he had, he could not write gossip.

This was such explosive stuff that when McKelway sailed to South America on the eve of its publication, it was rumored that he had done so to escape the furor. Winchell responded to the assault with unconcealed malice, repeatedly attacking Ross in his column. Ross outwardly shrugged off the salvos. When Winchell reported that Ross did not wear undershorts, the editor merely stripped off the pair he had on and mailed them to the columnist. When Winchell managed to persuade Sherman

Billingsley, the proprietor of his all-important base, the Stork Club, to bar Ross from the establishment, Ross told his staff that the snub was something he was doing "my best to take in my stride."

But privately, Ross seethed. "[U]nder the compulsion of violent personal animus," he said, Winchell was printing "slimy derogatory items" about him. The situation reached a head on June 21, 1942, when the gossip columnist excoriated Ross so viciously on the NBC Blue Network that Ross dispatched a three-page protest to its president, Mark Woods. Transcript in hand, Ross assailed the "vile and slanderous statements you have permitted to be shouted about me over the air waves of the continent":

> Winchell, in his broadcast, mentioned me, with the shrewd subtlety of the experienced character assassin, in juxtaposition with a group of infamous international heels, including the Nazis and "the Nazi hangman" [Reinhard] Heydrich, William Gerald Bishop, described as accused of trying to promote private armies for the overthrow of the government, Hans Von Stahremberg, the man who "did most of the printing for the German-American Bund and other Nazis" and George Sylvester Viereck.* The Nazis, Heydrich, Bishop, Von Stahremberg, Viereck—and Ross. Traitorous bastards all! Nice stuff, Mr. Woods.

When it came to tripping up subjects, Ross did not exempt his friends. Such was the case with his old army buddy Alexander Woollcott, who had had a profound influence on the early *New Yorker*. With its breezy, insider tone, his "Shouts and Murmurs" column was among the magazine's most popular features, laden with tantalizing stories of sex, murder, and the like. Many of his entries were hoary and ancient. But in the early

---

* George Sylvester Viereck (1884–1962), a German American writer and Nazi propagandist, was imprisoned by the State Department for five years.

days, when Ross was sometimes hard pressed for copy, even the proper Katharine White admitted, "Woollcott could be absolutely depended on to produce a page that would be a *divertissement* for the magazine."

At his height, Woollcott was a bona fide literary celebrity. As "The Town Crier" on CBS Radio clanging a bell and declaiming "Hear ye, hear ye!," he would issue proclamations on current books to rapt listeners. He was a tireless lecturer, appearing occasionally in plays and becoming immortalized as the insufferable Sheridan Whiteside in the Kaufman-Hart classic *The Man Who Came to Dinner.* "Woollcott was, above all, a personality—a very theatrical personality," recalled Danton Walker, one of his many secretaries. "His familiar first night entrances—galoshes open and flapping, scarf fluttering in the breeze he created—were frequently more dramatic than what occurred on stage."

Eventually, however, the limelight and his own ego corrupted him. He was a shameless name-dropper, plugging the latest celebrity with whom he was fascinated. With little discrimination, he would endorse any product—automobiles, whiskey, tennis rackets—if the check was big enough and if the deal afforded him sufficient exposure. His taste was often downright moronic, perhaps deliberately so. He thought Lizzie Borden "America's most interesting woman" and the folk rhyme about her ax murders "on the plane with Shakespeare and Sophocles." Walt Disney's *Dumbo,* he said, was "the best achievement yet reached in the Seven Arts since the first white man landed on this continent." What excited Woollcott, White said, "was so capricious that it occasionally made even his best friends wince." There also seemed to be no limit to his condescension. "By some miracle you have published a book which is not second rate," he wrote Bennett Cerf. "Please send me twelve copies at once."

The man's ability to "write literately and fairly well and, above all, turn in clean copy," Ross conceded, "was very rare." But the thin-skinned critic hotly resisted editorial changes. He also took a perverse delight in sticking it to Ross. "At a dinner party where both were guests," said

Walker, "Ross complained that his *amours* were being gossiped about by members of his staff. Woollcott sprang at this: 'No one,' he shouted, 'could tell more about your affairs than you do yourself!' This so upset Ross that he retired to the bathroom and threw up."

Such incidents, combined with Ross's increasing intolerance for Woollcott's peculiar prose, made a schism inevitable. Woollcott had become incredibly fussy about extending his deadlines, ever more resistant to editing, and much like O'Hara, consumed with his positioning in the magazine. Ross tried to placate him, to no avail. In 1934, after a showdown about a particularly racy "Shouts" column, Woollcott told Ross he was quitting. Fleischmann supported publishing the column; Ross was unimpressed. "That was, of course, Woollcott's one hundredth resignation," he told the publisher. "He always resigns under such circumstances. My opinion was merely that I certainly wouldn't run his stale and off-color anecdotes if I owned the magazine." He went on:

> I've heard a vast and an alarming lot of complaint about Woollcott's off-color anecdotes—people cutting them out of the magazine so the children wouldn't see them and so on—and actually there is damned little doubt in my mind. . . . In any event I don't think we ought to be bullied into running dirty stories if we don't want to run them. And I would point out that Woollcott can't get "five times as much for this stuff anywhere" because, pure as we are, we're the most liberal magazine he can write for and he can't print dirty stories anywhere. He doesn't try it on the radio, either.

Around this time Woollcott became "forever the deadly enemy of The New Yorker." Gibbs, meanwhile, had had his own fill of Woollcott. His editorial grudge dated to at least 1927, when he parodied Woollcott's style in the *North Hempstead Record,* employing such phrases as "an attentive but somewhat croupy gathering." He repeated the stunt in *The New Yorker* itself in 1935 with "Primo, My Puss," which he couched as an account of Primo Carnera telling Woollcott how he had lost to Max Baer: "To return, however, to the ostensible purpose of these somewhat desultory memoirs, it was, I think, in the eleventh round of our considerably less than Homeric conflict that Mr. Baer, animated by a sudden and rather repulsive vivacity, visited upon your indignant correspondent a succession of blows which left him, for the moment at least, both breathless and passionately disinclined for further combat."

Gibbs was frequently stuck with the thankless task of handling Woollcott's copy. "He took on this weekly chore when I was on vacation or working from Maine or out sick," recalled Katharine White. "I guess he had a harder time than I did because Aleck was ruder to men than to women." By nature direct and terse, Gibbs hated Woollcott's flaccid style. It was, he said, "sculptured from the very best Jello" and constituted a "terrible detriment of the English language." Further, "As other men fear and hate the dentist's drill, Mr. Woollcott is tortured by an unbalanced sentence. Adverbs and adverbial phrases ('oddly enough' is his favorite) and tender apostrophes to the reader ('my blossom, ' 'puss,' and 'my little dears') are judiciously inserted until the magic equilibrium is achieved."

Thus it was that Gibbs suggested to Ross, some four years after Woollcott had published his last "Shouts" column, that *The New Yorker* should undertake a Profile that would constitute a takedown of the egotistical raconteur. Woollcott, who for all his ostensible worldliness was easily hoodwinked, enthusiastically agreed. He invited Gibbs to come up to Neshobe Island, his retreat in the middle of Lake Bomoseen in Vermont, to get "the flavor of his personality." The eight-acre atoll was the site of storied croquet tournaments, nude swimming, parlor games, and other mandatory, full-throated activities with many of the Algonquin crowd. Many guests reveled in the experience. Others found Neshobe to be purgatory. "I was up there once and got claustrophobia, in spite of my analysis," Frank Sullivan recalled. For his part, Gibbs declined Woollcott's hospitality. REGRET CANT GET TO YOUR LAKE BUT HAVE MY OWN LIFE TO LIVE, he telegraphed.

As Gibbs exhumed Woollcott's past and scrutinized his present, he and his subject became quite entangled. Sullivan recalled dining with them some three months before the piece was published:

High spot of the evening came when Aleck let loose one of his benevolent diatribes on Gibbs. He had been talking about himself, but every once in a while he would ask Gibbs a question quite casually and pretty soon, without Gibbs being aware of it, he was in possession of a complete history of Gibbs' life including that first marriage to the brakeman's daughter in Long Island.* Then Gibbs said something that displeased Aleck and the latter cut loose on him, reciting a litany of the shortcomings of his life, all highly accurate and easily remembered because they had just been painlessly imparted to Aleck by Gibbs himself. The look that came over Gibbs was worth the price of the dinner (which was paid for by Aleck anyhow), I must admit. . . . Gibbs says he likes Aleck. I don't know whether that bodes well for the profile or not.

The result—titled "Big Nemo"—was a thorough dissection. Gibbs did not stint on Woollcott's many personal kindnesses and tender heart. But he also dwelt at length on his improbable, even preposterous, life story. Gibbs conveyed his fractured rearing on the Phalanx commune in New Jersey. He noted his "bizarre" attendance at Hamilton, where he routinely "wore corduroy trousers and a turtle-necked sweater and topped them off with a jubilant red fez." He related his conduct under fire in the Great War: "Other men dropped where they were, but Mr. Woollcott weighed close to two hundred pounds exclusive of hardware

---

* Sullivan was apparently unaware that Helen Galpin was the daughter of a butler. Many others also believed that her father had worked on the Long Island Rail Road, including Brendan Gill, who said so in his memoir of *The New Yorker*. It is not known how this misconception arose.

and his descent was gradual and majestic, like a slowly kneeling camel. Even when he had got safely down, he was still far from flat, and it is one of the miracles of the war that he came through it unperforated." Describing Woollcott's civilian appearance in evening clothes—complete with "a broad-brimmed black hat and flowing cape, carrying a heavy, silver-headed cane"—Gibbs adjudged that "on the whole he looked very much like Dracula."

He recounted Woollcott's slapdash journalism. "There could be no question that the *Times*' new man could write very nicely, though in a strangely lacy and intricate fashion, but as a reporter he was exasperating," Gibbs wrote. "He wasn't exactly hostile to facts, but he was apathetic about them." Woollcott was "sentimental, partisan, and maddeningly positive about everything even before he had been a critic long enough to know much about anything."

Gibbs also disclosed one of the more embarrassing episodes of his subject's career. It stemmed from an ostensible fan letter written by two elderly sisters in the vicinity of Albany. Though nearly destitute, they still owned a radio and on it they regularly listened to Woollcott, regarding him as "about the *best* thing in the world." Moved by the flattery, Woollcott serenaded the sisters over the airwaves by having the studio orchestra play songs like "Home Sweet Home" and "Old Folks at Home." Alas, it was not long before Woollcott was informed that both sisters had died within a week or so of each other. Woollcott earnestly sent forth inquiries about their identities, relatives, and any other relevant information. He came up empty, and no wonder: the unlikely yarn had all been an elaborate hoax, Gibbs reported, hatched by "a brooding author whose book Mr. Woollcott had dismissed too arrogantly as tripe."

Incredibly, upon receipt of the first set of proofs, Woollcott telegrammed Gibbs YOU HAVE MADE ME VERY HAPPY WITH CERTAIN RESERVATIONS. He did dispatch a nine-page letter pointing out any number of factual errors and what he regarded as misinterpretations. Nonetheless, Woollcott acceded that Gibbs had rightly pointed up his many foibles: "I have on my conscience certain sins of omission which the years do not offace [sic] and for which I expect to pay in hell. They were the result of indolence, contemptible cowardice and black-hearted selfishness."

When the three-part series appeared in March and April 1939, Woollcott was characteristically pleased by the publicity. His friends were not fooled. Alfred Lunt and Lynn Fontanne were so outraged by Gibbs's treatment that they canceled their subscription to the magazine. It took time, but Woollcott gradually became aware that he had been had. He was especially distressed by Gibbs's detailed recounting of the malefactions of an old army associate, Seth Bailey (disguised in print as "Sergeant Quirt"), a swindler on a grand scale. A naïve Woollcott had defended Bailey to the hilt, even pledging that "he would personally redeem every dollar's worth of false checks that could be shown to have originated with his virtuous friend." Confronted with several thousand dollars' worth of proof that Bailey was indeed a con man, "Mr. Woollcott was obliged to retract his offer and leave the Sergeant to the mercy of the State of California."

The Profile served as an excuse for a full Woollcott break with *The New Yorker*. After it appeared, he never printed another word in the magazine. And yet there followed a bizarre and protracted minuet of attempted and failed reconciliations. In 1942 Woollcott wrote Ross, "I've tried by tender and conscientious nursing to keep my grudge against you alive, but I find it has died on me."

Actually, it didn't; when Ross responded that he would be happy to visit him if he were up for it, Woollcott abruptly declined, citing the considerable "lying, cruelty and treachery" that accompanied the writing of the Profile. "For how much of this you were responsible and how much Gibbs, I am not sure," Woollcott fumed, "but as long as I live I could never talk across a dinner table with you or even play a game of cribbage without wondering."

Some months later Ross tried to mend the breach, assuring Woollcott that "I would be glad, God knows, to answer any questions you care to ask" in regard to Gibbs's handiwork. Woollcott could not have cared less. "To me you are no longer a faithless friend," he wrote from Neshobe. "To me you are dead. Hoping and believing I will soon be the same, I remain your quondam crony." At "21" one evening, Woollcott literally refused to shake hands with Ross "and asked him to leave before he really started to tear loose on him."

After Woollcott's death in January 1943, Ross tried to puzzle out his complex friend. "All the time Alec wrote for us he was a trial—something of a nuisance and an embarrassment," he told Woollcott's biographer, Samuel Hopkins Adams. "We had to fight to keep him printable, and he was harder to deal with than a Gila monster, which he sometimes resembled."

Even in death, Woollcott haunted Ross. Following his demise, the Algonquin donated to the Authors' Workshop for Veterans "a particularly monstrous lounging sofa" that Woollcott had favored, hoping that it might inspire the writing organization to new spiritual heights. When the workshop was forced to move to smaller quarters in 1947, a representative wrote Ross to ask if *The New Yorker* would be interested in having the furniture, humorously suggesting that Woollcott's ghost would accompany it. The answer was no: "We don't want any additional ghosts stalking the hall."

———————

Perhaps the best-known debunking in which Ross engaged—and certainly the project that not only made Gibbs's name but would define his reputation—was a 1936 parody of *Time* magazine that doubled as a Profile of its maximum editor and publisher, Henry R. Luce.

The burgeoning Time Inc. enterprise was riding high in 1936. The year before, the corporation's net profits had topped out at almost two and a quarter million dollars. Its holdings included *Fortune* magazine and the *March of Time* radio broadcasts and newsreels. The company would soon bring out the phenomenally successful picture magazine *Life*. *Time*

itself, founded just two years before *The New Yorker* and instantly identifiable by its red-bordered cover, had become something of a national
institution, with a circulation of 640,000. Its newsmagazine format—a
comprehensive digest of national and international affairs, drawn mainly
from newspapers across the country and supplemented by a small but
growing network of correspondents—was revolutionary.

Time was also widely reviled. Intellectuals hated its condensation
of the news, missing as it often did many of the finer points of important current events and framing unfolding stories with neat beginnings,
middles, and endings. Devotees of objective journalism were astonished
by *Time*'s sneaky bias in favor of the Republican Party and big business,
its admiration of Mussolini, and its outright disgust with Communism.
Members of the working press gnashed their teeth when they saw how
Time's editors appropriated and rewrote their copy without giving them
credit. Provincial subscribers resented the magazine's smug eastern
establishment attitude, and its penchant for mongering rumors turned
off upright readers. Sticklers for exactitude were frequently appalled at
Time's routine contempt for facts. As early as 1925, one reader had complained to the editors, "*Time*'s inaccuracies are chronic, flagrant and
even self-evident."

And purists of the English language hated the magazine's jarring,
often baffling assaults on their mother tongue. *Time* made a fetish of
obscure words like *tycoon, kudos,* and *pundit* and invented others, like
socialite. For quick identification, the magazine had perfected the art of
the neat, often embarrassing epithet, such as "wild-eyed" President Francisco Madero of Mexico, "torpedo-headed dynamo" Walter P. Chrysler,
"hen-shaped" New York City mayor Fiorello LaGuardia, and "duck-hunting dentist" Senator Henrik Shipstead of Minnesota. *Time*'s monikers
frequently ran to the absurd. Football star Red Grange was an "eel-hipped
runagade"; the prince of Monaco, a deep-sea diver, was a "bathysophical
enthusiast"; and supporters of Prohibition were "adherents of aridity."

The magazine's prose was conveyed in a weirdly fractured form that flouted many of the conventional rules of grammar and usage. For expediency's sake, the word *and* was often eliminated, with two-part thoughts mashed together via a comma or an ampersand. The article *the* was routinely jettisoned. The sentences themselves were often tortuously inverted and cluttered. "To Versailles (150 years ago) swarmed empurpled princelings, intent on an implicit mission of state," was typical. So distinctive was this bizarre argot that it acquired its own neologism: "Timestyle." Gibbs considered it "one of the great literary comedies of our time."

Timestyle was the invention of the brilliant, boisterous Briton Hadden who, with his Yale classmate Luce, had created *Time*. Hadden was a brash product of the 1920s, a party animal complete with pocket flask and a flip disregard for everything holy. Among his specialties was exposing the embarrassing middle names of such public figures as the automobile manufacturer William Crapo Durant and *Saturday Evening Post* owner Cyrus Hermann Kotzschmar Curtis. By laying bare these and similar personal details, his cousin and *Time* writer John Martin said, the impish Hadden was "undressing them in Macy's window."

"Hadden had not set out to create a new style of writing," wrote his biographer, Isaiah Wilner. But he did so out of the need for terseness and the reader's attention alike. Long denied his place in *Time* history, Hadden was the true originator of the magazine. When he died, tragically, of a streptococcus infection early in 1929 at the age of thirty-one, Luce assumed the company mantle. Unlike the rambunctious Hadden, he was an empire builder, politically minded, personally abstemious, and an altogether cold fish—in short, perfect for debunking.

In its own way, *Time* was actually much like *The New Yorker*—urbane, snappy, and self-assured. "Naturally," said David Cort, *Life*'s foreign editor, the two magazines "knifed each other at every opportunity." But Ross, unlike Luce, had no particular political ax to grind. He was fanatical about accuracy and grammar. He also had a personal feud with Luce.

The feud began when Hadden saw a prepublication announcement for *The New Yorker* in 1925. Seizing on Ross's famous declaration that his magazine would not be "edited for the old lady in Dubuque," Hadden snorted to his writer Niven Busch, "Damn it, the old lady in Dubuque is smarter than they are. Dubuque is a great place and just as sophisticated as New York. That's your angle, and make it plain that the magazine won't last." Busch's subsequent slam at *The New Yorker*'s start-up, in *Time*'s March 2 issue, concluded with a suspiciously pat quote from an elderly woman in that quintessential small town: "The editors of the periodical you forwarded are, I understand, members of a literary clique. They should learn that there is no provincialism so blatant as that of the metropolitan who lacks urbanity. They were quite correct, however, in their original assertion. *The New Yorker* is not for the old lady in Dubuque."*

More than anything else, it was a seventeen-page, full-blown look at *The New Yorker* in the July 1934 issue of *Fortune* that brought down Ross's wrath. The author was Ross's former right-hand man, Ralph Ingersoll, by this time a rapid climber of Luce's corporate ladder. Ingersoll's disclosure of juicy personal details about the magazine's prime movers proved jolting. Ross's face, Ingersoll wrote, was "made out of rubber which he stretches in every direction. Out of the lower half hangs a huge Hapsburg lip to which cigarettes stick. Widespread teeth diverge downward. . . . Ross's eyes are fierce, shifty, restless." Katharine White, he said, was "hard, suave, ambitious, sure of herself" and, being a woman, "may have recourse to tears." Ingersoll exposed her husband as "shy, frightened of life, often melancholy, always hypochondriac," while Thurber was "madder than White." As for the "slim, handsome, macabre" Gibbs, "He hates everybody and everything, takes an adolescent pride in it. To a simple honest comment on life he is likely to snap 'don't be banal!' "

---

* Not long afterward Busch left *Time* and met with Ross. "I wish you would do something for me," Ross told him. "Find out who was the stinker who wrote that snide article about *The New Yorker*." "I did," Busch confessed, whereupon Ross hired him.

The piece hardly caught Ross off guard. Several months before its appearance, he had written Ingersoll, "Hadn't you better show it to me to check for accuracy? I will promise not to try to soften the harshness, if any, but I do think you ought to get it right, and *Fortune* has made quite a few mistakes." He even said, "I would love to have a chance to write it myself." When the article finally hit the stands, Ross claimed he didn't read it, even though "every wise guy in town is speaking about it, or writing, or something." Still, he acknowledged, the story had "kicked up all sorts of unhappiness in subtle ways." Part of that unhappiness arose because Ingersoll printed the salaries of many of *The New Yorker*'s leading lights, not always correctly. In response, Ross put a notice on the office bulletin board that read, "I do not make $40,000 a year." By way of a potshot, White wrote a cryptic "Comment" entry that stated, "Gossip Note: The editor of *Fortune* makes thirty dollars a week and carfare."

Ross was particularly mortified at how Ingersoll had dumped on *The New Yorker*'s art arrangements: "Some artists are good on drawings, weak on ideas. Arno is one and much of his reputation is founded on wit that is not his own. Nowadays *The New Yorker* gives Gluyas Williams all his ideas." The barb so unsettled Williams that Ross reassured him, "Please stick with us, and please remember this: So help me, there's no sin, no harm, and nothing unethical in drawing up an idea suggested by a man who can't possibly draw it himself."

In the spring of 1935, Ross began contemplating a counterattack. The project was initially assigned to Allene Talmey, an editor at *Vanity Fair* and *Vogue*, and it may even have been proposed by her. Requests for information were made. Ingersoll, no dummy, was naturally suspicious and tried to draw Ross out about what he really had in mind:

> Thanks for your note telling us that the Luce Profile is a bona fide project. But what was all this you were telling me about on the telephone: that Miss Talmey was only a stooge, sent to us to get facts for someone else in the office to rewrite; that "someone

who knows Luce well" (whose name you wouldn't tell us because it might make us mad) was really going to do the job? Pardon my thinking it sounds like a gag.

God knows if the New Yorker feels like writing a Profile of Henry R. Luce there is nothing TIME INC can do about it. And we are all journalists together. Why the comic opera intrigue?

Come clean, pal, with (a) who's going to write the piece, (b) our rights in the matter of checking the factual contents, and (c) just what sort of a hearing, if any, we are entitled to at the trial of Mr. Luce and his magazines in print, and we will get down to cases.

The project was shelved for a while, likely in an attempt to elude Ingersoll's skepticism. Gibbs came into the picture after Katharine White suggested a parody of *Fortune* by way of retaliation. McKelway shifted the focus to a parody of *Time* "because nobody but business executives who are being written up and ambitious dentists ever see *Fortune,* much less read it." And he nominated Gibbs as the best man to undertake "such an antic job."

Apart from his unflattering depiction in *Fortune,* Gibbs had no personal quarrel with Luce. But he did hold a grudge against some of the publisher's people, including his second wife, Clare Boothe Brokaw. As ambitious in her own way as her husband, Clare had been an editor at *Vanity Fair* before she met Luce and was eager for freelance assignments. One day in 1931 she called up Gibbs to ask him over for drinks. Thinking he was being invited to a cocktail party, Gibbs responded in the affirmative—only to discover that he was the only guest. This was a familiar tactic for Clare. She would routinely have an editor over to her penthouse on Beekman Place and, "after giving him a cocktail, would inform him that she had a little time on her hands and thought it might be fun to dash off some articles for his magazine." In Gibbs's case, she suggested a Profile of the sculptor Gutzon Borglum, doing so with considerable snootiness. "Write that down," she told him. "Here, I'd better spell it for you." Gibbs was especially put off by her remark, "You Americans like your drinks sweet, don't you?," coming as it did from a fellow countryman. "This was the Vogue influence," he concluded. "Hanging around with foreigners or something."

The Luce endeavor gelled throughout 1936. Ingersoll remained dubious and tried to dissuade Luce from cooperating. "The fewer facts you give them," he said, "the less they'll have to twist to your discomfort." At one point he implored his boss, "They hate you over there. They'll take long knives and cut you into little pieces and put you over a fire." But Luce, as a fellow journalist, felt obliged to respond to *The New Yorker's* inquiries. Anyway, his ego would not allow him to avoid being featured in one of the country's most prestigious publications.

"It became an office project, the like of which I'd never seen," said McKelway of the Profile. The "Talk" staff dug up facts, and McKelway interviewed Luce in "deadpan manner," giving no hint that a bushwhacking was under way. Nor did he mention Gibbs, who had by this time acquired a reputation as a satirist. The background material included Talmey's preliminary research and the testimony of more than a dozen *Time* employees who were only too happy to pull the pants off their boss. Eugene Kinkead, an enterprising young *New Yorker* reporter, supplied some key facts. After Luce assured McKelway that he had leased the "smallest apartment in River House" at 435 East 52nd Street, dismissing it as a modest dwelling of four or five rooms, Kinkead somehow managed to wangle his way in. He discovered that the wealthy Luce was in possession of a grand assemblage of fifteen rooms and five baths.

Armed with a mass of information, Gibbs started writing, employing his natural wit and acid to weave a seamless send-up. When necessary, he improvised. Lacking the weekly salary of the average "Timemployee," he ran his index finger across the top row of his typewriter keys to arrive at the figure of $45.67890. Ross protested, "Look, this is too damned obvious. They'll get wise to it." So Gibbs changed the number to $45.67802. Though hardly accurate, the preposterous amount was a perfect touch for a satire. So sly was Gibbs's fictional accounting that the credulous critic Dwight Macdonald, who then worked for *Fortune*, later cited the $45.67802 tally as evidence that Luce had sweated his labor.

The resulting 4,500 words, running in the November 28 issue and titled "Time . . . Fortune . . . Life. . . . Luce," constituted a tour de force for Gibbs and *The New Yorker* alike. The peg was the launch of *Life*. "Sad-eyed last month was nimble, middle-sized *Life*-President Clair Maxwell as he told newshawks of the sale of the fifty-three-year-old gagmag to *Time*," the piece began. The first issue, Gibbs wrote, "pictured Russian peasants in the nude, the love life of the Black Widow spider, referred inevitably to Mrs. Ernest Simpson."

Following some background on the sale of the old *Life* title to the Luce gang and its reincarnation as a picture magazine, Gibbs struck with his nut graph: "Behind this latest, most incomprehensible Timenterprise looms, as usual, ambitious, gimlet-eyed, Baby Tycoon Henry Robinson Luce, co-founder of *Time*, promulgator of *Fortune*, potent in associated radio & cinema ventures."

From the first sentence to the last, the piece was an all-out assault on Timestyle.* "Sitting pretty are the boys," "In a quandary was Bridegroom Luce," "Doomed to strict anonymity are *Time-Fortune* staff writers," and "Shotup [as opposed to "upshot"] of this was that Luce, embarrassed, printed a retraction" were representative thrusts. Paragraph after merciless paragraph rammed home the point:

> "Tycoon," most successful Timepithet, had been coined by Editor Laird Shields Goldsborough; so fascinated Hadden with "beady-eyed" that for months nobody was anything else. Timeworthy

---

* One scholarly study determined that the Profile contained, among its other features, "51 full verb inversions, 12 quotations inversions (all verbs of quotation are inverted)" and "3 structures in which the predicate comes before the subject without a verb ('most brilliant he,' 'handicapped he')."

were deemed such designations as "Tom-tom" Heflin, "Body-lover" Macfadden.*

"Great word! Great word!" would crow Hadden, coming upon "snaggle-toothed," "pig-faced." Appearing already were such maddening coagulations as "cinemaddict," "radiorator." Appearing also were first gratuitous invasions of privacy. Always mentioned as William Randolph Hearst's "great & good friend" was Cinemactress Marion Davies, stressed was the bastardy of Ramsay MacDonald, the "cozy hospitality" of Mae West. Backward ran sentences until reeled the mind.

Countering *Time*'s neologisms, Gibbs concocted some of his own, tossing off the *March of Time* as "Cinemarch" and Luce's personal assets as his "Lucemolument." Gibbs even described McKelway, though not by name, as a "Newyorkereporter." And he tore into the "cold, baggy, temperate" Luce himself.

At work today, Luce is efficient, humorless, revered by colleagues; arrives always at 9:15, leaves at 6, carrying armfuls of work, talks jerkily, carefully, avoiding visitor's eye; stutters in conversation, never in speechmaking. . . . Prone he to wave aside pleasantries, social preliminaries, to get at once to the matter in hand. Once to interviewer who said, "I hope I'm not disturbing you," snapped Luce, "Well, you are." . . . He drinks not at all at midday, sparingly at all times, sometimes champagne at dinner, an occasional cocktail at parties.

---

* Senator James Thomas Heflin (1869–1951) of Alabama, also known as "Cotton Tom," was a leading advocate of white supremacy. The nationally known fitness enthusiast Bernarr Macfadden (1868–1955) published a successful string of magazines.

In the best *Time* tradition, the piece was sprinkled with such three-dollar words as *jocosities, necromancy,* and *transmogrified.* Similarly, it was laced with odd and arresting footnotes. A reference to a recent issue of *Fortune* weighing "as much as a good-sized flounder" was asterisked thusly: "Two pounds, nine ounces." When Gibbs noted in a humdrum passage given over to annual earnings that Time Inc.'s net profits had dropped more than $200,000 in 1932 from the year before, he jotted at the bottom of the page, "Hmm."*

Gibbs attacked the Lucean brand of fact gathering: "Typical perhaps of Luce methods is *Fortune* system of getting material. Writers in first draft put down wild gossip, any figures that occur to them. This is sent to victim, who indignantly corrects the errors, inadvertently supplies facts he might otherwise have withheld." In deference to Ingersoll's *Fortune* piece, Gibbs printed the salaries, known or assumed, of a number of key Time Inc. executives, along with their personality quirks. Not content with mentioning Ingersoll's $30,000 paycheck and $40,000 stock income, Gibbs sketched him as "Burly, able, tumbledown Yaleman Ralph McAllister Ingersoll, former Fortuneditor, now general manager of all Timenterprises, descendant of 400-famed Ward McAllister. Littered his desk with pills, unguents, Kleenex, Socialite Ingersoll is *Time*'s No. 1 hypochondriac, introduced ant palaces for study & emulation of employees, writes copious memoranda about filing systems, other trivia, seldom misses a Yale football game."

Gibbs finished with a grandiloquent Timestyle flourish: "Certainly to be taken with seriousness is Luce at thirty-eight, his fellowman already informed up to his ears, the shadow of his enterprises long across the land, his future plans impossible to imagine, staggering to contemplate. Where it all will end, knows God!"

Ostensibly in the interests of accuracy and courtesy, and certainly

---

* Seven decades later Ross's private secretary William Walden recalled, "I thought that was the funniest footnote I'd ever read. I really roared."

in the cause of revenge served cold, proofs of the piece were dispatched to Ingersoll. A couple of hours later, he telephoned McKelway. "Hearst tactics!" he shouted. "Time-Life was in an uproar about it; there was a continuous procession of people in and out of Mrs. White's office," recalled the newly arrived William Maxwell. "I sat taking in snatches of the excitement."

Ingersoll insisted that he and Luce meet with Ross that night. Drawing out the drama, McKelway replied that Ross had a dinner party going on. Why not make it tomorrow? Ingersoll persisted, and so it was arranged that the four men would meet at Ross's penthouse at 22 East 36th Street at 11:30 p.m. "Bulls like to fight," said a weary *New Yorker* staff member.

What followed was one of the most infamous intramural dust-ups in journalistic history. "Oh, that terrible night," Luce said years later. "I should never have gone over. Ingersoll dragged me there." For reasons not entirely clear, Gibbs was not present. According to Ingersoll, "[He] lost his nerve and didn't show. He hid out in some bar and got telephoned flashes from McKelway." By another account, Ross excused him as "a man of weak character" who would likely cave in to Luce's protests. Yet another story had Ross keeping him out of the fracas "on the grounds that no author should be subjected to such a strain."

When Ingersoll and Luce arrived at Ross's apartment, McKelway recalled, "Luce came straight across the room to me (he remembered me from the interviews) and said in a kind of whine, 'It's not true that I have no sense of humor.' I thought it was one of the most humorless remarks I'd ever heard."

And so it went. Luce stammered; Ross punctuated his retorts with refrains of "goddamn." Guaranteeing to heighten the tension, liquor was brought out. McKelway and Ingersoll freely partook, the virtuous Luce restricted himself to one drink ("making a valiant effort to get it down without gagging"), and the ulcer-ridden Ross abstained completely. The four quickly proceeded to spar, Luce and Ingersoll picking apart the proofs line by line, Ross and McKelway vigorously defending their material. Less important than any particular set of facts was Gibbs's overall theme. Luce wailed, "There isn't a single constructive thing in the whole piece."

"We didn't set out to do a constructive piece," Ross told him. "We simply tried to do a *fair* piece." Regarding Ross unbelievingly, a stunned Luce exclaimed, "Fair!" and shook his head, apparently resigned to a public crucifixion. Beseeching Ross again that the Profile contained nothing positive, Ross replied, "That's what you get for being a baby tycoon." An exasperated Luce managed to sputter, "But God damn it, Ross, this whole God damn piece is ma-ma-*malicious.*" Ross agreed. "You've put your finger on it, Luce. I believe in malice."

Among the many points to which Luce objected was Gibbs's merciless recalling of how Clare's drama *Abide with Me* had opened to disastrous reviews just a few days before she married the baby tycoon. Gibbs quoted verbatim a devastating passage by the *New York Herald Tribune*'s theater critic, Richard Watts, who had written that an overeager Clare had taken a curtain call in response to apparently nonexistent cries of "Author!" Clare, Watts said, "must have been crouched in the wings for a sprinter's start." Luce complained, "We didn't mention *your* wife in *Fortune.*" That gave Ross pause. He beckoned McKelway to follow him into the foyer and asked, "Did they mention my wife?" McKelway shrugged. "I can't say. I never read the damn piece all the way through." Ross agreed to downgrade the anecdote to a footnote—thereby guaranteeing that it would receive even more attention.

Luce seized on the absurd $45.67802 weekly salary figure, arguing that it was "far, far too low" and did not account for the Time Inc. mail clerks in Chicago. Lying through his gapped front teeth, Ross insisted, "That figure was arrived at only after the most painstaking research. We've checked it and *re*checked it and we have every reason to believe that it's accurate." When Luce declared that another tally was "completely, absolutely wrong," Ross replied mildly, "Wrong? Perhaps. Perhaps it is— but that, after all, is part of the parody of *Time.*"

That set Ingersoll off. He began shouting that the whole undertaking had been conducted under false pretenses and repeated his charge that it was in the worst Hearst tradition. A self-assured McKelway suggested that this was altogether appropriate for a portrait of Hearst's heir apparent. At that, "Ingersoll sprang from his chair and was advancing menacingly toward McKelway when Luce suddenly reached out, put his hand on his aide's head, and pressed him gently back." On that violent note the inconclusive, ill-conceived gathering wrapped up at about three a.m. A sodden Ingersoll leaned on Luce in getting out the door. Luce, looking crushed, may well have been blotto himself, giving the lie to Gibbs's assertion that he rarely imbibed.

A few days later Ross composed a remarkable five-page single-spaced letter to Luce that more fully set out the rationale for the tone and content of Gibbs's Profile. He prefaced it by stating, "The article went to your office in the form it did as a gag, a malicious playfully vindicative [sic] gag, from a gagmag. Ingersoll, with lofty arrogance, made this office sweat to the last drop when he could and we thought we would open *his* pores up. We did not foresee that you also would join him in the steamroom, but that just made the gag better."

His preliminaries out of the way, Ross disposed of Luce's objections. He disputed the publisher's claim that Gibbs hadn't written a single nice word about him. On the contrary: "It was generally felt that the total effect of the article and its being in existence at all were enormously favorable, and that our listing of your remarkable growth, the figures themselves, were complimentary in the highest degree, presenting you, in fact, as practically heroic."

In addition to many other points, Ross defended the use of the Watts quote "as being exactly the kind of item Time would pick up and use itself." He similarly defended a paragraph that dwelt on Luce's future plans, including a possible run for public office. "Vehemently denies this Luce, denies any personal political ambition," Gibbs had written.

"It was regarded," Ross explained, "as exactly the kind of thing Time is doing constantly: denying the weird and, as we call it, 'grotesque,' rumor after starting it, thereby getting the full news value of it.* Moreover Time enterprises are always speculating on people's ambitions." As for the disclosure about the palatial dimensions of the River House digs—which Luce was then subletting—Ross pointed out that Kinkead had dug up a real estate advertisement that accurately described the size of the space: "You are offering the place for rent as a fifteen-room apartment, a pretty state of affairs if it isn't true."

Threaded throughout this missive were Rossian thoughts on journalistic ethics. "I was astonished to realize the other night that you are apparently unconscious of the notorious reputation Time and Fortune have for insult," he wrote.† "I say frankly but really in a not unfriendly spirit, that you are in a hell of a position to ask anything." He also quoted from a memo that Gibbs had previously written him about the whole sordid undertaking:

---

* Actually, Gibbs had called the rumor not "grotesque" but "fantastic."

† In a portion of the letter that Ross struck from the final draft, there ensued after that sentence the following: "I would remind you that in the article in Fortune, for instance, you called Mrs. White a simple, sensitive gentlewoman, 'hard, suave, ambitious, sure of herself.' . . . 'She handles people smoothly, with a carefully studied courtesy and tact' . . . 'shrewd and able politically.' It is, so help me Christ, a positive crime that such a thing should have been printed, although the statements are so extreme as to be ridiculous and, like all such, are, partially at least, self-discounting. (You had her 'eloping' with White in the original draft; nice for her children.) Arno was 'losing his grip,' a damaging accusation in an artist's life. Gibbs was accused of responding to all simple, honest statements by saying 'Don't be banal,' a word which up to that time I am certain he never used in his life. I was '. . . not a large man (in the mental, not the physical sense), but a furious and a mad one.' I was 'without taste, either literary or good'. I '. . . was cruel and largely unnecessary. . . .' 'Elwyn Brooks White sold the only painting he ever made to The New Yorker's art board, on which his wife sits.' Damned if we aren't criminally corrupt, among other things."

I think Time has gratuitously invaded the privacy of a great many people; I think it draws conclusions unwarranted by the facts, distorts quotes, reprints conclusions unwarranted by the facts, reprints rumors it knows have little foundation, uses a form of selective editing in getting together a story from the newspapers that throws it altogether out of focus, and that Timestyle is an offense to the ear. I said that Mr. Luce was humorless because I could find nothing in the source or in the reports of people who had talked to him that indicated anything else. Also I doubt very much if a humorist would last a week as president of Time, Inc. I'm not even sure that "humorless" is a disparaging term. In any case all statements and editorial conclusions in the piece are matters of honest opinion with me, usually made after reading the evidence of a great many people. Don't know if Ingersoll and Luce realize just how much source material went into this thing, and from what widely divergent people it came. In almost every case I've tried to follow the most temperate estimate, throwing out a lot of stuff that would have made the boys' hair stand up.

Ross wound up with a body slam:

After our talk the other night I asked at least ten people about Time and, to my amazement, found them bitter, in varying degrees, in their attitude. You are generally regarded as being as mean as hell and frequently scurrilous. Two Jewish gentlemen were at dinner with me that night and, upon mention of Time, one of them charged that you are anti-Semitic, and asked the other if he didn't think so too. The other fellow said he'd read Time a lot and he didn't think you were anti-Semitic especially; you were just anti-everything, he said—anti-Semitic, anti-Italian, anti-Scandinavian, anti-black-widow spider. "It is just their pose," he said.

Ross signed this marathon dispatch "Harold Wallace Ross" and appended the words "Small man . . . furious . . . mad . . . no taste"— all of them epithets that Time Inc. had previously applied to him. The whole "childish" matter was now over, Ross said.* But there was no way that so bloody a feud could expire easily. A characteristically sour Luce shot back:

> Thank you for your letter of November 23. It was not "up to you" to make any explanations so far as I was concerned, but in any case I wanted to thank you for the personal trouble you took with the Time-Luce parody.
>
> Of course I regret you felt it necessary to print that Richard Watts quote. I only regret that Mr. Gibbs did not publish all he knew so that I might learn at once how mean and poisonous a person I am.
>
> Mr. Gibbs, like you, is undoubtedly sick of the whole subject. But, having located a poison more or less at large in society, he may perhaps like to help mitigate it. And this, I assure you, he can do if he will take any current copy of TIME and red-pencil every example of "cruelty, scandal-mongering and insult"—and send it to me.

It has been widely reported that Gibbs's barbed treatment managed to kill off Timestyle in one fell swoop, and that after the parody appeared, nobody at *Time* would dare employ it again. This is far from the truth. Thanks in part to Gibbs, much of *Time*'s prose did become noticeably less wacky. But many of its affectations—dropped articles, colorful descriptives, and especially, inherent biases—lingered for years.

Still, there was no arguing with what Gibbs had accomplished. For

---

* Frank Crowninshield, the former editor of *Vanity Fair*, thought Ross's response was "a gem of the purest ray."

once, Alexander Woollcott's enthusiasms were in order when he personally wrote Gibbs that his masterwork was "the most creditable thing that magazine has ever printed. Its publication renews my enthusiasm for the magazine and its guile as a piece of parody fills me with envy and admiration." In *Harper's*, Bernard DeVoto declared that Gibbs had executed "the most distinguished public service of American journalism in 1936." By one reckoning, the Luce issue was only the second number of *The New Yorker* that had sold out. (The previous one, in 1934, had been given over largely to a parody of *Punch,* titled "Paunch.") Winchell reported a rumor—which he probably started—that Luce had descended on *The New Yorker's* offices on Thanksgiving to personally beat Gibbs up, only to find that the place was closed for the holiday.

Ross considered the spoof "one of the best pieces ever run by a magazine, unquestionably, and my part in it was satisfying and wholesome." And he patted Gibbs on the back with the circulation figures to prove it:

> There is no doubt the Luce piece did something. . . . The issue of Nov. 14th, two weeks ahead of Luce sold 140,000. Nov. 21st was down to 138,000 and then Luce makes 141,000. That broke the record, but the next issue broke it again; sold 144,000. The plain fact is that the Luce Profile not only broke a season's record for the issue in which it appeared, but continued with the next issue and broke the record again. A peculiar, but gratifying effect.

Inevitably, the scrapping would continue. Less than a month after the parody appeared, *The New Yorker* ran a "Funny Coincidence Department" note that effectively accused *Fortune* of plagiarizing an item from *Magazine Digest.* Actually, the original had appeared in *Fortune,* prompting its managing editor, Eric Hodgins, to declare, "I find it hard to dissociate anything the New Yorker does these days from venality." When Hodgins told Ross about the mistake, and Ross fired back an impolitic response, Ingersoll told him, "The river looks very tempting this afternoon. I suggest—not entirely facetiously—that you go over and jump into it." In a subsequent "Department of Correction, Amplification, and Abuse," *The New Yorker* apologized grudgingly, stating that the matter seemed only "to be partially set in order."

In 1937 *Life* published a photo of Ross enhanced by the famed carica-turist Al Hirschfeld, who drew sinister eyebrows and a bushy mustache on Ross's grinning face to transform him into a dead ringer for Soviet dictator Josef Stalin. In 1938 Ingersoll mischievously added the name of Eustace Tilley, *The New Yorker*'s dandyish symbol, to *Time*'s masthead. After keeping the name there awhile, Ingersoll planned to drop it and explain that Tilley had been fired. But when Corey Ford, who had named Tilley, threatened to sue, Ingersoll abandoned the plan.

In 1940 a flap ensued when Freddie Packard supposedly sent a tele-gram to Hodgins that inquired DOES THE PRESENT MRS LUCE WEAR BLACK UNDERWEAR. Packard said he wasn't responsible and may well not have been; his first and middle initials were erroneously rendered as "R H." In any event, some months later Margaret Case Harriman published a two-part Profile of Clare titled "The Candor Kid" that began, "Once upon a time, in a far country called Riverside Drive, a miracle child was born and her name was Clare Boothe. Over her cradle hovered so many good fairy godmothers that an S.R.O. sign was soon put up at the foot of the crib." Shawn was delighted. "As for Harriman's bitchy tone," he wrote, "I think it's perfect; amounts to doing Boothe in her own terms, much as Gibbs did Luce in Timestyle."* In 1945 Charles Morton published in *The New Yorker* a casual that made sport of *Time*'s burgeoning editorial

---

* As part of an attempt to garner favorable coverage of her former plantation in Charleston, which had in the interim become a monastery, Clare told Ross shortly before his death that *The New Yorker* had "fulfilled its mission of laughter, which always provides a great tonic for the unnecessary miseries our human nature visits on itself." Apparently ignorant of Diogenes, she added, "A good friend of mine once said: 'It's better to light one candle than to curse the darkness.' You've lit lots of gay little candles in the gloom, bless you!"

roster, predicting that at some point Luce would be anointed "Exalted Supreme Editor-in-Chief."

Gibbs himself was happy to keep stoking the antagonism, almost to the point of exhaustion. In 1938 he gleefully noted in "Comment" that clerical workers, researchers, and writers for *Fortune* ("probably the third heaviest magazine in the English language") had been ordered to report to their desks by nine, nine-thirty, and ten a.m., respectively. In 1940 he reported that *Life* had conquered its struggle "to figure out a way to print a picture of a living, breathing woman with absolutely no clothes on" while making a significant cultural statement in the process. "They merely photographed a life class at the Yale Art School. This had Yale, it had Art, it had Class, it had America; it had everything, including no clothes on." There was also a Gibbbsian "Comment" from 1944 that described a Time Inc. worker who swore that one day he would destroy Luce's all-omniscient construct by shouting down its hallways, "I don't *know!*" Gibbs's subject summed up, "The whole damn thing will just come tumbling down."

Gibbs further published a casual called "Beauty and Gutzon Borglum" that was based very closely on his uncomfortable 1931 encounter with Clare. Disguising her as the "very beautiful and strange" Myrna Haskell, he concluded the vignette by having his alter ego exit Clare's apartment in a daze: "As he rode down Madison Avenue, he thought somewhat about the well-known sculptor but mostly about Miss Haskell's mind. For some reason he was never able to explain, it made him think of confetti."

"Time . . . Fortune . . . Life . . . Luce" may have been played for laughs, but Ross remained deadly serious about Luce and what he regarded as a truly dangerous enterprise. "*Time* is terrifying, and ought to be put out of business but it gets more powerful daily," he wrote Martha Gellhorn at the height of World War II. "If Clare isn't president Henry will be, and I'll probably get run out of the country." He subsequently told Gellhorn, "If either of the Luces become president I positively will leave the country and your suggestion of Cuba sounds fine. One or the other of them may make the White House if they don't tear each other to pieces on some occasion before they get there. I think they are the two most ambitious people I have ever encountered." In a lighter vein, Ross sent around a memo that recommended abandoning the use of the word *understandably*. He explained, "I saw it in *Life* the other day, and when *Life* takes up a word, it is time for us to unload, I think."

Luce eventually dismissed the Profile but he could never quite elude it. Two years after its appearance, a condensed version ran in *Scholastic* magazine. Long after that, when Luce was at Rollins College in Florida to make a speech, he decided to drop in on a class in contemporary biography. "And what do you suppose the class was discussing?" he complained. "*Me!* And what do you suppose they were using as their text? That goddamn article in *The New Yorker!* So now my question is, *Is* this thing going to be engraved on my tombstone?"

Curiously, Gibbs would have his own mild rapprochement with Luce. In 1946 he published a piece about Ethel Merman in *Life,* evoking at least one complaint of disloyalty. Two years later, when Ross accepted but killed a twelve-thousand-word Profile that Gibbs had written of Noël Coward, Gibbs returned to *Life* to peddle it. But he insisted that it not be cut, edited, or otherwise molested. Gibbs knew that those were impossible terms and practically dared the editor Robert Coughlan to reject the piece. "This brings me to money," Gibbs wrote, "about which in many ways I am a son of a bitch. If, by some miracle, like Luce dropping dead, you wanted to print it in two parts I'm afraid I'd want a price that would make *everybody* drop dead." The Coward story was never printed.

Gibbs would come to feel a strange ambivalence toward the parody. Privately, he was pleased to have given *Time* a well-deserved comeuppance and was gratified by the praise and the controversy. Over the years, though, he grew tired of having the piece being remembered above everything else he had written, especially when anyone quoted—or just as frequently, misquoted—its most deathless line. When Henry Holt anthologized the spoof in *More in Sorrow,* Gibbs confided to Thurber, "I wanted to change 'the famous profile on Luce' to 'the ill-advised,' etc., and they are still trying to figure out what to make of that."

Just the same, Gibbs stood by his work. Some twenty years after "Time . . . Fortune . . . Life . . . Luce" appeared, he considered expanding it. He resisted the temptation.

It seemed to me at first that Mr. Luce's career ought to be brought up to date, but my second, and final, decision was that this would be superfluous, not because of the extra effort involved, a matter naturally of small concern to me, but because whatever changes have taken place in him have had to do with increasing celebrity and scope rather than any fundamental shifting of personality. It is obvious that Mr. Luce occupies a more obtrusive position in the nation than he did in 1935 [*sic*], but I see no reason to suppose that he is a different man.

CHAPTER 7

"PRETTY GUMMY AT BEST"

Well after *The New Yorker* proved an editorial and financial success, Ross began pondering other ventures. In an echo of the days when he was hatching new projects to escape the grind of the *American Legion Weekly,* he toyed with the idea of a daily paper devoted entirely to ships' news, as well as a periodical given over entirely to detective stories. He even invested in a paint-spraying machine.

It was all of no consequence; Ross's commitment to his wunderkind was simply too single-minded. "Ross had no valid relationship with any creation excepting only *The New Yorker,*" said David Cort, who dealt with him on several occasions. "Ross did not care about the money in the enterprise; he cared only about the perfection of this insane impersonation of the sophisticated New Yorker, as a Norman in the year 900 might have wanted to look like a Gaul."

Not all his staff felt the same way. *The New Yorker* might have been emerging as the best general-interest periodical in the country, paying reasonably well and affording space and expression for its people that other magazines could not. But its very consistency, and Ross's insistence on uniformity of voice, proved frustrating for those who truly wanted to write from their hearts. And so it was, however improbably, that Gibbs, White, and Thurber all eventually began to make efforts to distance themselves from the magazine.

Thurber was the first to bolt. By the mid-1930s he was not only ready to settle down to a comfortable domestic life with his new wife, Helen, but was grappling with both progressive blindness and considerable ambition. His books *My Life and Hard Times, The Middle-Aged Man on the Flying Trapeze,* and *Let Your Mind Alone!* were popular and critical successes. For *The New Yorker,* he reached beyond "Talk" and casuals and cartoons to write columns about tennis and other indepth factual subjects. He wove the research of reporters like Eugene Kinkead into a popular series called "Where Are They Now?," a retrospective look at news fixtures who had once commanded the public eye, like Gertrude Ederle, the first woman to swim the English Channel. Another focused on Virginia O'Hanlon, whose plaintive inquiry of "Is there a Santa Claus?" to the *New York Sun* in 1897 had yielded the most famous editorial in American newspaper history, composed by Francis Pharcellus Church and answering in the affirmative, "Yes, Virginia, there is a Santa Claus."

One of Thurber's efforts went down in journalistic and legal history. It was an update of the life of William James Sidis, a onetime child mathematics prodigy who had entered Harvard at the age of eleven, the youngest student to enroll in the university's history. Thurber's examination of Sidis's pathetic downfall, complete with details of a reclusive existence in a shabby Boston apartment and an obsession with streetcar transfer tickets, became the focus of a celebrated invasion-of-privacy lawsuit. Perhaps because these works were such a departure from his usual milieu, he signed them with the pen name "Jared L. Manley."

Amid his writing, Thurber decided to "go away somewhere to get organized," as Helen put it. And so the two spent a couple of months in Bermuda, where both Gibbs and O'Hara had honeymooned and where he would return periodically. On that peaceful island, he formed a fast friendship with Jane and Ronald Williams. The latter was the publisher of *The Bermudian*, and Thurber would end up contributing light essays to the struggling Caribbean publication, gratis.

It was the beginning of a general branching out. Thurber left the formal ranks of the *New Yorker* staff but negotiated a freelance arrangement. Freed from the strictures of office work, he wrote widely for other publications. In 1940 and 1941 he intermittently published a column called "If You Ask Me" in his old colleague Ralph Ingersoll's upstart liberal newspaper *PM*. Eschewing most of the paper's avowedly progressive political coverage, Thurber tended to focus on humorous subjects. Ross complained, "You're throwing away ideas on *PM* that would make good casuals." Thurber shrugged off the charge. "I was out from under the strict and exacting editing for which the *New Yorker* was and still is famous," he said, "and I needed this relaxation and the hundred dollars a column Ingersoll paid me."

He further refined his reputation as a professional misogynist, as he revealed in a self-conducted interview for *Mademoiselle:*

MLLE: If you had been born a girl, Mr. Thurber, what kind of girl would you want to be?

THURBER: That's an interesting thought because I almost was a girl. My mother wanted a girl before I was born, so she did everything she could with prenatal influence to mark me—embroidered, cooked, sewed and looked at pictures of Mrs. Grover Cleveland all day long. But . . .

MLLE: It didn't work?

THURBER: No, shortly after I was born they discovered I wasn't a girl. A woman nurse brought me into this world—women have always influenced my life—and on top of breaking the news to my mother that I wasn't a girl, she then told her that I had a full head of hair, and that children born with a lot of hair are never bright. That's a prophecy still to be cleared up, of course.

MLLE: Supposing you had been a girl—

THURBER: Ah, I would have been a hussy. (*Thinking*) Or would I? No, on second thought I think I'd be the quiet, sympathetic-listener type of girl.

MLLE: Is that because, being a man, that's the kind of girl you like?

THURBER: Probably. I like a girl who'll listen while I talk—about myself.

By now he was beginning to return to Columbus, posturing as the local boy who had made good. And in 1940 he and his old friend Elliott Nugent triumphed on Broadway with *The Male Animal.* Nugent himself starred as Tommy Turner, a professor at a small university in the Midwest; the cast included a young Gene Tierney. The more typically Thurberian aspect of the comedy dealt with the romantic conflicts that arise when a football hero ex-boyfriend of Turner's wife returns for a campus visit. But at the heart of *The Male Animal* was the issue of free speech, which would increasingly concern Thurber. An unwitting Turner becomes embroiled in campus politics when reactionary trustees threaten to fire him because he wants to read to his class the statement of the anarchist Bartolomeo Vanzetti, made prior to the pronouncement of his 1927 death sentence. Turner is driven to share the speech not as a political manifesto but as an example of crude yet eloquent English composition.

The production was not without incidents. At one point Thurber tripped over the footlights and tumbled into the orchestra pit while at a rehearsal. Daise Terry, who went to see the play with most of *The New Yorker* staff, was not particularly amused; she compared it to "an unfunny Thurber drawing acted out" and reported that McKelway and Gibbs, among others, "didn't think it was a knockout by any means." But in general the critics loved *The Male Animal*, likening it to *Life with Father* and *The Man Who Came to Dinner*. It ran for nearly 250 performances and established Thurber not merely as a man of letters but as a literary celebrity in the mold of Woollcott.

Not everyone was happy about Thurber's new horizons. He received a poem from a fan who bemoaned his periodic absence from *The New Yorker*'s pages:

We Ask the New Yorker

Oh where has Mr. Thurber gone?
Admirers ask from night to sun (morn doesn't rhyme either)
Has he forgotten how to write,
Or is it just in rage and spite
He draws his women with a curse?
(How he must hate them, book and verse)
When Friday comes we watch the clock,
We wait the postman's cheerful knock,
The wrapper's torn with hungry look,
We leap from "Notes" to Fadiman's "Books."
Alas! No Thurber can be seen,
Except a dog of noble mien
(So different from his vicious gals
Or timid men who shrink from pals)
Oh, Mr. Thurber, come back home,
Or write more often, as you roam.

Thurber was so tickled by this doggerel that he adorned it with a caricature of himself waving at four stern-faced men labeled "Gibbs, Maloney, O'Hara etc." with the impish greeting "Hi, Fellas!"

White did not thirst for recognition as achingly as Thurber did, although the two did once make a half-hearted stab at collaborating on a play "about the difficulty people are experiencing in the decline of snobbery." In any event White, too, was restless. He was also genuinely unhappy. In the eight months between August 1935 and March 1936, his father and mother died. In between these two losses, Katharine had a miscarriage, and their close friend and *New Yorker* mainstay Clarence Day passed away. "I see him roaming the Hereafter / Racked with unregenerate laughter, / I see him chuckle as he sings / Of devil's tail and angel's wings," White pined.

On a professional level, he found himself chafing under *The New Yorker's* limitations. He achieved periodic public attention with endearing pieces like "Farewell, My Lovely!," his whimsical, nostalgic homage to his Model T "Hotspur" and his 1922 cross-country tour. But his energies were sapped by the demands and anonymity of "Comment." In 1934 he published a collection of his items, titled *Every Day Is Saturday*. It was well received; Gluyas Williams told Katharine that it was "about the only thing that has cheered me up this fall." His identity as the uncredited scribe behind the section now revealed, White asked Ross in 1935 if he could start signing his pieces. It had become "almost impossible to write anything decent using the editorial 'we,' unless you are the Dionne family," he said. Anyway, the paragraphs were beginning to take on a life of their own:

> Speaking for the writer of comment [*sic*], I can say that it tends to become (is) a mongrel department, or hybrid, half fish, half snail. . . . I feel that N & C are not, literally "the talk of the town." Maybe they were originally intended to be, but it hasn't worked out that way in practice. They are, specifically, editorial paragraphs with a bias or slant or conviction. And they are, to some degree, personal. . . . [I]t is pretty hard to write comment [*sic*]—or anything—over a long period of time without putting a lot of personal junk or notions into them.

But Ross, though he thought White's contributions "among the best stuff being written today," refused to divorce "Comment" from leading into "Talk" and rejected the notion of signed essays. "Your page is stronger anonymous, as an expression of an institution, rather than of an individual," Ross explained. "I feel this very strongly."

Impersonality and personal prejudice aside, White was also conflicted about the tenor of the section. "The suggestion has often been made," wrote one critic of *Every Day Is Saturday*, "that the distinctive prose which regularly fills the opening pages of The New Yorker has as its base a kind of ambergris resulting from a peculiar unrest growing out of actual fear of (a) the telephone company, (b) perambulators, (c) hoot owls, (d) locked doors." Though the observation may have rankled, it rang true. It was one thing to be irreverent during the Roaring '20s or, at worst, mildly neurotic. But with the Depression dragging on and Europe edging toward war, White felt a gnawing obligation to be serious.

Thurber thought this attitude absurd. "Never has there been so much to laugh at," he wrote White. He tried to convince him that a writer should be true to his métier:

It is the easiest thing in the world nowadays to become so socially conscious, so Spanish war stricken, that all sense of balance and values goes out of a person. Not long ago in Paris Lillian Hellman told me that she would give up writing if she could ameliorate the condition of the world, or of only a few people in it.* Hemingway is probably on that same path, and a drove of writers are following along, screaming and sweating and looking pretty strange and

---

* Hellman, as much a fabulist as Thurber, denied that this exchange ever took place. In 1975 she told White that she had not seen Thurber in Paris at the time he reported. Moreover, she said, "I never said any such thing and I don't believe anybody else ever said it, except maybe somebody in a nut joint pillow fight."

futile. This is one of the greatest menaces there is; people with intelligence deciding that the point is to become grimly gray and intense and unhappy and tiresome because the world and many of its people are in a bad way. It's a form of egotism, a supreme form. I've toyed with it myself and understand it a little. It's as dangerous as toying with a drug. How can these bastards hope to get hold of what's the matter with the world and do anything about it when they haven't the slightest idea that something just as bad and unnatural has happened to them?

White attempted to thread the needle of his trademark light touch with bona fide social awareness in a March 13, 1937, "Comment." With maximum indignation, he attacked FDR's misbegotten attempt to pack the Supreme Court. Denouncing as "balderdash" the president's insistence that those who opposed his plan were perforce anti–New Dealers, he called Roosevelt "a petulant saviour" and "an Eagle Scout whose passion for doing the country a good turn every day has at last got out of hand." But instead of recommending outright opposition to the court plan, White said *The New Yorker* would "sleep on it."

Ralph Ingersoll would not sleep on it. Having previously tweaked White's "gossamer writing" in his *Fortune* article, the increasingly activist editor now protested his former colleague's passivity. He accused White of "gentle complacency" and beseeched him, "Andy, Andy!! Doesn't that well-fed stomach of yours ever turn when you think of what you're saying? Let us sleep on suffering, want, malnutrition. Let us sleep too on young men who are so fond of phrasing things exactly that humanity never troubles them."

Within a couple of months, whether inspired at all by Ingersoll or not, White decided he would cease writing "Comment" and take a year's leave of absence. He was not interested in another job per se; the year before, he had turned down Christopher Morley's offer to be editor of *The Saturday Review of Literature*. He and Katharine even refused Fleischmann's

Wolcott Gibbs was *The New Yorker*'s workhorse—theater critic, writer of stories both serious and comic, expert parodist, "Notes and Comment" author, and cutting editor.

E. B. White (left) and James Thurber were close friends and occasional rivals. By setting *The New Yorker*'s whimsical yet sophisticated tone, they became legends.

The coarse, bull-headed, exacting Harold Ross admitted he was "the luckiest son of a bitch alive" when he founded his magazine in 1925.

Katharine White elevated Ross's early "gagmag" to serious literary heights and had the happiest of marriages, with its star writer.

The discriminating fiction editor and writer William Maxwell also served briefly and reluctantly at Ross's storied art conferences.

William Shawn—quiet, hard working and elusive—would succeed Ross as editor and make *The New Yorker* a journalistic touchstone.

Gibbs's first marriage, to college student Helen Galpin, was so big a mistake that neither spoke of it.

After cavorting at Vassar, Lois Long cavorted as the quintessential *New Yorker* tastemaker for nightlife and fashion.

Gibbs fell in love with the elegant writer Nancy Hale. She broke his heart by not abandoning her husband for him.

St. Clair McKelway, a consummate *New Yorker* reporter and editor, served with the fledgling air force in the Pacific. There his multiple personalities erupted.

The unreservedly gay John Mosher was *The New Yorker*'s first movie critic. He also rejected unsolicited manuscripts with gusto.

The talented and prodigious Russell Maloney, seen here with his wife, Miriam, unleashed his frustration at *The New Yorker* by tearing into Gibbs.

The self-indulgence and literary excesses of Alexander Woollcott were legion. After giving Ross invaluable early assistance, he broke with him irrevocably.

John O'Hara perfected the so-called *New Yorker* short story. He was a staple of the magazine—and a source of pride and vexation to Ross for years.

The kindly Robert Benchley, shown in a publicity shot for his short subject *Home Movies*, was a master of light *New Yorker* nonsense.

Charles Addams was synonymous with his namesake
ghouls and black cartoon humor. In real life, he lived
cheerfully and well.

Art editor James Geraghty set *The New Yorker's*
smart standard for all manner of illustration
and design.

Peter Arno's cartoons skewered "morons." This
rakish self-portrait conveys his devilish persona.

No item was too obscure to run down for Freddie Packard, head of *The New Yorker*'s storied fact-checking department.

"Burly, able, tumbledown" managing editor Ralph Ingersoll clashed with Ross on the job and later when Ingersoll joined Time Inc.

Gustave Lobrano took tasteful charge of *New Yorker* fiction after his friends E. B. and Katharine White left for Maine. Their return caused tension.

Elinor "Flip" Gibbs on Fire Island with son Tony and daughter Janet, ca. World War II.

On Fire Island, drenched in sun and cut off from the world, Gibbs was atypically at peace. "I guess I really like it here better than any other place in the world," he wrote.

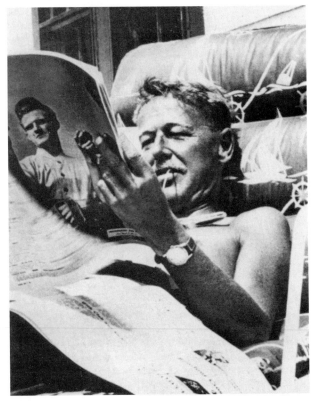

suggestion that they assume joint editorship of *The New Yorker*. What he wanted was what he had always wanted—to write as he pleased, even if he was not quite sure what that would constitute. He also needed to scour himself of more than a decade of Manhattan living. Besides, he told his brother, "I want to see what it feels like, again, to let a week pass by without having an editorial bowel movement." Assuming the pose of Eustace Tilley in the August 7 issue, he explained his rationale obliquely:

I want time to think about many people, alive and dead: Pearl White, Schoolboy Creekmore, Igor Sikorsky—I couldn't begin to name them. I want to think about the custom of skiing in summertime, want to hear a child play thirds on the pianoforte in midafternoon. I shall devote considerable time to studying the faces of motorists drawn up for the red light; in their look of discontent is the answer to the industrial revolution. Did you know that a porcupine has the longest intestine in Christendom, either because he eats so much wood or in order that he may? It is a fact. There must be something to be learned by thinking about that.

Otto Soglow illustrated these vague thoughts with a drawing of Tilley departing the Plaza Hotel in a horse-drawn carriage, doffing his hat to well-wishers, chased by a Thurber dog.

White left *The New Yorker* with no definite intentions. He could not even explain himself fully to Katharine. "In the main," he wrote her, "my plan is to have none." He did, however, expect to make any number of trips to "places where my spoor is still to be found." Katharine abided by her husband's decision, even as she grappled with his absence. "I don't think I ever missed you so much," she wrote within a month of his departure. Ross, too, was hit hard by the loss of arguably his best writer. White tried to placate him. "Enjoyed working in your shop very much," he wrote. "Will always remember it." But Ross was bitter about White's defection. "He just sails around in some God damn boat," he griped.

By his own admission, White made "an unholy mess" of his time off. He had hoped to use his freedom to work "on a theme which engrosses me"—a long autobiographical poem, assembled from notes he had been scribbling for some time. But he never finished it. Seventeen years after his sabbatical, he finally published six parts of it in his collection *The Second Tree from the Corner.* Entitled "Zoo Revisited: Or the Life and Death of Olie Hackstaff," it recounted his elusive feelings associated with some of the more significant locales of his past, places he revisited during his time away from *The New Yorker.* Among them were Mount Vernon, Bellport in Long Island—and especially Maine.

White had been drawn to Maine as a source of respite for years. Now he began to view it as a source of inspiration and even salvation. He reported to Thurber that he spent that Christmastime of 1937 "listening to the beat of tire chains against cold mudguards, studying tracks where the deer had pawed the snow under the little apple trees, sliding down hill, and ushering in the new year by going to bed and letting the Baptist church ring twelve clear holy strokes for me." Captivated by an atmosphere that was "almost Currier and Ives in its purity," he determined shortly thereafter that he and Katharine should relocate there.

Katharine acceded and found that the ensuing few years on the working farm that they purchased at Allen Cove were among her happiest. Fortunately, the experience was not quite the exile that it might have been; she ended up spending about half of each day working on manuscripts sent up to her from Manhattan and maintaining an active correspondence. Eventually, giving up her job for her husband's sake did turn out to be harder than she had expected. But in these early days she reveled in her rural domesticity, as she told Ruth McKenney:

My life here is fantastic. You should see me trying to be a good farm wife, picking, canning, mopping and dusting, and at the same time keeping my 7½ year old from drowning, and my 17 year old from killing himself and his girl friends in wild night rides, and making my big daughter-scientist be domestic when she'd rather be losing all her few dollars on late night poker parties. (Not one of the three pays the least attention to me.) And on top of this trying to be a long distance editor. Then there are the dogs, the pig, the chickens, the turkey (only one!), the cows who are our boarders, all meeting disaster daily, and the vegetables and flowers that I'm supposed to tend.

The Whites' departure from Manhattan ushered in a figure who would prove critical to *The New Yorker*'s continued success. Gustave "Gus" Stubbs Lobrano, born in the same year as Gibbs, had had a privileged upbringing in New Orleans, attending the excellent Newman School, a private institution originally designated for Jewish orphans. A couple of years behind White at Cornell, he met him on the *Cornell Daily Sun*. For a while in the 1920s they shared a Greenwich Village apartment with two other men; at one point the boarders included Lobrano's future brother-in-law, Jack Flick. His clumsy amours in the small space proved amusing. Once when Flick was trying not terribly successfully to make time with a companion, White stuck his head into the living room and announced, "If you haven't seduced her by one o'clock, forget it."

Upon marrying in 1927, Lobrano left this arrangement and moved with his wife, Jean, to Albany, where he toiled for years at her family's travel bureau. The business dwindled during the Depression. But in 1935, when White told him of a job back in Manhattan at *Town and Country* under Harry Bull, a fellow Cornell alumnus, Lobrano eagerly applied and was accepted. Three years later Katharine encouraged him to succeed her in the fiction department. Lobrano easily passed his editing test by expertly handling several pieces, Katharine assisting by providing him with a confidential copy of Gibbs's "Theory and Practice" guidelines. His elegant, patient presence proved a natural fit for *The New Yorker*.

Lobrano was "a tall, diffident man" with "soft eyes and a shy smile," remembered the Czech writer Joseph Wechsberg. "He was a Southern gentleman, a type I'd never met before. His politeness always put me on the defensive." At the same time, he had little patience for substandard work. "He showed me the proof of one of my pieces and asked me gently, as though he were embarrassed, whether I would mind clearing up a few minor points," said Wechsberg. "The proof had scores of penciled marks and remarks and queries written in the margins. I'd never seen such painfully edited copy."

Once described as "the nicest soul that ever lived," he was no pushover. When Edmund Wilson slammed Kay Boyle's novel *Avalanche* as "pure rubbish," Lobrano cheered him on. "Miss Boyle had exactly this sort of thing coming to her," he wrote Ross. "Her book, which I read, miserably, installment by installment in the Saturday Evening Post, is sickening mush. And I'm glad that Mr. Wilson singled out Kay Boyle's stylistic furbelows, including her exasperating trick of using the inanimate possessive." Lobrano's taste for good fiction was finely nuanced. "Something must be left to the reader's imagination," he once said. "After all, if he knows how to read, your reader probably knows how to think too."

"He did not enter lightly upon friendship, as many a writer has lived to discover, and to be his good friend was a tremendously satisfying experience," White recalled. "You felt you had hold of something solid." Moreover, "[h]e had a subtle mind, an engaging wit, an almost flawless taste in literary expression, and an impatience with all forms of shoddiness." Lobrano loved trout fishing, golf, and all manner of sports; he organized a children's Sunday softball game in his Chappaqua neighborhood that sometimes included visiting authors. When Emily Hahn dropped by, she created a small scandal by presenting a friend who had brought a large painting of a nearly naked African chieftain. After the game, Lobrano treated everyone to sodas and sundaes at the town drugstore.

Unlike many other *New Yorker* staff members, Lobrano did not attempt to trade in editing for writing. He had little interest in the latter, publishing only a few short pieces in the magazine, most of them in collaboration. He formed tight associations with many of *The New Yorker*'s best short story writers: he played tennis with Irwin Shaw, hobnobbed with his Westchester neighbor John Cheever, and endeared himself so much to J. D. Salinger that the eccentric author dedicated his acclaimed *Nine Stories* collection in part to him. So high was the regard of S. J. Perelman, not exactly a sentimental specimen, for Lobrano that in his office he displayed a photograph of him along with pictures of James Joyce and Somerset Maugham. Frank Sullivan extolled him as "Gustavus Vasa."

Lobrano was deeply grateful to the Whites for providing his professional deliverance. "I have been with the NYer for about nine months now (the period of gestation), and feel as though I have been born again," he wrote Andy. "My old life, before I had to write letters of rejection to Frank Sullivan and call up Peter Arno every Wednesday, was tranquil and sheltered; but in spite of fear and indigestion and heartbreak the new life is better. I shall die sooner but, all in all, happier."

As for White, when he wasn't "catching mackerel or building a laying house for the pullets," he was still keeping his hand, however reluctantly, in *The New Yorker*. At Ross's request, he continued editing newsbreaks and contributed an occasional piece. But as he once told Gibbs (addressing him as "Gibbsy"), "You can't support a farm on casuals—you have to get right out and sell the hay itself." And so he began writing a monthly, occasionally disjointed column for *Harper's* called "One Man's Meat." In addition to the three hundred dollars he would earn for each piece, the expansive 2,500 words he would contribute twelve times a year would afford him considerable creative freedom.

Just prior to White's departure for Maine, a friend told him snidely that he hoped he would "spare the reading public your little adventures in contentment." As it was, it was not contentment but concrete detail, undergirded by intelligent rumination, that marked much of "One Man's

Meat." Outwardly, White provided details of what it was like to run a farm, to interact with homespun neighbors, and to engage in life's daily business. But real emotion suffused the gentle prose. "Once More to the Lake," for example, was a reminiscent account of a visit with eleven-year-old Joel to Belgrade Lake, where White's father had taken him a generation before. Woven throughout were heart-seizing insights into such grand themes as aging, life, and death:

> I began to sustain the illusion that he was I, and therefore, by simple transposition, that I was my father. This sensation persisted, kept cropping up all the time we were there. It was not an entirely new feeling, but in this setting it grew much stronger. I seemed to be living a dual existence. I would be in the middle of some simple act, I would be picking up a bait box or laying down a table fork, or I would be saying something, and suddenly it would not be I but my father who was saying the words or making the gesture. It gave me a creepy feeling.

"I wish I could believe that I'd ever be able to write as well as that," Russell Maloney told White.

In "Clear Days," amid breaking news of the Munich accord that would tear Czechoslovakia apart and make war inevitable, White found himself "steadily laying shingles" on his barn roof. He combined these two disparate elements through deft rhetoric: "I'm down now; the barn is tight, and the peace is preserved. It is the ugliest peace the earth has ever received for a Christmas present. Old England, eating swastika for breakfast instead of kipper, is a sight I had as lief not lived to see."

"I think that 'One Man's Meat' was the making of him as a writer," said Roger Angell. "Freed of the weekly deadlines and the quaintsy first-person plural form of *The New Yorker*'s 'Notes and Comment' page, which he had written for more than a decade, he discovered his subject (it was himself) and a voice that spoke softly but rang true."

Unlike Thurber and White, Gibbs had a hard time making a name for himself outside the magazine. He took a stab in 1931 when he published a comic novella, *Bird Life at the Pole,* that poked fun at the Antarctic expeditions that were then making headlines. The jacket copy, accompanied by a photo of Gibbs taken before he acquired his trademark thin moustache, noted that the author was "fond of lying in warm water, of having somebody bring him his breakfast in bed, and of money." Around that time he also placed a couple of poignant short stories, "Another Such Victory—" and "November Afternoon," in *Harper's Bazaar.* The former carried strong hints of his impending breakup with Nancy Hale; the latter depicted a sensitive, Gibbs-like boy who tearfully breaks away from his preoccupied parents when, as a surprise, they come to see him play in a prep school football game.

But these efforts made little impression. *The New Yorker* seemed to be where Gibbs was destined to be. And so he remained in Manhattan, residing for almost twenty years in 317 East 51st Street. It was a spacious and comfortable duplex, but wall hangings in square or rectangular frames tended to emphasize its sagging structure. Therefore, in the living room, an oval frame circumscribed a portrait of Gibbs's ancestor Martin Van Buren. The master bedroom had a blocked-up marble fireplace and an unused wood locker built into the wall. The dark, dirty compartment, concealed by an unhinged door, fascinated young Tony. One day when he asked what was inside, the mischievous Gibbs replied ominously, "Injun Joe." The response terrified the boy, and Gibbs finally shone a flashlight inside the space to assure him he had nothing to fear. Out back was a small garden of "strangled vines" where Gibbs would amuse himself by using his hose to squirt his growing collection of cats as they tried to scale the fence.

By putting down roots in midtown, Gibbs tied himself ever more closely to *The New Yorker.* Following the *Time* parody, he attracted considerable attention with his 1937 volume, *Bed of Neuroses*. (The title contradicted Rule no. 24 of his "Theory and Practice'" guidelines: "On the whole, we are hostile to puns.") Many of the pieces were simply light bits of nonsense. "To Sublet, Furnished," took apart the subtle maneuverings of renting an apartment in New York; "Be Still, My Heart" concerned a fellow who could feign sickness at boring functions—and then, after curing himself, found he couldn't escape these ordeals. Gibbs didn't think much of the book; he called it "a perfect example of Nyer [*sic*] writing at its silliest—not a social dilemma in it that my six-year-old niece couldn't solve by walking across the room."

To come into his own as a writer, Gibbs found he needed to discharge at least some of his editing burdens. He never jettisoned this responsibility entirely, but he was relieved when William Maxwell came aboard in late 1936. Maxwell, like Gibbs and McKelway, was an editor who could also write. In Maxwell's case, he did so during periodic sabbaticals from his forty-year tenure. His finely attuned, frequently autobiographical short stories and novels won both fans and prizes. He was a tutor and encourager in the Katharine White mold, and his roster of writers was sterling—Salinger, Welty, Nabokov, Updike, and Isaac Bashevis Singer among them. Alec Wilkinson, a *New Yorker* staff writer who would compose an adulatory tribute, called him "a port in the storm," compared their relationship to that of a father and a son, and declared, "He so dramatically influenced my way of thinking about the world, and feeling about the world, and viewing the world."

It took Maxwell a little while to develop that talent. When he arrived, Gibbs was interested mainly in fobbing off his art conference responsibilities onto him. But he also began breaking the young man in to the fine points of dealing with contributors, as Maxwell recalled:

One day Wolcott Gibbs asked me if I'd like to try some editing. He handed me a manuscript and walked away, without explaining what he meant by editing. I didn't think much of the story, so I cut and changed things around and made it the way I thought it ought to be. To my surprise Gibbs sent it to the printer that way. And I thought, "So that's editing." The next time he gave me a piece to edit I fell on my face. I straightened out something that was mildly funny only if it wasn't too clear what was going on. Gibbs was kind, and said that my editing revealed that there wasn't very much there, but I got the point. In time I came to feel that real editing means changing as little as possible.

It turned out that after more than a decade of editing, Gibbs had accrued an unexpected benefit—a nearly pitch-perfect talent for assuming the voice of others. Gibbs, Thurber recalled, "was always able to fix up a casual without distorting or even marring its author's style." It was this ability that earned him his reputation as *The New Yorker*'s preeminent parodist.

Much of his work in this vein was a send-up of tired literary genres. In "Boo, Beau!" Gibbs skewered *Esquire*-type fashion trend pieces. Zippers, he declared, would henceforth replace suit buttons, "permitting the suit to be opened along the side, somewhat in the manner of a Parker House roll, and laid out on the floor. The customer, of course, will simply lie down on the opened suit, insert his arms and legs into the proper apertures, and zip himself up." Fed up with the extravagant claims that publishers made for prolific but mediocre authors, he wrote "Edward Damper," a book-jacket blurb whose eponymous scribe had, by age sixteen, already written one hundred novels and married five Miss Americas.

His specialty was parodies of particular writers. He imagined the tough-talking, red-baiting Hearst columnist Westbrook Pegler responding to little Virginia O'Hanlon's query about Saint Nicholas: "You're damn right there is a Santa Claus, Virginia. He lives down the road a piece from me, and my name for him is Comrade Jelly Belly." Gibbs's spoof of Sinclair Lewis, "Shad Ampersand," caught Lewis's overarching scene-setting ("The city of Grand Revenant, in High Hope County and the sovereign state of Nostalgia, has a population of 34,567") and his ham-handed dialogue ("'Shad!' she trilled, and now she was a bell. 'Wife!' he clamored through their urgent kiss"). In "Future Conditional," he captured Noël Coward's sparkling self-indulgence. Depicting Coward as carrying on "during a period of considerable stress," Gibbs wrote, "To this day I haven't the slightest idea why social upheaval should invariably be attended by extreme personal inconvenience whose interest in it is, to put the thing mildly, academic."

Gibbs pulled off parodies of writers as diverse as George Jean Nathan, John P. Marquand, and even his friend Sam Behrman. In "Shakespeare, Here's Your Hat," he displayed particular venom for William Saroyan's "customary prefatory notes" to his published plays:

> This play is a masterpiece. It is young, gusty, comical, tragic, beautiful, heroic, and as real as a slaughterhouse or some dame fixing her hair. It could only have been written in America, by an Armenian boy who is an artist and a lover and a dreamer. All at once. All mixed up. It could only have been written by Saroyan. ... The cure for the American theatre is more plays like this one. More plays by Saroyan.

Though Gibbs took little pride in most of what he wrote, these pieces gave him particular pleasure for particular reasons:

> The parodies are, I guess, my favorites because it is a form I like. Successful parody demands a good many things from a writer: it should be funny, as a piece of humorous writing, even to those who haven't read the book and are therefore unfamiliar with the style being imitated or the plot satirized; it should contain a certain amount of real criticism of what the author is saying as well as his manner of saying it; and it should be pitched so little above

(or below) the key of the original that an intelligent critic, on being read passages from both, might be honestly confused. Broad parody, or burlesque, is a tiresome and childish exercise.

After the Luce brouhaha, he began to branch out into full-blown Profiles as well. One of his earliest was of the gravelly voiced Amherst alumnus Burgess Meredith, who had recently made a memorable impression in Maxwell Anderson's play *Winterset*. "His friends call him Buzz, or Bugs, and either of these in some vague way seem descriptive," Gibbs wrote. He cited Meredith's former living arrangements with a "genial salesman of pornography," his peculiar talent for assembling acting troupes that always failed, and the time he got so plastered that he missed his stint on the NBC radio show *Red Davis,* resulting in $62,000 in canceled ad revenue. Naturally he took the usual swipes at his subject's physical features: "His pointed face might more reasonably belong to a jockey . . . at the moment it has seemed to him suitable to let his ginger-colored hair grow long on top, so that in dimmer lights he looks rather like a chrysanthemum." Far from being put off, Meredith thought that Gibbs's "whimsical evaluation was fairly accurate" and a warm friendship ensued.*

Gibbs also took on Ingersoll when he began making a splash with *PM.* In its subtly barbed way, the two-part "A Very Active Type Man" was, wrote Ingersoll's biographer, Roy Hoopes, "surprisingly gentle." But Ingersoll was not amused when Gibbs sent him advance proofs. Unlike the case with Luce, no physical clash resulted; Ingersoll merely responded with a four-and-one-half page, double-spaced memo. He didn't mind that Gibbs called him a hypochondriac, or recalled the time he was nearly thrown out of Yale, or wrote that "in general he has an air of having been rather loosely and casually assembled," with protruding

---

* His friendship with Gibbs notwithstanding, Meredith was one of many who mangled his most famous line. In his memoirs he reported it as "Backward go the sentences until boggles the mind."

eyes, a pouting lower lip, and jaundiced skin. He did, however, register certain other objections:

(4) So help me God, cross my heart and hope to die, that story about the Weegee picture is fictional.* It is also typical of the kind of emphasis of [Dashiell] Hammett which is [a] complete distortion of fact. You can pin many screwier cracks than this on me. . . .

(5) . . . . [F]or God's sake, lay off trying to pin on me that my operating technique or labor policy or whatever you want to call it is to embarrass me into resigning—which is standard Hearst technique. . . .

(6) and (6a) No kidding, I think that it is unfair to criticize me *as a writer* by quoting from a diary written on trains and obviously fragmentary and semi-garbled for the purpose of passing censorships. . . .

(9) There is no heating equipment connected with my 22 x 24 foot pool.

"I think I was offended," Ingersoll later wrote Gibbs, "by the over-all picture of me as a man without taste—either in my own life or in my editorial values."

In terms of sheer influence, Gibbs's most potent Profile was probably "St. George and the Dragnet," about Thomas Dewey, in 1940. Always suspicious of authority, Gibbs painted Manhattan's Republican district attorney as so hard-driven that he was necessarily suspect. It was part of Dewey's genius, Gibbs wrote, "to make the jurors feel that they are

---

* Arthur Felig (1899–1968), aka "Weegee," was a famous realist photographer of New York City street scenes, lowlife, crime, accidents, and similar subjects.

part of the prosecution, not a difficult feat with a blue-ribbon jury, which usually imagines that it has been divinely appointed to convict, anyway." He imparted the DA's inordinate passion with a couple of arresting sentences about his eyes: "These are brown, with small irises surrounded by a relatively immense area of white, and Dewey has a habit of rotating them furiously to punctuate and emphasize his speech, expressing horror and surprise by shooting them upward, cunning by sliding them from side to side behind narrowed lids. At climactic moments he can pop them side to side, almost audibly." Far from impugning the man's integrity, Gibbs thought it beyond belief, noting that reporters often called him "The Boy Scout" or, more simply, "The Boy." He left out no obscure detail, down to Dewey's admission that he drank more than three quarts of water a day.

The piece, with legwork supplied by John Bainbridge, was explosive. Suspecting that the Democrats had employed Gibbs, Dewey impounded his generally overdrawn bank account. Pegler, not yet the target of Gibbs's pen, was in awe. The Profile was "a beautiful operation," he wrote, one that "must command the respect of any colleague and the awe of those cleaver-and buck-saw butchers who cut a man up with woodsman's strokes." In fact, he thought the Profile was perhaps *too* good: "I submit that such a job as the boys have done on Dewey is likely to discourage any public servant and deter good men from entertaining public life."

Amid these undertakings, Gibbs found himself stuck taking over "Comment." Although White contributed sporadically to the section, Gibbs now assumed the magazine's editorial voice. If his jottings lacked White's unique panache, they were no less memorable. Here he was on the newly opened World's Fair:

We spent an hour in the library looking at pictures of Old World's Fairs and reading what contemporary opinion had to say about them. It might all have come out of Flushing this week. How strange and gratifying, our fathers wrote, that civilization should have culminated in their lifetime, that *their* Fair should have been the stick in the stand to mark the highest reaching of the tide. How quaint, we said to ourself, looking at the scrolled and tur-reted buildings at the old Chicago Fair. How quaint, we suppose our grandson will say when he comes across pictures of this one in all its streamlined and functional majesty. We tried to think what *his* Fair will look like, fifty years from now, but our mind, too, wouldn't go beyond the miracles of the present. Perhaps, after all, we thought, 1939 will be remembered as the year when the human mind actually did reach the limit of its ingenuity, and Grover Whalen, the flower of a race, built the towers that could not be improved.

When hard-pressed for copy, he wrote about his children. Once he reported on a weird little ditty that four-year-old Tony chanted in the bathtub; it was sung "entirely on one note except that the voice drops on the last word in every line." It began, *He will just do nothing at all, / He will just sit there in the noonday sun. / And when they speak to him, he will not answer them, / because he does not care to.* Gibbs called this remark-able achievement "one of the handsomest literary efforts of the year" and took a perverse pride in getting its key word, *wee-wee,* into print.* He also wrote a touching paragraph about Tony escorting Janet to her first day of kindergarten. Years later, at a party at the house of the *New York Post* theater critic Richard Watts, a precocious young Jonathan Schwartz approached him. "I asked Gibbs what his favorite piece was," Schwartz recalled. Standing by a bookshelf, Gibbs picked up one of his collections and pointed out the anecdote.

And when World War II began on September 1, 1939, Gibbs com-bined astonishment, revulsion, and prescience. The conflict, he pre-

---

* The composer Celius Daughtery later set the incantation to music. Titled "Declara-tion of Independence," it was recorded by Pete Seeger.

dicted, would be waged against flesh and spirit alike, with the best military brains consumed with their murderous task:

> [They] will now think continuously and cleverly of death—planning new and better ways to annihilate an army in the open field (the planes will be very useful this time); planning ways to crush and stifle men in their impregnable shelters (it is a tribute to our ingenuity that no shelter these days remains impregnable very long); planning bombs that set incendiary fires which can't be put out (a much more economical way of destroying a city than the old-fashioned one of just trying to blow it up); planning death just as thoroughly and competently for old men and women and children as for the soldiers (this war will be quite impartial; it will play no favorites).

And yet Gibbs's fit with "Comment" was strained. Back in 1931, when he had temporarily filled in for White on the section, Ross had not been impressed. "The trouble with Gibbs' stuff is that it's in one tone," the editor said. "He hates everything, without qualification." Almost a decade later Gibbs found himself not so much hating everything without qualification as being periodically paralyzed about speaking for the magazine on a regular deadline. He had no illusions about his strengths. He wrote White in Maine, "We all try very hard to keep Notes & Comment up there where you put it, but I'm afraid it is pretty gummy at best."

How to escape the gumminess? Gibbs determined that the theater might be his ticket out. He had his reasons. Many years before, at Riverdale, his teachers had made him "a member of the rabble, a senator, a soldier, and assorted offstage vocal effects" in *Coriolanus.* The experience taught him mainly that "small boys are likely to make rather convulsive Romans." Still, he was cast as a conspirator who stabbed Harold Guinzburg, the future founder of the Viking Press, in *Julius Caesar.*

His most memorable Riverdale Shakespeare experience was an

open-air production of *A Midsummer Night's Dream*. As he recounted in his casual "Ring Out, Wild Bells," Gibbs played Puck, wearing a motley costume of his mother's own devising that came equipped with myriad tiny bells. Telling Gibbs that he envisioned Puck as a mischief-maker in perpetual motion, the director instructed him to dance up and down continually, waving his arms and cocking his head. "I want you to be a little whirlwind," he said. The results were predictably catastrophic. The tintinnabulation— "a silvery music, festive and horrible"—drowned out all the dialogue and so unnerved one of the fairies that when it came time for his big speech, the panic-stricken child unwittingly launched into a recitation of the Gettysburg Address.

Obviously Gibbs was not destined to be an actor. Perhaps, though, he could be a playwright in the mold of Thurber and *The Male Animal*. His attempts to mount a theatrical had begun as early as 1935, when he tried to collaborate with McKelway on a comedy whose main character would be Ross. "Gibbs wrote a perfect opening scene by himself and then we wrote some kind of draft of a couple of acts," McKelway recalled. But they gave up almost immediately. "As others have done since, we had made the mistake of trying to do a play about 'The New Yorker' itself and about the real Ross, instead of a play about some believeable people who work on a magazine like 'The New Yorker.' "*

Gibbs got much further with a musical that he wrote sometime during the war. It was based in part on two of his short stories—"Feud" and "The Courtship of Milton Barker," both of them concerned with comedic mishaps on the Long Island Rail Road. In developing the material for the stage, Gibbs wove a plot around a "virtuous brakeman" named Martin,

---

* Gibbs cannibalized the opening scene for his November 27, 1943, casual "Miss McManus and the Muse," about an exasperating encounter between a frustrated poet and a by-the-book telephone operator in the switchboard room of *The New York Literary Messenger*, "a magazine of deep thought." In McKelway's estimation, the casual's source material "was the only publishable thing in those whole two acts."

his innocent girlfriend, Selena, and a traveling circus. In brief, Martin foils a plot hatched by a crooked railway cop and the nearly destitute circus owner—the father of a seductress named Juanita—to wreck the show for the insurance money. In the process, Martin wins the hand of Selena, who happens to be the yardmaster's daughter. Gibbs called it *Sarasota Special.*

Written with an eye for visual spectacle (the suggestion of the circus pulling into the yards would make for "a nice, noisy night effect") and an ear for appropriately placed musical numbers, it held some promise. Gibbs wrote an entire script and hoped that O'Hara, still triumphant from *Pal Joey*, would join him in bringing it to the stage. He did want proper credit. "I don't want to be taken over by you, winding up as 'additional dialogue by Wolcott Gibbs' or based on a story by," he told O'Hara. "In fact, [I] want it basically something like this now. Maybe I ought to get two thirds of the book as a matter of fact." Gibbs even considered enlisting White to compose the lyrics because "[h]e isn't doing anything that I know of."

Sarasota Special never got off the ground.* Though competent and entertaining, it offered little to distinguish it from much of the Broadway dross against which it would have competed. It was "just the bunk," Gibbs admitted years later. "It's a faulty play. There's one good scene in it that goes on for twenty minutes, but twenty minutes is not a play." Anyway, he told O'Hara, "I am a hell of a writer to try a collaboration, being generally against other people's ideas."

As it turned out, Gibbs would indeed make a name for himself in the theater. But it would be from the audience, not the stage.

---

* NBC broadcast a modified version of *Sarasota Special,* sans music, on May 6, 1960. Titled *Full Moon Over Brooklyn,* it was produced by David Susskind, directed by Jack Smight, and starred Robert Webber, Barbara Barrie, Elaine Stritch, and Art Carney. "It did not get uproarious," wrote John P. Shanley in *The New York Times,* "but except for a tedious longish stretch in the middle, made for a pleasant enough hour."

CHAPTER 8

"A SILLY OCCUPATION
FOR A GROWN MAN"

"There is nothing like an Opening Night to make the performer wish he were temporarily dead or at least slightly numb," wrote Louis Sobol in 1945. "The producer doesn't feel too frolicsome either." Describing "that second of throat-catch and heart-pause when the house lights dim out," he noted that at that moment,

> [B]ackstage folk shiver with the swoon-droops, a sinister ailment germinated not by the thought that out front are notable First Nighters like Fannie Hurst, Herbert Bayard Swope and Irving Berlin, Hope Hampton, Moss Hart and Gilbert Miller, or that relatives are in back seats or in the balcony, but by awareness of a dozen or so deadpanned gentlemen and unemotional ladies of varying ages, moods and eccentricities, generally referred to by the honest and the fearless as Dramatic Critics. These exalted personages draw handsome salaries from the newspapers or magazines they represent in return for submitting a candid report on the latest play. On this report may hang the fate of the producer's investment—anywhere from $20,000 to $250,000. Similarly, on

the critics' decision may rest the length of the actor's job—the yardstick which measures the difference between being able to dine at "21" and the Stork and standing in line at the Automat.

The bottom portion of the opening spread of Sobol's magazine piece caricatured nine of those critics clustered in the front row, their faces registering expressions ranging from mild skepticism to outright hostility. Third from the left was Gibbs, looking directly at the reader with a countenance that was quite unsmiling.

When Gibbs composed a review, he did so "in the manner of a little boy plucking the wings off a nasty insect." Gibbs, it was said, set "standards so high that even he could never attain them," as these snippets attest:

The Man with Blond Hair, which vanished from the Belasco after seven performances, was a striking example of the effect of lotus-eating on the human mind.

In the course of the piece known as *I Killed the Count,* which bounced into the Cort one night last week, the audience was permitted to see the same man killed three times by three different people and to hear a fourth confess to the crime. It remained, nevertheless, about the dullest exhibition you can imagine.

Very soon after the curtain rose on *A Boy Who Lived Twice,* a society matron from Oyster Bay declined a cup of tea offered her by the butler and ordered up a slug of Scotch. "Braxton," she said frankly, "I'm pooped." This established the approximate comedic level of last week's entry at the Biltmore.

Sea Dogs, which blew into the Maxine Elliott, was hard for me to accept as a serious dramatic enterprise, undertaken for profit. The ship was on fire, the captain was drunk, and from where I sat, the audience appeared to be either dead or asleep.

[*Abie's Irish Rose*] had, in fact, the rather eerie quality of a repeated nightmare; the one, perhaps, in which I always find myself in an old well, thick with bats, and can't get out.

"God, he's brilliant," said an anonymous admirer. "He doesn't like anything." To which Ross supposedly replied, "Maybe he doesn't like anything, but he can do everything."

Actually, Gibbs was always ready to praise good work, often at length, and he was generally perceptive enough to recognize its merits. He found Noël Coward's *Blithe Spirit* to be "as deft, malicious, and fascinating a comedy as you could hope to see." Of *Guys and Dolls* he declared, "I don't think I've ever had more fun at a musical comedy than I had the other night." On a more serious level, he was appropriately moved by *Death of a Salesman*. In describing Arthur Miller's masterpiece, he acknowledged, he had not done justice in conveying "the quality of his work, of how unerringly he has drawn the portrait of a failure, a man who has broken under the pressures of an economic system that he is fatally incapable of understanding."

Nonetheless Irwin Shaw, the author of the archetypal *New Yorker* short story "The Girls in Their Summer Dresses," made a telling point when he wrote,

Critics in New York are made by their dislikes, not by their enthusiasms. Their bon mots, which are quoted and remembered, are always capsule damnations, cutting and sour. Their reputations and, I suppose, their pay, depend, then, upon disliking plays. Wolcott Gibbs, of the *New Yorker,* despite his firm resolve to learn nothing about the theatre and to treat it like a garrulous mother-in-law who will stay the winter if given any encouragement, is, in his hand-

somely written, cranky tirades, often uproariously funny. But when
he is trapped into praising a play, his review reads like a paper by
an intelligent, somewhat snobbish sophomore at a nice college in a
course in contemporary literature, and is forgotten as soon, except
by the actors and playwright he reluctantly patted on the head.

Shaw's use of "snobbish" was fitting. Once, when sitting next to Gibbs
during a "godawful, sentimental" offering called *A Roomful of Roses* that
had the women in the audience weeping into their handkerchiefs, Henry
Hewes of *The Saturday Review* ventured, "Isn't this terrible?"

"Yes," Gibbs responded.

"But I feel like some kind of snob," Hewes continued, "when I see
all these women very moved by all this."

To which Gibbs replied, "What's wrong with being a snob?"

There were other reasons why Gibbs was not enthused by his bailiwick. "I've always felt that play criticism was a silly occupation for a
grown man," he said.

The roots of Gibbs's dramatic antagonism were planted in childhood. He generally found that whenever his mother took him to see
a play, the performance rarely matched his expectations. *Ben-Hur* and
Peter Pan let him down at a young age. So, especially, did *The Wizard of
Oz*. The young Wolcott did not like Dorothy's adult demeanor or her habit
of "detaching herself suddenly from the events around her and singing
a song." He particularly hated the palpably costumed Cowardly Lion:
"I was sad enough to cry about him, and whenever I read the Oz books
after that, it was never a living lion I saw, but a cloth-and-cardboard one,
prancing idiotically on its hind legs." From incidents like this, Gibbs said,
he "began to suspect that all so-called 'children's entertainments' were
designed to provide adults with a bogus and condescending nostalgia."

Yet it was precisely Gibbs's sharp eye that made him the ideal candidate to replace his good friend Benchley when Benchley began spending
long stretches in Hollywood making his film shorts and leading what

Gibbs called "one of the most insanely complicated private lives of our day." Gibbs's first theater column, about Eugene O'Neill's *Ah, Wilderness!,* appeared in 1933, and as the decade progressed, he pretty much became Benchley's designated successor. Gentle to the core, Benchley encouraged the arrangement. "Once, shortly after Robert returned [from Hollywood], Gibbs told him that he was going to give up theater reviewing, because no matter how hard he tried, his prose sounded awful," recalled Benchley's son Nathaniel. "Robert took him out and bought him a drink, and told him not to worry, that his stuff was fine. 'I wish I could write as well,' he concluded. It was what Gibbs described as a grotesque thing to say, but he almost believed that Robert meant it, and that borderline belief was enough to encourage him to continue." In fact, by late 1938 Benchley was telling Ross that he thought Gibbs was "obviously better on the job than I am in my dotage."

And so it was that Gibbs settled into Benchley's job and an idiosyncratic routine. Typically, he would arise at about ten o'clock. After some coffee and a small breakfast, he would compose his review of whatever he had seen the night before. He usually paced in his living room, scattered with copies of *Playbill,* as he worked out in his head what he wanted to say. Always there would be three Lucky Strikes smoldering in ashtrays that he had positioned at either end of the room and on a coffee table in the middle. As he walked back and forth he would pick one up, take a puff, set it back down, then continue on to the next ashtray. He thus worked his way through three packs of cigarettes a day while actually smoking only about half that amount. He rarely dressed before he went out in the evening, preferring to do his work in pajamas and a dressing gown. This embarrassed Tony, who avoided bringing friends home, lest they see his father looking as if he had just rolled out of bed.*

---

* Gibbs's work habits caused Tony embarrassment of another sort when he was about seven and was assigned a classroom report on what his father did for a living. "I had not the foggiest notion, so I came home and asked. And he said, 'Well, what do

When Gibbs sat down to write his review, he would work in the living room on a Royal portable. He could type only with his right thumb, right forefinger, and left forefinger, having once broken the other digits when jumping down a flight of stairs on a drunken bet. (His left pinky was adorned with a family signet ring made of twenty-two-carat gold so soft that he kept it together with a Band-Aid.) But he more than compensated for his infirmity by typing with such speed that his fingers would quite literally become a blur on the keyboard. He hit the keys so forcefully that after six months of constant pounding, the Royal would begin to break down. After another six months, the machine would be beyond repair, and *The New Yorker* would supply him with a new one. Between the broken-down Royal, his mangled fingers, his own rapidity, and his mania for expressing himself clearly, his copy was usually full of mistakes. So he would hand this mess, complete with Eagle number-one pencil corrections, to Elinor, who would unscramble it and type a clean copy.

Eventually Gibbs would get dressed and, with Elinor frequently in tow, proceed from the East 51st Street apartment to the theater district, where he would dine out before the curtain.* Making it to a playhouse should not have been a major ordeal, but it often was. "[T]here are seldom any cabs in the slum area in which I live," he told his readers, "so that I have to progress dismally and circuitously from East to West underground, usually winding up somewhere in the mysterious catacombs underneath Times Square, where it is said many a man has been lost forever." He continued:

---

you think I do? I get dressed up and I go to work at night and I come back long after you're in bed.' I couldn't come up with anything. So he said, 'A burglar.'" A naïve Tony duly conveyed this information at school, causing something of an uproar.

* One of Gibbs's preferred restaurants was an Italian establishment called Zucca's on West 49th Street. Rita Zucca, the daughter of the proprietor, gained notoriety as one of the fascist propagandists during World War II, known as "Axis Sally."

The theater itself, on an opening night, isn't a very comforting place for a nervous man. The old faces (and some of them are getting very old indeed) have the effect of a recurring nightmare: the off-stage conversation is loud and generally facetious, for there is hardly a first-nighter who doesn't fancy himself as a humorist; the air is almost always either too hot or too cold and strongly charged with the scent of alcohol, perfume and disinfectant; there is rarely any adequate place to dispose of a hat and coat; and again there is the anxiety about getting a cab in the end—a doomed project, since only the first ten or twelve people leaving the theater are likely to be so accommodated and there are those who, after years of experience, can run rings around an antelope.

These are by no means all the physical discomforts attached to my career—there is, for instance, the matter of trying to make notes on a program in the dark which are apt to say, "Why she keep that goat in the attic?" on inspection the following morning—but they are probably enough. It has sometimes occurred to me that managements would be well advised to furnish each critic with a good stiff drink of something or other on his arrival at his seat, but I'm afraid this idea will never really take hold, the consensus among producers being that a writing man operates best in a state of faint uneasiness and melancholy.

From time to time, Gibbs would try to ameliorate these conditions. He brought Elinor with him as much for her ability to magically find a taxi amid the postcurtain crush as for her companionship. And periodically he would buy unreliable trick pen-and-flashlight combinations at novelty shops, hoping they would help him scrawl his notes with some degree of legibility in the dark. But they never quite worked. He was forever jotting cryptic, even indecipherable messages like "Lanchstr get face stuck I these nights awful if."

What with his job challenges, his natural irascibility, and the mediocrity he so often witnessed onstage, Gibbs quickly acquired a reputation as a hanging judge. Frequently he would be so unimpressed by what was being unfurled that he would simply cross his arms and glower. Or he would cup his chin in his hand and feign sleep. Not infrequently he did pass out, either from inebriation or from sheer boredom. So did Elinor. Once she awoke suddenly in the middle of an act and blurted out, "What are all these people doing in my bedroom?"

Often he was so appalled by the proceedings that he would not stick around. Regarding *Sleep, My Pretty One,* by Charlie and Oliver H. P. Garrett, he wrote, "There was said to be a brief flurry of excitement toward the end of the third act, but unfortunately, I wasn't there by then." When it came to the "massacre" that was Stanley Richards's *Marriage Is for Single People,* he departed "while the malady was still in its primary stages."

He may have left early, but his judgment was usually acute. "He was always right," said Geraghty's assistant, Frank Modell. In *The Yale Review,* Vernon Young said that Gibbs's criticism was "unique and indispensable" and "surely unsurpassed for its purpose by any weekly jester since The Age of Dryden." Young exulted, "I would forgive him anything—even poisoning."

But if he had admirers, he had far more detractors. Charles Cooke, a former *New Yorker* employee, once told Ross that Gibbs not only had a "sick critical viewpoint" but that his old boss had begun to "confuse Gibbs' little-boy 'I hate everything' complex with true sophistication." ("You don't suck me into any argument on Gibbs," Ross shot back.) After Gibbs dismissed Lillian Hellman's *The Searching Wind,* Dashiell Hammett consoled her: "I read the Gibbs review last night and a nasty little puppyish affair it is. Jesus, the impudence of the little when they happen not to like something! It fills them with all the power of a beauty contest judge." His pan of *The Biggest Thief in Town* by Dalton Trumbo, which lasted all of thirteen performances, brought this outraged letter from the author:

Dear Mr. Gibbs:

I have just read your obstinately wrong-headed review of *The Biggest Thief in Town*.

I call to your attention the sentence, "Unfortunately, Mr. Trumbo, whatever his gifts as a political thinker may be," is a dull dog, etc.

The very wording of the comment indicates that here I have you on unfamiliar ground. Please, therefore, be informed that my gifts as a political thinker are of a very high order.

Other assaults were even more savage. A dozen supporters of *Flahooley*, an overblown puppet show whose book and lyrics were the work of no less than "Yip" Harburg ("I'd avoid it if I were you," Gibbs wrote), called his review "the most stupid thing we have ever read." Above their collective signature they wrote DOWN WITH GIBBS. Calling Gibbs "egregious," Eric Bentley said he disguised his "barbarism in the sheep's clothing of a dilettante" and that his "special contribution is an attempt to legitimize philistine prejudice." Raymond Chandler felt similarly:

The fact that Gibbs (together with other *New Yorker* critical minds) is gifted with a talent for derogatory criticism doesn't necessarily make him a good critic. I remember, long ago, when I was doing book-reviews [*sic*] in London, that my first impulse always was to find something smart and nasty to say because that sort of writing is so much easier. In spite of its superficial sophistication, the whole attitude of the *New Yorker* seems to me to have that same touch of under-graduate [*sic*] sarcasm. I find this sort of thing rather juvenile.

For a while, Gibbs felt obliged to respond to the criticisms of his criticisms. But this quickly proved impossibly time-consuming. He solved the problem very simply. To anyone who questioned his judgment, he would send a form response that read, "Dear Sir [or Madam]: You may be right. Sincerely, Wolcott Gibbs."

Gibbs was quite capable of missing the mark. By his own admission, he was tone-deaf and so could not wholly appreciate musicals. "I have no idea how the damn things get there in the first place," he acknowledged. Mel Brooks once asked him, "Mr. Gibbs, why did you never give a musical a good review?" He could be as capricious as anyone. "When youth and beauty walk on the stage," he said, "to hell with Sarah Bernhardt." And like other critics—Alexander Woollcott included—he was capable of putting himself out on embarrassing limbs. "Every now and then he goes off on a book or a play, liking it when nobody else can stomach a word of it and it is usually a one-joke book or a one-joke play," observed *The Harvard Crimson*. "A few years ago he liked a musical called *Park Avenue* which flopped. It was one long, dull joke about intermarriage and divorce in the Park Avenue set. But Gibbs raved about it, for what must be curious reasons."

Gibbs could sometimes be grievously wrong not just critically but factually. Although he admired *South Pacific,* he thought it bore little resemblance to James Michener's original source material. Michener and his friend Herman Silverman were outraged. "We decided to call Gibbs and tell him what a jerk he was," Silverman recalled. "To our gratification, Gibbs apologized and explained that he had used as his reference a paperback edition of Jim's book which omitted the two stories upon which the musical was based." Gibbs's explanation seems improbable in the extreme, but Silverman bought it.

He engaged in a delicate balance with playwrights, producers, cast members, and all the other interrelated parts of the incestuous Broadway culture. Fair comment being what it is, there was usually no recourse for the stricken. At one point James Reilly, executive director of the League of New York Theatres, protested that Gibbs was guilty of "continual carping," having sneered at nearly half of Broadway's recent twenty-five openings, dismissing Tennessee Williams's *Summer and Smoke* as "cloudy and monotonous" and Jean-Paul Sartre's *Red Gloves as* "slightly irritating." In an internal memo, Ross brushed aside the charge: "Mr. Reilly's is funniest letter of the month."

Still, blood was occasionally drawn. When *Apple of His Eye,* by Kenyon Nicholson and Charles Robinson, failed to impress Gibbs early in 1946, the producer, Jed Harris, refused to send him press tickets to his fall production of *Loco,* the undistinguished handiwork of Dale Eunson and Katherine Albert. Gibbs outwitted Harris by quoting several negative reviews from some of the New York dailies and deduced, "On the whole, it seems possible that Mr. Harris sent his tickets out to quite a lot of undesirable people." The incident became so well publicized that when Congressman Emanuel Celler scrutinized the Shubert organization some years later, he cited it as one of the reasons for his investigation.

Curiously, Gibbs enjoyed a respectful, even admiring, relationship with many of those on whom he passed judgment. Theater people would often genuflect before him. Linda Kramer, a childhood friend of Gibbs's daughter, Janet, saw them do so at "21" and other pre- and post-Broadway venues. "It was quite exciting because he was terribly important. He was sort of an idol."

Of course, it helped if he liked their work. Even before he publicly declared Rodgers and Hammerstein's *Oklahoma!* "a completely enchanting performance—gay, stylish, imaginative, and equipped with some of the best music and dancing in a long time," he crossed the length of Sardi's to shake hands with the choreographer, Agnes de Mille. "I want to congratulate you," he said. "That was most distinguished." The praise, de Mille said, left her "in a sort of stupor." Similarly, when he extolled Tallulah Bankhead in *The Circle,* she was so taken that she later entertained him while he was in the hospital. "I put on a one-woman floor show designed to cure or kill," she wrote in her memoirs. "The nurses swore it was the most exciting vaudeville ever seen on the floor. Without music, too! After the drubbing I had taken in *Cleopatra,* Gibbs' words had been nectar. I would have married him on the spot, had not the venture involved double bigamy."

———————

Gibbs's most gratifying, problematic, and complex relations with the Broadway set were with his fellow critics and columnists. In the 1940s and 1950s their pronouncements on live dramatic entertainment were practically gospel, and they were accorded commensurate respect. The producer Mike Todd once commissioned a four-by-thirty-six-inch painting of six of the day's leading critics—Gibbs included—holding up their enthusiastic reviews of his musical *As the Girls Go*. This was transmuted into a billboard measuring 26 feet high and 156 feet long above the Winter Garden Theatre, where the production was playing. All together Todd paid more than ten thousand dollars for the effort. Dozens of Broadway tastemakers were similarly canonized in an Al Hirschfeld mural called "First Nighters" that once adorned a curving wall behind the bar of the Hotel Manhattan on West 44th Street at Eighth Avenue. Gibbs, squeezed in at the far left, was caricatured with a boutonniere, sallow expression, cigarette in drooping hand and rail-thin corpus.

Amid the first-night crush, and the competition with the other press, Gibbs navigated his way among his fellows. His closest confidant was John Mason Brown, the elegant, Harvard-educated reviewer for the *New York Post* and, later, *The Saturday Review*. "[F]rom time to time I seem to be in disagreement with a great many of your opinions," Gibbs told him, "but it is all so literate and charming and persuasive that I am often almost convinced against my own strong, interior judgments." When, in 1942, Brown left the *Post* to fight the war, Gibbs remarked that opening nights seemed "pretty bleak and strange" without him. In turn, Brown congratulated Gibbs as "the best parodist to have written since Beerbohm."

But for the most part, Gibbs regarded his peers askance. Some, like George Jean Nathan of *Esquire* and *The American Mercury,* merely amused him. "Mr. Nathan can be moderately silly when his special prejudices are involved" and "I am embarrassed to admit that Mr. Nathan fascinates me somewhat more as a genial essayist than as a critic" were representative jabs. When Russell Crouse found himself captivated by a blond actress named Lorna Lynn, he told Gibbs that he hoped to marry her. After a moment's thought, Gibbs responded, "George Jean Nathan probably will."

In a rather different fashion he actively despised Burton Rascoe of the *World-Telegram.* Their enmity dated to the 1920s, when Rascoe was writing for the *Great Neck News,* the regional rival of Gibbs's *North Hempstead Record.* By the 1940s Gibbs thought that Rascoe, like his old nemesis Woollcott, had become excessively self-indulgent; he called his column "Burton's Anatomy of Rascoe." To Brown he confided, "I'm sure Mr. Rascoe is a moral man, but he isn't decorative and I'm damned if he knows what he's talking about most of the time." Rascoe in turn called Gibbs "the New Yorker's tired young man of the theater." More seriously, he accused Gibbs of plagiarism. In 1943, after Rascoe wrote a review of *Men in Shadow* by Mary Hayley Bell, he noted curious similarities between some of his phraseology and certain Gibbs sentences that appeared in *The New Yorker* some days later. This raised Gibbs's hackles. "I have done many terrible things in my life," he said, "but I have never robbed the poor box."

Gibbs's prejudices against his contemporaries were cemented by his inclusion in the New York Drama Critics' Circle. He found their formal gatherings to be pointless, going so far as to skewer the Circle in a casual called "The Jukes Family Revisited" (the title being a reference to the recidivism and mental retardation of the extended and pseudonymous "Juke" family of upstate New York, who were often invoked as a defense of eugenics). Gibbs composed the piece as a broad stage farce and in the opening aired some of his grievances toward the organization:

The curtain goes up on a scene of unimaginable squalor, in a base-ment dining room in some second-rate Broadway hotel. There is a long table at the rear of the stage and most of the critics are seated at it, behind a formidable array of glasses and bottles. Two or three of the brothers have collapsed in drunken sleep and sev-eral of the others are clearly far from sober. On the walls there are a great many indecent pictures. A young woman, dressed like a French maid in a 1905 farce, fills the critics' glasses from time to time, often finding it necessary to sit on their laps as she does so. There is a small piano in one corner of the room, at which a typical disorderly-house musician is batting out "Mademoiselle from Armentières." On the floor, there is a crap game, involving three prominent members—Mr. [Brooks] Atkinson, Mr. [Howard] Barnes, and Mr. [Richard] Watts.

After a raucous call to order, it is proposed to add to the rolls such unlikely characters as a thirteen-year-old girl and the critics for *National Orthodontist* and *Furtive Detective* magazines. At one point, the assem-bled chant to the tune of "Onward Christian Soldiers" a ditty that begins, "Welcome novice cri-atics/To this den of vice/Brothers, ye are treading/ Where things ain't so nice." The sardonic touches include ten absurd motions, e.g., "Each critic who is paid more than five hundred dollars a week shall be entitled to one full extra vote" and "Any critic not personally acquainted with Henry L. Mencken shall be penalized one whole vote."

Nor did Gibbs consider his fellow members to be good company. Louis Kronenberger of *PM* (a "correct and literate" type, Gibbs allowed, whose "active social conscience makes it difficult for him to approve wholeheartedly of any product without a serious purpose") recalled a memorable scene to this effect: "While having an altogether placid con-versation with two fellow members, Gibbs suddenly drew himself up, said to one of them, 'I will not be talked to like that!' and then to the other, 'How dare you insult my wife, sir!' and, not staying for an answer, flung out of the private dining-room door and, clattering down the stairs, escaped from what had obviously bored him beyond endurance."

Despite his frequent contempt for the Circle, Gibbs did from time to time find common cause with them. One occasion was the 1943 opening of Maxwell Anderson's *Truckline Café,* with a cast that included Karl Malden, Marlon Brando, Kevin McCarthy, and Frank Overton. The reviews were scathing. Ward Morehouse of the *Sun* called it Anderson's "worst play in nearly a quarter of a century of valiant service as a dramatist"; in the *Daily News,* John Chapman thought it "the worst play I have seen since I have been in the reviewing business." The wounded producers, Harold Clurman and Elia Kazan, closed the production almost immediately—but not before taking out a large protest ad in *The New York Times.* In it, they raged against the "group of men who are hired to report the events of our stage and who more and more are acquiring powers which, as a group, they are not qualified to exercise." The diatribe, which combined a defense of the play with an attack on the "blackout of all taste except the taste of these men," went on for some five hundred words. Gibbs spoke up for the Circle in his own left-handed way. "I'd say offhand that there are only about three newspaper reviewers here who are competent to write about anything," he said, "but it is absolutely absurd to make an issue out of this play, which has no merit whatsoever."

A rather more serious incident took place a few months hence when Gibbs joined Rascoe, Nathan, and Stark Young of *The New Republic* in quitting the group for reasons that remain obscure; it seems there was a fierce internal brouhaha over the kind of exclusivity that Gibbs would later send up in his Jukes Family sketch. Adding to the drama, Joseph Wood Krutch of *The Nation* stepped down to take a year's leave of absence, and Robert Garland immediately resigned when he was officially elected to the group to fill one of the slots. About four months after his resignation, though, Gibbs rejoined the Circle. Having been implored by Howard Barnes to return, he replied with customary nonchalance, "Why not?"

In his critic's capacity, Gibbs was distracted by Broadway personalities outside of the Circle. In the 1940s and the 1950s there existed in Manhattan a unique collection of newspaper columnists who were closely yet nebulously associated with the entertainment world. They breezily dished industry dirt, occasionally reliable commentary, and related items. Their ranks included Ed Sullivan, Earl Wilson, the pseudonymous Cholly Knickerbocker, and of course, Winchell.

The New Yorker made special sport of one of them, Leonard Lyons, the author of "The Lyons Den" column for the *Post;* Russell Maloney ripped into him in a 1945 Profile, declaring, "Aside from his immediate relatives, Lyons knows nobody but celebrities." His tired reportage was widely regarded as untrustworthy. Freddie Packard, with his usual scrupulousness, found some of Lyons's items to be so vague and absurd that he fired at the columnist a dozen or so specific queries each in two separate casuals, demanding pertinent details. McKelway spoofed the lame tone of "The Lyons Den" in a casual called "The Mare's Nest." Among his fictional items was an anecdote that he attributed to Assistant Secretary of Agriculture Grover B. Hill: "Many farmers in recent years have been using a machine that works on much the same principle as the military tank. Called 'tractors,' because, working on much the same principle as the military tank, they have potent traction and can cross rough fields, etc."

Gibbs tended to stay clear of hack writers, but he could not avoid them entirely. One was Dorothy Kilgallen. Her column "The Voice of Broadway" reached beyond show business to encompass such Winchellian subjects as politics and the mob. Against his better judgment, Gibbs in the early 1940s collaborated with her on a fanciful musical about a "sporty, cosmopolitan" female writer of a daily radio soap opera. Through her dreams, she is transported into the role of Scheherazade. But after a first treatment, Gibbs disentangled himself. When the show's costume designer, Miles White, ran into Gibbs at the Algonquin and asked how things were going, Gibbs explained that he had been forced to throw up his hands over the troublesome project. "I can sum up the whole show in one phrase," he said. "It's the phrase that Miss Kilgallen opened every one of our story conferences with: 'Wouldn't it be cute if . . .'"*

On the other hand, Gibbs had respect and even a strange affection for Lucius Beebe, who owned several newspapers around the country and wrote a chatty, amiable society column called "This New York" for the *Herald Tribune.* His interest in Beebe extended beyond the fact that Beebe's first name was that of his, Gibbs's, late father. Both were born in 1902. Both had attended the Roxbury School. Both had had problems with college; Beebe was thrown out of Yale after he hurled an empty bottle at the stage of the Hyperion Theatre in New Haven and roared, "I am Professor Tweedy of the Yale Divinity School!"

Despite this fracas, Beebe managed to transfer from Yale to Harvard, with President James Angell of the former supposedly telling President Abbott Lawrence Lowell of the latter, "I apologize for sending you such a bad potato." As Gibbs had been a prankster at Hill, so Beebe was one at Harvard. According to legend, he circulated a ballot to see if it would be worth trading President Lowell and three professors for "a good running backfield." The motion, drawing more 2,300 responses, failed by only seven votes.

Both Gibbs and Beebe were fascinated by railroads. But whereas Gibbs had been a mere brakeman on the LIRR, the wealthy Beebe personally owned two plush pieces of rolling stock, the *Gold Coast* and the *Virginia City.* The latter was a "pretty toy, a jewel box, a dream on

---

* Other writers, including Sidney Sheldon, replaced Gibbs, but there was no saving the production, which opened as *Dream with Music* in 1944 and ran for only twenty-eight performances. On opening night, the acclaimed ballerina Vera Zorina slipped and fell onstage. Two scenes later, during a tender interlude between her and her lover, there was a power failure. The stage manager tried to compensate by holding a flashlight over the heads of the infatuated partners, at which point the audience began giggling and the house lights were suddenly restored. Sheldon called it "probably the most disastrous opening in the history of Broadway." Gibbs agreed with a friend that the fiasco was an example "not of good taste or bad taste but simply of no taste at all."

wheels," said Gibbs. It was "ninety-three feet long, weighs a hundred and eighty-five thousand pounds, and consists of a twenty-three-foot observation-drawing room, three master staterooms (each with its own toilet facilities), a small Turkish bath, a dining room seating eight, a galley with a fifty-bottle wine cellar, an extra seven-hundred-pound refrigerator on the forward platform, and crew quarters for two." The whole rig was wired for music and equipped with three telephones for outside communication. When Beebe welcomed visitors aboard, he would cry, "Welcome to Walden Pond!"

Beebe was an aesthete supreme, and Gibbs was particularly taken with his sartorial self-indulgence. At any given time Beebe owned about forty suits, ten of them formal outfits ("I would no more think of appearing in a restaurant in the evening out of dinner dress than I would in swimming shorts"). He had a mink-lined, astrakhan-collared dress coat that he insured for $3,000. For a ten-day visit to Hollywood, his wardrobe included seventy-two shirts. His accoutrements included three gold cigarette cases worth some $700 apiece, a cashmere sapphire cabochon ring worth $1,200, and a platinum watch that cost $1,000. He was, Gibbs said, "menacingly well-groomed." For his part, Beebe understood Gibbs perfectly; he called him "a fiend in human form."

A cadre of publicists and press agents fed Gibbs's Broadway chroniclers—from Beebe to Sullivan—a steady diet of tickets, interviews, and exclusives. The best known was Richard Maney, whom Gibbs called "the most prosperous gnome of the lot." Jack Gould of *The New York Times* estimated that Maney could "spout Elizabethanisms by the hour and recite Shakespeare even longer." He had a dispassion about his work to which Gibbs could relate. "Press agentry is no business for people with nerves," Maney once said. "But it can be a gay life for one with detachment, with sympathy for the deranged and with an understanding of why the theater's children behave the way they do." Gibbs admired Maney's ability to treat his own people "with the genial condescension of an Irish cop addressing a Fifth Avenue doorman." The condescension was not always so genial; from time to time Maney would tear into a client with the dreaded sneer, "You *actor,* you!"

Gibbs was also taken with Maney because he had a passion for fly-fishing and Gibbs, as a devotee of the sand and surf, loved to cast his reel. He published a typically barbed yet smiling Profile about Maney in 1941; the title, "The Customer Is Always Wrong," hinted at the treatment. He quoted Maney as once saying that "All female stars have one thing in common: after you stand on your head to arrange an interview, they break the date because they have to go and get their hair washed." The press agent was featured several times on the NBC radio show *Information, Please,* moderated by Clifton Fadiman; calling his appearances "cerebral ambushes," Maney remembered, "My most hair-raising moment came when, casting a furtive look at the studio audience, I caught the eye of Wolcott Gibbs, The New Yorker's critic and bon vivant. Mr. Gibbs leered at me like a hyena from the front row, and whirled his forefingers about his ear in a circular movement."

Yet Maney respected Gibbs. He thought him "a perfectionist, a stickler for syntax and symmetry and sentence structure" and a master stylist who was "pained by the prose of many of his fellows."

CHAPTER 9

———

"I AM A CHILD OF THE SUN"

A s World War II approached and materialized, and *The New Yorker* became not merely an editorial jester but a reliable literary and journalistic institution, the extracurricular diversions of its crew generally diminished. The end of the forbidden pleasures of Prohibition, coupled with the growing Depression, tended to put a crimp on hijinks in general. Increasingly rare were such occasions when the likes of Edmund Wilson, John Chapin Mosher, Peter Arno, Lois Long, the Whites, and similar company would gather at Louise Bogan's place in Tudor City, where her husband, Raymond Holden, poured what was reported to be the best bathtub gin in town. "O those wonderful summer evenings when the cream of New York literary life played craps on my floor," lamented Bogan in 1939, "and I was hard put to choose between the charms of Scudder Middleton, Ogden Nash, and Wolcott Gibbs!"

True, there was still horseplay to be had. When Tallulah Bankhead was starring in *The Skin of Our Teeth* in the early 1940s, she decided to cap a revel at four a.m. by bringing her friends back to her place at the Elysee Hotel. Present were Gibbs; his good friend the former *Herald Tribune* sportswriter John Lardner, who would do many nonsports pieces for

The New Yorker; Cole Porter; Stanley Walker; and the future CBS News producer Leslie Midgley. "When we all trooped into the lobby long after closing time," Midgley recalled, "Tallulah stalked up to the desk clerk and waved toward the closed door of the Monkey Bar. 'Open the bar,' she thundered. And I do mean thundered." Without saying a word, the clerk unlocked the bar, and the interlopers helped themselves. "It was an exhibition of raw power. The hotel could have lost its liquor license by serving booze at that hour, but the clerk knew he didn't have a chance."

But by this time, things had begun to settle down. When contributors encountered Ross in the middle to late 1930s, he had "virtually none of the manic attributes that amazed and cowed their counterparts from the middle and late Twenties." In Manhattan he maintained well-appointed digs on Park Avenue and other fashionable addresses. He found himself adjusting to middle age with all its trappings, buying a weekend place on Wire Hill Road in Stamford, whose grounds would eventually grow to 157 acres. There he would come to relish private time with his only child, Patty, and engage in such decorous activities as playing solitaire and listening to the radio news.

As he could, he would retreat to Aspen and its environs for fishing and pure relaxation. His impulse, vaguely tied to a desire to revisit his past, was typically idiosyncratic. "I'm going to Colorado, or somewhere near there; I don't quite know yet," he told Katharine White at one point. "I won't fly. Not by a damned site [*sic*]." And in one of his few successful non–*New Yorker* business ventures, he invested heavily in his friend Dave Chasen's famous restaurant in Beverly Hills. There he hobnobbed respectably with celebrities and writers alike, his solid financial backing and physical presence eventually being celebrated with an oil portrait of him upstairs in a private dining space called, appropriately, "The New Yorker Room."

Gibbs captured this kind of advancing maturity well in his Profile of Woollcott, when he reflected on the demise of the Algonquin mob: "Hollywood got some of them and others moved to Connecticut, partly to escape the New York state income tax and partly under the sad old delusion that a man can write far more rapidly and beautifully while raising his own vegetables. Those who didn't move away were by now temperamentally unfit for the old close association, since there is nothing more enervating to the artist than the daily society of a lot of people who are just as famous as he is."

White, of course, had already made his move in a major way. Far less gregarious than his compatriots to begin with, he also had a working farm to run in Maine.

> I carry dry shavings by the truckload (I now own a truck), cordwood from the woodyard, rugs to the dry cleaner, and old cedar fence-rails for building yoke fences. I am always carrying something—a burdensome life, but kind of soothing. My sheep are soothing, too. They come up out of the pasture at this time of year and stand around in the barn, and that is very soothing to me, to see sheep standing around, waiting. Quite a few of my ewes look as though they would have early lambs, and all are thrifty. I have begun graining them—feeding out a mixture of five parts oats, three parts whole corn, one part bran, and one part linseed oil meal. I am as fussy with a mixture like that as with a mixture of gin and French vermouth. My poultry operations have expanded considerably since you were here: I have a large laying house and a flock of would-be layers that turned and bit me in mid season.

His homespun efforts were not always successful. "The missus, who is a New England girl and thrifty, personally put up 71 jars of strawberry jam before she discovered nobody much ate it in the family," he wrote Gibbs. "Yesterday we picked the cherries off the cherry tree, following close on the heels of the robins, and last night, ate the pie, so you see it's hand to mouth all right." The Whites had to contend with everything from freezing farmhouse water pipes to the encroachment of various forms of vermin. Though hardly cut off from civilization, they were rather removed from it. It was nine miles to the grocery store, 23 miles to the train, 47 miles to the Frances Fox Institute (where Katharine got her hair washed), and a 56-mile round-trip excursion to the movies. White made it back to New York periodically, but the sorts of activities that had defined Corey Ford's time of laughter were now infrequent. Katharine, never entirely as enamored of rural life as was Andy, nonetheless adjusted to and even embraced it. She found a love of gardening, helped her husband in his various farm-related activities despite periodic health problems, and derived considerable satisfaction from continuing to deal with contributors from afar.

Conversely, White wrestled with his decision to exile himself. He conscientiously tended to his agrarian responsibilities, to Katharine, and to *Harper's*. But as war began to rage, he felt somehow obliged to do something more, even as he realized he would likely stay on the sidelines:

> Maine suddenly seems too remote to satisfy my nervous desire to help in a bad situation. My reason tells me that I can contribute most effectively by staying right here and continuing to produce large quantities of hens' eggs and to write my stuff every month; but the human system seems to demand something which has more of the air of bustle and confusion. I may try for a job in Washington, in the high realms of propaganda. Or the draft board, locally, may settle the whole matter for me with one quick swoop. I'm only 42, and most of my teeth still show through the gooms [sic]. Here, anybody with natural teeth is taken for the army. There are only three or four of us in the whole county. My wife being an earning girl, gives me no deferment, and I expect none.

Soon enough he would make his particular contribution to the war effort and continue to break through as a writer by putting together a memorable *Harper's* essay collection—one that he told Harper and

Brothers would not be "another one of those Adventures in Contentment, or as an Escape from the City, or How to Farm with a Portable
Corona." For the moment, he contented himself editing, with Katharine,
A Subtreasury of American Humor. This 804-page anthology, published
just before Pearl Harbor, was a cross-section of its title subject, its nearly
two hundred entries running the gamut from Benjamin Franklin to
Mark Twain to S. J. Perelman. Immodestly, nearly a third of the pieces
came from *The New Yorker,* with seven entries by Thurber, six by Gibbs,
and four by White.

But beyond his glib assertion that the preponderance of *New Yorker*
material "should surprise nobody," White scored a poignant point in his
preface: "One of the things commonly said about humorists is that they
are really very sad people—clowns with a breaking heart. There is some
truth to it, but it is badly stated. It would be more accurate, I think, to
say that there is a deep vein of melancholy running through everyone's
life and that a humorist, perhaps more sensible of it than some others,
compensates for it actively and positively." As proof of his ever-deepening
commitment to Katharine, he gave her free rein to edit his words: "[G]et
right after it and give it the works," he told her. "I trust you absolutely to
doctor it any way you think it should be doctored. . . . The most important
thing, of course, is that you bring a ruthlessly critical mind to my facts
and my theories."

The book, translated into French and German, was a success, selling
tens of thousands of copies. The Columbia University philosopher Irwin
Edman not only likened White to Thoreau and Montaigne but called him
"our finest essayist, perhaps our only one." Gibbs gave the Whites the
highest praise he could, declaring, "Everybody thinks it is a fine book,
including me." That was not quite true; O'Hara, thin-skinned as usual
and not especially funny, was miffed that he was not represented. But
Gibbs assured Andy and Katharine, "The O'Hara omission isn't anything to worry your heads about, I think. John says he is a God damn
[*sic*] sight funnier than Clarence Day, but more or less dispassionately.

At the moment he is sore at too many people right here in New York to fuss about anybody in Maine. Anyway, he is drunk most of the time."

Thurber, meanwhile, was feeling his age. He was a relative latecomer to fatherhood; his only child, Rosemary, was born in 1931, when he was thirty-six. By late 1938 he was confiding to White, "I am an older man, with my youth definitely behind me and fifty around the corner." Like White, he had a taste for the rustic; when married to Althea, he had lived for a time in a 125-year-old farmhouse on twenty acres near Sandy Hook, in Connecticut. There he found himself comforted by "the intermittent fall of apples from my apple trees." Later, with Helen, he settled in Litchfield. Its pastoral nature, while still not too far removed from Manhattan, proved to be the perfect tonic for Thurber's ever-active mind, Helen recalled: "He could *feel* the greenness." Thurber would operate from Connecticut for much of the rest of his life, eventually moving to West Cornwall, where his cherished friends would come to include Mark Van Doren.*

As was the case with Ross in Stamford, Thurber found his Connecticut digs to be far enough removed to give him breathing room from New York but still close enough to take advantage of its amenities. When in Manhattan, Thurber would often stay at the Algonquin. On one excursion he ran into Gibbs, McKelway, Dorothy Parker, Mosher, Robert M. Coates, and Lois Long, among others, in rapid succession, in the lobby. The experience left him "worn and a little depressed," and he was relieved to retreat from Gotham: "It is nice to be back under the 200-year-old maples and the apple trees." To complicate matters, his blindness was becoming worse; in June 1941 alone he had five eye operations. "[H]e cannot go out alone, has to be led around, except indoors, where he is very agile," Helen confided. "And the worst is that he cannot read or draw. He writes in longhand on yellow paper, but cannot see what he writes, and you know his painstaking method of writing and rewriting."

---

* The actor Sam Waterston currently lives in Thurber's West Cornwall house.

Thurber did his best to make light of the situation. "A blind man benefits by a lack of distractions," he explained. "I remember sitting with Ross at a table in this restaurant. He picked up a bottle of Worcestershire sauce and then threw it down, saying, 'Goddamit, that's the 10,000th time I've read the label on this bottle.' I told him, 'Godammit, Harold, that's because you're handicapped by vision.'" Thurber also claimed that his blindness benefited him with the writer's blessing of total recall.

Still, when not recovering, he traveled widely, not only within the United States but to Europe and Bermuda and entered the most creatively satisfying and wide-ranging period of his life. Stories like "The Whip-Poor-Will" (1941) and "The Catbird Seat" (1942) were among the pieces that established him as the leading sardonic authority on the battle of the sexes. There was, too, the success of *The Male Animal* and of *Many Moons,* a 1943 fairy story about a sick princess who pines for the moon; the latter won the prestigious Caldecott Medal for the most distinguished American picture book for children. Within the calendar year of 1939, Thurber published the more than two dozen vignettes that constituted "Fables for Our Time." Populated with animals that generally learn life's lessons the hard way, these Aesop-like yarns were so brief and cleverly constructed that their counterintuitive punch lines, like "It is better to ask some of the questions than to know all of the answers," came as genuine surprises.

And, of course, there was 1939's "The Secret Life of Walter Mitty," starring the archetypal Thurber man. In this case the hapless husband escapes from domestic routine and his pushy wife by recourse to outlandish fantasies—envisioning himself as a heroic navy pilot, a dexterous surgeon, a fearless courtroom defendant, et al., ending with his defiant death by firing squad—only to be constantly brought back to reality. The story became one of the most anthologized in American literature, its immortality guaranteed when it was reprinted in *Reader's Digest* in 1943 and devoured by troops who, like their civilian counterparts, saw at least some Mitty in themselves. Robert Benchley starred in a 1944 radio adaptation (of which Thurber approved); there was also a 1947 Technicolor Danny Kaye vehicle (of which Thurber did not approve). So impressed was Ross with this jewel of a piece, which deftly conveyed the daydreams of Everyman, that he told Thurber, "In your way you are just about the all-time master of them all, by Jesus, and you have come a long way since the old N.Y. Evening Post days."

Gibbs had also come a long way from his cub reporter background. Despite the distractions of work and family, he now had at least some time to devote to his few cherished pastimes. He had enjoyed tennis since prep school and had honed his skill under the tutelage of his publisher cousin Lloyd Carpenter Griscom at Huntover, Griscom's country place on Long Island's Gold Coast. If Griscom had hired him at the *East Norwich Enterprise* at their cousin Alice Duer Miller's urging, Gibbs also suspected that his ability to bat a ball back and forth with his weekend guests got him the job. Not that he had any objection. "As much as anything else, I guess, I would have liked to instruct an endless succession of beautiful young women to play tennis," Gibbs said. "The only trouble with that was that I didn't really play tennis very well." Still, he held his own with his colleagues Lobrano and Kinkead.

For such a physically slight man (he weighed only 135 pounds while standing five foot ten), Gibbs had an active interest in burly sports. He would diagram baseball proceedings painstakingly, sometimes sending detailed reports to such like-minded friends as Alec Waugh. "As you will note," Gibbs told him following a Dodgers-Cubs encounter, "there was a rather interesting play in the second inning when [Gil] Hodges reached first on a single and then scored on two successive errors by the Chicago first-baseman, who dropped the ball on an easy pick-off play and then overthrew second, with the ball winding up in the outfield." His real passion, when it came to the diamond, was going to the Polo Grounds, even though he knew his trips were usually wasted. "He kept on rooting for the Giants, as he once said, as if he were rooting for the brontosaurus," recalled Tony.

He was intensely interested in boxing as well, as evidenced by his part ownership of Eddie Edge. In keeping with his feel for the aesthetics of the theater, he appreciated the pure movement of the sweet science, cheering on true pugilists and disparaging mere hitters. He admired Sugar Ray Robinson, found Rocky Marciano boring, loved Joe Louis, and felt Max Baer underrated, faulting him only because "he sleep-walked through his talent." For a man so finicky about what he witnessed on stage, Gibbs took a perverse pleasure in boxing's seamier aspects; with his compatriots John Lardner and A. J. Liebling he lapped up the fouls and other low-blowing that took place within the ring. Nor did he restrict himself to the reasonably respectable forum of Madison Square Garden; among his preferred venues was the "really seedy, smelly pigpen" that was the St. Nicholas Arena.

Gibbs's nonsporting interests were few. He enjoyed poker and took on such well-heeled opponents as Raoul Fleischmann. Sometimes the stakes got a tad high. Louis Kronenberger of *PM* once came late to a Gibbs game and ended up sitting "next to a man I had never seen before who, I suddenly discovered, was packing a rod, or at any rate wearing a holster containing a revolver."

For all his interest in sports and cards, the high-strung Gibbs found he needed relief of a far more elemental sort. As Ross went to Aspen to reconnect with his roots, and Thurber paid court to Columbus, so Gibbs tried to get in touch with his own background by dropping in at Hauxhurst, the one-time estate of Alice Duer Miller's grandfather, in Weehawken. He recorded this haunting snapshot for Nancy Hale:

There is still a hollow place in the lawn where my cousin and I and two Townley girls dug a cave where we could get undressed and paint ourselves, or each other, with water colors [*sic*]. The dawn of the biological urge, and look where it's got me. There is also a place under a tree where I buried, with more horror of the spirit than I have ever known since, a stray cat I shot. Up in the attic

. . . I have found a trunkful of children's books, which suggest a New Yorker piece long enough to buy you a small automobile. Things like "Slovenly Peter," "Little Black Sambo" and so on, and the interesting thing about them is that they're the cruellest [*sic*] books I've ever read, full of pictures of children who were unkind to animals and were subsequently eaten, in full view of the reader, by irritated cats and dogs.

These were morbid memories. Gibbs found more genuine relaxation in a place he had occasionally visited when he spent his prep school summers with his aunt Elizabeth, uncle Carroll, and cousin Dan in Merrick. It was a spit of land thirty-two miles long and less than a mile wide, "stretched out like a basking lizard" about five and a half miles south of Long Island across the Great South Bay.

John Chapin Mosher had preceded Gibbs as a Fire Island denizen by a couple of years, staking out turf with his boyfriend Philip Claflin. They did so at Cherry Grove, a haven for what were then called "nances" who required discretion and distance. Mosher helped bring Fire Island to public attention, publishing three short stories about it in *The New Yorker* in the spring and summer of 1939. By this time the place was already becoming a refuge for writers, entertainers, advertising executives, "party animals and old-fashioned families" who craved summertime peace.

If Hauxhurst reawakened Gibbs's childhood jitters, Fire Island rejuvenated its joys. During his young summers, it had been a place where he could, however temporarily, get out from under the death of his father, the separation from his mother, and the miseries of boarding school. Now he was determined to turn back the clock, reminiscing, "Most people these days seem to have had miserable childhoods, but I had a hell of a time." Soaking up the rays, his toes scrunching the shore, he was atypically happy. "I am a child of the sun," he told Nancy Hale, "and in the summer I am happy, singing from morning till night, but when it gets cold I die."

Gibbs and his Merrick relatives had sailed all over the South Shore during the years before, during, and after World War I. His cousin Dan, a natural seaman, had taken Wolcott in hand, literally showing him the ropes as he instructed him in the basics of boat handling. Gibbs wrote any number of paeans to Fire Island for "Comment," none more heartfelt than the one he composed about the clinker-built Sea Bright dory powered by a one-cylinder, two-cycle inboard make-or-break Eagle engine that his family presented to him in 1916, when he was fourteen. "It could do three miles an hour," he remembered fondly, "except when the weedless propeller enmeshed itself hopelessly in weeds."

When Gibbs began coming out to Fire Island as an adult in 1936, it was a true getaway; the only telephone within reach was at the local firehouse. A telegraph office connected the island to the outside world, and it was here that Ross, much to Gibbs's annoyance, would periodically try to reach him. Then as now, no automobiles were permitted. Once they departed from their various ferries, visitors would pile their luggage and belongings into little wagons and trundle them along a maze of interconnected boardwalks until they reached their residences. Local boys would make a killing by charging less able-bodied vacationers for this service. So ubiquitous were these carts that when John Lardner bought a Fire Island home from a psychoanalyst, "she told him solemnly that the natives were a strange species indeed, biological mutants somewhat on the order of the centaurs. 'Their front portions,' she said, 'are human, but their rear portions are shaped like a boy's express wagon with a suitcase in it.'"

Although there was some overlap and mixing among the cultures that constituted Fire Island's twenty or so communities, most had distinct identities. Cherry Grove, of course, was for gays, as was the neighboring Pines. Saltaire, on the other hand, was "stuffy or Victorian, perhaps even mainlandish." Fair Harbor would come to attract many actors; Seaview was known as "Scarsdale-by-the-Sea," whereas Gibbs characterized Point O'Woods as "a sort of Brooklyn Southampton." Straight, single men and women came to favor Davis Park. Gibbs chose Ocean Beach, a family-oriented enclave that, by virtue of its size and amenities, including the telegraph office, was the de facto capital. Each house in every community had its own name; before settling into The Studio, Gibbs rented a one-story, green-trimmed affair called The Normandie. It was dubbed after a painting of the famed ocean liner that hung over the fireplace; another painting of the ship also adorned the back of the living room, a double image that thoroughly confused some guests.

The collection of boldface names that flocked to Fire Island in those days included Fanny Brice, Billy Rose, Bea Lillie, George and Ira Gershwin, Jimmy Durante, Leslie Howard, Moss Hart, and Helen Hayes. Another notable was Polly Adler, a notorious New York madam whose clients included Benchley. "Everyone's absolutely up in arms and appalled and horrified that this Adler creature's roaming around loose on the island, and *they say* on a talent hunt," exclaimed a regular. Still, like most of her neighbors, Adler kept a low profile, as nightlife was generally confined to one's home. The few night spots included Flynn's, Maguire's, the Bayview, and Goldie's, this last the personal provenance of Lou "Goldie" Hawkins, an accomplished cocktail pianist and Manhattan nightclub owner. He hailed from Fort Deposit, Alabama, and referred to his namesake establishment as "my caravansary."

The locals were as memorable as the summer people. Blanche Pastorfield, the hunchbacked landlady of the hotel in Crest O'Dune, was a "demon" who treated her customers with contempt. "She insulted them and overcharged them and threw them out when she got sick of them," Gibbs recalled, "but they'd got the idea that she was a picturesque old character, a wonderful, rather obscene joke that they'd made up all by themselves, and so they put up with her." The unofficial chief of the beach was her husband, Jerry, "a man with a face like Punch and a body like Santa Claus. . . . There were no shoes on his feet, which he washed intermittently by the lazy October tide." Pastorfield didn't hesitate to throw his weight around. Following a major hurricane that swept away a number of beachside houses, a major debate ensued about whether it made more sense to plant sea grass or create more dunes to prevent further erosion. Although the majority of residents voted in favor of sea grass, Pastorfield owned the only bulldozer around and was thus able to impose his minority will by piling up the sand.

This mix of personalities and attitudes, so closely jammed together, made for many neuroses. When the vaudevillian Joe Laurie first beheld Fire Island, he declared it "an island booby hatch," "a sandy insane asylum," and "a whole island loaded with nuts, running around and playing with toys." Gibbs himself acknowledged, "They are a very strange people out there, either imperturbable or mad." Many were also unfaithful. During the summer, wives and children would unwind in the sun for weeks at a time while their menfolk toiled in New York; in their absence, the women would have casual affairs with the resident gardeners, local merchants, and handymen. That would all come to an end every late Friday afternoon, when the ferry known as the "daddy boat" arrived, carrying husbands and fathers. Upon its approach, many a blue-collar Lothario would beat a hasty retreat out a rear door or bedroom window.

On Fire Island, at least, Gibbs was not much of a canoodler. Sometimes, emboldened by booze, he would make a pass. Arthur Gelb, who married the stepdaughter of Gibbs's firm friend Sam Behrman, remembered an occasion when Gibbs was seated between two women who were wearing shorts. "At one point—there were a few people in the room—he put his left hand on one's thigh and his other on the other woman's thigh. And he started creeping up. They were admirers and they were paralyzed." Finally, Gelb remembered, one victim grabbed the other, and together they left. "If they hadn't moved, I think he would have gotten there."

Though content to be ensconced in his sanctuary, Gibbs was within striking distance of O'Hara in Quogue and Addams in Westhampton

Beach. He kept in rather less close touch with the cantankerous former than with the outgoing latter. Fire Island inspired one of Addams's better-remembered cartoons; it entailed the two Addams Family children being delivered to their mother and father in animal cages, with the slim wife announcing to her creepy husband, "It's the children, darling—back from camp." As Addams recalled much later, "My then-wife and I were sharing a cottage at Fire Island with another couple and the children were especially recalcitrant and the wife said, 'Well, the children are coming from camp next week,' and there was the idea already for it. I mean, the animal carriers was the instant thought."

Gibbs regarded the summer as sacrosanct, reserved for a genuine recharging of batteries, and he felt that others should follow his example. With simultaneous awe and horror, he recalled Moss Hart being the only writer he had ever known who could type a play in the sand. For a while he lived up the street from Alfred Bester, who would write his stories on his front porch. "Every time he passed our cottage and saw me working," Bester remembered, "he would denounce me."

Dyspeptic though he was, Gibbs came to love many of the locals and summer folk. There was a perennial parade of comers and goers; an obese Liebling once got caught in a deck chair and couldn't get out. Behrman was a neighbor, and Gibbs attempted to strike up an uncle-type relationship with his son, David, by discussing sports, in which David had no interest. "He would say something about the baseball season, and I wouldn't know what to say." David had a rather more successful relationship with Janet, Gibbs's daughter; as teenagers, they would end up dating.

Other good friends from Manhattan were Nancy and Henry Stern. The latter, always known as "Bunny"—because he hopped as a baby— was president of a men's clothing manufacturer; the former was a theater producer. Susan, their daughter, recalled seeing plenty of Addams on Fire Island: "I especially remember him standing in back of my mother while she was trying to get me to finish a meal, making faces and making me laugh, but every time mom turned around to see what was going on, he was deadpan."

And as he did with David Behrman, Gibbs took a shine to the Sterns' son, Morley, who was confusingly nicknamed "Tony." One time he invited the young man out to Ocean Beach on a lonely weekend. But as Sunday afternoon drew on and Tony Stern was preparing for the ferry back to Long Island, Gibbs began drinking heavily at the prospect of a separation. "He started getting mean," Tony said, "as if I was walking away and he was alone again."

The most colorful member of the cadre was Valentine Sherry, a diamond merchant by trade, a producer by occasional whim, and a bon vivant and true eccentric at all times. Generally sporting a cravat and a silk handkerchief, the chunky Sherry wore a Jerry Colonna–type moustache dyed as black as his hair. At his many dinner parties, he served hot grapefruit as an appetizer. He had a taste for offbeat gifts, once giving the singer Joanna Simon, the daughter of the publisher Richard Simon, a diamond "smaller than a grain of rice" and trying to track down some of Elinor's silent movies to present to her. For Sherry, mechanical objects were objects to be mastered and abused. He once arranged for a cherry picker to smash through the outside wall of his third-floor diamond office on Canal Street at four in the morning to retrieve a safe. His odder qualities notwithstanding, Sherry was a talented amateur photographer and, on Gibbs's porch, snapped the critic's favorite picture of himself—lying with shirt off in a deck chair, its cushioning decorated with nautical motifs, while flipping through the Sunday *New York Times,* sunglasses dangling from his lips. The photo reflected Gibbs's peace with his environment and adorned the back cover of *More in Sorrow.*

Gibbs's best friend on Fire Island, and perhaps anywhere, was the Ocean Beach realtor Bill Birmingham. Born in Brooklyn, he worked on commercial fishing boats and, like Gibbs, became acquainted with Fire Island as a teenager. He joined the Coast Guard during Prohibition and cruised Lake Champlain on the lookout for Canadian whiskey smuggling. Come World War II, he was attached to the British wing of the Normandy invasion. Birmingham was rock solid physically and emotionally; broad-shouldered, six feet tall, and two hundred pounds in his prime, he had huge hands and looked like a prizefighter. But "he had an almost boyish enthusiasm about him, and he was quick to lend a helping hand." Gibbs was fascinated by his mechanical abilities, his natural skill as a raconteur, and his dependability in general. "He was as good a friend to my father as Charles Addams," said Tony. "A marvelous guy, marvelous." It was to Birmingham whom Gibbs dedicated *More in Sorrow*.

With the raw material of these and other acquaintances, his ever widening familiarity with Fire Island, and some imagination, Gibbs set about writing a group of short stories about his favorite place. In doing so, he was treading on what was by now familiar *New Yorker* literary ground—the semiconnected series. Among the better known examples were O'Hara's "Pal Joey" letters; Frank Sullivan's "Cliché Expert," which employed nothing but threadbare expressions to testify on everything from war to tabloids; Ruth McKenney's autobiographical yarns about herself and her free-spirited sister, Eileen, which became the musical *Wonderful Town;* and of course, Clarence Day's "Father" stories.

Appearing in issues that spanned November 10, 1945, to September 14, 1946, Gibbs's nine entries ran under the rubric "Season in the Sun." Among the island folk he thinly disguised were the Pastorfields as the "Jermyns" and Polly Adler as "Molly Burden." At the core of the stories was the Crane family: George (Gibbs), his wife, Emily (Elinor), son Billy (Tony), and daughter Marcia (Janet). Curiously, Gibbs revealed very little about his alter ego, George. Instead, he assigned much of his own background to a bland, Princeton-educated construct named "Mark Anderson." To Anderson, Gibbs ascribed his unfortunate marriage to Helen Galpin, his Long Island newspaper days, and what he regarded as his own mediocre way with words: "He had one of those polite, derivative talents that are often regarded as terribly promising on the campus but never seem to come to very much later."

The format proved flexible enough to accommodate a variety of approaches. "Song at Twilight" was a droll, meandering sketch about a shaggy-dog story being told amid general booziness on a porch at dusk, while the fairly serious "The Foreign Population" concerns a little boy who is rebuked for his budding anti-Semitism. The most haunting of the bunch was the deeply allegorical "Crusoe's Footprint." Against the backdrop of an approaching hurricane, George and Emily walk along the beach, making small talk until they encounter a woman's moccasins, along with her eyeglasses and a watch. Having seen no one in either direction, they conclude she has drowned. Despite Emily's protests, George plunges into the churning surf to find her and nearly dies in the process. In the end, the young woman is discovered to be safe, and the Cranes are taken home in a Coast Guard jeep to escape the storm—with George feeling foolish and Emily sound asleep.

At the other extreme was the out-and-out comedy "The Cat on the Roof," based on a visit of the "extremely disreputable" playgirl Leonore Lemmon, who achieved her greatest fame as the girlfriend of the actor George Reeves. Disguising her as "Deedy Barton," Gibbs composed a vignette drawn almost entirely from real life. "What happened was that her cat got stuck up on my roof and she drunkenly turned in a fire alarm and the whole village came to my house to watch," he told Sam Behrman. "It's just the kind of thing that would really drive the character in these stories crazy."

It was the kind of thing guaranteed to drive Gibbs crazy as well. As gregarious as he could be with friends and associates, he distrusted strangers and interlopers. A solid wooden railing encircled The Studio's porch, and Gibbs would routinely drop down behind it to shield himself from the gaze of passersby. He relished his quiet. "We ourself would like to see it made a federal offence [sic] to play a portable radio on a beach," he wrote in "Comment."

In contrast to his dapper appearance at *The New Yorker*, Gibbs would neglect his appearance while on vacation, routinely going for a week without shaving. He donned khakis or a bathing suit and sported a light Mexican Guayabera shirt of which he was so fond that he wore it until it literally dissolved in the wash. He became a heliotrope, lying on the beach for hours at a time, his thin knees tucked up under his chin, his hair becoming so bleached and his skin so dark that he would come to be likened to a photographer's negative. "A man with an impressive coat of tan may still be an almost total physical wreck, a perennial bankrupt, and a stupefying bore," he wrote, "but so powerful is the tradition that a well-bronzed skin postulates health, wealth, and strange adventures in distant lands that his chances for social, financial, and even amorous advancement are usually excellent."

When not tanning, Gibbs could often be found, like White, afloat. Whereas White sailed, Gibbs cruised in a succession of powerboats, all named after Elinor. And he fished, usually for fluke or flounder but sometimes for weakfish and bluefish. To attract blues, Gibbs would chum with ground-up menhaden—an oily, bony specimen otherwise used for fertilizer and cat food—through a most unusual means of dispersal: he would purchase a five-gallon drum of the stuff, open it up, then turn it upside down onto a makeshift toilet built under the port front seat. He often went fishing alone but would frequently pair up with Birmingham or Tony; at one point he went out daily with Richard Adler, the composer and lyricist of *The Pajama Game*.

Gibbs was a good enough angler, and sometimes he lucked out. One Sunday he caught a twenty-pound striped bass and went over to Behrman's house to make a present of it. There he found Arthur Gelb, who told him that Behrman "had locked himself in his room and might not reappear until summer's end. Gibbs, crestfallen, left. But he returned with his fish a few hours later, wobbly from the effects of alcohol. Berrie was still in his room, I informed him.

" 'By God,' said Gibbs, 'he's a hard man to give a fish to.' "

CHAPTER 10

———

"ALWAYS POISON"

G ibbs's bizarre fish episode was shorthand for a whole catalog of alcohol-related misbehavior by *New Yorker* types. Alec Waugh might have put it most succinctly when he wrote, of the crew's bibulous habits, "Every drink was an adventure; every drink was a protest against an outrageous imposition of authority."

The New Yorker had been forged during the Noble Experiment of Prohibition, and befitting its stated purpose as a conveyer of metropolitan wit and gaiety, the magazine devoted no small portion of its early contents to the nightlife that surrounded the flourishing and surreptitious trade in illegally manufactured potables. In those days, it was officially estimated that there were as many as one hundred thousand speakeasies in the five boroughs. In his 1927 story "Speakeasy Nights," Niven Busch painted a memorable portrait of one such establishment that came equipped with a side entrance, a tinny piano playing "Baby Face," and an electric dumbwaiter that would, at the touch of a button, dump liquor bottles into the cellar in case of a raid. Even before he began at *The New Yorker,* Gibbs drove from Long Island to Manhattan "to spend the afternoon at a resort known as 40 East 60th Street, where tired young men gather to drink tea and jerk bored damsels through the Charleston and Black Bottom." And after he arrived at the magazine, he wrote of a hangout that was ostensibly located in the basement of the Argonaut National Bank. "The liquor," he said sourly, "is not very good—you're apt to find bits of paper—torn bonds or currency—floating around in your glass."

Lois Long's "Tables for Two" column typified the coverage of this decadence, as she recalled long after the Eighteenth Amendment had been repealed:

> You went out—how quaint it seems now—to have fun. Every time I think of the childlike verve with which we visited the dingy joints of those days, I am ashamed to look the clear-eyed young people of today in the face. It was a foolhardy, collegiate, naïve era, and the miracle is that any of us survived it. Nonchalantly we romped through hole-in-the-wall speakeasies that were here today and gone tomorrow. There were gentlemen in most of them who used a gun so casually that murders weren't News [sic] unless the murderee was a somebody in gangland. At closing time, headwaiters of perfectly proper night clubs gave you cards to late places that turned out to be grim little apartments full of hostesses where you got a check for $18.75 for four drinks—and the waiters were awfully big.

After Prohibition died, it turned out that drinking had taken so firm a hold that it pervaded the off-hours of the Manhattan literati. Such minutiae as the ratio of the perfect martini and the best barware became manias. "Preciousness almost engulfed us back then," wrote Roger Angell. "Tiffany's produced a tiny silver oil can, meant to dispense vermouth." When Ross suggested to Dorothy Parker that she contribute to the column that would become "Onward and Upward with the Arts," he said half in jest that she should write about drinking as if it were an art form. "And then I thought that this wasn't really such a bad idea and then

I thought that perhaps you would be the writer to write on the subject," he told Frank Sullivan. "I had in mind your mint julep piece, which I will always remember as something sweet and tender in my life.* With prohibition going, or gone, the art of mixing drinks will be important, and a timely subject."

Ross was a tad naïve about the effects of demon rum. "He once said to me 'Eighty percent of the people I know are sound about liquor,'" Thurber told Gibbs. "I have never forgot that. Two things about it impressed me deeply, the utter conviction with which he spoke, and the complete untruth of the statement."

Simply put, drinking suffused *The New Yorker.* "Everyone seemed to drink back then," said Helen Stark, the magazine's longtime librarian. The extent of this activity astonished Thurber's brother, Robert. "I never could figure out how all those people could drink all that stuff and stay so sharp," he said.† "I don't think I finished one dinner on theater night before curtain time, so much was spent on cocktails." The young writer Walter Bernstein once saw A. J. Liebling in action: "He ordered a martini straight up and drank it down like a glass of water." Every night Russell Maloney would come home with a bottle of gin, once prompting his toddling daughter Amelia to lisp, "Bat's mo," i.e., "That's more." These were among her first words.

As the speakeasies morphed into respectable outlets, *The New Yorker*'s leading lights moved readily among them. For straightforward cocktails and dinner, the Algonquin, "21," and Martin and Mino's on East 52nd Street were the destinations of choice. For slightly more exclusive surroundings, the personnel gravitated toward those hallmarks of café society, El Morocco and the Stork Club. The former became famous for its

---

* Sullivan's piece, "Agosto Port and Mint Juleps," about a customer who walks into a bar on a warm day and offers absurdly explicit instructions on how to make the drink of the title, ran in the July 22, 1933, issue of the magazine.

† Instancing Benchley, White once remarked, "A man can do a lot of drinking and still turn out a lot of work."

zebra-striped motifs, commemorated in myriad photographs by Beebe's photographer boyfriend Jerome Zerbe. The latter is today remembered for its equally famous pictures of notables clustered at tables that were graced by its trademark ashtrays and top-hatted stork centerpieces. This was where Winchell held court, and from which Gibbs's Fire Island nemesis Leonore Lemmon reportedly became the first woman to be ejected for fist fighting.

New Yorker people did not necessarily go to these places to see and be seen. (Peter Arno, in the company of Brenda Frazier, was a notable exception.) Their preferred watering holes were both conveniently located and tended to have a quirky ambiance. An Italian immigrant named Tony Soma, a former waiter, opened a namesake restaurant at 57 West 52nd Street that drew Ross and his brood in part for his outlandish stunts. Soma was an early yoga fanatic, frequently doing headstands on the premises during the height of business hours and even on the sidewalk to attract customers.

Another immigrant, this one from Ireland, also operated an establishment named for himself. Tim Costello, though possessed of little formal education, was a devotee of the English language and often conveyed his literary tastes as might a college professor. Costello's was far from classy; its food was often terrible, with green vegetables simmered beyond recognition into a pulpy mess. Physically, it was "a long narrow shoebox of a space, with the bar itself running along the south wall and a number of cheap wooden booths facing it on the opposite wall," recalled Brendan Gill. "In the space that remained between the last booth and the serving pantry were a few tables, covered with white, much-mended tablecloths." But it achieved a certain kind of perverse immortality thanks to a few mainstays of *The New Yorker*. In one often-retold story, a drunken O'Hara, equipped with a blackthorn walking stick, encountered Ernest Hemingway there in the wee hours. Supposedly a bullying Hemingway, not believing an equally bullying O'Hara's assertion that he possessed the best blackthorn walking stick in New York City, bet O'Hara that he could break it over his head and proceeded to do so. Costello saved the pieces and mounted them over the bar.

Costello's, located first at the corner of Third Avenue and 44th Street and then next door at 699 Third Avenue—under the shadow of the El— was a forum for "some of the best arguments" in New York City, the journalist Charles McCabe recalled after presenting the place with a copy of *The World Almanac*:

> I remember one about what the "B" in Rutherford B. Hayes stood for. This one was settled when Dick Maney, a theatrical press agent, entered the joint. . . . One day I asked Tim Costello, who with his brother ran the place, why he didn't invest a half buck in the invaluable reference book of which we are speaking. Tim was visibly taken aback. "What!" he said indignantly, "and have them settle all those arguments?" There spoke the true Irish tradesman. All Tim thought of was selling spirits and beer, and prolonged arguments increased his income. Having a "World Almanac" in his pub would in his view be in the same category as the return of Prohibition.

One of the major celebrants of Costello's was the writer John McNulty, who published a series of short stories about the place and its offbeat denizens without ever quite identifying it, employing such euphemisms as "this gin mill on Third Avenue" and "this place on Third Avenue." His contributions were often rambling yarns with titles almost as long and shaggy as the stories themselves, e.g., "Barkeep Won't Let Anybody at All Shove This Handyman Around" and "They'd Have Taken Him If He Was Only a Torso." Thurber wrote an affectionate introduction to his collected stories, which were gathered under the title *The World of John McNulty*.

Thurber made his own literal impression on Costello's—on its walls, in the form of his customary doodles. Among them were three rabbits chasing a Thurber dog downhill and a Thurber Woman tackling a Thurber Man. So flattered was Costello by this artistry and its consequent publicity that he ordered that the place was never to close as long as Thurber was there. This could be rather tiresome to the staff when he stumbled in at two or three in the morning, "prepared to talk and sing until dawn." When Costello moved his establishment around the corner in 1949, he transported the wallboard with particular care.*

Just as popular as Costello's, if not more so, was Bleeck's (pronounced "Blake's") at 213 West 40th Street. It was the de facto retreat for the *Herald Tribune,* which had an employees' entrance just a few feet away. When a *Trib* man said, "I'm going downstairs," he meant he was on his way to Bleeck's. So close were the two institutions that "when the presses rolled, the walls of Bleeck's trembled symbiotically, and reporters and editors would leave their martinis on the bar and go upstairs to check their stories in print. Their drinks would be waiting when they got back."

The owner, John ("Jack" or, less frequently, "Dutch") Bleeck, was born in St. Louis in 1880 and made his way east via boxcar at age twenty. He opened his place in 1925 and, under the pretense of legality and with a dubious dispensation from Albany, christened it the Artist and Writers' Club. It soon acquired about six thousand members, all of them men; the only female allowed was a cat called Minnie. When Prohibition ended, Bleeck tried to keep things stag. But after customers began patronizing coed establishments, costing him an average of five hundred dollars a month, he relented. In 1934, when the first anonymous woman entered Bleeck's, one charter member muttered, "There'll be mayonnaise on the steaks next week."

Actually, the only major change in the place was in its name. It was rechristened the "Artist and Writers' Restaurant (Formerly Club),"

---

* As the years went by, and cigarette smoke and grease darkened the murals' contours, attempts were made to brighten up and retrace them. When Costello's closed for good in 1994, the originals were believed to be lost. However, a patron rescued a sketch that Thurber had drawn on a tablecloth stained with whiskey and steak juice and presented it to Helen.

leading many to call it "The Formerly Club." Its name notwithstanding, Bleeck's remained a mainly male citadel, its clientele comprising not only writers and editors but actors, publishers, painters, cartoonists, publicists, singers, and all manner of those somehow associated with the arts and letters—so much so that it was commonly known as a latter-day Mermaid Tavern.

As was the case with Costello's, the decor, described as "early Butte, Montana," was not designed to impress. "The tables and chairs were battered dark oak and the walls a particularly ugly shade of brown, darkened by years of exposure to billowing cigar smoke," said Leslie Midgley. "It was grand." The bar itself was a staggering forty-two feet long; along the wall facing it was a single row of small tables devoid of tablecloths. Just past this arrangement were two dining rooms separated by a partition, in front of which stood a suit of armor that once belonged to the nearby Metropolitan Opera. Perhaps to keep it erect, it was filled with cement, and many a boisterous drunk broke his knuckles on it. Above the bar was a stuffed fish caught by J. P. Morgan off Newport. Other odd memorabilia included a radiogram sent by the *Times* reporter Russell Owen from the South Pole during Admiral Byrd's first Antarctic expedition and a painting by the *Trib* cartoonist Clare Briggs that depicted a golfer lifting his glass on the nineteenth hole. Radios and jukeboxes were verboten, as were certain foods. Heavy German fare like sauerbraten, red cabbage, and potato pancakes were Bleeck's staples; anyone who wanted to indulge in French fries or ice cream was curtly informed to patronize Schrafft's, down the street.

The booming, florid-faced, white-haired Bleeck was devoted to his patrons. He was especially pleased when it began raining around dinnertime, which encouraged them to linger. His "subterranean grotto" had only one window that looked out onto the bottom of a twelve-story airshaft, an arrangement that he used to his advantage, as Nunnally Johnson attested: "Jack fixed up a kind of shower bath effect over this one window and would turn it on around 5 or 5:30, whereupon the customers would glance toward the window, see the downpour and decide to have another until the shower passed over."

Bleeck probably didn't need the fake rain. When his clients were in his care, time stood still, much to the consternation of many wives; whenever they would ring up to ask where their husbands were, the standard response was, "He just left." But Richard Maney's feisty wife, Betty, was not easily put off. Once, when her husband did not come home for his evening meal of cherrystone clams and bluefish, she stomped over to Bleeck's, put it before him, and announced, "All right, Mohamet, here's your dinner." When Maney declined to eat, she began lugging the clams and fish to bewildered customers at the surrounding tables, "suggesting to them both items were better than anything on the menu, and could be had for a fraction of what Bleeck would ask."

"Bleeck's, when you analyze it, is very much like a front line dugout—the noise, the dogged courage of the men holding on till zero hour, the fits of hysteria, the sitting around in sullen gloom," said Thurber. One *New Yorker* editor stood on a table and, denouncing Isaac Newton, declared that he would fly to the men's room. Only quick intervention kept him from breaking his neck. There was organized horseplay as well: the regulars enjoyed their own form of the Dead Pool, which they called "The Ghoul Pool" and "The Grim Reaper's Sweepstakes." For two dollars apiece, participants would draw one of a hundred names of celebrities "who were either aged or likely to die through violence," for a payout of two hundred dollars, two or three times a week as they expired. Darts, too, were popular, until Gibbs boasted that by using a mirror, he could score bull's-eyes by throwing them over his back. But after he nearly skewered a relative of *Saturday Evening Post* editor George Horace Lorimer, the game was played no more.

Far more pervasive than the Ghoul Pool or darts was the match game, "one of the daffiest pastimes ever devised by man for his own confusion." The idea was simple, based on guessing how many matches— from zero to three—the other players were holding in their closed hands. But the execution could quickly become complex and expensive, as Maney recalled:

> Each of the fanatics guesses at the total of matches concealed in all the visible fists. If seven are playing, the possibilities range from nothing to 21. The player guessing the correct number is eliminated. Further rounds with further eliminations continue until but two players are left. The finalists play best two out of three guesses. The doomed man then pays each of his jeering opponents the sum fixed at the start, usually compounding his fiscal folly by buying a round of drinks. The flaw in the game, by any mathematical standard known to Einstein, Euclid or Copernicus, is that with seven playing, a competitor can lose as much in one game as he can win in six.

This childish nonsense was so addictive that it spawned its own subculture. Stanley Walker, the *Trib*'s legendary city editor, once played a hundred straight games to see if there was an advantage to going first or last. (He found a slight advantage to the former.) A few of the game's better practitioners toyed with the notion of making a career of it. Some were good enough that they attributed their success to clairvoyance; others, less successful, resorted to voodoo in an attempt to turn their fortunes. Lucius Beebe would play with his own solid gold matches, complete with diamond heads. For less well-heeled players, Bleeck would distribute thousands of sets of plastic matches at Christmastime. When the bar closed at four in the morning, diehard matchers would sometimes continue their game on the sidewalk. When John Lardner died and was laid out, *Pogo* cartoonist Walt Kelly put three matches in his hand.

At one point, though, even as devoted a gamesman as Maney decided he had had enough during a particularly riotous bout involving nine people, including himself and Gibbs. Gibbs was so drunk that he couldn't recognize his opponents. Still, it befell him to be the first one to venture how many matches all nine participants were clutching. Against all logic and experience, he guessed none. "And before God, he won!" said Johnson. "Not even Ripley would have believed that." Whereupon Maney bowed out, explaining that "he wouldn't play in a game subject to miracles."

There was a downside to this drinking culture, of course. Some of it is—in retrospect—funny. On an occasion when Packard was cat sitting, he found himself so deeply hung over that he couldn't be bothered opening a tin of cat food. So he reached into the refrigerator, grabbed a dish of cooked peas, and set it down. The disgusted cat whapped the peas with a paw, sending them across the floor. Gibbs found himself on the floor any number of times; once, when his steak slipped off his plate, he simply swore, bent down, and continued to carve it. Another time, after heckling his nemesis Leonore Lemmon in a nightclub, he ended up practically prostrate. This prompted Lemmon to shout, "Hey, Wolcott! You're out three days before your magazine."

But any such amusement was the exception. Far more often, drinking would lead *The New Yorker*'s people down miserable paths, as Walter Bernstein discovered during a lunch with three of his colleagues:

Their talk was keen and witty, but their eyes had the faraway look of drinkers, fixed on some invisible watering hole in the distance. Still, they always heard what you were saying. Sober, they were talented professionals, proud of their craft, not easily fooled. ... Drunk, they became mean and sloppy and belligerent. One in particular [Richard O. Boyer], a lapsed Catholic, liked to sit in bars and assault convivial clergymen, regardless of denomination. He had an uncanny eye for picking out men of the cloth, even when they were dressed like anyone else. Another [Robert Lewis Taylor] would sit on the porch of his farmhouse, a bottle in one hand and a pistol in the other, and shoot at anyone who crossed his property. Most of the time he missed, which only irritated him further. A third [Croswell Bowen] backed his car out of his garage and ran over his child.

Sometimes this deviance was on public display. Richard Maney remembered a party that Gibbs and Elinor, along with *New Yorker* contributor Philip W. Wrenn, Jr., and his wife, gave for several hundred guests on the East Side; the attendees "embraced the flower and chivalry of Bleeck's and 21." The gathering was set for the odd hour of nine p.m., by which time any number were already sodden and collapsing. At one point the butler fretted aloud that Sanderson Vanderbilt, who had passed out amid his own vomit under a rosebush, was dead. Upon viewing the sickening scene, Lillian Hellman and Dorothy Parker chorused, "Even a Vanderbilt can throw up and roll in it."*

It was at parties like these that McKelway's particular brand of behavior while inebriated emerged. As Edward Newhouse told it, the charismatic writer had a habit of taking women by the hand and leading them into bedrooms piled high with coats to impregnate them, producing progeny who bore an uncanny resemblance to their illegitimate father. One of these offspring, supposedly, was the guitarist Sandy Bull, who would spend considerable time playing in the Greenwich Village folk scene and with Bob Dylan.

With the possible exception of Thurber—who could pick fights with or without liquor under his belt—O'Hara may have caused more scenes in his cups than any of his peers. The writer Helen Lawrenson called him "an ugly drunk" and recalled a double date she went on with him, his first wife, Petie, and Gibbs sometime in the early 1930s:

---

* Vanderbilt died in 1967—a suicide, according to Gardner Botsford.

The four of us started drinking at the O'Haras' apartment, moved on to a restaurant, and ended at the Algonquin, where John and Wolcott played Ping-Pong for five dollars a game, while Petie and I sat and drank brandy. The more he drank, the nastier John got—to every one of us—and he and Gibbs got in a fight, throwing money at each other until finally Gibbs got up and went out. We thought he had gone to the men's room. When he didn't return, John went to look for him and discovered he had left the hotel. John and Petie took me home and I kept thinking, "I bet if I looked like Ruby Keeler, he wouldn't have walked out on me."

O'Hara eventually quit this sort of behavior after a perforated ulcer rendered him semiconscious on a bathroom floor and he nearly bled to death; he was put on a regimen of bland foods that consisted mainly of mashed potatoes and steak juice. It was, he said, "a hell of a way for booze to treat me after I've been so kind to it." Not long afterward, following the death of his second wife, Belle, he poured a bottle of whiskey into the sink and never took another drink for the rest of his life. Curiously, the prim Katharine White remarked, "I think he wrote better when he was drinking than he did later. His subject matter and style seemed fresher then."

Unlike O'Hara, Gibbs never stopped. "There is no such thing as one martini," he would say, and he proved it. The effects of alcohol on him varied. Sometimes his speech would simply become rambling and disjointed. At other times, he would literally fall down, marking his fragile corpus with myriad bruises and scars. Edith Iglauer Daly, the wife of Philip Hamburger, personally witnessed one such incident at her apartment. "He actually did fall over, I can see it yet, he was so drunk. That whole generation of *The New Yorker* seemed to me to be drinking all the time; I felt I was running a kind of salon every Sunday afternoon in our apartment on East End."

Nancy and Bunny Stern's daughter, Susan, once encountered Gibbs passed out in her parents' duplex on East 95th Street as she was getting ready for school. "He faded into the couch. He didn't move. I remember taking a wide berth around him." This accorded with the recollections of David Cort. "At a party Gibbs was good for about two hours," he said. "After that he didn't fight, he dissolved, and had to be carried." Frequently, after a bout with the bottle, Gibbs would fall asleep smoking in bed, in an echo of his casual "Wit's End." According to Beebe, he managed to nearly immolate himself one night, but the night operator of his building refused to contact the fire department, thinking his panicky call was a joke. The truth was likelier less colorful. "Occasionally he would burn himself," said Tony. "A typical cigarette burn between his fingers. And you really have to be out cold not to notice that."

It was no way to live, and yet Gibbs somehow thought booze was a necessary personality lubricant—even essential to his central identity. "Most of the time I lie on the sofa and think about you and what a God damn [sic] bore I'll be when I've been sober for six months," he told Nancy Hale. He once wrote a casual called "A Man May Be Down" in which his alter ego, a fellow named Munson, goes on the wagon. Munson's appetite, health, finances, appearance, and love life all improve dramatically. Unfortunately, "[t]he gift of repartee left Munson the day he drank his last Martini." Munson, Gibbs observes, "was outrageous at times—a liar and a bankrupt and the enemy of order—but I liked him. He was a man living on a volcano who had no confidence in any tomorrow, and he gave you and the moment all he had. The new Munson, this sepia changeling with the hard stomach, leaves me cold."

For the most part, his inebriation somehow did not interfere with his work. "Gibbs would quite often come to the theater drunk, and I would say, now how is he going to write a review of this?" remembered his colleague Henry Hewes. "But sure enough when the review came out it was all there. He was aware of everything." Jane, his wife, had similar recollections. "I'd say, 'Oh my God, he's going to sleep' and I'd miss some of the play because he fascinated me. But his review would come out and he'd be right on the ticket."

The calls were sometimes close. Gibbs was so blind on the opening night of *The Crucible,* said the play's assistant press agent, Merle Debuskey, "he had to be carried into his seat." The irate producer, Kermit Bloomgarden, complained to Jim Proctor, the head press agent, "He can't possibly review the play. You have to talk to him." Proctor reluctantly called Gibbs; the critic interrupted him to say, "Jimmy, tell Kermit not to worry. It'll be a rave." And it was.

But this sort of behavior could not go unnoticed indefinitely. There were lapses, embarrassing ones. On November 27, 1946, the executive secretary of the League of New York Theatres sent Ross a furious telegram:

ON BEHALF OF A NUMBER [OF] THE PLAY PRODUCERS OF NEW YORK CITY WE WISH TO PROTEST THE BEHAVIOR OF YOUR DRAMATIC CRITIC ON OPENING NIGHTS. ON TWO RECENT OCCASIONS HE HAS BEEN UNDER THE INFLUENCE OF LIQUOR AND WE CANNOT BELIEVE THAT A FAIR AND IMPARTIAL REVIEW CAN BE OBTAINED UNDER SUCH CIRCUMSTANCES. WE ARE SENDING THIS IN ADVANCE OF THE PUBLICATION OF THE REVIEW OF TWO RECENT PLAYS AT WHICH SUCH CONDUCT WAS OBSERVED SO THAT NO CHARGE CAN BE MADE THAT THE REVIEWS WHATEVER THEIR CONTENT HAVE INFLUENCED THIS ACTION.

On paper Ross took this matter seriously, especially when Richard Rodgers and a cohort of peers from the Dramatists Guild made a similar complaint. "I concur in your opinion that the interests of the theatre and the dramatists require that a critic be in a competent condition," Ross told Rodgers, "and that we shall accept the responsibility for our representative." Privately, though, he sensed that certain members of the guild simply "wanted to depose and eat a critic." He was referring primarily to the imperious Lillian Hellman, who was fuming over Gibbs's dismissal of her drama *Another Part of the Forest.* "Serious critics should treat writing seriously," she told Gibbs. "On two occasions at least you did not do that.* . . . Because I respect you as a writer I am more sympathetically sorry for that than you would probably believe." The unfortunate business quickly blew over, but not before Ross found time to gripe to Maney, "Why don't that dame go down to Palm Beach and lie in the sand until her menopause has passed?"

Still, there was no way to dismiss other complaints—like the one that was filed by Cheryl Crawford, the producer of *Flahooley*. Gibbs, she informed Ross, "was seen being held up against the wall in Shubert Alley by his wife and their conversation was overheard. He was seen staggering to his seat and he was seen leaving after the first act. Whatever his opinion of the show, I feel a producer has the right to expect sobriety and attention. . . . I feel incensed at such treatment."

That was Manhattan. On Fire Island, Gibbs could damage himself without fear of professional repercussions. The Studio was often the site of raucous parties; in their aftermath, Elinor—who was as addicted to rye as Gibbs was to martinis—would announce to visitors, "The cat has a headache. Just keep it down, boys." It was all intensely painful for young Tony, who was sometimes pressed into playing bartender at Ocean Beach revels. As he became aware of the alcoholism of both of his parents, he made his displeasure known to them:

> On Fire Island, I used to drive them crazy. My bedroom was in one of the balcony bedrooms, and I would just sit up there on the balcony and stare down at them while they were drinking, which probably must have been kind of a gauntlet in the house. I didn't need to say anything, it was just obvious that this disapproval would just radiate out. And I think it made them quite unhappy, but not unhappy enough to stop. I had no idea what to do; I didn't know if there was anything to do. I mean, for somebody my age it was a position of total helplessness.

---

* The name of the other play that Gibbs did not take seriously is not known.

And there was nothing he could do to prevent them from going out to one of the few local establishments. At Goldie's, Elinor Gibbs and John Lardner's wife, Hazel, would sometimes fall off barstools and find themselves escorted home by the police. Bel Kaufman, the future author of *Up the Down Staircase,* remembered seeing Gibbs frequently at Maguire's in the mid-1940s. "He looked old and shriveled and always drunk." But she wanted to tell him how much she admired his work. So one night, "I gathered up my courage to talk to him with some flowery words of praise. He weaved over to me and he said, 'Are you pretty? I can't see a damn thing.'" Kaufman remembered Gibbs, like Elinor and Hazel, occasionally being carried out. "It was heartbreaking."

Heartbreaking, too, was the personal conversation that McKelway once set down in his journal about his relationship with his foul seductress:

> Alcohol is one of the chief things that have been interfering with both my work and my marriage. I do not want to forbid alcohol, because forbidden things are apt to take on an additional charm, especially in the case of a Presbyterian like myself. If I can use alcohol—under certain rather rigid circumstances—without letting it interfere with my work or my marriage, well and good. But if alcohol in any way at all prevents me from being at my best in the morning—when I work—or in the evening—when I play—it can go and fuck itself. It will no longer be on my list of friends. It will, in that case, not be forbidden, but will simply be clouted over the head, kicked in the ass, and abandoned. So, Alcohol, you watch your step if you want to remain a friend of mine.

But internal ruminations could only go so far. Almost invariably, what was then known as "taking the cure" was a necessary antidote. There were a number of refuges for this purpose. "John McCarten, our old drama and movie critic, used to joke that they had a special New

Yorker dry-out wing at Payne Whitney," said Helen Stark, referring to the historic Upper East Side psychiatric facility. "He was a naughty man. When his wife had a child I told him he'd soon have to stop partying and stay home with his wife and baby. He said, 'In a pig's ass I will.'"

Payne Whitney was often not enough. To truly escape the temptations of New York and regain some semblance of composure, the cast of characters periodically fled to a collection of sanitariums in pastoral settings. Two of the most popular were the Foundation Inn, aka Austen Riggs Associates, in Stockbridge, Massachusetts, and Nonkanahwa in Kerhonkson, New York. The former was usually referred to as "Riggs" and the latter as "Foord's" after its chief physician, Andrew Green Foord. Ross went to Riggs at least once. But given his ulcers, he was not a boozer by nature and so managed to steer clear of the establishment. For many others, though, these places were necessary evils. On his first known visit to Foord's, in 1934, Gibbs telegrammed Elinor: ARRIVED AT THE MINES JOEY IT IS ALL RIGHT BUT YOU MUSTN'T VISIT THE OTHER INMATES.

Admission for the agreed-upon length of commitment—which usually ranged from two weeks to a month or more—was not automatic. When McKelway checked into Riggs to write his Winchell series, he had to secure an endorsement from an outside party and a supporting letter from Ross to one of the resident physicians. "I have had a talk with McKelway, and I have told him to take your treatment seriously, which he has promised to do so," Ross reassured the doctor. Ross stated that *The New Yorker* would meet McKelway's expenses, which McKelway estimated would come to $800 for two months, apart from approximately $70 per week for room and board.*

Things didn't always go that smoothly. Around Christmas 1941, Thurber and Honeycutt tried to check into Foord's while both were three

---

* This figure did not initially include a charge of $2.50 that McKelway incurred when he placed a lit candle next to his bedside lamp and ended up burning the lampshade.

sheets to the wind, with "Thurber shouting and waving bottles, Honeycutt hysterical and screaming," Daise Terry recalled. "They just about scared the pants off the old ladies gathered in the lounge having tea. Foord would have none of them and kicked them right out, threatened to get the police. . . . [I]t ended up [with] their being thrown out and having to spend the night at an inn. They came back to town the next day, very meek." In one of his casuals, "Eden, With Serpents," Gibbs depicts himself alighting at Foord's in a similarly riotous fashion. Disguising the place as Mink-a-wonk-it Lodge, he writes of arriving on the grounds in a taxi direct from the city, accompanied by a couple of empty bottles and an unnamed companion who was almost certainly a stand-in for McKelway. Despite having insisted that he be brought to the place, the Gibbs character roars, "I'm not going to any god-damn asylum," and runs away, while his sidekick allows himself to be taken into the kindly care of the facility.

If a patient did stick it out, the results were usually beneficial. "It's nice here, the place, the people, the country," Thurber wrote Honey from Foord's in 1935. "I do not accept that lank, sick, nervous man who for years wandered from the N. Yorker [sic] to the Algonquin to Tony's. I don't accept the things he said or did. I never want to see him again. I don't marvel that you & everybody else avoided him. . . . I don't miss drinking at all." In another dispatch to her, he reported, "The food is excellent, the rooms bright and easy, the people easy, the woods and cascades and cliffs make you silent like stout Crotz [sic]* (who would have run some of the fat off his adventurous ass up here). There is no vista in Tony's and where there is no vista the people perish." In yet another communiqué, he admired the mild discipline of the outfit. It was, he said, "not strict or rigorous, but gently firm—the hours, the meals (including a quiet tea time), the walks, the baths, the mas-

---

* A misspelled reference to "stout Cortez" from "On First Looking into Chapman's Homer" by John Keats.

sages. It makes the rusty wheels of my mind begin to turn in rhythm again—old thoughts and plans and ideas fall into line; I can think already, straight again."

Gibbs also benefited from the treatment; any number of times he wrote Elinor to tell her he was feeling better, such as: "So nice not to wake up and wish you were dead." But his relief was mixed with boredom, especially when he found himself "playing anagrams with old ladies every night (can you take CHOIR with an E?)." His fellow inmates, he found, ranged from plain dull to "pretty terrible." Among the specimens were a Miss Whelen ("cries herself to sleep at night"), a Mr. Tierney ("always gets gas on his stomach immediately after eating"), and a Mrs. Martin and Miss FitzHugh ("quieter and just shake, but you can see they aren't happy either"). Their respective conditions filled him with self-loathing. "It's miserable to think that I can't cope with life any better than these other lunatics, and worse to realize that it's a regular thing with them—a week at Foord's every year to put your character together again," he wrote home. "I can't face a prospect like that, if I have to spend the rest of my life on the wagon."

There were some rudimentary attempts at rooting out the psychological problems that undergirded all the drinking and depression. When McKelway checked into Riggs during his Winchell interregnum, one of its specialists informed Ross vaguely, "Among his sources of satisfaction is the deepening degree of insight into the genesis of certain of his handicapping personality traits. He also says that certain of his values are clearing themselves of the emotional fog which previously surrounded them and they are now standing out in a more clear-cut manner."

In general, however, the inebriates' personalities received little attention. Rather, the emphasis was on cleaning them up and keeping them busy with enforced activities whose discipline would serve them well as an example when they returned to their normal routines. There was some emphasis on arts and crafts. In fact, it was that aspect of Ross's brief stay at Riggs that one of the physicians remembered most vividly:

"Ross just made one bench, very quickly, and went back to town!" Among the therapists who worked for Dr. Foord was his son, Fritz, who was close to many of the Algonquin crowd; when not designing movie sets, he taught painting classes on the premises. He can be seen in a famous 1938 photograph featuring Gibbs, Thurber, Maloney, McKelway, Frank Case, Parker (wearing what appears to be a fez), and her husband, Alan Campbell, in the lobby of their preferred hotel.

The doctors considered exercise, to tone up the body and purge it of toxins, more important than basket weaving. Such physical activity could include long walks, dumbbells, throwing around a medicine ball, or more strenuous pursuits. This hit-or-miss approach did have its beneficial aspects. On one occasion, after walking five miles one morning and playing tennis all afternoon, Gibbs found himself "lame as all hell and covered with blisters, but otherwise fine," although he also grew "stupefied" by the procedures.

The most curious aspect of the sanitariums' treatment was their emphasis on hydrotherapy. This was not a case of merely relaxing in whirling, warm Jacuzzis or floating aimlessly in a pool. Rather, the subjects would periodically be marched into a huge tiled room and squirted with hoses. Somehow, it was thought this would relax them and improve their circulation. It was an ignoble procedure. "I have just been hosed and pummeled (one 'l'; they beat the other one out of me)," Thurber reported to Honey. "Every day for an hour I'm hosed and pummeled." He even drew a caricature of his ordeal that depicted his nude self being drenched, incongruously, with his glasses on. He captioned it, "Just warm them cold as a son of a bitch, as my Aunt Caroline used to say."

Topping off the process, at Foord's anyway, was an attempt to bring the charges back into the routine of normal domestic life. To that end, Foord kept his own family on the four-thousand-acre compound and often allowed them free access to the residents. When the main house grew too cold, he would have them sleep on one of the asylum floors. "I can't think of a stranger environment for the young," Gibbs reflected. It was through such proximity that Foord's granddaughter, Carol, came to play with Gibbs and become acquainted with McKelway and Thurber. Foord further expected his guests to dress in evening clothes for dinner to instill some sense of decorum and order. "His ideas about what was best for these people was very unusual," said Carol.

After a stint at Foord's or Riggs, the affected parties would generally return healthier and happier. But this rarely lasted. Thurber went into and out of drinking phases for most of his life, as did McKelway. In some cases, like that of Benchley, boozing would literally be the death of them. "Drinking did kill him in the end—got him in the liver," White said.

As for Gibbs, Ross monitored him closely. In the summer of 1937 he wrote Katharine White, "Gibbs hasn't had a drink in months, is clean-eyed and in command of everything since he came back from the sanitarium, and there is no theatre to speak of this month. He could carry on all right." A year later he wrote Andy with confidence, "Gibbs hasn't had any jitters lately that I've seen or heard about. I thought they were going to be recurrent and maybe they are, but if they are the interval is apparently longer."

There may have been intervals, but there were no permanent respites. A good ten years after Ross made his observations about Gibbs's jitters, the critic confided to Behrman:

[H]ere is a nervous, melancholy letter from Fifty-second street, from a man just back on the wagon after a ten-day's bender. Son of a bitch if I know how these things happen to me because they're always poison, or anyway no damn fun and the pieces nearly impossible to put together again afterwards. . . . I'd say arrogantly, Sam, that the big trouble with getting soused, really soused, is that you give too many awful people an edge on you. You wouldn't know. You'll just have to take my word for it.

Gibbs might not have understood how such things happened to him, but the novelist Dawn Powell did. Instancing Gibbs, Dorothy Parker, and Arthur Kober, among others, she pegged their essential insecurity:

They challenge each other by being seen at certain parties, places; they are each other's sores and are half-fascinated, half-repelled. They are ruined by not being able to want what they individually want, but most want inevitably what the other wants. They are spoiled nursery children who really want to go on playing with an old clothespin, but seeing Brother happy with an engine, must fight for engine. Winning it, they are discontented, ill-natured.

Most of all, they have perverted their rather infantile ambitions into destruction of others' ambitions and happiness. If people are in love, they must mar it with laughter; if people are laughing, they must stop it with "Your slip is showing." They are in a permanent prep school where they perpetually haze each other. They destroy their own happiness by being ashamed of whatever brings it; they want to be loved but are unloving; they want to destroy but be themselves saved. They are afraid of being used, even while they use.

CHAPTER 11

"FLYING HIGH AND FAST"

A round midday on December 7, 1941, Gibbs was tuned in to the radio in his apartment to listen to a game between the Brooklyn Dodgers and the New York Giants—the football teams, not their baseball counterparts. When the news broke, he twisted the dial, combing for information amid Christmas carols and department store advertisements. When it was time for him to compose his "Comment" for that week, he took his cue from White and resisted the temptation to succumb to grandiloquence. Instead, he led with the initial shock of confusion. "War came to us with the ball in Brooklyn's possession on the Giants' forty-five-yard line," he wrote. " 'Japanese bombs have fallen on Hawaii and the Philippine Islands,' a hurried voice broke in to announce. 'Keep tuned to this station for further details. We now return you to the Polo Grounds.' No more than that."

He continued, "Gradually all the voices—in reality, one voice, the placid, rather foolish voice of America on Sunday afternoon—took up the incredible story from the Pacific. It came in slowly—disjointed, fragmentary; contradicting itself every now and then." Gibbs discussed the preliminary gabble but gradually summoned hold of the enormity of the disaster, conveying what details he could snatch from the airwaves—"A man in a private plane over Diamond Head, just flying for fun, shot down by two planes," "three hundred and fifty men killed by a direct hit on the barracks at Hickam Field," and so on. For the summing up, he registered controlled disbelief:

> The old nightmare of the Yellow Peril, a comic bugaboo almost as long as we can remember, is a strange thing to have come true in the early afternoon, with the radio on and the Sunday papers still only partly read. Like practically everybody else, we've been sure for a long time that war was bound to come, but we never thought that it would come like that.

Years before war arrived on America's doorstep, the staff of *The New Yorker*, like most sentient people in the country, had known it was on the way and that the United States was destined to be part of it. But following the government line, and absent a casus belli, they did not say so explicitly. Ross, though fully aware of the danger approaching, was terribly conflicted. Never much of a crusader, he determined to steer as middle a course as he could until the United States entered the conflagration. So he sounded ever-more ominous warnings and printed unhappy dispatches from overseas while refusing to straitjacket the magazine into any particular stance.

In a three-page, single-spaced letter to White he agonized over the life-and-death prospects at hand. He was not at all sure that the country would prevail, but he knew that the United States had for all intents and purposes joined the cause:

> Internationally, there is no question that there is a way of dodging the fight (your phrase) indefinitely. . . . We can cut ourselves off from the rest of the world, reorganize our economy to exist on

our domestic activities alone, and live happy ever after. . . . We can sit tight for a generation or a century, until things blow over. We can't be invaded or bombed, or harmed. . . . People are saying everything. Thurber wants war at once, and a hell of a lot of other people do. To most of these people, our entrance into the war can only mean victory. They don't see a possibility of a German victory. Pinned down, there isn't one in one-hundred [sic] of them who can go further with an outline of future action than a stand-off of Germany. . . . All the talk and all the thought, including mine, is beside the point, however, I think. My solemn conviction is that we are going into the war, and going in soon, for better or for worse, whatever the responsibility, whatever the chances. In fact, we seem already to be in it.

As far as the magazine's stance was concerned, he had no doubts. "The policy of the paper to date is generally approved," he declared. "Flanner, who spent the week-end [sic] with me, thinks our policy has been right—to my astonishment. Lobrano does and so do most others. I think even Thurber doubts if we should try to become a leader at this time. Christ there are enough leaders, from Dorothy Thompson, Winchell and the Evening Post down. It isn't leaders of opinion the U.S. lacks now."

Individual contributors were allowed to follow their own consciences. Finding himself "depressed and shaken" by Germany's invasion of Poland, Thurber sat down in his room at the Algonquin and within a few hours sketched out the thin text and extraordinary drawings that constituted *The Last Flower*. This allegory about the fallout of "World War XII," and the fragile potential that humanity might be able to recover from it—with both hopes for peace and the prospect of another war simultaneously emerging in the last pages—turned out to be his favorite book. It was White's, too, and he commended his good friend's artistry and perception:

It is a fearsome picture. Centuries seem to hang motionless, time crawls like a slug on a garden wall. There is an unspeakable hopelessness in the drag of its years. Then suddenly, turning the pages, you find motion and pace in the world again. You see the rebirth of beauty, culture, love. Groves and forests flourish again, children run and laugh, dogs come out of exile, towns and cities spring up, and the world quickens to the singing of troubadors and the antics of jugglers. There is a magnificent sweep to this rebirth. Thurber does it all in just a few pictures, using his stock characters, yet you feel his agitation. Then you turn the penultimate page and find, once again, soldiers on the march, soldiers in unending columns, harbingers of the dreary familiar death of men and painting and love, and the new shooting of young students against the wall, and the burning of the books, and all the revolting sad contemptible rigmarole which we know so well.

Clearly, White was no warmonger, but he knew that America's hour was at hand. Drawing on the political consciousness he had begun summoning during the Depression, he set about quietly preparing the country for battle. In *Harper's* he registered disgust at the slipshod logic of Anne Morrow Lindbergh's best-selling anti-interventionist jeremiad *The Wave of the Future*. White thought some of her observations about the character of the German people and their grievances were sound enough. But he found her notion that there was something to be said for fascism appalling. "The fascist ideal, however great the misery which released it and however impressive the self-denial and burning courage which promote it, does not hold the seed of a better order but of a worse one, and it always has a foul smell and a bad effect on the soil," he wrote. "It stank at the time of Christ and it stinks today. . . . There is nothing new in it and nothing good in it, and today when it is developed to a political nicety and supported by a formidable military machine the best thing to do is to defeat it as promptly as possible and in all humility."

Following the day of infamy, such arguments were moot. As usual, White rendered the attack in approachable terms:

My wife was getting a hot-water bag for somebody, and somehow she managed to lose the stopper down the toilet, beyond recall. This grotesque little incident seemed to upset her to a disproportionate degree: it was because she felt that, now that the war had begun in earnest, there was no excuse for any clumsiness in home nursing. The loss of the stopper suddenly seemed as severe a blow as the loss of a battleship. Life, which for two years had had a rather dreamlike quality, came instantly into sharp focus.

Any irresolution that Ross may have still possessed on December 6 evaporated when the bombs dropped on December 7. For a few desperate days, there was little he could do editorially. "The Japs got me this week," he wrote to Gibbs. The cover of the December 13 issue, a peaceful early wintertime barnyard scene by Ilonka Karasz, remained in place. Ross did tear up small chunks of "Comment" and "Talk," giving the lead spot illustration over to an amalgam of shells, submarines, parachutists, gunners, tanks, and planes; the spot drawing on the next page was of two sailors sharing a smoke.

Apart from Gibbs's ruminations about the sneak attack amid a football game, though, the only written evidence in the front of the book that the United States was now mobilized was a "Talk" piece by Russell Maloney and Philip Hamburger. Describing a visit to the Japanese consulate at Radio City "the day before the bombers flew over Honolulu," it captured the calm yet surreal scramble for visas on the eve of battle that spilled over into the Japan Institute across the hall:

We had a conversation, somewhat irritable on both sides, with a Mr. Shimanouchi, the assistant director of the Institute. He said there wasn't going to be any war, that the only reason the Institute was folding up was lack of funds, caused by the recent freezing of Japanese credits here. "The war bloc in Japan is just a small, influential group, like your America First people," Shimanouchi told us soothingly. "Japan is friendly, and desires peace in Asia." We mumbled something about the bombings in China, but he had a ready answer. "Chinamen are always dying anyway, in floods or epidemics," he told us. We hissed at Shimanouchi, without bowing, and broke off relations with him.

It was all quite preliminary. The next week, the December 20 issue was filled with reaction and outrage. "We're sure that a lot of very unpleasant things still lie ahead of us," Gibbs wrote in one of several paragraphs of "Comment," "but we doubt if anything can be much more unpleasant than the uncertainty, frustration, and bitterness that lay between Munich and Manila. On the whole, we'd say we feel much better now." There were "Talk" stories about blackout preparations, air raids, and similar domestic precautions. "Soldier," a poem by Harry Brown, drew on the Trojan War as an allegory ("It is not known what happened to his body./Dogs got it, perhaps, though it is to be presumed/That his wife and children, granting, of course, he had any,/Became slaves in, say, Argos. And Troy, of course, went down"). McKelway turned in a densely detailed "Reporter at Large" feature about fourteen compatriots who were inspired to enlist in the navy simultaneously.

There were also relevant cartoons. Charles Addams drew a pack of wolves chasing a German staff car. Carl Rose depicted a stout businessman asking a Japanese American from behind a chain-link internment screen, "Tell, me, Togo, where did you put the Napoleon brandy?" And Irvin turned in a grotesque, full-page image of two Nipponese dignitaries—complete with buck teeth, top hats, and swastika-swathed kimonos, backed by bombers and parachutists—announcing, "If you want to know who we are/We are the gentlemen of Japan."

Within a couple of weeks Gibbs made his own personal statement in a short story called "Some of the Nicest Guys You Ever Saw." Most of it was given over to a desultory barroom reminiscence of his days as a cadet in the Student Army Training Corps at the Hill School. It wrapped up with a haunting vision:

> The clear sky pricked with a million stars reminded him of the Germans. It was just the night for them. He looked up at the thin, silver spire of the Chrysler Building towering on his left, a block or so ahead. That would probably be the way the bastards would come, if they did—over from Long Island, flying high and fast, in strict and orderly formation.

The New Yorker had gone to war. And before long, that war would alter the fundamental character of the magazine—transforming it from a "gagmag" into a journalistic enterprise of unparalleled depth and dimension.

––––––––––

In many ways World War II was the perfect subject for *The New Yorker,* offering as it did the opportunity to cover readily identifiable, robust subjects in articles larded with the sort of tangible facts that Ross loved. And the sheer enormity of the conflict afforded the magazine an international scope that it could scarcely have imagined upon its founding. Staff members and freelancers like Walter Bernstein, E. J. Kahn, Jr., Joel Sayre, Daniel Lang, and Robert Lewis Taylor reported from far afield. The domestic front was rife with material, too. The draft, military training, gas shortages, ration booklets, gold-star mothers, military bureaucracy, shipbuilding, factory quotas, and other stateside issues were all grist for the pages.

The correspondent who set the tone for much of the coverage was A. J. Liebling. A Francophile, he wangled an assignment to the Continent in October 1939. He did so, as he put it, "by telling McKelway how well I could talk French. McKelway could not judge." For more than six months, he grappled to cover the boredom and strangeness of the *sitzkrieg*. But when the Germans smashed into France, he got caught up in the fate of Paris and fired off pieces filled with Rossian worm's-eye detail:

> By now there were perceptible changes in the daily life of Paris. There was no telephone service in the hotels, so you had to make a special trip afoot every time you wanted to tell somebody something. Taxis were harder than ever to find. My hotel, which was typical, had six floors. At the beginning of the war in September the proprietor had closed the fourth, fifth, and sixth floors. Now I was the only guest on the second floor, and there were perhaps a half dozen on the first. The staff, naturally, dwindled like the clientele. Every day somebody said goodbye to me. One by one the waiters left, and then it was the headwaiter, who had been kept on after all of his subordinates had been dismissed.

When Paris fell, Liebling groped his way back to the States. But he would soon enough return to the front, spending months in Tunisia and memorably setting foot on Omaha Beach on D-Day sixty-five minutes after H-hour. His account of a German shell fragment that hit both personnel and rations in a landing craft, turning its deck sticky with a sickening coagulation of blood and condensed milk, remains one of the best-remembered images of *New Yorker* war reporting. On battlefields and in tents, Liebling set down the same blunt prose that he had displayed with such fleshy domestic characters as Father Divine and the con man Hymie Katz.

"Liebling treated war as if it had been Times Square with bullets," wrote his biographer, Raymond Sokolov. His gusto extended to the off-hours; whenever he could, the gourmandizing correspondent indulged in all amenities available to him. Before leaving New York for Normandy, he took the precaution of shipping a pound of caviar to himself. "Then on Xmas Eve," he boasted, "I 'shared' it with some friends—8 oz. for me and the rest for them." He also reported, "At the price of a few tears you can sleep with any woman in England."

Another major war contributor was Gibbs's friend John Lardner. Although he wrote about the war for *Newsweek*, his most memorable pieces were done for *The New Yorker*. He filed memorable dispatches about the action in North Africa and Italy, ultimately ending up in the Pacific for the invasion of Okinawa. "John was naturally brave," wrote Liebling. "When he saw blinding bomb flashes at night, he used to walk *toward* them to see better."

In Lardner's case, the war struck home more personally than it did with any other contributor. His brother, James, had already been killed fighting for the Lincoln Brigade during the Spanish Civil War. Then in 1944 his brother David insisted on becoming a correspondent. While still in his early twenties, David was doing a yeoman's job at *The New Yorker*, writing "Talk" pieces, film reviews, the "Notes on Sports" department, and even Lois Long's old "Tables for Two" column. But he wanted to go to the front. Reluctantly, Ross acceded. David Lardner filed one dispatch while attached to the First Army—a "Letter From Luxembourg" that ran in the October 21 issue. Even before it appeared, however, Liebling telegraphed grim news to Shawn:

URGENT GET THIS TO BILL EVEN IF HE NOT IN OFFICE STOP DAVE LARDNER WAS KILLED THURSDAY NIGHT OCTOBER NINETEENTH STOP DAVE AND ANOTHER CORRESPONDENT WERE COMING OUT OF AACHEN IN JEEP STOP THEY GOT INTO MINEFIELD AND SET OFF THREE MINES STOP JEEP DRIVER WAS KILLED IMMEDIATELY STOP DAVE HAD MANY WOUNDS AND DIED THREE OR FOUR HOURS LATER STOP PRINCIPAL WOUND WAS HEAD INJURY RECEIVED WHEN HE HIT GROUND AFTER BLOWN FROM JEEP STOP.

Liebling signed off SORRY SORRY SORRY

Gibbs had the sad task of writing the brief obituary. He saluted the young Lardner as "a remarkably able and perceptive writer, and he was still very young—twenty-five—with almost everything left to be written. We liked and admired him as much as any man we have known, and we have never printed a paragraph with deeper sorrow than we print this one." Thurber, as always persnickety about *The New Yorker's* tendency to be "more bloodless than sophisticated," was responsible for that final wording. "I insisted that 'regret' be changed to 'sorrow,'" he wrote Lobrano, "telling Ross for God's sake not to let the magazine deteriorate into that vein." A dozen years after Lardner's death, he was still crowing about the change.

David Lardner may have been the only literal *New Yorker* casualty of the war. But losses of another sort arrived in the form of a manpower drain. At one point, more than thirty writers or artists were out of the office, and not all were reporting from the front. Many were simply in uniform. Their absence distressed Ross no end. "I don't know what will become of us," he told White. His concerns were not exaggerated. "The office is quite literally putting up a struggle for existence these days," Maloney said.

It did not help that John Mosher passed away suddenly on September 3, 1942, at the age of fifty. His death followed a tumultuous year during which his companion, Philip Claflin, enlisted in the army, his dog died of poisoning, and his heart began giving out. "I always had the feeling that the first serious thing that happened would knock him over," said a rueful Ross. Admire Mosher though he did, the resolutely heterosexual Gibbs had not particularly liked him, especially when the two shared an office and Mosher was having romantic trouble. ("I don't remember ever being more uncomfortable with anybody in my life.") But when he composed Mosher's obituary, Gibbs extolled the man as "witty, perceptive, and informed by a deep and tolerant knowledge of the world." It was not just public praise. Privately, Gibbs confided, "I wouldn't be surprised if he was the greatest wit I ever knew."

Ross, whose commitment to *The New Yorker* was total, could forgive death more readily than what he regarded as misguided notions of patriotism. Gus Lobrano put in for a navy commission pretty much over his boss's dead body. After lauding his fiction editor to the director of naval officer procurement as "sober, tactful, thoughtful, kind, patient," Ross added, "It is a wry pleasure that I take pleasure in commending him to you because he is what is called an important key man on this magazine, and I deplore the fact that the government is not, for the present, exempting from military service such important, older men, with wives and children to support." Lobrano didn't get his commission, so he spent weekends working as a stevedore for the Lehigh Valley Railroad, getting up at five a.m. to get to the North River docks along the southern Hudson. He made a good enough impression that he was able to lunch with the Lehigh's president; on that occasion, he complained about the conditions in the lavatory. "I'll bet you're the only man who uses it," the official responded.

Other editors accomplished what they could at a remove. Rogers E. M. Whitaker ended up at the Pentagon, attached to the supply service and working in the office of the chief of transportation. He managed some editing but made clear to Shawn that he was overwhelmed:

I am still shaking down into my work, have no secretary yet (she arrives *next* week), am going to school six hours a week, may be sent away to school (another one, which will be my third) for six weeks, may be transferred from Specialist Corps to the Army of the United States (I have already been told to make application), have a swollen arm (four injections in it), have to salute five hundred times a day, don't get enough sleep or enough to eat, have been too busy even to phone Hamburger and Hellman, think the Army is unnecessarily underrated by civilians in general, wish I didn't have to live in Washington, am losing a little weight, don't get The New Yorker (will someone put me on the mailing list?), haven't been paid a nickel yet, don't know when I'll ever see New York again, would like to know Hobey's address, and expect the war to end Sept. 17, 1945 (please file for reference).

In an altogether dissimilar vein was the curious case of St. Clair McKelway. Like Lobrano, he faced stiff opposition from Ross when he determined to sign up. "He considered that I was a deserter because I accepted a commission in the Air Force when the Air Force asked me to take one," he told Thurber. As if to tweak the editor, McKelway once underlined his rank of "Major" ten times in closing a letter he sent to the office and jotted, "Pvt. Ross please note."

The war brought out both the best and the worst in him. In 1942, after the famed Doolittle Raid on Tokyo, he published a trenchant "Comment" on how the military might have improved the promotion of this audacious, morale-boosting attack. McKelway's piece so impressed the top brass that he soon landed a spot as a public relations officer on the staff of Curtis LeMay. Assigned to the 21st Bomber Command of the Twentieth Air Force, he attained the rank of lieutenant colonel and was awarded a Presidential Unit Citation that Arthur Kober mistook for a Purple Heart.

Under LeMay, McKelway seemed to be in his element. He had long had a fascination with flying; back in 1919, perhaps inspired by the nonstop transatlantic journey of Alcock and Brown, he had penned a boyishly romantic ode to taking wing:

I

If you were a great big soldier man
With gold braid on your coat
How would you like to go up in a 'plane? [sic]
In a great big flying boat.

II

If you were a great big soldier man,
With gold braid on your pocket
How would you like to sail in a plane
And let the big wind sock—it?

III

If you were a great big soldier man
With gold braid on your cap
How would you like to sit in a cloud?
As you would in your mother's lap.

IV

If you were a great big soldier man
With a nice little boy like you
Don't you think you'd come down some nice spring day
And let him nose dive too?

McKelway saw duty in the China-Burma-India Theater and the Marianas and published an arresting four-part series shortly before Hiroshima about the activities of his unit, which conducted the first high-altitude precision bombing raids over Tokyo. In addition to relating the activities and the nuts and bolts of his unit, McKelway offered a vivid impression of his commander, LeMay: "He had the kind of toughness that comes from, or with, innate goodness and hard, clear honesty, especially when the possessor of such qualities has been faced, in his youth, with reality at its damnedest." He offered a soldier's stolid reflections on the conflict, e.g., "I do not know when again, in war or peace, any of us will have exactly the same feeling of a secret gathering of strength in a remote place for a great cause."

And he discussed his brothers in arms, concluding with the story of Staff Sergeant Henry Eugene Erwin of Bessemer, Alabama. During a March 1945 incendiary strike over Japan, a phosphorus bomb that he was supposed to drop on the enemy blew up in his face. Its smoke and fumes sent his B-29 into a spin. Blinded, scarred, spattered with white-hot phosphorus, Erwin somehow managed with his bare hands to toss the still-live twenty-pound monster out the window and save the plane. For this, he received the Medal of Honor.

McKelway faced his own form of danger. At one point, based in Guam, he was forced to land in a Japanese jungle and hide out incommunicado for three weeks for fear of any radio signals being intercepted. The incident was not without humor. An air force surgeon who was with him took the unexpected opportunity to psychoanalyze his current writer's block. At the end of the ordeal, the doctor declared, "I have the answer—it's very simple—you are a very lazy man!"

St. Clair McKelway was hardly lazy. His problem, rather, on top of his alcoholism, was bona fide mental illness. His symptoms did not become apparent until the war. But when they did, they exploded. By all indications, he suffered from some form of a multiple personality condition, convinced that within his brain there dwelt no fewer than "twelve separate and distinct heads." Shawn reckoned that eleven of them "were acutely romantic, one of them was practical and sensible, nine of them were imaginative, three of them were dangerously imaginative, three or four of them were industrious, and none of them were earthbound."

McKelway accorded each of these fellows a name in the form of a number and tried desperately to sort out their respective traits. Six, Seven, and Eight, for instance, were "on the whole, fairly level-headed chaps." Two and Three were a tad flighty, having once "gone off on a wild goose chase of overenthusiasm [sic] connected with the Times Literary Supplement." At the outset of his illness, he appeared to have had only two personalities, "one of them Presbyterian and the other King Henry VIII." But manifold visitors within his skull finally lanced him. By far "the most useless, reprehensible and all-round delinquent of the McKelway dozen" was "poor, doleful" Twelve, who "had never in his whole life had so much as a word of encouragement from the other eleven."

In Guam, McKelway's internal mental battle came to a head; he began having boozy blackouts and disappearing for a week at a time. Once he accidentally sent an uncoded message that gave the route of a B-24 that was carrying seven generals, including "Vinegar Joe" Stilwell and Field Marshal Harold Alexander. Had the Japanese intercepted it, they surely would have shot the plane down. Gradually, against a backdrop of liquor, four bouts of malaria, and the hothouse atmosphere of the jungle, McKelway came unglued. At the same time, in a classic case of interservice rivalry, he was convinced that the all-powerful navy was hampering the operations of the fledgling air force and grabbing credit for its victories.

The blow-up came in the spring of 1945 when the navy prepared to issue a press release that McKelway somehow thought would endanger future B-29 operations and maybe even goad the Japanese into bombing Iwo Jima, which was by now under American control. Invoking an obscure regulation that allowed a press censor to protest directly to the War Department under certain circumstances, he fired off to Washington an obscenity-filled dispatch that accused Admiral Chester Nimitz of high treason. "I got more and more worked up as I wrote," McKelway recalled, "and toward the end the things I said seemed to me muddle-headed if not hysterical." Among other rants, he charged Nimitz with the "compulsive practice of fellatio."

The fallout was rapid. As soon as McKelway's superiors got wind of what he had done, they gently confined him to the medical ward. Word of the incident reached all the way to General of the Air Force Henry "Hap" Arnold, who reportedly yelled, "Kill the s.o.b.!" McKelway was neither killed nor court-martialed but rather was whisked out of Guam and shipped stateside into the arms of Walter Reed. Years later he would record the bizarre episode in a rambling, detail-choked but wholly coherent story called "The Blowing of the Top of Peter Roger Oboe." By his account, when he subsequently met Nimitz at a cocktail party at the Overseas Press Club, they greeted each other cordially, the admiral perhaps not realizing who he was.

Back in midtown, Ross faced concerns of his own. The government was clamping down on the use of paper for civilian purposes. *New Yorker* employees had to endure such preemptive measures as blackouts and air raids—mixed up with their usual neuroses, as Maloney told the Whites:

> As you doubtless know, we had our first genuine air-raid alarm last week. The alternate senior post warden, Post 6 and 10, Sector B, Zone 1, 17th Precinct (me) was out on the street in a twinkling, fully equipped and still sound asleep. Lee Simonson came charging out of the house next door, waving a flashlight, so I said to him, in the reasonable tone of a warden soothing a frantic citizen, "Lights out, sir." "Don't go Captain Stanhope on me," he said.* Miriam and I are both wardens, but we have only one helmet between us, as yet. With the most chivalrous intentions in the world, I can never make up my mind whether to make her wear it, or wear it myself. If it's a real raid, the helmet is useful armor, of course; but the chances are heavily against any given helmet being genuine, and in that case the wearer of the helmet just looks like a fool. Generally speaking, the wardens were pretty efficient in the emergency; it was the higher-ups that fell apart. Probably

---

* A reference to a central character in R. C. Sherriff's *Journey's End*, originally played in 1928 by Laurence Olivier.

you read that the big siren in Radio City never sounded, because the man who was supposed to sound it somehow got the door to the roof stuck so he couldn't open it.

Far more important, the staff was hemorrhaging. Maloney referred to those who were left in the office as "little 4f's and 4h's at 25 West 43rd st [sic]." Daise Terry reported to Katharine White that of the fifty-nine people on one editorial floor, "a dozen or more are wandering through the halls with batches of proofs till 9, 10 and 12 o'clock at night, and on Sundays a crew of 6 or 8 is here till all hours." To Andy, Terry confided, "I practically live in the office now. It's a funny place; Mr. Gibbs says The New Yorker is now a bunch of giggling women and pickaninnies—the latter category being made up of two office boys, the most colorful and interesting members of the staff at the moment."

The lack of able bodies was so acute that the magazine was forced to hire a substitute telephone receptionist. He was 4F, supposedly because of a bad heart. Little did the staff realize the real reason he was available. "About 7 o'clock the old board was blazing with lights and the buzzers roaring and nobody responding," said Terry. "Bashing out to see what was wrong, [we] found the boy writhing on the floor in an epileptic fit!" At one point, she simply surrendered to the realities of the war: "Things move in such mysterious and underground methods that I've given up trying to figure out who is who and what he does. I honestly don't believe anyone here knows the whole setup at present; one hears on all sides the question 'who is he (or she) and what does he do?'"

There was one bright spot to this disorganization—namely, the blossoming of William Shawn. In his own quiet way, he was a formidable character, his soft yet indomitable persona earning him the nickname "The Iron Mouse." Born "William Chon" in Chicago in 1907, he put in two years at the University of Michigan and, when not playing piano in nightclubs in both the States and in Paris, struck out as a reporter for various papers and news services, including the obscure Las Vegas (New

Mexico) *Optic*. He was drawn to *The New Yorker* in the early 1930s and got his start by contributing freelance "Talk" pieces.

Shawn's specialty was carrying out legwork for Alva Johnston and other reporters. He earned minor sums for background research into such varied subjects as the Roosevelt family, the New York City bartenders' union, deaf-mutes, the ushers at Radio City, the Gulf Stream, General Electric, gangsters, bridges that spanned buildings, and "freaks." By the end of 1933, Ross had hired him for the "Talk" staff. Slowly, unobtrusively, he set about carving out a domain; by 1939 Ross was calling him "shepherd of the fact stuff." Unlike the boisterous, roughhewn Ross, Shawn was courteous, soft-spoken, and discreet.* But to Ross, what mattered was that this small, slight man had an enormous capacity for clear thinking and all manner of editorial work. Ross was palpably relieved when it became evident that the army would not snatch him. "Shawn is now highly eligible, on paper," he told White, "but by God I don't think he would make a soldier."

Shawn was a perceptive judge of talent, especially as the staff became ever more thinly stretched. He was quick to grasp Gibbs's value in many capacities to the magazine. "Gibbs is the perfect New Yorker personality in Ross's mind," he said. "Ross feels that Gibbs can do no wrong."

Yet even as Gibbs's all-around utility was manifesting itself more strongly than ever, he was beset by personal challenges. His father-in-law died in May 1939. His mother passed away the following January. Uncle George, who had footed the bill for Gibbs's education, and seen to it that his nephew was brought up in safe surroundings, followed her a few months later. Then in May 1942, Gibbs's cousin and mentor Alice Duer Miller succumbed. Amid these family heartaches, rais-

---

* After Shawn died, his image would be tarnished by revelations—not exactly unknown to many associates—that he had long had an extramarital affair and raised a child with *The New Yorker* reporter Lillian Ross, who was no relation to Harold Ross.

ing Tony and Janet, and doing his theater work, Gibbs largely stopped going to the office ("too many children and fairies," he grumbled) and functioned almost exclusively "in squalor" from home. At the same time, absent various workhorses, Ross had to lean on Gibbs to fill in on miscellaneous duties.

So on top of writing "Comment" and the theater column, contributing stories and sketches, and editing in general, Gibbs reluctantly returned to the cartoon slush pile. And in the wake of David Lardner—who had followed Mosher as movie critic—he got stuck with reviewing films. With increasing weariness, from December 1944 to September 1945, he found himself screening such divergent fare as *Son of Lassie, The Three Caballeros, A Tree Grows in Brooklyn, Colonel Blimp,* and *God Is My Co-Pilot.* Occasionally he was entertained, but on the whole the experience left him disillusioned and exhausted. When he turned in his final cinematic copy, he hoped it would be "the last movie piece I'll have to write this side of the grave." He summed up his frustrations in a fierce essay, "The Kingdom of the Blind," for *The Saturday Review of Literature.* "It is my indignant opinion," he wrote, "that ninety percent of the moving pictures exhibited in America are so vulgar, witless, and dull that it is preposterous to write about them in any publication not intended to be read while chewing gum." Content and aesthetics aside, he spent a good deal of space attacking the "small but fascinating literary comedy" of film reviewing itself. He scored the racket in general, pointing up the average movie critic's tendency to rely on flabby adjectives when afforded only a limited amount of time and equally limited space:

The result is that he has developed a very special vocabulary in which words come to transcend their exact and customary meanings—in which, in a sense, they are detached from the language and inflated like little balloons, and presently sent spinning, lovely, iridescent, and meaningless, into the wild, blue heaven of critical prose. "Luminous" is such a word. . . . "Taut" is

another . . . There are a great many of these wonderful words—
"haunting," "lyric," "brave," "tender," "compassionate," and, above
all, "poignant" occur to me in passing—and they are invaluable in
imparting such a comic air to a conversation that it is never quite
apparent just what precisely is being discussed.

White was so impressed by this analysis that he included an excerpt of
it in *The Elements of Style*.

That was to come later. For the moment, Gibbs was more concerned
about keeping the pages filled. The grind of the war was wearing. "It
probably doesn't sound exhausting to write 2500 words of criticism a
week; it is, though, especially when you have to look at ten or twelve
of the God damn things, film and flesh," he told the novelist Joseph
Hergesheimer. "Last week I reviewed no less [*sic*] than four moving pictures and three plays, and the next few weeks look no easier. All this stuff
(and, by the living God that made us, stuff it is) has to be written over
the week-ends [*sic*]. I think I shall just have to be denounced by you and
Mr. Mencken, with whom, however, I'll be in spirit. I'm sorry, but I am
employed by a war and there is nothing to be done about it."

He broached his burden to Shawn:

Unlike White I am capable of turning out two or at the most three
pieces a week which to me seem respectable. Confronted, however, with the responsibility for an entire department, I find (A)
that the pressure keeps me from doing good originals and (B) that
the rewrite, naturally written in various idioms, usually ends up
by sounding like an inane parody of White. The fact, I'm afraid, is
that I have very little enthusiasm for messing around with other
people's work and, although I spend hell's own amount of time
on it, it comes out dead as a mackerel. . . . I want to go on record
as saying that I can't work this way permanently, spending at least
fifty percent of my time doing stuff that bores me to death, or else

sitting around worrying about it, so that I can't write anything I want to.

Quite apart from the crushing workload, Gibbs felt he was doing a poor job with "Comment" and could not live up to White's standard. "The last time I looked at it," Gibbs confessed, "all the items began 'Plucking at the counterpane of the future' and wound up 'his broken heart comma his little bankrupt dreams.' Readers are not going to stand much more of this kind of crap, and I myself am tired of people in restaurants whispering 'That's Gibbs, the pansy mystic.'"

Ross was aware of Gibbs's struggle. Even before Pearl Harbor, the editor fretted that the writer was "fidgety" about filling "Comment" and confided to Katharine that he was always relieved when her husband could submit editorial observations:

At least three of those comments, [sic] were superb, absolutely first class White and there's nothing better. The rest were all right certainly, and all told they were a God-send [sic]. They braced Gibbs up considerably. My diagnosis of his panics on Comment is that he gets the quakes when he thinks of the long yawning gap ahead with no help in sight and spends his time worrying instead of working. If he has help he relaxes and works. White's sending in a big batch of comment [sic] resulted in Gibbs doing an equally large batch and putting us well ahead. . . . Gibbs is worn out and stale and needs help, and God knows is entitled to it if we can give it to him.

Strangely, even after almost twenty years of speaking for the magazine on and off, White continued to wonder about his ability to do so. He was proud of his "Comment" contributions, as signaled by his desire in the mid-1930s to sign his name to them. Still, he was not entirely sure that he had mastered the form in particular or his voice in general. "Don't be discouraged if you never learn anything about the English language," he once told Alice Burchfield. "She is a very fickle mistress. I have made love to her for ten years with scarce a smile for my pains."

Ross had no such doubts. He was determined to get White back into the book and was frustrated when he couldn't. "He has gone to Maine and writes about ewes," Ross told Benchley. "If I ever read about another ewe I am going to cut my throat and leave my body to the Office of Production Management to be made into soap." It was true enough; White was focused on his farm and *Harper's*. Some of his entries for the monthly publication were strained ("Morning comes and bed is a vise from which it is almost impossible to get free") and even inaccurate ("Hitler and I are about the same age").

But in general White was becoming more broad-minded and worldly—quite a change from the time when writing about "the small things of the day" contented him. A good example is one of his last "One Man's Meat" pieces, wherein he took up the subject of capitalism and profits and the nature of *homo sapiens* in relation to both. He began his essay with an account of a hook that had been put through his cow's nose. From there, he transitioned easily into a reflection on the controlling, dehumanizing effect of money:

> The true shape of man is an elusive thing. One thing I am sure of—he is a natural-born gambler whose normal instincts in this regard have long been frustrated. He has commonly been interested less in security than in gain, less in safety than in risk, and he has always been a fool for anything that gave him a chance at the jackpot . . . Low wages infuriate him, but all wages bore him. The trouble with the profit system, as far as this man was concerned, was that he seemed to bear no relation to the result. It could prosper without his prospering too. He felt lonely and out of things. It could fail and he still felt lonely and in need of another job.

Shawn seized on these words. "I found it distinctly painful to read White's piece," he told Ross. "If ever anything belonged in *The New Yorker,* that did. It's White in one of his best veins, I think, and on a theme that is exactly right for us. In a wartime Comment department, we need something like that occasionally, something of importance—solid but not heavy. I wish that you, or we, could prevail upon White to do more along these lines for us."

As it turned out, Ross didn't have to. White had done well enough with his *Harper's* stint, and his collected columns won the Limited Editions Club's Gold Medal, presented every three years to the author of a book likely to achieve "classic" status. So powerful was the reach of this anthology that when a Japanese sniper broke into the office of a public relations officer in the Marianas, the intruder stole a copy of it. "Although some one might accuse you of giving aid and comfort to the enemy," Roger Angell confided in his stepfather, "at least it is an enemy with pretty good literary tastes."

But while "One Man's Meat" had given him space and a byline, White realized he was bound by inclination and expression to *The New Yorker.* "Running a column in your paper has been a lot of fun, not to say a privilege, and I'd like nothing better than to feel that I was able to go right on doing," he told *Harper's* editor Frederick Lewis Allen in March 1943. "But I don't, and I know that nothing can change that."

And so, with as much wiggle room as he could negotiate, White agreed to resume writing "Comment" on a more or less regular basis in early 1943. Ross could not have been happier, given that he could not afford Gibbs's self-proclaimed inability to weigh forth weekly on an entire world locked in mortal combat. He offered White considerable freedom and emoluments:

Well, I am, of course, greatly pleased. The [*Harper's*] column was always a sour dish to me because of the circumstances, the principal circumstances being that I thought it deprived us of your

Comment and casual writings, and that was always hard to take. You'll have to admit, however, that although I was dutifully persistent, I was tactful. What I'd like tactfully to do now is divert that wordage here but I haven't got any arguments other than the old ones, and I won't go into them, except to say that I think the opportunity for you to do something with the Comment department is golden and that I wish for all concerned, including the people of the United States, that you would size [sic] it. Or I'll say that I hope you do. . . . We're willing to make any kind of deal you want on Comment, as well as on anything else, as you so well know from wheedlings [sic] in the past. If a regular income is a factor (I will treat of [sic] this subject very carefully) that can easily be arranged, too, possibly with a bonus to pay your taxes with at the end of the year. Or any such. . . . Of course, we can fix up a weekly income proposition without any specific oblications [sic] on your part, any that might be a burden.

Ross's blandishments notwithstanding, White found it difficult to return to *The New Yorker*. He and Katharine had made a life for themselves in Maine, ewes and all. Resettling in busy Manhattan would be an adjustment. There were other issues: in Katharine's absence, Gus Lobrano had established himself as master of the fiction department. He had not only inherited from his predecessor a stable of contributors "whom Katharine was not quite comfortable handling" but had recruited many others. Now he was faced with the return of his self-assured mentor to the office. Lobrano may not have been caught entirely by surprise. Katharine's observations to him about office procedure and editing amid the flurry of her departure for Maine were as clear as her hope that she could somehow continue to have a hand in executing them:

Now, of course, promptness in handling [manuscripts] involves much more than sending out the check. It involves getting the piece read and getting Mr. Ross to read it and okay it. Then it involves getting the piece edited. We used to keep in our minds the pieces that we had written opinions on and sent to Mr. Ross and if he seemed to delay in replying on them we followed him up through Mr. Winney or Mr. Shuman. More often than not a piece that is delayed in his reply you will find in your discussion folder. I used to wander in to Mr. Winney's desk and look through my discuss folder almost every day. If there was stuff in it that it would be advisable to have an answer on before the regular weekly Mr. Ross-discuss-period I would ask for a special session if he were in town. This doesn't often happen but once in awhile [*sic*] it is advisable. As soon as Mr. Ross says to buy a piece, unless it can be paid for by a flat payment, Mr. Gibbs and I used to put the editing of that piece as a first call, the only thing taking precedence over it being red tag timely stuff to read for opinion. Occasionally we would get stalled in editing a piece and keep postponing it. That will happen to anybody. You try editing a piece and it just doesn't work. If that were the case we would sometimes admit defeat and ask the other person to try editing it. Perhaps you too will find me useful, and each other useful, on such occasions.

There was no doubt that Katharine was useful, or that both she and her husband loved Lobrano. He was their "dear friend," Katharine said, and indeed "Andy's oldest and closest, almost." The feeling was mutual. "Everybody thought she was wonderful," said Lobrano's daughter, Dorothy. "But everybody had their problems with her. She was very regal." With her return, things were never quite the same among the three old comrades. Katharine did not insist on completely recapturing her domain, yet she would not be ignored. To her credit, she sensed the tension inherent in her reappearance. She acknowledged it was "a difficult, sticky situation calling for tact on both our parts. I had trained Lobrano to be an editor, and now he was my boss." Compounding the matter,

Lobrano suffered from what Thurber called a "unique cycle of apprehension." Still, despite occasional disagreements over manuscripts, they had "many, many happy times together during that period."

As for White, he was soon busy batting out weekly "Comment" again with his customary aplomb. Almost immediately he would be making some of the most far-reaching political observations of his life. In the meantime, he allowed himself an ample measure of his old fun. Shortly after D-Day, he applauded the adjutant general's order to keep "books which are full of political implications" out of the hands of servicemen. This list of banned works included *One Man's Meat*. Reveling in being placed on a sort of literary enemies' list, White cheekily fessed up that at least three of this subversive volume's entries "were deliberately calculated to influence the soldier vote."

> One of the essays was about the catarrhal trouble of Daniel Webster, a notorious Whig; another was about the opening of the World's Fair, a bald excursion into internationalism; and the third was a thinly veiled fiction piece about a boy and a sick sheep, a story so drenched with political implications that it gives us the Republican twitches just to think of it.

CHAPTER 12

—————

"THE MORAL CLIMATE
IS AGAINST IT"

In 1946 Simon and Schuster published a book called *While You Were Gone: A Report on Wartime Life in the United States,* a collection of essays meant to appeal both to those on the home front, as a sort of taking of domestic stock, and to returning veterans, as a primer on what they had missed. The contributors included Allan Nevins, Margaret Mead, Norman Corwin, Carey McWilliams, Lewis Gannett, Thurber, and Gibbs. Gibbs's entry, titled simply, "The Theatre," offered many examples of plays both good and bad from the previous four years, as well as some critical thoughts about drama in general. He concluded with what was for him an uncharacteristically humane observation—that the Broadway he had been so glibly covering would never be the same, with much of its future content to be informed by an unprecedented holocaust of man's own making:

> The young men who have known the dull, dirty, murderous business of war at first hand are still to be heard from. Many of them are still in Europe or the Pacific, and it is still too soon to expect very much from those who have come back. The atom bomb, too,

is bound to call for certain readjustments in any serious play-wright's thought. The appalling explosions that mushroomed over Hiroshima and Nagasaki shook the foundations of every idea in the world, and men need a little while to look around and think.

Gibbs knew what those "appalling explosions" meant. So did Ross. When, in *The New Yorker* of August 31, 1946, he put forth the 31,347 words that would later be issued in book form as *Hiroshima,* he took the magazine in an irrevocable new direction. This journalistic landmark by John Hersey was, *The New Yorker* suggested upon his death in 1993, "the most famous magazine article ever published." For Ross, it was certainly the most significant. "I don't think I've ever got as much satisfaction out of anything else in my life," he told Irwin Shaw.

Hersey was an expatriate of the Luce domain. His uncanny biograph-ical overlap with Gibbs's "baby tycoon"—birth in China, education at Yale, membership in Skull and Bones, postgraduate work in England—had been fortuitous. But Hersey broke with Time-Life when he realized he could no longer abide his boss's ever mounting slanting of the news. He found a more conducive atmosphere with Ross, for whom he filed a number of fine war stories, including "Survival," which pretty much enshrined John F. Kennedy as the hero of *PT-109.* His Pulitzer Prize for his novel *A Bell for Adano* was another coup. Now he found himself grappling with the human toll of the atomic bomb.

The idea for the piece was Shawn's. After all the newspaper ink that had been spilled about the twin atomic attacks, Ross's right-hand man was not especially concerned with the scientific principles or the military thinking that lay behind the bombs. With an editor's instinct, Shawn sought a close-up angle on the actual effects of their unique horror. The story came together in improvisation and haste. Hersey arrived in Japan in late May 1946 and spent a mere three weeks collecting material from both official and unofficial subjects. Soon enough he produced some 150 pages that floored Ross, despite some 200 queries on his part. *The*

New Yorker's founder grasped the power of Hersey's understated, close-up reporting and its focus on six survivors. It was, Ross told Rebecca West just as Hersey's work was about to hit the stands, "one of the most remarkable stories I have ever seen." Moreover,

> It wasn't a series of pieces, as our series go, and it couldn't be, by its nature, and we finally decided that it wouldn't work as a serial, so we decided to use it all at one time, although it would take most of an issue. After a couple of days more of reflection, we got into an evangelical mood and decided to throw out all the other text in the issue, and make a gesture that might impress people.... [N]ext week's issue will be a very peculiar one. I don't know what people will think but a lot of readers are going to be startled.

Originally scheduled for the first anniversary of the Hiroshima bombing, Hersey's work ran a few weeks later. The timing didn't matter; the piece was pivotal and, by most accounts, changed the orientation of the magazine. Never before had *The New Yorker* engaged in such a radical departure from its familiar format; virtually the entire number was given over to Hersey's account, the better to heighten its impact. No cartoons graced the sixty-eight pages, lest they detract from the tenor of the story. As unhappy as much of the magazine's war reporting had been, it had generally included dabs of irony and dark humor.

But this was different. "I've just read that long Hiroshima article from beginning to end," one woman told Helen Hokinson, "and I just wish you'd tell me what was funny about it!" She would have done well to have read the editor's preface: "The New Yorker this week devotes its entire editorial space to an article on the almost complete obliteration of a city by one atomic bomb, and what happened to the people of that city.* It does so in the conviction that few of us have yet comprehended the all

---

* This was not quite accurate; the "Goings On About Town" listings ran as usual.

but incredible destructive power of this weapon, and that everyone might well take time to consider the terrible implications of its use."

Apart from showmanship, Ross had a handle on his readership. A veteran himself, he realized that the millions of servicemen who had come back were forever changed. Many were now *New Yorker* readers, having gotten hooked on an undersized, slimmed-down "pony" edition of the magazine distributed to them overseas. Above all, he grasped that a new world was dawning for humankind and his brainchild alike.

Like Ross and Gibbs, White recognized what was going on. In a bitter poem called "Alamogordo," he despaired of manmade fission and envisioned the site of the first atomic blast as a national tourist trap:

Build the museum, O builders! Have it ready for me when I come.
Then, when the radioactivity has been dissipated and the rays no
    longer threaten my white corpuscles,
Letter the proper sign and let me in. And don't forget
To give the date. I like dates.
July 16, 1945.
Give the hour, the minute, the very second of the blast.
Exactly five-thirty A.M. "Beginning of the atomic age."
Alamogordo, Alamogordo—my last pilgrimage. Earliest bomb crater
    in the atomic world. Most famous deathsite [sic].
Note, ladies and gentlemen, how the effect radiates in all directions,
With color and shading gradually growing darker like the petals of
    a flower.
Those who are hungry will find an appetizing, moderately priced
Meal in the Nuclear Snack Bar, just outside the gate, and
Clean rest rooms.
Take home a souvenir of atomsite [sic] for the children.

For much of the first half of the 1940s, White had been concerned with war. Now he determined to occupy himself with peace. This he did by pressing the cause of world government. At the time, the notion that nations might cede their own prerogatives and spheres of influence, and form a sort of global congress, was not preposterous. After all, it was inevitable that other countries would get the Bomb and bring about the specter of utter destruction. Anyway, if democracies could join Communists to defeat fascists, then anything was possible.

It was a romantic, even messianic mission that had begun as long before as 1940 when White declared, "I have given up planning a perfect state for America, as it is too small a field. Henceforth I shall design only world societies, which will include everybody and everything." Now White stumped regularly for globalization in "Comment." By one estimate, nearly a third of his contributions to that section, starting in the issue of April 10, 1943, and extending into 1947, contained at least one paragraph about his vision. "Science is universal, music is universal, sex is universal, chow is universal, and by God government better be, too," he wrote Ross in 1944. His exhortations accelerated when, in April 1945, he covered the San Francisco Conference, which yielded the United Nations. In two "Reporter at Large" dispatches, he could barely contain his enthusiasm at the prospect of supranational cooperation:

> I just went on down the hall to the big press room, where forty or fifty men and women, of several shades of color and many shades of opinion, were belaboring the keys. The room had the wonderful sound that orchestras make just before they swing into action. I sat down and began tuning an Underwood and studying the notes of the New World Symphony. Next to me sat a girl reporter from, I think, one of the local papers. She was relaxed in front of a still typewriter and was deep in a magazine. I glanced cautiously at the title. It was called *Fantastic Adventures*.

A typical "Comment" entry of his during this period attempted to debunk the idea that countries were inevitable, organic constructs:

Neither the Russian people nor the American people nor any people have as yet seen the essentially fictitious character of the nation. The nation still persists in people's minds as a tangible, solid, living and breathing thing, capable of doing and thinking, feeling and believing, having and enjoying. But the nation is not that at all. A nation is a state of mind. . . . [T]here is no such thing as Russia—unless you are satisfied with a bear. . . . There is no such thing as the U.S.—unless you are satisfied with an uncle.

In writing this way, White fretted that he was going too far with his opinions. The largely apolitical Ross offered reassurance, albeit more along editorial than ideological lines. "I say dismiss any fear that you might make the magazine a crank publication," the editor told his resident idealist. He called White's squibs "the most eloquent things you have ever written and magnificent. My viewpoint is that if the people of the earth don't get a new set-up, they are being offered a very remarkable line of writing and thinking anyhow." On that basis White in 1946 accepted an offer from Houghton Mifflin to publish a collection of his editorials. Reviewing the result, *The Wild Flag*, in *Partisan Review*, Robert Warshow said that the author "has good will and intelligence, and he is trying to live up to his responsibilities as a citizen."

Unfortunately, as history proved, White's earnest efforts went nowhere. He later admitted to "eating some of the words" in *The Wild Flag* and would come to regard it as "a little uninformed and half-baked." He had written his pieces before China turned Red, and he realized that in their naïveté, he and other do-gooders "had no conception at that time of what the Soviet Union would do." Nonetheless, he would continue to stress the need for cooperation. "I don't think there's an independent country any more," he said. "All are interdependent."

For the moment, interdependence was elusive. The prevailing ethos was one of anxiety laced, when possible, with black humor, as the longtime *New Yorker* secretary Tom Gorman signaled to the staff:

The Civil Defense Organization of this building will hold a practice evacuation at exactly 3 P.M. on Wednesday, February 28,
1951. At that time whistles will be blown. Please leave your offices
immediately and gather in front of the elevators. The operators
have been instructed to take 20th Floor personnel to the 10th
Floor. Of course, there will be the usual trumpet solos and other
entertainment during the descent.

As they had during the prelude to World War II, individual contributors
reacted in their own ways. Identifying himself with Eisenhower, Thurber
thought it "rather foolish to hold the respect we do for ex-Communists,
that is, people who once tried to overthrow the Government" [sic]. But he
made clear his distress that excessive worry about the Red menace was
hampering free expression: "If we don't stop suspecting all writers, it will
be a severe blow to our culture. I think all writers, even the innocent ones,
are scared. There's guilt by association, guilt by excoriation, there's guilt by
everything the politicians invent. . . . [W]e're living in the most frightened
country in the world."

In late 1947 White won widespread approval for publicly opposing
the firing of the Hollywood Ten. His prewar "genteel, hand-wringing
style" had been "about half-Thurber and half-Zasu Pitts," wrote the
Springfield, Ohio, *Sun*. Now, said the newspaper, "this talented fellow
looks a lot better in his shirtsleeves, out in the arena, than he ever did in
his Brooks Brothers jacket, dreamily sniffing the carnation in his lapel."
At this time as well, White published in the *New York Herald Tribune* one
of his most famous declarations of conscience, which began,

I am a party of one, and I live in an age of fear. Nothing lately
has unsettled my party and raised my fears so much as your editorial on Thanksgiving Day, suggesting that employees should
be required to state their beliefs in order to hold their jobs. The
idea is inconsistent with our Constitutional theory and has been

stubbornly opposed by watchful men since the early days of the Republic.

Even Gibbs, whose politics were as hard to pin down as Ross's, signed his name—along with about forty others, ranging from Norman Cousins to Helen Hayes—to a statement by Americans for Democratic Action that opposed Communism and hysteria alike.

This social consciousness may have been laudable, but it was not exactly consistent with *The New Yorker*'s ostensible focus on gaiety and satire. Part of this was due to the passage of time; the magazine had been born in a raucous age more than twenty years earlier. On many an occasion, Thurber publicly regretted the accelerating absence of jocular writers like Frank Sullivan, Ogden Nash, S. J. Perelman, Dorothy Parker, and Corey Ford. "No one has come along to take their place," he complained. "The depression did something to us. The kids became serious after 1930. The colleges don't turn out men who write humor."

His ever more irascible comments in this vein, while not always well received by his colleagues, could not be entirely dismissed. Ross himself moaned to Nash, as *The New Yorker* was on the cusp of its twenty-fifth anniversary, that "not one (or more than one or two at the outside) humorous writers" of any note had lately emerged: "I don't know whether it's the New Deal or Communist infiltration or the law of averages, or what, but I do know that if I'd known how little talent was going to develop I'd have got into some other line of work years ago."

Ross did his best to serve the God of humor and the Caesar of seriousness. In one of his few public appearances during this interval, he managed to appease both simultaneously. In 1949, finding himself with some frequency in Grand Central Terminal as he commuted to and from Stamford, he backed a *New Yorker* campaign that opposed the airing of commercial broadcasts and music over the facility's public address system. This quixotic crusade inspired many protests to the New York

State Public Service Commission about the broadcasts and culminated in a widely covered public hearing shortly before Christmas. Turned out nattily in a necktie monogrammed with his initials, Ross as the star witness characterized himself as an "editor of an adult comic book." As a transcript reveals, he remained more than capable of humbling the mighty by mocking them.

Q: Would you like to give your impression of the advertising by this public-address system?

A: In the first place, I think it is a semi-swindle. No person can think of two things at the same time. You try to read a newspaper and that thing is going, and you don't hear that, either; so these advertisers are being largely swindled. You don't hear anything distinctly; there is just a ringing in your ears.

Q: Why is that? Because of the volume of tone or the quality of sound?

A: I am no radio engineer. The New York Central seems to be able to run trains, but they do not seem to be able to run their elevators or a radio system.

Q: Do you find that in different parts of the station the radio volume varies?

A: It varies, but it is all bad. As to the employees there, I I [sic] would like to advocate one thing, and that is a secret vote of the employees in the Terminal who must be going slowly nuts there, and I also think that the Fact Finder ought to be examined. He found that 84.7 per cent [sic]—whatever it is—love this kiddie stuff. There is an organization I am told about in our place, called Datum Diggers, who found that 86.8 per cent [sic] do not like it.

The broadcasts were discontinued not long afterward, even though Ross thought his testimony "practically incoherent" and wished he had been better prepared.

There was joshing to be had on other fronts. In his casual "Preposterous Parables: The Decline of Sport," White predicted that by 1975 spectator pastimes like football games, horse racing, and boxing would be vaporized by such events as a deranged shooting spree and a mass crash-up on one of the country's emerging superhighways. Gibbs applauded this mordant contribution while despairing its atypical appearance:

> Your sports parable is a very fine piece, though quite a shock since I had an idea humor was supposed to be against the rules around here. The moral climate is against it. Right at this minute there is a son of a bitch down the hall (Bainbridge) writing a thirty-two part profile of Stalin, and somewhere east of th [sic] water cooler Liebling is trying to beat a little social consciousness into the Wayward Press department, and somebody else is writing a short story beginning "Cress Delahunty, who was thirteen years old but looked awful, asked her mother if she sould [sic] stay all night with her friend Irma in a sump hole."

Quite apart from postwar politics, the core of *The New Yorker* crew found itself confronting personal considerations that often kept them from writing in a lighthearted manner. For one thing, there were health issues.

It was inevitable that by the war years, the *New Yorker*'s guiding lights would not be exempt from physical maladies. White had already had a vague "nervous crack-up" in the summer of 1943; he cured it mainly by taking showers, drinking dry sherry, working with hand tools, and playing old records until there was "no wax left in the grooves." But the following March he "decided to go to a doctor about my head, as there seems to be a kite caught in the branches somewhere." At the beginning of 1945, he complained about how it had taken eighteen months to get rid of certain "mice in the subconscious." Reflecting her affinity with her husband, Katharine underwent a spell of depression just as Andy was having his own; in her case, the main underlying problem was a hysterectomy. Ross's ulcers became legend; they were bad enough that a drink for him was a rarity. So foul was his potent medication, Amphojel, that he diluted it with the cream that his assistant Dan Pinck regularly purchased.

Gibbs, never exactly robust, was sick as well. For much of the first half of 1947, he was hospitalized for lung problems related to his heavy smoking; the diagnoses ranged from pneumonia to tuberculosis. His condition was so severe that when one physician examined his dark X-ray, he thought he was looking at a photographic negative. Still, Gibbs continued to dispatch correspondence to the office. "I'll close now," he wrote to Lobrano, "as somebody wants to look down my throat." It was finally determined that he was suffering from pleurisy. The treatment was brutal: just to get a scope into Gibbs's lungs required pulling some of his teeth. The surgeons ended up taking out two of his ribs, leaving him lopsided enough that afterward he sometimes wore suits tailored with extra padding; the scar extended from his rib cage to the back of his shoulder blade. But the radical procedure worked. "The spot was the size of an orange," Gibbs reported, "[and] now is the size of a lime."

Ross was happy to provide him with some respite. "Do not bother your beautiful head with financial worries," the editor told him. "Don't give it a second thought."* For his feeding and care, Ross got his money's worth. Despite his illness Gibbs managed to publish a casual, "Where Was I?," which made sport of his recovery: "I've still got a little deficiency. You know, on the hemoglobin. Couple of million or so. Hardly worth

---

* Liebling admitted he was jealous that Ross had extended this generosity to Gibbs: "That was white of him, I thought, but he had never said that to me. It was a true sibling emotion."

mentioning." Not much later he offered up a sequel of sorts, "Mewow, Mewow, Mewow," wherein he described a postconvalescent reunion with Janet that was both gossipy and poignant. "*Dear* Daddy!" she exclaims in welcoming him back from the hospital. "Goodness I love you so!"

McKelway also had his struggles with the flesh. Although he shook off his jungle fever, he found himself convalescing in a hospital in Pasadena a good year beyond war's end with a leftover insect infestation. "The damned things are like tapeworms, each being from five to ten inches in length," he informed Lobrano, "and they have been sitting down there in my intestines eating expensive food and drinking light wines and beer for God knows how long, evidently since Guam."

Nobody had more heartbreaking bouts with bad health than Thurber. His need to draw, to write, to communicate, was soul defining. As his eyesight dissolved, he talked ever more and literally reached out, his hands insistently twitching and feeling as if they were antennae. With Helen's help, he managed well enough, and his sensitivity to his surroundings, both physical and emotional, was keenly attuned. "He was the least *blind* blind man I ever knew, and the most independent," said Katharine. "He should be given great tribute for that."

There was, however, only so much he could navigate. On those occasions when Thurber dropped by the office, he required special attention and handling. He sometimes resisted it, as Frank Modell recalled upon espying him one day while everyone was at lunch:

> He had a manuscript under his arm, and he was going right to a stairway. And I was thinking only of me, which was usual: "If I sit here and let this million-dollar talent fall down the stairs and kill himself, they're all going to say, 'Why the hell didn't you help him?'" So I said, "I'd better do something; I can't just stand there." . . . So I went up to him, like the nice good boy that I am, and touched his elbow and said, "Mr. Thurber, might I help you?" And he said, "Get out of here, you sons of bitches!" Down the steps he

went, like a bunch of plastic dishes, the manuscript flying all over the place. And he didn't hurt himself at all. But I was standing up there with tears in my eyes.

Walter Bernstein found himself similarly positioned, albeit more successfully. Following a lunch at the Algonquin, a preoccupied Ross somehow left Thurber in the middle of the street. Bernstein seized the initiative and pulled the million-dollar talent out of harm's way.

Thurber's infirmity made him downright irritable. He picked fights indiscriminately. By one account, he never quite forgave Gibbs for failing to visit him during any of his eye operations because Gibbs was "so goddam sensitive" about hospitals. And so Thurber struck back in his casual "The Cane in the Corridor." Casting himself as "Joe Fletcher," fresh out of the operating theater, Thurber contemplates revenge on "George Minturn"—i.e., Gibbs—in a scenario whereby Minturn is hospitalized. To make Minturn miserable, Fletcher visits him every day for the six weeks of his convalescence, during which time the latter is unable to escape Fletcher's annoying company. At one point Fletcher even lambastes Minturn because he does not feel sorry for his, Fletcher's, cane of the title; Fletcher refers to it as "poor tap-tap."

There was another reason for Thurber's mental state—he was beginning to suffer from severe hyperthyroidism. Undiagnosed at first, the condition had the effect of making him unreasonably vicious, even borderline paranoid. When *The New Yorker* printed John McNulty's "Back Where I Had Never Been," Thurber lashed out at Ross, surprised by its very publication: "The surprise comes from the fact that it was not run through our formidable prose machine, in a desperate and dedicated Ross-Shawn attempt to make it sound like everybody else. . . . The machine has left almost no differences in tongue or temperament or style." He resisted editorial changes and accused his British publisher, Hamish Hamilton, of "tampering with my books." A visit to his Bermuda friends Ronald and Jane Williams was a disaster. "Ordinarily Ronnie and Jim enjoyed their fights," said Jane, "but at dinner during his bad periods, I didn't dare serve the Jell-O; I knew it would be thrown."

Happily, the right diagnosis and combination of drugs did Thurber some good, and he apologized accordingly. Even during the worst of his ordeals, there was a chuckle or two to be had. When Ross gave a book party for Rebecca West following the publication of her monumental volume about Yugoslavia, *Black Lamb and Grey Falcon*, someone knocked over a table. Following the crash and the ensuing silence, Ross called out, "Is that you, Thurber?" On another occasion, Ross and Thurber found themselves as hemorrhoidal customers of the same proctologist.

"The doctor would have them undress," said the physician Melvin Hershkowitz, having heard the tale directly from Ross, "turn around, bend over, and would then identify them by name, according to the pattern of their rectal anatomy."

––––––––––

The downturn in *New Yorker* jokiness was not merely a symptom of the Cold War climate or personal health. The voices that had begun to plumb their literary potential in the 1930s continued to do so, their work growing ever more varied and individual. They could not always fit into Ross's "adult comic book."

St. Clair McKelway was a case in point. He did not return immediately to *The New Yorker* following his discharge. Instead, he spent some time with Gibbs on Fire Island (HOPE YOU GET SOME GOOD REST AND SUN, Shawn wired him shortly after Japan's formal surrender) and ran into Sam and Bella Spewak, the husband-and-wife team who had just devised the book for *Kiss Me Kate*. They suggested he try writing for Hollywood and set him up with their agent. Two days later he was off for California.

From the start, McKelway's time in the movies was inconclusive and frustrating; he found it "more like carpentry, interesting but not quite gripping" and practically "like a continuation of the war." He worked first for Columbia, where his labors "consisted largely of spicing up with additional dialogue and other appropriate condiments a number of scripts which it seemed to me had already been spiced and seasoned far beyond their capacity as vehicles of public entertainment." After seven weeks, he decamped to join Leo McCarey at RKO in writing a vehicle for Ingrid Bergman, Jimmy Stewart, and Charles Boyer. "I wound up after two weeks with a determination to do the story of Adam and Eve, with Bergman and Stewart. In such a script, obviously, there was no part for Boyer."

He returned to Columbia to craft a barely recognizable version of *The Front Page* in which the action was moved from Chicago to Brazil, the hard-boiled editor Walter Burns was transformed into a theatrical producer, and whiz reporter Hildy Johnson was "transmuted into a shapely girl dancer." From there he went to Triangle Productions and *Sleep, My Love,* a psychological thriller with Bob Cummings, Claudette Colbert, and Don Ameche. "Production was frequently halted while all of us engaged in prolonged debate as to whether it was more in keeping, say, for a character to say: 'How do you do?' 'How are you?' or just 'Hi?'"

Besides *Sleep, My Love,* McKelway also managed a credit on *The Mating of Millie* with Glenn Ford and Evelyn Keyes. But by this time he realized he was kidding himself. Though his salary was "reasonably fabulous," he found that after taxes and expenses, it was buying him no more than about three hundred dollars a week had bought him in Manhattan before the war. "I am in my usual shape," he told Katharine White, "just ahead of the waiter with the check."

So McKelway retreated to *The New Yorker,* convinced he was in the grip of a professional downturn. "Melville once said that there is a Cape Horn in every man's life," he wrote Ross. "White says he's been rounding it now for about six years and that a heavy fog seems to be coming up ahead. It's the sixth or seventh time around for me, of course." Working for the first time on salary, without "the illusory comforts of unsound salary advances," he had a brief but unhappy stint as a fiction editor, filling in for Lobrano, who had just suffered a heart attack. He also flirted with becoming a foreign correspondent. He spent most of his working hours "scheming not writing," prompting his physician to characterize him as an "ambitious beach-comber and unsuccessful businessman."

Finally he found his strength, as he had years before, with the "Annals of Crime" section, drolly relating the rascally malefactions of colorful felons in prose laced with offbeat revelations and a straightforward arrangement of facts. In "Mister 880," he examined the peculiar case of the counterfeiter Edward John Wellman:

> He was a personable middle-aged man, an Estonian by birth, an unlucky horse player, and an accomplished ice skater. When he began to glide and pirouette, other skaters would slow up, or stop altogether, to watch him. He was known at all the ice-skating places in and around New York. He picked up pocket money at some of them from time to time as a skating instructor. He was jolly with the children and had a courtly manner with the ladies. Descriptions and photographs of him were sent by the Secret Service to all race tracks and all skating rinks, and a little over three months after he skipped bail he was arrested at Tropical Park race track, in Florida. He had been passing pewter fifty-cent pieces all over Miami and vicinity and betting on the races with his profits. In his car, the Secret Service found seven hundred and eighty-nine phony half dollars, thirty-five pounds of pewter, a bottle of silver chloride, a can of sodium cyanide of potassium, some silver that he used for plating the coins, and the other paraphernalia he required to turn out finished fifty-cent pieces. He could make them without even getting out of his car, a 1941 Buick.

With pieces like this, McKelway stayed firmly within *The New Yorker's* orbit.

John O'Hara, on the other hand, did not. Almost from the beginning, his relationship with the magazine had been by turns sycophantic, boastful, humble, and maddening. In 1934—the same year Woollcott announced his ostensible resignation—the prickly O'Hara had lit into Ross for failing to sufficiently appreciate his first and best novel, *Appointment in Samarra*. "I felt that The New Yorker, that great impersonal organization The New Yorker, might have taken the book a little less in stride," he groused. "As Woollcott would say, you-all flew into a great state of calm, when I thought that since I am practically exclusively a New Yorker product, you might have taken cognizance of the book in somewhat more concrete fashion."

It would be as unfair to characterize O'Hara as entirely self-centered as it would be to say the same about Woollcott. Many, including Katharine White and O'Hara's stepson C.D.B. "Courty" Bryan, would attest to his essential humanity; the latter characterized him as "an intensely shy, warm, *gentle* man" (emphasis in the original). When it came to his reputation and reception, however, O'Hara was uncompromising. Hence he erupted when Brendan Gill slammed his 1949 potboiler *A Rage to Live* as tantamount to "a catastrophe." Much has been written about the fracas—that Thurber supposedly claimed Gibbs had written the review, that the clue was the use of the adjective "discursive," that Gill was out to shaft O'Hara, and so on. The upshot was that O'Hara broke off relations with Ross, infuriated by what he regarded as a betrayal. Ross, O'Hara fumed, "had called me the master. Then this clown comes along and flays me as a bumbling incompetent. You can't be both. There are various degrees of treachery, and I consider *The New Yorker*'s printing such a scurrilous review to be treachery of the lowest kind."

Gibbs did what he could to patch things up, writing to Lobrano:

I went down to Princeton last weekend and had lunch with O'Hara. He would really like very much to write for us again, because there is really no other place for his short stories, but his conditions, of course, are grotesque. He wants an apology, from somebody in authority, for Gill's review of his book, and he wants what you might call a punitive punishment payment for the pieces he might have written if we hadn't annoyed him so. I asked him how much he thought this would amount to, and he said that, well, in a good year he had made as much as $10,000 from us and so, since he had lost five years, he felt that morally we owed him $50,000. He has a feeling that this may be a little excessive, but that it is a figure at which negotiations might start. . . . In any case, I felt that he wanted this intelligence passed along to you, and I do so. You might offer to pay him ten dollars and shoot Gill. Your problem, of course.

A break, at least for a while, might have been inevitable. For some time, O'Hara had wanted more money than *The New Yorker* could pay him. And with *A Rage to Live,* it was clear that he would be focusing not on stories but on novels, notably *Ten North Frederick* and *From the Terrace.* O'Hara also needed the sort of self-expression that *The New Yorker* could not always accommodate. Less than a year after *Rage* was published, he issued in *The New York Times Book Review* a fulsome endorsement of Hemingway's *Over the River and Into the Trees,* in which he called Papa "the most important author living today, the outstanding author since the death of Shakespeare." Arthur Kober was astonished. "All the people I spoke to thought the guy had gone off his rocker," he told Gus Lobrano. "Me, too. His style, a combination of kiddie-stuff and hard-guy writing, makes me think that his pubic hairs have gone to his chest."

Even Gibbs, close to O'Hara though he was, rolled his eyes at his old friend's steadily mounting self-indulgence, never more so than following one of his "Appointment with O'Hara" columns in *Collier's.* O'Hara had written,

I have lived an extremely full life, experiencing exquisite pleasure and all but unbearable sorrow and pain; loving some, hating a few, pitying many and scorning the contemptible; joyful of my accomplishments and stung by my failures. Throughout it all I have been pleased by the circumstance that has enabled me to earn my living at the job I love best, which is writing. I am a simple, worldly-wise man and practically nothing except stupid cruelty can shock me, and I never have written a word for the purpose of shocking anyone else. But I have often been disgusted by people who take pleasure in scatological humor, in the telling and the listening, and yet are genuinely or otherwise offended by any and all reference to the function called sex.

Those sentences "made me jump," Gibbs told Thurber. "He sounds like Lincoln's Second Inaugural. It must be wonderful to think of yourself so majestically and even more wonderful to have no misgivings about putting it all down for a national magazine."

If O'Hara's growing preoccupation with sexual frankness and his own ego were keeping him out of *The New Yorker,* the flights of fancy now being taken by Thurber and White were another matter. Thurber was putting down longish, downright experimental works, some of them almost phantasmagorical. One of these was *The White Deer.* This fifteen-thousand-word children's book, he told friends, was "a new version of the old fairy tale of the deer which, chased by a king and his three songs, is transformed into a princess." It was considerably more than that: in conveying the narrative, Thurber demonstrated his linguistic virtuosity with alliteration, inside references (he deployed Ross's catchphrase "Done and done"), and weird words, e.g., *whinkering.* With such facility, he was with increasing frequency turning verbal cartwheels.

He admitted as much in his foreword to *The 13 Clocks.* Calling this inventive contrivance an example of "escapism and self-indulgence," he explained, "Unless Modern Man wanders down these byways occasionally, I do not see how he can hope to preserve his sanity." In many ways, it was perhaps Thurber's most self-consciously literary effort to date. Much of it was purely whimsical: to win the hand of the Princess Saralinda, a prince must secure for her uncle—an evil duke—a thousand precious jewels. He attempts to do so through a woman who weeps not tears but gems. However, she can produce them only via laughter, as opposed to sorrow. In the course of this adventure, the duke cruelly murders time itself by stopping his castle's thirteen clocks. *The 13 Clocks* was a literary tour de force, replete with limericks, Jamesian allusions, unconventional narrative constructions, and even code words that the author had retained from his army-clerk days, among them *Golux, Todal,* and *Hagga.*

White was not entirely enthused. He praised *The 13 Clocks* as "a wondrous tale and very musical and melancholy." Still, he suggested it was too complicated—"so concentrated a diet, with new characters and events and twists appearing in almost every sentence." He was also baffled by Thurber's offbeat paragraphing and found his foreword "defensive—as though you were prematurely sore because the wrong people were reading your book or the right people weren't." White tweaked his old friend: "I think you are just sticking out your zatch, and many a tosspan and stutfart will run you through." Taking the criticisms in stride, Thurber revised.

When it came time for White to compose his own children's confections *Stuart Little* and *Charlotte's Web*, he adhered to conventional storybook narrative. Still, he broached quite grown-up themes in his plain prose. Fern's tenderhearted concern for Wilbur, Charlotte's selfless rescue of the runt of the litter, and her own aging and death—offset by the legacy of her many progeny—are wholly moving. As for Stuart's never-ending journey at his eponymous book's end, White over the course of myriad letters always resisted letting readers know what was ahead.

He was already a household name among adults. Now he was a familiar figure to children as well. Indeed, in the case of *Stuart Little,* youngsters warmed to the work more than some grown-ups did. Edmund Wilson enjoyed the first page but told White he was "disappointed that you didn't develop the theme more in the manner of Kafka." Anne Carroll Moore, the former children's librarian of the New York Public Library, thought the book "non-affirmative, inconclusive, unfit for children, and would harm its author if published."

No such controversy attended the publication of *Charlotte's Web*. Read aloud by countless teachers in countless classrooms, consumed by youngsters themselves, it would become one of the top-selling children's paperbacks of all time. Curiously, it took a while to take hold. "So far," White told his editor, Ursula Nordstrom, not long after its initial printing, "*Charlotte's Web* seems to have been read largely by adults with a literary turn of mind. I have had only a sprinkling of childhood reaction to the book—those vital and difficult precincts—and will not know for a little while how it sits with the young." Soon enough he would, with volumes of juvenile fan mail to prove it.

In some respects, *Stuart Little* and *Charlotte's Web* may have represented the best expression of White's tentative, not always successful, ventures into fabulism. One of his most unusual *Harper's* contributions had been a dreamlike elegy to New York City. In it, a Manhattan expatriate named Volente returns to town and checks into a mysterious building called "The Hotel of the Total Stranger." On his way there and once settled, he fantasizes:

> New York lay stretched in midsummer languor under her trees in the thinnest dress, idly and beautifully to the eyes of Mr. Volente her lover. She lay this morning early in the arms of the heat, humorously and indulgently, as though, having bathed in the night, she had emerged and not bothered to put anything on and had stretched out to let the air, what air there was, touch her along arms and legs and shoulders and forehead, he thought, admiringly.

Memories trickle back—including the Childs' restaurant incident with the buttermilk, which had revealed "the enormously important discovery that the world would pay a man for setting down a simple, legible account of his own misfortunes." White concluded, purplishly, "Oh inscrutable and lovely town! oh [sic] citadel of love."

In 1952, more than a decade after this enigmatic piece saw print—and in the same year that he published *Charlotte's Web*—White teamed improbably with McKelway to work up a screen treatment, expanding and trying to deepen it by having the hero visit his office on a deserted Saturday afternoon. There he encounters a nameless and mysterious girl who is determined to leave New York for vague reasons—"money, disappointment in love, unsuccess," etc. He does his best to persuade her to stay. Though he fails, his own on-again, off-again romance with New York comes through in the last lines. There, he hears the sound of the *Queen Mary*'s horn, carrying "the whole history of departure and longing and loss."

It was a bizarre excursion, and White was aware of its shortcomings. "I vacillate between thinking that this is the most promising thing to hit the screen since Theda Bara and thinking that there is really very little here to work on," he told McKelway. In the end, the strange film was never made. But if it had been, it would have given White the opportunity to "swipe stuff directly" from his notable essay "Here Is New York" and given it even wider exposure.

White had written the seven thousand words of "Here Is New York" at the Algonquin during the sweltering August of 1948, having been commissioned to do so by Roger Angell for *Holiday* magazine. The tone was bittersweet. Much of the piece is a love letter. "New York is to the nation what the white church is to the village—the visible symbol of aspiration and faith, the white plume saying the way is up," White wrote. He retreated into youthful nostalgia—his memories of the El, the profusion of daily newspapers, his life in Greenwich Village.

He also bewailed the city's gigantism: "It is a miracle that New York works at all. The whole thing is implausible. Every time the residents brush their teeth, millions of gallons of water must be drawn from the Catskills and the hills of Westchester. . . . Long ago the city should have experienced an insoluble traffic snarl at some impossible bottleneck. It should have perished of hunger when food lines failed for a few days. It should have been wiped out by a plague starting in its slums or carried in by ships' rats." And in a chilling foreshadowing of September 11, he despaired of the city's vulnerability: "A single flight of planes no bigger than a wedge of geese can quickly end this island fantasy, burn the towers, crumble the bridges, turn the underground passages into lethal chambers, cremate millions." Of one thing White was sure: the place was on its way to "becoming a capital of the world."

It was one of White's best-remembered efforts. "I regard you as I do one of two teachers I know—irreplaceable," wrote Jack Arbolino, a Columbia University admissions officer. "I already feel foolish in praising you. Just take this as a fan letter."

For Gibbs, meanwhile, little gelled outside *The New Yorker*. He got nowhere with adapting Joseph Hergesheimer's novel *Balisand* and his literary idol Max Beerbohm's *Zuleika Dobson*. His attempt to revive the nineteenth-century musical *The Belle of New York* similarly fizzled.

Still, he remained convinced that he could do as good a job on Broadway as any of the hacks who were succeeding there. In 1946 he published some Mittyesque daydreaming (dedicated "with a Peck on the Cheek for James Thurber") with the title "The Secret Life of Myself." In it, he imagines himself effortlessly doctoring a stinker of a script and saving the play from disaster. For good measure, he even condescends to take over the lead role at the director's behest. It is all a fantasy, conceived in the brief interval during which he has fallen asleep while watching the actual production, only to be rudely awakened by Elinor.*

---

* Repaying the compliment, Thurber later wrote a spoof of Gibbs's "Theory and Practice of Editing *New Yorker* Articles." He titled it "The Theory and Practice of Criticizing the Criticism of the Editing of *New Yorker* Articles" and dedicated it to Gibbs "with a lighted candle."

Finally, Gibbs hit on a largely autobiographical approach that worked. While recovering from his pleurisy operation, he decided to cannibalize his nine "Season in the Sun" stories and craft a comedy with the same title. In some preliminary notes, he sketched out his theme:

[A] time is apt to come in almost every innocent writer's life when it occurs to him that he ought to be making rather larger or anyway deeper footprints in the sand. With White, this took the form of the Brotherhood of Man and packing his whole family rather arbitrarily off to Maine. With the writer in this play, it is reduced and simplified to the point where he just feels it is high time he got away from a corrupt and urban environment and wrote a novel inspired by the feeling a man is apt to get about America—if he picks up Walt Whitman rather late in life. There is, however, a minimum of social signifigance [sic] in the play; it is mainly just silly.

In assembling his disparate pieces into a dramatic whole, Gibbs depicted his alter ego George Crane as a reformed drinker. Though a respected and successful writer at an unnamed weekly humor magazine, he approaches middle age upset by his perceived lack of achievement. So he has quit the periodical and holed up on Fire Island to work on a great American novel. As the play opens, George unloads to his wife, Emily, about life, conventionality, and the hell of other people. His central statement is a cri de coeur about how Manhattan has wrecked his compatriots. "They're vacant, used-up people," he complains. "Most of them came to New York—as I did—full of all kinds of hope about the fine jobs they were going to have and the wonderful lives they were going to live. It took quite a while for it to get to them, but it did."

As the play progresses, though, Crane finds that even in his paradise, there are plenty of disagreeable characters. Some, like Mae Jermyn (the real-life Blanche Pastorfield), are wacky. Others, like Molly Burden (Polly Adler), are disreputable. And a couple of specimens are downright dangerous. At one point, as the cracks in her marriage to George become painfully apparent, Emily is almost snatched away by John Colgate, a Pulitzer-winning "journalist and dipsomaniac" modeled on O'Hara.*

The most problematic serpent in Crane's Eden is Horace William Dodd, his editor, patterned to the life after Ross. Dodd is not about to let one of his best writers go without a fight and lights out to Fire Island to retrieve him. Gibbs gave Dodd some of his play's best lines. "Say, this is quite a community you got," Dodd tells Crane. "No telephones, no taxis, I wouldn't be surprised no interior plumbing." When he reads aloud Crane's earnest despair over the rootlessness of New Yorkers, he croaks, "Water! Water!" Dodd's only concern is getting Crane back to Manhattan; it matters little to him that his writer's marriage is on the verge of breaking down after years of alcohol, cynicism, and mutual disaffection.

Things come to a head when Emily learns of a budding extramarital affair between George and Deedy Barton (the Leonore Lemmon character from "The Cat on the Roof"), and she prepares to leave him. Things get so bad that Crane falls off the wagon and picks up the bottle again. At this moment, Gibbs writes, Crane comes to life: "It is an amazing metamorphosis. This is probably the first time we've seen the fundamental George." In short order his imbibing is back, and he is singing with sodden self-pity, "Nobody loves me, I wonder why?" Coming from someone as reticent as Gibbs, it is an extraordinary self-revelation.

To get *Season* off the ground, Gibbs turned to his old friend Burgess Meredith, who took the script to the flamboyant producer Courtney Burr. "He tottered between being either dead broke or dead rich," said Mer-

---

* Brendan Gill thought Colgate was based on the *New York Herald Tribune* sportswriter Don Skene, "whose invariable modest boast in his cups was that he was a descendant of the man who discovered Skene's glands, which lubricate the female genitalia." But Gibbs specifically stated that O'Hara inspired the character.

edith, who also recalled that Burr "went to many bizarre places to find investors, including two famous whorehouses, where the madams were friends of his." The filthy lucre of sporting houses, however, couldn't cover all the costs, so Burr brought in Malcolm Pearson, the producer of Clare Boothe Luce's ill-fated *Abide with Me*. Meredith staged the production, his first major directing job. And Burr found a confidante in Elinor. "She spent a lot of time in his ear," said Burr's friend Joan Castle Sitwell, "crying on his shoulder."

Production of *Season* proceeded more or less smoothly through the spring of 1950. Richard Whorf, who had played opposite Jimmy Cagney in *Yankee Doodle Dandy*, was Crane. Nancy Kelly was his wife, Emily; she would go on to win a Tony Award for *The Bad Seed* and replace Uta Hagen in *Who's Afraid of Virginia Woolf?* Anthony Ross (no relation to Harold Ross) took the Dodd role. Seven years before he had been Jim O'Connor, the bright, enthusiastic gentleman caller, in the original *Glass Menagerie*.

The cast and crew were perversely perfect for a Gibbs play. "Almost everybody connected with that show was an alcoholic," said George Ives, who played one of two minor gay characters. "Nancy Kelly was. I was. Courtney was. Malcolm was." So were Anthony Ross, such supporting members as Charlie Thompson and Grace Valentine, and the star. "Dicky was drinking at that period, which at first made a lot of us nervous," said Meredith, "but he never let us down."

Not all of the choices worked out. Ives recalled that his onstage partner—a homosexual in real life—somehow couldn't impart his orientation to the public. Finally "[t]hey had to let him go because he couldn't do it the way they wanted." By far the most compelling member of the company was Joan Diener as Deedy Barton. "Joan was amazing," Meredith recalled. "Her acting wasn't great but she was beautiful and had the most astonishingly large breasts in proportion to her body that Broadway had ever seen." To Deedy falls the task of offering Crane a possible way out of his travails. Consumed with latching on to a sugar daddy, she dangles the prospect of a house in Bucks County so he can write his magnum opus in peace, strongly hinting that she will be available to reassure him of his worth.

The resolution, however, is never in doubt. When Emily gets wind of a drunken offstage fling between Crane and Deedy, her husband crawls back to her. In the process, Crane—channeling Gibbs—realizes he is running from his own fears while pretending to merely be fleeing the company he keeps.

EMILY: I know they're awful. Molly runs a hook-shop, in your own happy phrase, and Johnny drinks too much, and Mrs. Jermyn has what you might call a rather carefree outlook on life. But they're *people*. They're funny and they're *alive*. I'm only guessing, but I think you're afraid of them.

GEORGE (turning to her): Afraid of them?

EMILY: Yes. Because they're real, and this damn world you've made up, this absurd little boy's world—can't exist with real people in it.

Later, Dodd tells Crane essentially the same thing—that by trying to hole himself up and create a work of art, he is pursuing an illusion. So Crane literally rips his book in half and returns not only to his family but to the familiar, if unchallenging, world of his magazine.

That summer some of the crew trekked to Ocean Beach to soak up the atmosphere and develop their characters. Their raucous presence didn't sit well with Gibbs's neighbors; some even picketed his house in protest. On August 27, Arthur Gelb visited with Gibbs to convey the brewing conflict for *The New York Times*. He found the novice playwright dressed in a bathing suit and a wrinkled white linen shirt, a two-day-old growth of stubble on his face. "He holds a colorless martini and idly depresses and releases the shift lock of his typewriter with his big toe," Gelb wrote. The interview included this exchange:

VISITOR: Are you aware of the resentment against you for bringing the island publicity via your writings?

GIBBS: Yes, but I don't think it's too widespread. When Boris Aronson wandered around the island looking inside houses to get ideas for the set, he was welcomed very cordially by everyone.

VISITOR: Who is going to review your play for the New Yorker?

GIBBS: Don't know yet. If it's a quick flop, I might review it myself.

Thurber dropped by the rehearsals and, drawing on his memories of *The Male Animal* ten years before, predicted various agonies. "During rehearsal you discover that your prettiest lines do not cross the footlights, because they are too pretty, or an actor can't say them, or an actress doesn't know what they mean," he wrote Gibbs. "There comes the horrible realization that phrases like 'Yes, you were' or 'No I won't' are better and more effective than the ones you slaved over. . . . On the thirteenth day of rehearsal, the play suddenly makes no sense to you and does not seem to be written in English."

By Gibbs's estimate, he rewrote *Season in the Sun* thirteen times. "Cut out any sentence in the play that needs a comma," he told himself. "A semi-colon is disastrous. In fact, the best play has no punctuation whatsoever." If he was hard on himself, he had considerable respect for the cast. "How do they manage to rehearse for so many hours?" he asked. The going was tough. "When we opened in Boston, we got panned," said Ives. "We really thought we were going to get killed in town [Manhattan] as well."

The problem was a basic lack of coherent narrative and novelty. For all of Gibbs's rewriting, *Season* remained a series of largely random run-ins with his Fire Island neighbors and detractors. Among the skeptics was Ross. "He told me it was a funny play," Gibbs informed Thurber, "but that the central dilemma (whether a man ought to write paragraphs or a novel) struck him as practically nonexistent." Gibbs's indirection wasn't lost on Elinor Hughes of the *Boston Herald*. While praising *Season's* "sharp, witty dialogue and the cruelly comic characters," she was not happy about Gibbs's "indifference to plot construction and his conventional triangle story." Overall she found herself "amused" but signed off,

> With a New York opening just around the corner, I think Mr. Gibbs had better take a few more pains with the relationship between the husband and the wife, who have a way of behaving as discontentedly as the rest of the characters while purporting to be normal people. . . . [B]efore this particular vessel is launched on the Broadway sea, it should have all its seams caulked and its rigging taut, for there'll be a strong wind blowing.

The New York premiere took place on September 28, 1950. As he had for the play's eponymous book four years before, the ever-faithful Charles Addams supplied the cover illustration for the *Playbill*—in this case, a little boy pulling an express wagon laden with a buxom blonde in a bikini past an apprehensive Crane. On opening night, Gibbs was fidgety. As the zero hour approached, he swore off his ringside seat and retreated with Elinor to stand at the rear of the theater.

"I thought my colleagues, some of whom dislike me intensely, were going to be rough," he said. "If the reviews had been very bad, I guess I would have quit *The New Yorker* and perhaps even the country." Perhaps still in search of retribution for the Luce Profile, *Life* dispatched the photographer Leonard McCombe to shoot Gibbs during opening night as he fretted. "I don't think I spoke a word to him," said McCombe more than fifty years later. "I was just hoping that something would come out—I'd never shot like that. So *I* was nervous."

In the end, all of Gibbs's anxiety was for nothing. "The opening night," said Ives, "we got laughs from the minute the curtain went up."

The triumphant assemblage retreated to the Q Club to await the reviews. At about one in the morning, Gibbs dialed the *Times* to get a preview of Brooks Atkinson's all-important column. Much to the novice playwright's annoyance, McCombe clicked away madly as he listened to the playback over the pay phone. "The photographer kept telling me to bite my nails. I told him I had caps on my teeth and couldn't," he complained. As the night went on, the news came back reassuringly. Atkinson called the play "vastly amusing" and praised its "wit, drollery and humor." William Hawkins of the *World-Telegram and Sun* thought it "a sophisticated uproar," Howard Barnes in the *Herald Tribune* declared it "a glittering comedy of manners," and John Chapman of the *Daily News* raved, "I nearly busted myself trying to keep from laughing." In the final photo of McCombe's *Life* spread, Gibbs and Meredith can be seen poring over a copy of Chapman's review, Meredith looking pleased and Gibbs grimly vindicated.*

Though he didn't get to bed until after four, Gibbs showed up at *The New Yorker* that Friday. Ross greeted him curtly: "I suppose you're going to quit the magazine, now you're a millionaire." Gibbs spent the rest of that day receiving plaudits. "At each fresh assurance," wrote Arthur Gelb in the *Times*, "he scratched his head in bewilderment." After a day of being pelted with praise, he fled for Fire Island, where he spent four days fishing and losing $1.60 at poker.

The reactions of Gibbs's *New Yorker* colleagues varied. In the magazine, John Lardner—a tough customer—found *Season* to be "gaily, sharply, and consistently satirical," enacted by a "cheerful and competent" cast. Ross's assistant William Walden, who saw *Season* with his

---

* Although some critics were lukewarm about *Season*, Claudia Cassidy of the *Chicago Tribune* actively dumped on it when it opened in Chicago, calling it "a turkey if ever you saw one." A little more than two years later, Gibbs got revenge by declining to review Cassidy's book *Europe on the Aisle*. He told the editor who had solicited him that he was not enamored of such phrases as "Rivers swirled into silver dragons," "Blurred pastel bouquets of a lyric come to life," and "capacious maw."

wife, Tippy, was astonished that so slim a piece had garnered such accolades; he suspected that the critics had simply closed ranks around one of
their own. By his estimate, there wasn't a single laugh for the play's first
twenty-six minutes.* "It was not a great play," agreed Mary D. Kierstead.
"It was perfectly agreeable, but no great shakes." Janet Flanner reported,
"Office very happy at his success but no one understands jocularity of
play as subject very bad, and only one good comedy character in it." As
for Ross, he swore he wouldn't see the play until he was satisfied that
no one in the audience would recognize him. He ended up seeing it not
once, but twice.

The play brought Gibbs a substantial two thousand dollars a week.
His plans for the extra income were modest; he wanted only to build two
dormers atop the Fire Island house and buy Tony a new boat motor. But if
Season did not affect Gibbs that much, it did put Fire Island on the map.
As Gelb predicted, the small number of curious onlookers and visitors
who had been drawn there during the run-up descended in droves in the
summer of 1951. "To think that I wrote my play with the express intention
of discouraging people from coming here!" Gibbs wailed.

Season settled down to a healthy run, and at the 1951 Tony Awards
Boris Aronson came away with the prize for Best Scenic Design. Eventually Victor Jory, best known as the brutal overseer Jonas Wilkerson
in *Gone with the Wind,* replaced Whorf as George Crane. Walter Matthau took over from Anthony Ross as Horace Dodd and spent much
time with Gibbs, slightly sozzled and talking baseball. By then the cast
had grown restless and mischievous; they began engaging in no-holds-
barred water-pistol fights out of sight, lying in wait around corners as victims approached. Dressed only in a towel, Jack Weston—who eventually

---

* Less than a year before, Gibbs had slammed *Metropole,* Walden's own Broadway
  effort, about *New Yorker* types. However, Walden was never particularly embittered by the review because every other critic in town savaged him as well. Despite
  being directed by George S. Kaufman, *Metropole* closed after two performances.

filled the role of Ives's gay partner—ran around backstage screaming and firing madly. The curtain came down for the last time on August 11, 1951. There was talk of exporting *Season* to London, but when Gibbs learned that he would have to spend any of his consequent profits in England, he balked. Besides, he couldn't bear to fly across the Atlantic.

Considering how long Gibbs had worked to bring his creation to life, he had surprisingly little affection for it in the years to come. He disparaged *Season* as "a bunch of vaudeville routines hooked together by some crap about whether a guy writes a novel or paragraphs, a non-existent dilemma if ever I heard one." He even bet Meredith a hundred dollars—and lost—that the production would not still be running by Independence Day. He could have afforded to let up on himself, having set out to accomplish what he wanted and, in the process, discovering a hard-won appreciation of the playwright's craft.

"Now that I've found it isn't as simple getting a play into production as I thought," he said, "I will probably become a more benign critic."

CHAPTER 13

"A LOT OF SUICIDAL ENTERPRISES"

I n February 1950 *The New Yorker* celebrated its twenty-fifth anniversary. If it had been up to Ross, the occasion would have passed quietly. But on the night of March 18, he found himself in the grand ballroom of the Ritz-Carlton presiding over a mammoth black-tie affair for contributors, friends, and associates. Among the seven hundred attendees were plenty of old-timers who had been with the magazine from its rocky founding a quarter of a century before. "It ran until about 4 in the morning," reported Gus Lobrano, "and seems generally to be regarded as a success, despite the fact that nobody got insulted, nobody fell down stairs, and there were no fist fights. In fact the key-notes seemed to be good-will and good-humor." The man who had made it all possible was appalled by the crush. "I'm sorry I didn't get to see more of you at the party," Harold Ross told a friend. "The whole thing was like a movie run off five times too fast." To Jay Hormel, of the meatpacking dynasty, he wrote, "I never got pulled and hauled so in my life." So heavy with history was the atmosphere that Gibbs quipped, "That party proved one thing. It proved that lady writers don't die. I danced with Harriet Beecher Stowe twice."

Coupled with his onstage immortalization in *Season* several months hence, Ross was marking a signal year. It was also his penultimate one. He was dying.

Ross had been ill for some time, his slouching and loping becoming ever more pronounced. For a while, he blamed his ulcers. He was so convinced of their baleful effects that he contributed—with an uncharacteristic byline—an introduction to the healthful-living cookbook *Good Food for Bad Stomachs.* "I write as a duodenum-scarred veteran of many years of guerrilla service in the Hydrochloric War," he declared. But it was not his duodenum that was killing him. At a preliminary diagnosis at the Lahey Clinic in Boston in April 1951—and in an echo of Gibbs's condition—pleurisy was suspected. Then, as they continued to prod their patient, Ross's physicians determined that he was suffering from cancer of the windpipe, almost certainly the result of years of heavy smoking. Without knowing quite what was happening, his friends worried accordingly.

"Runners keep telling me you're sick," wrote Ann Honeycutt. "I am very, very sorry and wish I could do something to help you feel better. Would you like my stomach, for instance? Ask the doctor if he could make such a transfer. Or the whole torso if you need it. I'm the spiritual type and don't really need an earthly home and care less and less about it furthermore, so keep it in mind."

But no stomach or torso transplant would have helped Ross. He rallied and faded through the rest of the year, enduring thirty-nine separate radiation treatments. In September, he mounted a brief return. "I have taken back about one-third of the work I used to do at the office," he told Rebecca West in October, "but that has kept me busy, partly, because, I suspect, I just got out of the habit of working and partly because I am only about fifty percent efficient yet, although I am pronounced and seem to be eighty-five percent recovered."

Actually, he was not. On December 6 Ross underwent exploratory surgery at New England Baptist Hospital to determine if his cancer had metastasized. Just before the procedure, he managed to place a phone call to George S. Kaufman, who was in town. The editor told him, "I'm half under the anesthetic now." He never came out of it: After the surgeons removed his cancerous right lung, he died at about six-thirty p.m.

"Ross won't leave my thoughts, and probably never will to the end of my days," said Frank Sullivan, "and it is all right with me." White felt as if he had been "disemboweled." The word went out, and instinctively the faithful gathered at one another's apartments, in bars, anywhere they could commiserate. The next day a pall hung over the *New Yorker* offices. A blind Thurber somehow found his way there and, in a heart-rending scene, clutched the corridor walls and wailed, "Andy! *An*-dy!"

By unspoken consensus, it fell to White to compose the obituary. Jettisoning hearts-and-flowers writing, he emphasized Ross's unrelenting commitment to *The New Yorker*, his preoccupation with his people, and his many eccentricities. White's tribute was laced with typical rhetorical touches, such as, "Ross always knew when we were in a jam, and usually got on the phone to offer advice and comfort and support. When our phone rang just now, and in that split second before the mind focusses [*sic*] we thought, 'Good here it comes!' But this old connection is broken beyond fixing." He allowed himself a few indulgences: "We love Ross so, and bear him such respect, that these quick notes, which purport to record the sorrow that runs through here and dissolves so many people, cannot possibly seem overstated or silly."

Readers concurred. "I started reading your article on Harold Ross as I was crossing the street at 33rd St.," one of them wrote. "I couldn't go on because I was crying. I tried to read it again at the office and again I was crying. Perhaps I shall never have the heart to read the complete story." Carl Rose wrote to Katharine:

You know, these days, it's difficult for me to apply the word "beauty" to many current creative efforts. I mean beauty in the sense that a da Vinci or a Pisanello or a Rembrandt sketch is "beautiful" or that marvelous Michelangelo sculpture "Pieta" is "beautiful," but what Andy wrote about Ross had true beauty. I say it with no qualifications whatever. I've read it half a dozen times. It's better than a hundred headstones, and in the long run, will prove more durable.

White disagreed. "No, Ross wouldn't have liked it," he said. "He would have written in the margin 'writer-conscious'—an adjective he invented for just such pieces." By contrast, he would have been amused by a telegram that the magazine sent to Elmer Davis in Washington, D.C., informing him about the funeral; it referred to him as "Reverend Harold Ross." Circling that peculiar locution, Davis scrawled, "Ross would print that."

The service at Frank Campbell's was an ordeal—"about four hundred of the most restless and noisy people in town, silent as a horned toad and a thousand times sadder," said White. "My job was to be sure that nobody but *New Yorker* people got in," said Frank Modell. "It was like suddenly a military exercise."

The fallout was worse. There was, to begin with, the matter of Ross's estate. Many of his friends had not taken to his widow, Ariane, with whom he was engaged in messy divorce proceedings; they thought her simultaneously greedy and clinging. Thurber even reported that Julius Baer, who made the arrangements with Campbell, did so with Ariane in person at her apartment at midnight—because he was "afraid Ariane would take it over herself and might make the services private." Ariane resented such talk and denied it specifically in a letter to the Whites within two weeks of her husband's death. She pleaded for understanding amid a lawsuit that she insisted she had pretty much been forced to launch against him:

> I cannot bear to think that anyone Harold cared for should think
> I did not love him or would have, willingly, hurt him in any way.
> Although we had been living apart since September, 1950, I lived

that time in almost complete retirement, always with the hope that we might eventually work [out] our problems and be happy together again. . . . [I]n spite of our differences, I loved Harold with all my heart. . . . I wish people he cared for could know the truth. I hope he will understand my writing this letter. He meant so much to me.

Though it took six years to settle the estate, the issue was resolved unsurprisingly: "a third of the money to Ariane, a third to Patty—and a third, naturally, to the lawyers."

More relevant for the staff was the question of how *The New Yorker* would carry on. Its key people, consumed with contracts and personal histories that they had developed with Ross, were bewildered. When they wondered what would happen, Liebling supposedly replied, "The same thing that happened to analysis after Freud died." The conclusive answer came on January 21, 1952 when, after more than six weeks of official silence, Raoul Fleischmann posted on the bulletin board an announcement stating, "William Shawn has accepted the position of editor of The New Yorker, effective today."

Shawn's anointing was inevitable. He was a fact man in the Ross mode and had, more than anyone other than his boss, pulled the magazine through World War II and its aftermath. Although he was "as different from Ross as *The New Yorker* is from the *National Geographic*," he worked up to fourteen hours a day and inspired considerable confidence. "I like to do a New Yorker piece once a year," Sam Behrman said, "just to get the benefit of Shawn's editing."

His elevation, however, was not unanimously acclaimed. Within a few months of the handover, Thurber—never shy about sharing his opinions—complained to the staff writer Peter De Vries, "I'm beginning to worry a little about Shawn's sense of humor and I hope you will tell me it is simply a case of an old magazine passing through the tail of a comet." Thurber specifically bewailed what he regarded as an influx of hackneyed cartoon situations: "I don't want to believe [Rea] Irvin is back. I wish to Christ Ross were." Others had simply favored Gus Lobrano over Shawn, John Cheever among them. Not long after Shawn got the nod, the writer found himself playing a roughhouse football game at E. J. Kahn, Jr.'s place; he made "a particularly bullish charge" and, careening into the defensive line, knocked Shawn over. "My father took such delight in telling that story," said Cheever's daughter, Susan.

Suggestions to the contrary, when Lobrano died on March 2, 1956, at the age of fifty-three, it was not of a broken heart but of cancer. His daughter, Dorothy—who herself would work for the magazine—was always upset by rumors that the rite of succession had somehow helped kill her father. The self-effacing Shawn, she insisted, never trumpeted his triumph. Of the affection and loyalty Lobrano inspired there was no doubt; Perelman and Salinger were particularly hard hit by his passing. White never forgot how his old roommate and Cornell brother left "a trail of friendship that penetrates the literary scene in every part of the globe." The short-story writer John Collier told Katharine, "A great part of my pleasure in writing stories again was based on the hope that I might do some that would please him." It was a sentiment that moved her deeply. Collier's condolence letter, she told William Maxwell, was

> the most remarkable summing up of what Gus meant to contributors, and it had a message for you in particular. This tribute really said what Andy was groping for in his obituary. That, by the way, was the most awful ordeal for Andy—far harder than to write about Ross, because he was closer to Gus. He felt that he had failed Gus, but Shawn felt just the opposite—that he had summed up both his personality and his career. . . . Gus can never be replaced.

The Whites marked Shawn's official debut at a party on March 1, 1952, at their duplex at 229 East 48th Street, overlooking Turtle Bay Gardens. Katharine scrupulously divided the guests into "Staff," "Writers and Artists," and "Outsiders." All together, 130 people attended. In homage to The New Yorker's origins, some of the women wore flapper garb, and at least one came equipped with a feather boa. At first the atmosphere was chilly, given the deference to Ross and the uncertainty about Shawn. "No one was used to a party like that," said one guest. "They all just sat around and stared at each other." But as the night went on, acquaintances warmed. Lillian Ross met Peter Arno for the first time and spent a good stretch charmed by him as they sat on the sofa; Shawn loosened up matters by playing jazz piano. Toward evening's end, however, the tiny Maeve Brennan began shouting drunkenly, "Charlie Addams, you're a pig!" Even after Katharine decorously arranged for Gardner Botsford to take her home, she continued to yell from the taxi, "Charlie Addams is a pig! Charlie Addams is a pig!"

Brennan had just begun to make herself known as one of the leading chroniclers of the Irish diaspora, with many exquisite short stories in The New Yorker. Later she would achieve semianonymous renown in "Talk" as "The Long-Winded Lady." In private life she had a talent for bewitching her fellow contributors. According to Botsford, she was involved not only with Addams but with Brendan Gill, Joseph Mitchell, and supposedly, Gibbs. She also became the fifth Mrs. St. Clair McKelway. The marriage took place in New Jersey, Gibbs said, "because the other states around here are getting bored with him."

By this time, McKelway's romantic existence had become hopelessly convoluted. He and Ann Honeycutt had long been divorced. In 1944 he entered into a short-lived fourth marriage with Martha Stephenson Kemp; in the four previous years she had been both the widow of the bandleader Hal Kemp and the ex-wife of Victor Mature. A debutante and a starlet, she was an "execrable" woman, said Edward Newhouse. "I was gonna shake her hand," Harold Ross grumbled, "but hands that have touched Mature will never touch mine." McKelway's marriage to Martha had been bracketed by his involvement with the free-spirited

Eileen McKenney (who, as previously mentioned, had inspired her sister Ruth's *New Yorker* stories about her) and a fling with the actress Natalie Schafer.* In 1954 McKelway capped these amorous misadventures by marrying Brennan—as big a drinker as he and, for all her talent and productivity, just as nutty.†

"It may not have been the worst of all possible marriages," William Maxwell reflected, "but it was not something you could be hopeful about." When the couple held a reception at their new place on East 44th Street, near the United Nations, Shawn shook his head slightly at Philip Hamburger as he beheld what was obviously a doomed union. McKelway and Brennan, said Roger Angell, were "like two children out on a dangerous walk: both so dangerous and so charming." Still, McKelway did his best to make a go of it, writing to himself:

> My objectives in life are now two. To revel in my marriage, by being at my playing best when not working, and to revel in my work by being at my working best when not playing. Since I can only play well when I have worked well, work, in a sense, must be the main objective—but only because it leads me to the best objective—that of being happy with Maeve. Nothing must be allowed to interfere with my work, and it will follow that nothing *can* interfere with my marriage. Even my marriage must not be allowed to interfere with my work, because that would constitute interference with my marriage, and that I won't put up with.

No amount of effort, however, could salvage the misguided joining. Before and during their marriage, Brennan would publish half a dozen

---

* Schafer would achieve dubious immortality as "Lovey" Howell on the TV series *Gilligan's Island.*

† In 1981 Maeve camped out slovenly in *The New Yorker*'s reception room for a couple of days. She died in 1993, having long wandered the streets of Manhattan when not in a nursing home.

stories in *The New Yorker* about their riotous life. Barely disguising their place at Sneden's Landing as "Herbert's Retreat," she would chronicle a series of sodden, disillusioned get-togethers with their literary friends. In real life, her marriage to McKelway would last all of five years. As it vaporized, Maeve clipped and sent to him a syndicated newspaper question-and-answer column that asked, "Are geniuses aware of their special gifts?" The response: "Not in early adulthood, and apparently many never come around to that realization."

As disheartening as his breakup may have been, McKelway suffered worse grief on another front. In the early 1930s he and his second wife, Estelle, had had a son, St. Clair McKelway, Jr., aka "Saint." The young man had gone to Cornell, where he formed a friendship with Joel White and become editor of the humor magazine *The Widow*. "Since he draws and writes pretty well, [he] hopes to use both talents as sidelines—which I think is very sound," his father told Katharine. Saint graduated from Cornell in 1952 and, following St. Clair, Sr.'s, example, entered the air force. Stationed in France, he trained to fly the H-19B Chickasaw rescue helicopter. It was in one of these vehicles that, on a routine flight near Bordeaux on June 3, 1954, the twenty-two-year-old lieutenant and three other crew members died. A main rotor blade became detached, and several explosions sent the craft plummeting.

The news, coming shortly after the marriage to Maeve, was shattering. McKelway retreated into his past, publishing in *The New Yorker* several moving pieces about his childhood and his early newspaper days. But his personality disorder kicked in again; he became convinced that Saint was sending him coded messages via automobile license plates. On these plates, too, McKelway saw the initials of many of his colleagues—Thurber, Liebling, Whitaker, Maeve, Gibbs, and Shawn, "to mention a few." He envisioned Katharine "directly behind me" on the road, and White "scooting on ahead." McKelway's published literary excesses climaxed in "The Edinburgh Caper," a frequently unreadable trip into paranoia involving a CIA conspiracy, a Soviet-inspired kidnapping plot against Eisenhower and the British royal family, and similar delusions. Though reminiscent of "Peter Roger Oboe" it was far more lunatic and lengthy.

Gibbs struggled under Shawn for his own reasons, even though the two had a good working relationship. Back in 1941 Shawn had called Gibbs's Profile of Richard Maney "a miraculously skillful, funny piece of prose." Lillian Ross personally witnessed the editor's regard: "I remember Bill Shawn thinking that Wolcott was much better than E. B. White." Shawn, said the editor's son, Wallace, "adored" Gibbs. But adoration went only so far. As was always the case with Gibbs, self-doubt and depression made their appearances. A few weeks after Shawn's coming-out party at the Whites', Sam Behrman expressed his concern to McKelway:

> I've been worried about him off and on for years. He goes through these bad periods and then suddenly and unaccountably turns some kind of corner, cheers up, and does a lot of work. I don't know what we can do for him. . . . I heard from Charlie Addams that Elinor had said she was more worried about him now than she had ever been before. . . . Gibbs being the man he is, I wouldn't be at all surprised to hear that, since I last talked to him on the phone, he has completed his new play and has written a novel comparable to *War and Peace*. On the other hand, the fact that his success with *Season*, and the security that should have come to him . . . have not made him less anxious but seem to have made him more so, and more melancholy, suggests to me that his trouble may be deeper than I ever thought.

His rare office visits became even rarer. It was not until 1954, after she had been on the staff for eight years, that Lillian Ross finally spoke with him. Gibbs poked his "slim, dapper, jaunty-looking" corpus into her office one day to congratulate her on a recent piece that had made considerable fun of the Junior League's precious planning of their Mardi

Gras Ball. "'You really gave it to those bores, I can't abide them,'" he said, grinning. "'Great writing!'" More typical was the experience of William Murray, the son of Janet Flanner's lover Natalia Danesi Murray. When he arrived to work at *The New Yorker* in 1956, he was installed in Gibbs's office. "He hadn't been seen around the premises for years, but he had never officially withdrawn," Murray remembered. Gibbs's desk was still cluttered, and one of his khaki shirts was hanging from a hook. Staff members referred to the office as "The Shrine." Its status was so sacrosanct—and office space so coveted—that at around the time Murray arrived, Katharine White wrote a lengthy and strangely agonized personal memo to Shawn about how it should remain assigned to the fiction, rather than the art, department.

In January 1955, Gibbs endured the passing of his sister, Angelica. Although she had successfully juggled her work with raising a son and a daughter, her domestic life came apart when her husband, the respectable Republican lawyer Robert Canfield, had an extramarital affair. Not long after they divorced, she died at age forty-six. To Behrman, who offered condolences, Gibbs expressed atypical introspection: "She was a fine girl, and I'm sorry that more people didn't know her better. We grew up apart, and I didn't see much of her myself, which seems a great pity to me now."

Gibbs's troubles extended to his freelance activities. He completed a domestic comedy called *Diana*, but despite announcements that Nancy Stern would bring it to Broadway, she did not. More serious was his failure to deliver an eighty-thousand-word novel, *Starry Stranger*, to Random House. Four years after he was due to turn in the manuscript, Random sued him for his $2,500 advance; in 1953 the New York State Supreme Court issued a judgment against him for $3,104.16, the figure including interest and costs. "I owe so much and can only say that I am probably the most improvident son of a bitch who ever lived," he once told Ross. He was not exaggerating. After a while he and Elinor did not pay their bills; rather, they stuffed them in shoeboxes in their closet. "That was my mother's way of dealing with financial crisis," said Tony. "I'm surprised at how often it worked."

Gibbs was also souring on his job, he told Thurber:

My own secret feeling about The New Yorker is that it is deteriorating at almost exactly the right rate for me. I seem to be wearing very thin as a writer and the theatre stuff I am doing now would be embarrassing if it appeared in the magazine we used to know. It seems adequate enough, though, when it runs along with twenty-thousand-word literary enigmas, exhausted little jokes by S. J. Sullivan-Perelman, and book reviews pointing out that in many ways O'Hara is a better writer than Hemingway, Fitzgerald, and Faulkner.

He now found himself subjected to gratuitous blue pencils. "I figure there are seven people who edit me in one way or another and they try to earn their money by making little lunatic last-minute changes, particularly the man in charge of superfluous punctuation," he wrote. "I have no objection to clarity but I don't like having jokes twisted around in order to be perfectly comprehensible to my cleaning woman." So, determined to maintain what remained of his own voice, he embarked on a project that turned out to be uniquely close to his heart.

———

Gibbs was not entirely enamored of what was lately happening on Fire Island. The intrusive arrival of telephones and television paralleled the growing crassness of certain summer people. Mel Brooks, who literally lived next door to Gibbs, typified this devolution. Once, trying to get a rise out of his neighbor, the in-your-face Brooks asked the aloof Gibbs what it would mean if he saw his, Brooks's, house being swept out to sea. "I think, Mr. Brooks," Gibbs responded, not especially interested in

Brooks's home or Brooks himself, "that it would mean it would be about half an hour until mine went, too."

Nonetheless Gibbs remained devoted enough to his summer retreat to launch the seasonal weekly newspaper *The Fire Islander* in 1954. His motives were various. In part he wanted to annoy one of his neighbors, Leo Shull, the founder of the *Fire Island Press* and the entertainment-focused *Show Business* magazine. Gibbs could forgive Shull for dedicating himself to "the exposure of unlisted private telephone numbers, home addresses of active producers, playwrights, and directors, their favored haunts, and the most likely time they may be reached at any hour of the day or night." But his choler rose when Shull showed up Fire Island's impostures—editorializing, for instance, "The parties are incessant. We used to cover 3 to 4 a day and up to 7 on Saturdays, besides making the 4 nitespots [sic]. Cocktail parties start at 5 . . . and run till 2, usually, sometimes till dawn."

Anyway, Gibbs wanted to publish a newspaper that would be "written in something resembling the English language—a project hitherto unheard-of in the short and troubled annals of Fire Island journalism." His most keenly felt editorial declaration was his terse pronouncement, "I'm in love with the goddam beach."

It was indeed a romantic enterprise, reminiscent of his Long Island cub reporter days nearly thirty years before. Gibbs's statement of purpose repudiated his past and embraced his present:

We worked once on a Long Island weekly where the lady in charge of social notes saved herself a good deal of time and bother by confining herself almost exclusively to the activities of a Mr. and Mrs. Gil Manifold and their charming daughter, Belle, all of whom happened to be cousins of hers. The subscribers were told practically everything about this pleasingly named family, right down to what they ate for breakfast, but they heard very little about anybody else. It was generally felt that the Manifolds got a little monotonous. *The Fire Islander* will try to avoid this kind of reporting.

Gibbs floated *The Fire Islander* with a thousand dollars, kicked in by himself and Bill Birmingham and a third local partner, Herman Wechsler, a fine art dealer who owned the FAR Gallery at East 65th Street and Madison Avenue. Wechsler, a tasteful and literate graduate of New York University, brought considerable intellectual cachet, having known Ezra Pound and the art historian Meyer Schapiro. The operation was conducted on "one half of a desk" at Birmingham's waterfront office. For legwork, Gibbs turned to a series of young men, some of them recommended to him by a minor dean at the Columbia Graduate School of Journalism. In general he was less than enthused by the recruits; he declared one of them "as dim as Miss Bush League."

One of his more successful candidates was Constantine Karvonides. A young veteran of Scholastic Magazines, the Bowdoin College graduate saw an ad in the *Herald Tribune* announcing that Gibbs was recruiting reporters for a new newspaper and realized, "Jesus Christ, this job is for me." Though it was only May, Gibbs was already out at the beach, but Elinor suggested that Karvonides join them there. The trip was memorable; Elinor called on a local veterinarian to chloroform the family's eight cats for the ferry ride. About halfway across the bay, they arose from the anesthetic and began screeching. When the party alit on Ocean Beach, to be greeted by Tony and a convoy of express wagons, the feline howling climaxed, with local shopkeepers sticking their heads out of windows and doors to see what was going on. Once the entourage was in the house, the cats started climbing the walls. "That was my introduction to the family," said Karvonides.

The Fire Islander was assembled at the Ryder Press in Freeport, an establishment that also printed an in-house newsletter for American Airlines and literature for a religious sect that emphasized prophecy. After putting the paper to bed on Thursdays, the small crew would try to get the last ferry back to the island, sometimes making do at various bed-and-breakfast type establishments. For Tony, that was a luxury; usually he would find himself crashing in the car of his "totally incompetent" colleague St. George Bryan, Courty's brother, or at the printing plant itself. "I could just find a big stack of crumpled-up papers and sleep on that. It was pretty soft."

The production of the first issue was fraught with drama. As the deadline approached, a nervous Gibbs—who had not been drinking for the week prior to publication—started up again. On this occasion the print shop owner joined him and, as the presses began to roll, passed out. Rather than return to Ocean Beach, Gibbs got into a taxi with Karvonides back to Manhattan. He had no money, so he had the driver pull up to "21," where he pressed the doorman for fifty dollars; the astonished attendant gave Gibbs twice that amount. "At that point, the cab driver was thinking, 'Get me the fuck out of here,' " said Karvonides.

The bulk of the May 28, 1954, debut number of *The Fire Islander* constituted the sort of small-town items Gibbs had known at the *East Norwich Enterprise*, the *North Hempstead Record*, and the *Nassau Daily Star*. "Police Boat for Islip," "Group Seeks Support of Land Owners," and "Seasoned Angler Forecasts Usual Woes for Fishermen" were typical headlines. There was a good dose of inside information and innocent gossip, such as "William Randolph Hearst, Jr. [is] a guest at Flynn's Ocean Bay Park Hotel this Decoration Day weekend." But Gibbs, determined to bring as much sophistication to the enterprise as he could, called on friends for literary and artistic ballast. In that first issue, the self-described "visiting gourmet" Nathaniel Benchley had a funny piece about favored local recipes, including "Potage P. W. Wrenn, Jr.," in honor of *New Yorker* contributor Philip Wrenn. John O'Hara scraped up some surly memories of a 1938 Fire Island visit, his ego on full display: "I am a venal man, a mercenary, and a true artist." Charles Addams made the most on-target contribution, a cartoon of a beach house equipped with a lifeboat hanging from its side. The caption, uttered by one passerby to another, was "They worry about hurricanes."

The backbone of *Fire Islander* copy came from local talent. Bill Birmingham turned out to be a fine writer and did a column called "Beach Combings." Another column, "On the Beach," was written by Roger Hall, a maverick veteran of the OSS who once predicted that had the organization not existed, he would "have been shot by a firing squad on his own side." To distribute each week's 2,500 copies, Gibbs enlisted able-bodied boys, including Tony Stern, to trundle the ten-cent newspaper to local shops via the ubiquitous express wagons. The paper would not be hawked on the boardwalks, said its founder, because "I don't like kids yelling around the streets."

In a small way, Gibbs became a crusading editor. He and his cohorts covered and editorialized about the need for a proper boat basin, a youth center, decent tennis courts, and more authority regarding overnight guests. Their biggest issue was control of the dunes. On the front page of the August 20, 1954, edition, Gibbs spotlighted the proposed purchase of a ten-thousand-dollar "Tracto-Shovel" that could move up to a thousand yards of sand in a day. The matter was clotted by local interests like the Pastorfields and turf wars among state legislators and such nettlesome parties as Robert Moses.

Gibbs wanted to transcend these parochial concerns by drawing on the skills of professional writers. They were, he remarked, "as abundant out here as crabs." Nonetheless, the solicitation process mortified him. "I'm sure this is the God damndest [sic] request you ever got," he told George Price by way of asking for a drawing. He suggested that Thurber write a piece that began, "I've never been to Fire Island, and the ideas I've formed of it from people I know are etc etc. . . . but I do [know something] about country journalism. It is a sucker's racket." Admitting that his venture was "hell's own imposition," Gibbs beseeched White:

I have been mixed up in a lot of suicidal enterprises in my life, but nothing like this. As you can see from the samples, I've been printing a writer of sorts each week, and I'm committed to go on doing it. At the moment, though, the summer looks terribly long, and I'm damned if I can see how I'm going to make it. You ought to be the last person I'd try to drag into all this, because I know damn well that you don't write much for fun, but it is quite a situation for me. Five hundred words or so, dealing with anything you know about rural journalism, beaches, fish, birds, or just the weather would be the best thing that could possibly happen to me. I am embarrassed about the whole thing, but certainly not enough.

Gibbs ultimately printed material by Lucius Beebe, John Lardner, Al Frueh, John McNulty, Whitney Darrow, Mary Petty, Robert Day, William Steig, Frank Sullivan, Saul Steinberg, John Crosby, Ann Honeycutt, Carl Rose, Allan Dunn, and Arthur Kober. He even paid *The New Yorker* five dollars to reprint one of Mosher's Fire Island stories and persuaded Frank Modell to draw the newspaper's banner—a couple of small houses, the island's water tower, and its landmark lighthouse. Not everyone enjoyed their dealings with *The Fire Islander*: after Gibbs's neighbor Herman Wouk turned in a piece, he solicited a contribution from his old radio boss, Fred Allen; Allen registered his dissatisfaction, with a distinctive lack of capital letters:

mr. gibbs promised to send me a copy of the paper the week the piece was used. after waiting for two weeks for the paper to arrive i sent him a note and one dollar enclosed to send me a copy. he returned the dollar and said i was lifetime subscriber. i still have not received the paper. i am thinking of withdrawing as a contributor. i don't mind not getting paid for my product but i resent being ignored. i may go over to the Shull group next summer.

Under Gibbs, *The Fire Islander* was an informative, literate, and quirky start-up. It even garnered attention on an NBC news segment ("We simulated a publication meeting on the porch," said Karvonides). But it was just too big an undertaking. Shortly before Independence Day 1956, Gibbs turned the paper over to a new group that included a collection of teenage editors. In a farewell both fond and jaundiced, he expressed pride in what the scrappy newspaper had accomplished. "Contrary to persistent rumors, the reason we felt obliged to abandon it ourselves was not financial," he wrote. "The real trouble was that each of us who ran it was primarily engaged in another business from which unhappily his living came." He signed off, "We expect to be visible as contributors from time to time, and the paper will, of course, always have our best wishes and our first spiritual support. . . . Beyond that, however, we are as dead as so many dinosaurs. It may be just as well."

For other *New Yorker* mainstays, much of the Eisenhower decade was mainly comfortable, productive, and rewarding. A. J. Liebling had ongoing problems with obesity but published a worthy stream of "Reporter at Large" and "Our Footloose Correspondents" pieces. He also found a growing reputation as a newspaper critic in the magazine's "Wayward Press" column.

John O'Hara did not particularly suffer from his break with *The New Yorker*. Indeed, from his memorabilia-lined study in Princeton, "thousands of good words were issued every week," encompassing novels, short stories for slick magazines, and his "Appointment with O'Hara" column. Although he never realized his dreams of winning the Pulitzer and Nobel prizes, he did snare the National Book Award for fiction for *Ten North Frederick* in 1955. The book was a popular success as well, selling more than 65,000 copies in its first two weeks and, after passing the million-copy mark, earning him an engraved silver cigarette case from his publisher, Bennett Cerf.

Amid his amorous misconduct, Charles Addams remained reliably macabre and funny, his career proceeding "in an ever-rising, unbroken curve"—an accomplishment, Irwin Shaw said, that "none of the rest of us" could claim.

White did not coast on the critical acclaim of *Stuart Little* and *Charlotte's Web*. He continued to turn out "Comment," casuals, spoofs (Gibbs regarded one of them, a take-off on Hemingway titled "Across the Street and Into the Grill," as among the funniest things he had ever read), assorted dispatches, and personal essays. White collected the best of these in *The Second Tree from the Corner* in 1954. Befitting his gradual recognition as a latter-day Thoreau—his literary idol—he returned periodically to Allen Cove and the semihomespun life. There, following the death of Ross, he lived on and off for several months out of the year. Finally he and Katharine returned to Maine for good. He made clear where he would hang his hat from now on in the first of his "Letter from the East" pieces, which appeared shortly before Christmas 1955. He affectionately referred to his domicile as "Wormwood":

At Wormwood, each season carries a hundred foreshadowings of the season that is to follow—which is one of the things I love about it. Winter is rough and long, but spring lies all round about. Yesterday, a small white keel feather escaped from my goose and lodged in the bank boughs near the kitchen porch, where I spied it as I came home in the cold twilight. The minute I saw the feather, I was projected into May, knowing that a barn swallow would be along to claim the prize and use it to decorate the front edge of its nest. Immediately, the December air seemed full of the wings of swallows and the warmth of barns.

It was from Maine that White completed his updated version of his mentor Will Strunk's *The Elements of Style*. Jack Case, an editor at Macmillan, wished the project on him after reading his "Letter from the East" of July 27, 1957; it had been a rambling essay that somehow ended up with a reminiscence of Strunk and his "little book." In revising the work and adding his afterword, "An Approach to Style," White departed from Strunk in some ways, emphasizing certain grammatical and rhetorical bugbears of his own. But he did not disagree—nor would Ross have —with the professor's most forceful observation: "Vigorous writing is concise. A sentence should contain no unnecessary words, a paragraph no unnecessary sentences, for the same reason that a drawing should have no unnecessary lines and a machine no unnecessary parts. This requires not that the writer make all his sentences short, or that he avoid all detail and treat his subjects only in outline, but that every word tell."

"My single purpose," the ever-modest White told Case, "is to be faithful to Strunk as of 1958, reliable, holding the line, and maybe even selling some copies to English Departments [sic] that collect oddities and curios." In that he succeeded. Although there has lately been a small backlash against the prescriptive, even rigid tone of *The Elements of Style,* it remains a touchstone of prose composition, required reading in uncounted classrooms and a phenomenon in terms of the millions of copies it has sold. White gave Katharine leave to redact his handiwork. "She is a better grammarian, organizer, teacher, editor, and mother than I am," he said.

The death of Gus Lobrano had taken place at an awkward time for Katharine, just as she and Andy were contemplating their permanent retreat to the Pine Tree State. With circumstances mounting, she set about preparing the future of the fiction department. However, when she resigned in 1957, she left no designated successor. Rather, Shawn and Maxwell and others would deal with particular authors. For several years Katharine would continue to edit manuscripts from the farm, much as she had done back in the late 1930s and early 1940s.

But her editorial expression now found its voice mainly in columns under the heading of "Onward and Upward in the Garden." In these pieces she delighted in seed catalogs, horticultural history, the process of planting, and related backyard matters. Not all readers were fascinated. In *Fact* magazine, the feisty David Cort, late of the Luce empire—with whom both Katharine and Gibbs had crossed swords over some rejected contributions back in 1930—summed up one of her contributions thusly:

> Mrs. White has a lawn. Lawns are great. George Washington's lawn, or bowling green, was "just north of the vegetable garden." (Remember that.) Her father's handyman. Mumblety-peg, played on lawns. Grass. Lady gardeners. Espaliered fruit trees back of lawns. Firewood. Jane Austen. Berries, bamboos, house-plants. Finally, the marigold must not be made our national flower, because it is Mexican. Up the goldenrod.

The assumption that anyone might want to pay to read such material was "sheer insolence," Cort wrote. Nonetheless, Katharine's disciples remained beholden to her. "I am very sad, for myself and for the magazine, for I think as an editor you are irreplaceable, and probably personally responsible for a giant part of the magazine's excellence in the last thirty years," John Updike wrote when she stepped down. "I don't know much about editors, but you have a freshness of reaction to printed words whose effect on me has always been tonic."

On the surface, there was much happiness in Thurber's life. In 1953 his daughter, Rosemary, a senior at the University of Pennsylvania, married a fellow student, Frederick Sauers. While the father of the bride was opposed to early marriages, he blessed the union; the guests at the "wonderful and perfect" wedding included the Mark Van Dorens and the Whites. Garlands were accumulating in the form of honorary degrees from Kenyon, Williams, and Yale.

But Thurber exploded when another bastion of higher learning—his alma mater, Ohio State—succumbed to the climate of the times. Hearkening to *The Male Animal*, the university in September 1951 instituted a gag rule for campus speakers, requiring that its president grant permission for them to utter their thoughts, lest they spread subversion. Calling OSU "that terrible institution," Thurber fumed, "I wish the entire faculty and student body would resign." A couple of months later, apparently trying to placate their upset son and get him to tone down his public pronouncements, OSU offered him an honorary degree. On the day of Ross's death Thurber wrote to the university's president with terse regret that such an acceptance would be construed as "approval or as indifference to the situation."*

Thurber's refusal was almost certainly as much the result of his own cantankerousness as it was a defense of free speech. His blindness was permanent. Fans offered heartfelt, if unhelpful, advice—watch Mexican jumping beans, they said, or rub lemon juice in your eyes, or even apply a hot flatiron to the side of your face. His recurring thyroid condition also cursed him on and off. "I have been much worse the past eight weeks," he complained in the fall of 1952. A year later he told the Whites, "I feel better than I ever have in my life."

Whatever his physical condition, and probably in part because of it, he continued to hound *The New Yorker* for becoming gray and humorless. Now the matter was personal: the magazine was holding back and rejecting his pieces. Thurber resented this disrespect, as he did the picayune queries to which he was subjected. Under Lobrano and Ross, he wrote, "no violent pencil was ever laid upon my manuscripts." But this was dif-

---

* Thurber had his own brush with charges of disloyalty: the FBI kept a file on him. In 1953 the self-appointed political defense organization AWARE—which made its money by "clearing" creative artists of subversion—suggested to the ABC television network that it would "run a serious risk of adverse public opinion" by featuring Thurber on its airwaves. For this warning, and Thurber's subsequent exoneration, AWARE received twenty dollars. In 1962, arguing the celebrated lawsuit of AWARE's most famous victim, John Henry Faulk, Faulk's lawyer Louis Nizer praised Thurber—who was by then deceased—as "one of the great figures that we ought to be proud of in America."

ferent, a bevy of editors picking apart his copy. Thurber responded with a string of complaining letters.

> [A] letter of mine to the *New Yorker,* in which I accused the magazine of being "editor conscious," drew a denial of this charge in the most editor conscious letter I ever got. It contained this sentence, "We thank God every day for Shawn." I wrote an answer to this, but I didn't send it, in which I said, "I forgive God every night for having created editors and I thank God for no editor on earth." It seems to me, as I have told Shawn, a healthy state of affairs when writers heckle editors. If the *New Yorker* writers ever become editor-dominated, the end will be clearly in view.

He grew so combative that Whitaker asked him one day, "What's the matter? You been sick or something? You haven't threatened this place in a month." But he was not so fixated on himself that he could not acknowledge his own sapping spirit. "I fear that where my fancy flowered and my wild invention grew, there is now a small and arid space," he informed John McNulty. "The fresh spaces are wilted and there is rust on my metaphor mixer." And yet he continued to produce enough good material that he was still able to issue books like *Thurber Country, Alarms and Diversions, Further Fables for Our Time,* and especially, *The Wonderful O,* all of which solidified his reputation not only as a master humorist but as an incomparable fantasist.

By contrast, Gibbs broke little new literary ground after he gave up *The Fire Islander.* He published virtually nothing in *The New Yorker* except for his regular column. And at a time when provocative, experimental works were challenging Broadway audiences, he clung to convention. He found *Six Characters in Search of an Author* "rather painful" and *Waiting for Godot* "a very sad and confusing situation all around." In his eyes, musicals that pleased both the critics and the crowds fared only somewhat better. Gibbs singled out *The Music Man* as "an exceptionally cheerful offering" but dismissed colleagues who compared it with *Guys and Dolls, My Fair Lady,* and *Oklahoma!* At the end of 1956, he published in the upstart magazine *Playboy* a rueful reflection on the current theater scene that said as much about his state of mind as about what he had witnessed: "With the passing years, my judgment, I'm afraid, has grown increasingly detached, and my feeling for the stage, once so miraculously like that of a young man afflicted for the first time with love, is now rather more like that of a middle-aged husband."

In that regard, he was becoming alienated from the people closest to him. "They couldn't live with each other and they couldn't live without each other," said Tony of his parents. Though Janet was only in high school, her father was already making absurd plans for her domestic future. He hoped aloud that she would first marry a man with money, then one possessed of creativity, then a third with royal blood, and then—finally—someone she could actually love. "That was shocking to me," said Karvonides, "to talk about one's daughter this way."

He also had sharp thoughts about his son. "Gibbs used to complain to me about Tony because he was so damn straight," Karvonides said. "He used to say to me, 'Why don't you take him out and get laid? When I was his age, I was screwing chorus girls.'" Tony, however, had a more respectable agenda. After graduating from Princeton, he found himself in the army, working at Fort Hamilton and avoiding contact with his parents. On Fire Island he met a straightforward, presentable young graduate of Wheaton College from Garden City, Long Island, named Elizabeth ("Tish") Villa, the daughter of a Swiss-born cheese importer. Gibbs was not happy about their conventional coupling; when he saw them walking hand in hand, he would say, "I think I'm going to throw up." Tish had no illusions about her persona. "By his standards, I was certainly dull," she said.

But before long they were engaged. Gibbs and Elinor took the news hard. "I think they just had this vision that Tony should maybe be a playboy or something," said Tish. Come the wedding day in January

1958, Gibbs bewailed the nuptials at the Cathedral of the Incarnation in Garden City. "He found the prospect absolutely intolerable," Shawn said. "He said it was so damn *middle-class*" (emphasis in the original). In the end, Gibbs got drunk and inexcusably didn't show up. Elinor attended but, under the influence herself, spent most of her time at the reception at the Garden City Hotel in an anteroom bemoaning the union. Tony— whose best man was Bill Birmingham—was unmoved by his parents' woes. "They were so continuously unpleasant about all the women I went out with that I had simply written off their opinion."

As 1958 proceeded, however, things seemed to get better. Throughout the first half of the year, Gibbs did "a complete 180" about the marriage, telling Birmingham that he was actually pleased by it. Sometime in July he gave up booze and cigarettes alike. He even began seeing a psychoanalyst—this despite having declared only a few years before, "I am just about the only member of my little world who has never been 'in analysis,' as the sorcerous [sic] jargon seems to go." He was happy about the forthcoming publication of Thurber's *The Years with Ross,* personally editing two chapters and, in early August, responding to one of Thurber's many inquiries with information that would round out the idiosyncratic work. "It was a letter typical of Wolcott Gibbs at his best—sharp, ironic, funny, and I am glad to say, cheerful," Thurber remembered. "Wolcott was not a man easy to please, and no one's pleasure gratified me more than his, and no one's judgment meant more to me."

Gibbs returned the compliment. He thought that *The Years with Ross* "should serve always as a model for such reminiscences. In addition to a phenomenal memory, Mr. Thurber has enormous perseverance in research, a wit and style that have always commanded my stunned admiration, and, I should say, a romantic heart that has enabled him to think of his place of business as the most picturesque establishment in publishing history."

As it was, Gibbs was looking forward to his own upcoming collection, *More in Sorrow.* "Because of a late-blooming and therefore more than usually passionate energy, I have contributed more words to *The New Yorker* than anybody in its thirty-odd year span," he wrote in his introduction. Given the physical limitations of the book and his prodigious output, the oeuvre constituted the barest taste of a fillet. A quarter of the book's contents had already appeared in *Bed of Neuroses* in 1937. Another 25 percent had been reprinted in *Season in the Sun and Other Pleasures* back in 1946. Irrespective of their previous appearances, the entries were generally worthy. Among them were notable theater pieces, the Profiles of Alexander Woollcott and Thomas Dewey, a salute to Robert Benchley, a "Wayward Press" column on gossip writers' reactions to Pearl Harbor, a couple of the better Fire Island stories, Long Island Rail Road reminiscences, certain casuals, and the best parodies—of Hemingway and Sinclair Lewis, of Aldous Huxley and Westbrook Pegler. "Time . . . Fortune . . . Life . . . Luce" ran first.

"In my opinion, the selection that follows contains the best of this staggering output, or at any rate the part that pleases me most," Gibbs wrote. "I will be grateful, and rather startled, if anyone agrees." With these words in hand, Gibbs ascended the stairs of The Studio on the night of August 16.

CHAPTER 14

"WHOSE DAYS, IN ANY CASE, WERE NUMBERED"

"I'll be here when I'm sixty, snarling," Gibbs once predicted to Nancy Hale. He was off by four years.

In his final nontheater piece for *The New Yorker,* the short story "A Fellow of Infinite Jest," Gibbs assigned himself the alter ego of Bardolph Martin, "the last of the fashionable literary humorists." He transmuted Elinor, Tony, and Janet into "Perdita," "Cyril," and "Ariadne." In a mordant and extended scene, Gibbs had them discuss his past accomplishments, his decline amid changing public tastes, and the possibility of dispatching him for his insurance money. Ariadne thinks he is worth about a dime, whereas Perdita estimates a return of about $300,000. The story ends with the arrival of Bardolph. His "halting footsteps were audible in the hallway," Gibbs wrote, "clearly those of a man whose days, in any case, were numbered." It was an ending that Katharine White thought "masterly."

His actual departure was as mysterious as his marriage to Helen and the suicide of Elizabeth. Winchell, with his penchant for inaccuracy, reported, "Mrs. Wolcott Gibbs was upstairs in their Fire Island home confined to a wheel chair [*sic*] when Gibbs died at his desk downstairs.

Charles Addams, whose cartoons are usually connected with macabre things, dropped in and found him." Forty-five years later Botsford conveyed a similarly garbled version. "Gibbs was upstairs in his bedroom, reading proofs," he wrote.

> Periodically, Elinor would call up to him to remind him of lunch, but there was never an answer. Finally, she asked the maid to go up and rout him out. The maid came back and said, "Maybe you'd better go up, Mr. Addams." Charlie went up, and there was Gibbs, dead in his chair. "He had his feet up on the windowsill," Addams told me later, "and the proofs of his book *More in Sorrow* were in his lap. He had a cigarette in his hands and it had burned right down to his fingers."

Some of these details are correct. Elinor was indeed in a wheelchair, having recently injured her ankle. And every reliable account places Gibbs with some form of *More in Sorrow* and a cigarette in hand. But no maid was likely in attendance. Nor, definitely, was Addams. And Gibbs was not sitting up. The most authoritative version comes from Tony. Though not present—he was with Tish at her parents' place in nearby Seaview—he pieced together what happened:

> My understanding was that he had taken the first copy of *More in Sorrow* upstairs the previous evening to look it over. He hadn't seen it; it had only just arrived. And then he didn't come down to breakfast the next morning, didn't come down at all. And my mother grew mildly concerned, and went up to see what was wrong and discovered that he was in bed and dead with the book. And I don't know if she saw a bottle of pills or what, but my understanding, again, is that she called—because I think we had a telephone at that point—Bill Birmingham and their doctor, or Bill may have called the doctor, because she probably didn't want doctors or

didn't know how to get hold of them. I don't think the town had a phone book at that point. But I guess Bill went up and had a look at him and knew immediately he was dead.

Amid the grief and confusion, it would not have been surprising for the ever-supportive Addams to place himself in the scene to somehow take some of the burden of the discovery off Elinor. It was not surprising, either, that Birmingham insisted that no autopsy be performed. When the attending physician mentioned the procedure, Elinor became quite upset, at which point Birmingham drew the doctor aside.

"What he did say, I was told, was, 'If you insist on an autopsy, you are finished in this town,'" said Tony. "I'm sure Birmingham probably also at the time reassured him and said, 'Look, I know this guy and he's not healthy and he just slipped away in the night. So why are you making this production about it?' And certainly there was no sign of foul play or anything like that, so the doctor probably had no great problems squaring it with his conscience." Therefore, the official record was fudged. The coroner entered "Congestion and Cyanosis of Lungs" as the cause of death, with notations that an investigation and a chemical analysis were pending. It was further stated on the certificate that an autopsy had been performed, when in fact it never was.

Elinor suspected that her husband had killed himself. More than once he had overdosed, intentionally or unintentionally, on a combination of sleeping pills and alcohol. Gibbs's access to drugs increased in his last years when the family moved from their semiprivate East 51st Street digs to a large apartment building on Park Avenue and 82nd. Mail was often left on a communal table in the lobby; among the parcels were pharmaceutical samples that were dropped off for the three physicians with offices on the ground floor. Elinor took full advantage of them. "She would sweep through without a second thought," said Tony. "Anything that looked interesting, she'd take it."

Tish, among others, was dubious about a suicide. "He seemed rather, for him, in a more up cycle," she said. "I don't think that I can remember a bad time. . . . It wasn't like he'd been ailing."

The news made the front page of the *Times*. Thurber, in London with Helen, telegraphed Shawn: DEEPLY SHOCKED AND GRIEVED PLEASE HAVE [DAISE] TERRY SEND FLOWERS FOR US TO FUNERAL AND TO ELINOR. Tom Gorman of the secretarial staff told Katharine he was "drenched in grief." When word reached O'Hara, he wept. He concluded that his old friend had drunk himself to death. "I had hoped, without much hope, that he might last out this phase and be one of my old-age cronies as he had been of my youth, but the whole business of life was stacked against Gibbs," he told a friend. "I know of no one who had better reasons for being soured, and he is all the proof you need that things do not even up in the end. They never evened up for him."

"We can't bear it," wrote John Mason Brown and his wife, Cassie, to Elinor. "We can't believe it."

The wake was held, as Ross's service had been, at Frank Campbell's. The funeral proper took place at the Protestant Episcopal Church of the Ascension at Fifth Avenue and Tenth Street, not far from where Gibbs once lived with his sister. It was an odd ritual; Rev. Peter Wilkinson, the assistant rector, did not once mention the name of the deceased, having never met him. "He wasn't about to take the chance of pronouncing the name 'Wolcott' from a standing start," said Tony. A number of Gibbs's brothers in theatrical criticism were at the burial at Ferncliff Cemetery in Hartsdale. So were McKelway, Perelman, Liebling, Mitchell, Meredith, Burr, and Maney; Sam Behrman's son, David, handled Elinor in her wheelchair. When he returned from the services, Sam found a copy of *More In Sorrow* waiting for him in his hallway, presumably sent either by Henry Holt or by *The Saturday Review*; the magazine was hoping he would write a review. "Just can't," he jotted in his diary a few days later.

White offered *The New Yorker*'s official farewell—with typical affection, humor, and personal insight. Gibbs probably would have been most pleased with White's estimation of his nontheatrical editorial abilities:

Often the editor would have been far happier to publish a Gibbs opinion sheet than the manuscript to which it was attached. In fact, if these spontaneous and unguarded written opinions of his could be released to the world (and they most assuredly can't be), they would make probably a funnier and sounder critique of creative writing in the late twenties and early thirties than has ever been assembled.

"Terrible that it had to be written," Thurber told White, "but a fine thing that you were there to write it."

Unlike Gibbs, Thurber had a repeat triumph on Broadway. It was *A Thurber Carnival,* a 1960 revue based on his best stories and drawings. Burgess Meredith directed the unconventional show, which featured Tom Ewell, Paul Ford, John McGiver, Peggy Cass, Alice Ghostley, and Eddie Mayehoff, a veteran of *Season in the Sun.* But seventeen weeks into its run, bad luck nearly ruined everything when an actors' strike forced a closure from June 25 to September 5. When the strike was over, Ewell, who had played such central parts as Walter Mitty and Thurber himself, was no longer available. And then something of a miracle occurred: Thurber stepped into the role.

"He literally jumped at the chance," said the actress, writer, director, and producer Haila Stoddard. "It was the only way to save the show. He was always performing, anyway." It was an audacious move. But when Meredith asked if Thurber had memorized his lines, he erupted, "Memorized! I wrote the goddamn thing. I have the whole play memorized."

For the author it was a wonderful experience, even if he could not see the audience. "He was a born actor," said Stoddard. "He was suddenly a happy man again, full of involvement with the show and in love with being the new star on Broadway. And for the three months he was acting, the box office was fine. He saved his own show." Thurber and

Meredith both ended up winning a special Tony Award for their efforts, and *Carnival* ran for 223 performances.

Thurber's *New Yorker* work, what remained of it, was less happy. "My old relationship really died with Ross and Lobrano," he told Milton Greenstein, the magazine's counsel and guru. Roger Angell agreed. "Thurber's copy often came in clean and poor," he recalled. "He'd shout and carry on. 'Do you know who I am?' he'd yell at me over the phone. 'I sat at the Long Table at *Punch!*' Once Shawn pulled me aside in the corridor and asked me, 'Do you think Thurber is crazy?' " Nor were Andy and Katharine, among others, pleased with the pieces he issued in *The Atlantic Monthly* about Ross, which—loving as they were—by turns made his subject out to be an editorial moron, extolled Thurber's own importance, and dwelt on such touchy matters as *New Yorker* payments and the sex lives of his colleagues. Little wonder, then, that between the sweetness of *Carnival* and the sorrow of the magazine, when he slipped away on November 2, 1961, his famous last words were reportedly the double-barreled "God bless . . . goddam."

When it came time for White, inevitably, to have the last word, he conveyed it with his characteristic generosity and compassion: "I am one of the lucky ones. I knew him before blindness hit him, before fame hit him, and I tend always to think of him as a young artist in a small office in a big city, with all the world still ahead. It was a fine thing to be young and at work in New York for a new magazine when Thurber was young and at work, and I will always be glad that this happened to me." He observed, poignantly,

> His waking dreams and his sleeping dreams commingled shamelessly and uproariously; Ohio was never far from his thoughts, and when he received a medal from his home state in 1953, he wrote, "The clocks that strike in my dreams are often the clocks of Columbus." It is a beautiful sentence and a revealing one.

St. Clair McKelway's denouement was strung out and pathetic. In 1963 he secured a six-week summer residency at Yaddo, the writers' colony in upstate New York. There he intended to finish up a book "about an impostor, a Brooklyn man now dead" that would, he said, be a "study of imposture, and the odd relation of the impostor to the artist." But after checking in, he almost immediately checked out—to the Albany Medical Center. Yaddo canceled his residency; John Cheever, who had helped sponsor him, was compelled to apologize, "I did not know he was this seriously unhinged." Some years later McKelway ended up in Bellevue and submitted a self-obsessed account of his stay there. Titled "A Reporter at Large: A Journalist in Bellevue," it was never printed.

Poverty went in tandem with McKelway's dementia. He had begun running up major debts after his return from the Pacific; when he was in Hollywood, Ross was "amazed that creditors didn't grab money out there." By the time he married Maeve and Saint died, the New York State Tax Commission reckoned he was in hock to *The New Yorker* for $7,138.76—in part as the result of incessant advances of fifty dollars a week. At intervals his creditors included the Rockland Light and Power Co.; the Uplifters Club of Rustic Canyon, California; the Algonquin; Dave Chasen's restaurant; and the kennel where he kept his cats. Toward the end of his life, he had his mail forwarded to such disparate venues as the Hotel Esplanade in Locarno, Switzerland, and a Holiday Inn in Temple, Texas. At one point McKelway tried to check into the Mansfield Hotel in midtown, but the front desk refused him—not only because of his appearance but because he had left his wallet, containing three hundred dollars, back at *The New Yorker*. As he could, he ventured forth to the magazine, where he would often doodle on the walls, much like Thurber, although the quality of his work was not recorded.

He passed away on January 10, 1980, penniless and "dotty."

John O'Hara prospered. After he returned to *The New Yorker* with "Imagine Kissing Pete" in September 1960, nearly forty more of his stories graced the magazine's pages during the decade. Dedicating his 1961 collection *Assembly* to Gibbs, O'Hara continued to pay homage to his deceased champion by placing much of his work in Gibbsville. He wrote major novels, especially *The Big Laugh, Elizabeth Appleton,* and *The Lockwood Concern.* Critical reaction to his output was mixed, with reviewers tending to favor his stories over his longer works. But despite his not being awarded any honorary degrees—an omission that rankled—he received deference in the form of a *Newsweek* cover story in 1963 and, the following year, the Award of Merit Medal from the National Institute of Arts and Letters.

O'Hara treated the oscillating reception with his particular brand of gratitude and contempt. But so long as the money kept coming in he was happy; in 1963 his income tax payment alone was $135,000. He grew consumed with material objects, acquiring a veritable fleet of Rolls-Royces and other high-end cars, an expensive wardrobe, and tchotchkes of various kinds. He also turned reactionary, his conservatism reaching its peak with his 1960s *Newsday* column "My Turn." His most embarrassing moment may have occurred when he expressed astonishment that Martin Luther King, Jr., was a contender for the 1964 Nobel Peace Prize. "I maintain that much of the guilt for [the] evil race situation must go to the liberals, whose conventional, strictly conformist view is that anything and everything the Negro does is right, and everything the white man does, vis a vis the Negro is wrong," he wrote to an acquaintance. "This is a gutless, irresponsible attitude."

Nonetheless his frank, revolutionary fiction—as opposed to his social commentary—has endured, passing through cycles of critical evaluation and re-evaluation. The former *New Yorker* editor Charles McGrath recently praised O'Hara's "toughness and grittiness, a determination to

succeed and prove others wrong, that made him get up every morning—
or, more likely, every afternoon—his head pounding, light another cigarette, and start typing." Frank MacShane, one of his several biographers,
did not flinch at confronting O'Hara's snobbery, his arrogance, and his
reflexive defensiveness. But ten years after O'Hara's death on April 11,
1970, at the age of sixty-five, MacShane proclaimed his subject "one of
the half-dozen most important writers of his time."

Charles Addams retained his unique combination of artistic morbidity
and personal cheer to the end. But there would be almost no more
Addams Family cartoons after 1964, when their namesake television
series debuted; the decorous Shawn apparently didn't want any crossover
between his refined magazine and Hollywood commercialism. At one
point, when Addams tried to submit a Family cartoon, the editor replied
quietly, "I don't think we want to revive them." Nonetheless the clan
lived on not only in reruns but in various animated appearances, TV
and theatrical films, and profitable merchandising. In 2010 *The Addams
Family* debuted as a Broadway musical to mixed reviews but lucrative
box office. One can only wonder about the judgment that Gibbs, who
had wanted to collaborate on a live-action version of "that haunted house
bunch" some sixty years before, would have passed on it.

Irrespective of the Family, Addams still had plenty of offbeat material with which to work. One of his most famous later cartoons was
of an old man securing himself in his room with seven locks on the
door, unaware that directly beneath him someone is sawing his way up
through the floor. His *New Yorker* oeuvre came to include more than
thirteen hundred illustrations and covers. Thanks in part to his productivity and Family tie-ins—from the TV series alone he made $141,276—
Addams lived well. To his collection of esoteric items (at one point he
acquired a pair of biopsy scissors), he added a variety of foreign cars,
including an Aston Martin, a Bentley, a Bugatti, and a supercharged

German army staff vehicle. Unlike O'Hara, Addams did not deploy these acquisitions as status symbols; they were reflections of a fun and imaginative personality.

Addams's devil-may-care attitude continued to find expression in his love life, through which he ran without much thought of the consequences. In the 1960s he dated the newly widowed Jacqueline Kennedy, an admirer of his work, until she began putting him down, indicating that as a mere cartoonist he was not quite in her league. "She may be the moodiest woman I've ever met," Addams complained. He also had a tempestuous relationship with Joan Fontaine that was so public it set off marriage rumors. Ignobly, he seems to have seduced Gibbs's daughter, Janet, when she was a young woman who was just beginning to exhibit symptoms of bipolar disorder. After two failed marriages, to Barbara Jean Day and Barbara Barb (nicknamed "Good Barbara" and "Bad Barbara" because of their respective personalities), he settled down in 1980 with Marilyn "Tee" Miller. The wedding took place in Tee's pet cemetery at her home in Water Mill, New York. "It's my favorite place in the world," Tee told the *Times*. In many ways it was a perfect joining; the bride wore black.

He succumbed to a heart attack on September 29, 1988, slumped behind the wheel of his Audi in front of his apartment building. By that time he had been pronounced "an American landmark, one of the few, by which one and all have learned to steer. An Addams house, an Addams family, an Addams situation are archetypes that we see all around us." His ashes were buried in Tee's animal graveyard.

E. B. White became something of an elder statesman of American letters. Honorary degrees, along with such accolades as the National Medal for Literature and the gold medal of the American Academy of Arts and Letters, poured in. In December 1963 he was given the Presidential Medal of Freedom, the country's highest civilian award. However, he "muffed" his attendance at the ceremony in Washington, remaining at home because of one of Katharine's ever-mounting bouts of ill health. Even without that excuse he probably would have found a reason not to attend. "I dislike cameras and airplanes," he told Andy Rooney. "The camera is unforgiving; the airplane is impractical in thick weather. So I avoid both." A few months after the ceremony, Senator Edmund Muskie was dispatched to present the prize to White on their mutual Maine turf, a gesture that rather embarrassed the author. "I really had not intended to put anyone to any trouble," he wrote. In 1978 he received a special Pulitzer Prize citation for the collective body of his work.

For White, prose was more important than accolades. He lived long enough to write memorable "Comment" about the assassination of President Kennedy and the first moon landing. Both entries reflected his continued ability to turn an unexpected phrase. Noting that JFK disdained hats, he remarked that the president "died of exposure, but in a way that he would have settled for—in the line of duty, and with his friends and enemies all around, supporting and shooting at him." When it came to Apollo XI, his devotion to one world remained as strong as ever. Disdaining the planting of the Stars and Stripes on extraterrestrial soil, he transcended nationalism and reached for universalism:

> Like every great river and every great sea, the moon belongs to none and belongs to all. It still holds the key to madness, still controls the tides that lap on shores everywhere, still guards the lovers who kiss in every land under no banner but the sky. What a pity that in our moment of triumph we did not forswear the familiar Iwo Jima scene and plant instead a device acceptable to all: a limp white handkerchief, perhaps, symbol of the common cold, which, like the moon, affects us all, unites us all.

Many of his *New Yorker* "Letters" from various locales were collected in *The Points of My Compass*; much of his correspondence made it between hard covers as well. And he published his last children's novel, *The Trumpet of the Swan*. If not as well remembered or quite as beloved as *Charlotte's Web* and *Stuart Little*, it endeared him yet to young readers who knew nothing of what he had done for Ross's magazine.

Katharine, meanwhile, found herself not quite able to adapt to changing times. While she was still editing fiction, she had asked Norman Mailer if he would care to contribute to *The New Yorker*. Mailer refused, explaining that he would not be free to use the word *shit* in its pages. "White wrote back to suggest that perhaps Mr. Mailer did not understand the true meaning of freedom," wrote the future *New Yorker* critic Louis Menand. "Mailer answered that he did indeed understand the true meaning of freedom: freedom meant being able to say 'shit' in *The New Yorker*." Not that Katharine wholly resisted the New Journalism; Truman Capote's *In Cold Blood*, she told Behrman, was "a feather in Shawn's cap."

In her official retirement, she preferred to focus on projects that were within her power—namely, her gardening columns. But her health was declining rapidly. Escaping the Maine winters, the Whites began spending time in Florida. The change of climate, however, could only do so much. By the early 1970s Katharine was suffering from shingles, dermatosis, a fractured vertebra, osteoporosis, a kidney infection, and congestive heart failure. Within a short time she found herself relying on various friends and aides some eighteen hours a day. In her own way she hated her downward spiral as much as Thurber had hated his; she called herself "a bent and horrible looking old crone" and "a burden to myself and poor Andy." Collaborating with her husband and Philip Hamburger, she published her final *New Yorker* item, a minor "Talk" entry about a Medicare claim conducted via telephone and computer, in 1971. She died six years later, a week after writing a letter to Jean Stafford that she acknowledged was "dull and feeble."

Andy had written her many a poem in their decades together. This was one of Katharine's to him, composed twenty-two years before her passing:

Saint Valentine and I one day a year
Go shopping for my sweet, my only love,
And then I would my minute prowess move
To choose a necktie he would want to wear
Of fabrics silky, staunch, or very sheer.
Alas, though I the heavens move
In [working?] Cupid's many-colored dove,
I turn up nothing that will please me, dear.
O Garrell, Keep, and Saks! O Brothers Brooks! [Jarrell?]
What horrors do you lead me on to buy?
What spotted outrages you like to call a tie
Constructed to undo a Greek god's looks?
Forgive, my dear, this annual charade,
And only wear my love when you parade.

"This place doesn't fit me since Katharine died," Andy told the *Times* in 1980. "Only just lately have I been free to explore the depths of despair you get into. I don't have friends here my own age. Everybody I know is below ground."

White's last years were far from unhappy. He reveled in his grandchildren, his periodic writings, life on the farm and his extensive correspondence. After some initial reluctance, he cooperated with Scott Elledge, a professor of English at Cornell, on *E. B. White: A Biography*. On the whole he was pleased by the result. "I was reduced alternately to tears and to laughter," he told his chronicler. "The laughs were generated by rediscovering what a consummate ass I was, early and late." He remained his own man, writing what he wanted and somehow balancing his need to be heard while keeping great chunks of his life, which informed so much of his output, to himself. Linda H. Davis, who wrote definitive biographies of both Katharine and Addams, captured this dichotomy in a fond but unflinching *New Yorker* reminiscence:

> A vulnerable, intensely private man, White put up a lot of fences and opened the gate to a select few. Even those who got past the gate could quickly find themselves back on the outside.... A writer used to a self-centered existence, a man whose close relationship with his wife had left other people on the periphery, he was also an affectionate person, quick to sign "love" to his letters to a new friend, and he needed the warmth of human contact. But his personality said, "Come here, come here. Get away, get away."

When he left, at eighty-six, on October 1, 1985, the cartoonist Brian Duffy of the *Des Moines Register* seized on the Garth Williams illustration of *Charlotte's Web* that depicted Charlotte having spun out the words SOME PIG. Duffy rendered a mournful Wilbur poised beneath the silken epigraph SOME WRITER.

POSTSCRIPT

In June 2007 I visited Tony Gibbs's ex-wife, Tish, now long married to Bill Collins, at her home in Norwalk, Connecticut. Over iced tea in her backyard, she chatted informatively and cheerfully about her father-in-law and his family, even when broaching the more disturbing aspects of their domestic life. At one point she said she had something to show me. Ducking into the house, she returned with an old blue Brooks Brothers box.

In it was the Puck costume that Gibbs had worn in his Riverdale production of *A Midsummer Night's Dream* nearly a hundred years before—the one he had written about in "Ring Out, Wild Bells," the one whose "festive and horrible" noise had obscured all the dialogue. The harlequin colors were now muddy; one bootie was missing. Still, there it was.

Gibbs's director had told him to be "a little whirlwind," and in his obituary White said that Gibbs remained one even beyond the end: "In these offices can still be heard the pure and irreplaceable sound of his wild bells." In closing "Ring Out," Gibbs had written that during the intermission, "the director cut off my bells with his penknife, and after that things quieted down and got dull."

But the bells of this motley coat were attached. I lifted the garment gently from the box and shook it slightly. It all still jingled.

ACKNOWLEDGMENTS

This book began life in 2005 as a straightforward biography of Wolcott Gibbs. Along the way, it took a couple of sharp turns. Although the final content of *Cast of Characters* may not directly reflect the specific contributions of everyone I have contacted over the past decade, all have informed my writing. I therefore tip my hat to them.

From first to last, I owe an enduring debt to Tony Gibbs. When I first approached Tony, he knew nothing of me and could have easily demurred. But within a week of my sending him some pieces I had published in *The New York Times,* he told me he was happy to cooperate. Early on he explained that if he could not supply particular information, it was because he simply did not have it on call—a consequence of having distanced himself as a young adult from his parents' frequently tumultuous lives. As it was, Tony subjected himself time and again to my inquiries. A fine and fair writer, he understood my probing and never hesitated to give me what he thought was the best version of the truth. This book would have been literally impossible without him. I cannot thank him enough.

My thanks go as well to Tony's immediate and extended family and their associates who helped me trace the elusive past of his father. They are Lynne Gibbs, Tish and Bill Collins, Eric Gibbs, Susan Ward Roncalli, Sarah Smith, Phoebe Frackman, and Virginia Canfield. John Speed, Keats Vincent Thackston, and Lawrence Crutcher clued me in to the later years of Angelica Singleton Duer. Linda Kramer and Ruth O'Hara fleshed out much of Gibbs's domestic existence.

There are few survivors from what I call the golden age of *The New Yorker*, but all those I reached were most gracious. Among them are Roger Angell, Lillian Ross, Mary D. Kierstead, William Walden, Jim Munves, Walter Bernstein, Don Mankiewicz, Gordon Cotler, Frank Modell, Dan Pinck, Charlotte Maurer, and Betsy Flagler.

I received invaluable assistance, remembrances, and documentation from survivors and relations of many *New Yorker* personnel and associated individuals. They include Rosemary Thurber, Sara Sauers, Jonathan Meredith, David Behrman, Carola Vecchio, Susan Lardner, Mary Jane Lardner, Charles Price, Dorothy Lobrano Guth, Allen Shawn, Wallace Shawn, Martha White, Amelia Hard, Maeve Kinkead Streep, Duncan Kinkead, Christina Carver Pratt, Joan Bryan Gates, Roberta Bryan Bocock, Courty Bryan, Wylie O'Hara Doughty, Brookie Maxwell, Katharine Maxwell, Patsy Blake, Patricia Arno, Molly Rea, Meredith Brown, Preston Brown, Nat Benchley, Edith Iglauer Daly, Jeanne Steig, Susan Packard, Penelope Lord, Sarah Herndon, John Wunderlich, Robert Ballard, Liza Gard, Bill Wertenbaker, Alexander Waugh, Peter Waugh, William Edge, and Peter Powers.

Obscure and fascinating information about the Long Island Rail Road of Gibbs's day came from Sam Berliner III, Art Huneke, Frank Zahn, and John Teichmoeller. John Hammond of the Oyster Bay Historical Society made clear Gibbs's efforts on behalf of the Boy Scouts and Mortimer Schiff. Gilbert Stancourt, Laurene Hofer, Pat Barry, Terry Hamilton Wollin, Helen Farrell, and Bill Carew gave me glimpses into the hidden history of Gibbs and Helen Galpin. Rufus Griscom kindly discussed his grandfather's career as a newspaper publisher.

ACKNOWLEDGMENTS

It took a veritable battalion to help me assemble my documentation. That battalion comprises Albert Harris at the Riverdale Country Day School; Philip Moore and Ann Moriarty at the Cheshire Academy; Cathy Skitko, Denise Spatarella, Ryan Merriam, and Robert Cope at the Hill School; Mary Richter at the Brearley School; Ann Hamilton and Wilma Slaight at the registrar's office at Wellesley College; Sandy Stelts at the Special Collections Library of Pennsylvania State University; Donald Glassman at the Barnard College Archives; Jocelyn Wilk at the Rare Book and Manuscript Library of Columbia University; Dean Rogers and Colton Johnson at the Archives and Special Collections Library and Historian's Office, respectively, of Vassar College; Katherine Reagan, Hilary Dorsch Wong, Eisha Neely, Elaine Engst, and Ana Guimaraes at the Division of Rare and Manuscript Collections of Cornell University; J. C. Johnson at the Howard Gotlieb Archival Research Center at Boston University; Peter Nelson at Amherst College Archives and Special Collections; Elizabeth Frank at the Louise Bogan Charitable Trust; Graham Sherriff, Karen Spicher, June Can, and Moira Ann Fitzgerald at the Beinecke Rare Book and Manuscript Library of Yale University; Marianne Hansen of Special Collections at Bryn Mawr College; Maida Goodwin at the Sophia Smith Collection of Smith College; Jennie Rathbun at Houghton Library of Harvard University; Geri Solomon and Victoria Aspinwall at Special Collections of Hofstra University; Monica Mercado and Christine Colburn at the Special Collections Research Center of the University of Chicago; Jean Cannon and Arcadia Falcone at the Harry Ransom Center of the University of Texas; Rebecca Jewett at the Rare Books and Manuscripts Division of Ohio State University; Linda Hall at the Archives and Special Collections of Williams College; Mark Woodhouse and Lesia Fadale at Elmira College; Geoff Smith, Michael Rosen, and Susanne Jaffe at Thurber House; Michael Barry Bernard at Washington Group International; Jill Gage at the Newberry Library; Kevin Miserocchi at the Charles and Tee Addams Foundation; John Printz at the Newcomen Society of the United States; Elizabeth Botten at the Smithsonian Institution Archives of American Art; Tara Anderson at Trinity Church/Grace Church; Mark Young at the Conrad N. Hilton College of Restaurant Management at the University of Houston; and Mark Ricci at Hilton Worldwide. Tom Mathewson courteously withdrew certain important books from the Columbia University library system on my behalf. Barbara Hogenson and Lori Styler granted kind permission to reprint many Thurber-related materials.

The New York Public Library, which houses the *New Yorker* Records, offers a most generous and enlightened fellowship at the Dorothy and Lewis B. Cullman Center for Scholars and Writers. I regret that this program saw fit to turn down my four separate applications. So I am indebted to the excellent and efficient staff of the library's Manuscripts and Archives Division who facilitated my persistent researches into its trove of *New Yorker* memos, drafts, and other ephemera. They are Tal Nadan, Susan Malsbury, Philip Heslip, Weatherly Stephan, Lea Jordan, Thomas Lannon, John Cordovez, Nasima Hasnat, and Kit Messick. They navigated me through the S. N. Behrman Papers, the Joel Sayre Papers, the James M. Geraghty Papers, the Harriet Walden *New Yorker* Papers, and the Yaddo Records as well.

For retrieving certain articles about *The New Yorker* and related subjects, I commend Rachel Vincent, Tatianna Hunter, and Lisa Luna at *Harper's Bazaar*, Alex Hoyt and Sarah Yager at *The Atlantic Monthly*, Anna Peele at *Esquire*, Victoria Kirk and Ann Wright at *Cosmopolitan*, and Jeremiah Manion at *The Boston Globe*. No question about *The New Yorker* was too trivial for its archivist supreme, Jon Michaud, or his colleague Erin Overbey. I delighted in revelations from the *New Yorker* cartoonist Michael Maslin, who is writing what will be a fine biography of Peter Arno. Others who worked for *The New Yorker*, like Dana Fradon and Charles McGrath, were most solicitous. Lew Powell furnished a nice reflection about St. Clair McKelway.

ACKNOWLEDGMENTS

Jamie Katz, Edie Lieber, Janice Birmingham Webb, Rushelle Wechsler, Toni Wechsler, Richard Wechsler, Tony Stern, Susan Cookson, Sarah Morgan, Nicole Pressley Wolf, Jay Trien, Herman Wouk, Bel Kaufman, Linda Hall, Constantine Karvonides, and Arthur Gelb enriched my appreciation of Fire Island. Betty Rollin, Joanna Simon, and Isabel Konecky shared wonderful reminiscences of Valentine Sherry. *Season in the Sun* came to life thanks to George Ives, Jada Rowland, Gregor Rowland, Leonard McCombe, and Courtney Burr III.

For crucial information about Foord's sanitarium, I salute Carol Hazlehurst and Roma Lisovich. Regarding Gibbs's theater days, I pay tribute to Judy Rascoe, Dorianne Guernsey, Irvin Ungar, Susan McCarthy Todd, Eric Bentley, Alexandra Bracie, Bernard Gittelman, and Jane Hewes. Joan Castle Sitwell and Jonathan Schwartz offered wonderful anecdotes. Miscellaneous help in other areas came from Park Dougherty and Alan Brinkley.

Many books have been written about *The New Yorker* and some of its outstanding figures. I am especially thankful for the encouragement and support of the authors of some of these more recent and excellent volumes, among them Thomas Kunkel, Ben Yagoda, Harrison Kinney, and Linda H. Davis. Regarding William Maxwell, I thank Chris Carduff, Michael Steinman, and Barbara Burkhardt. I had some most pleasant exchanges with Gilbert Leigh Bloom and Howard Fishlove, who wrote informative and analytical doctoral and master's theses, respectively, about Gibbs's theatre criticism. I consulted, too, with Ari Hogenboom and Mary Kalfatovic about their noteworthy Gibbs encyclopedia entries. Chuck Fountain generously forwarded a copy of George Frazier's unpublished book about Time, Inc.

I respectfully tweak my fellow Philolexian Society alumnus Jason Epstein, who informed me that the last thing the world needed was another book about *The New Yorker*. I shake the hand of another Columbia friend, Adam Van Doren, for his continuing interest, informed as it was by his knowledge of the Algonquin crowd. Kevin Fitzpatrick of the Dorothy Parker Society was also most supportive.

Some groundwork for this book was laid in 2008, when I published an essay in *The Weekly Standard* tied to the fiftieth anniversary of Gibbs's death. My *Standard* friends include the Old Lion Matthew Continetti, the indulgent Terry Eastland, the constantly encouraging Joseph Epstein, and the all-wise Phil Terzian. Matters accelerated in 2011 when I published the anthology *Backward Ran Sentences: The Best of Wolcott Gibbs From* The New Yorker. My editors, production personnel, and marketing crew at the Bloomsbury Press—Rachel Mannheimer, Nate Knaebel, Carrie Majer, Anthony LaSasso, Michelle Blankenship, Peter Miller, Jeremy Wang-Iverson, and of course, Kathy Belden—were consummate professionals. P. J. O'Rourke supplied—no surprise—a hilarious foreword.

My handlers at W. W. Norton were superb. First among them is editor-in-chief and vice president John Glusman, my old *Columbia College Today* compatriot. With his customary editorial acumen, he helped me define this book's scope and focus and guide it toward its conclusion. Alexa Pugh did fine administrative work; she and Jillian Brall steered me through the permissions process, as did Leigh Montville at Condé Nast. Janet Biehl's copy editing was masterful. My diligent agent, Glen Hartley, took me on with maximum conscientiousness.

Over the last few years I was fortunate to have delivered several talks and discussions about my subject at the Yale Club, the Coffee House, the Dutch Treat Club, and the Port Washington Pubic Library; I thank the personnel who coordinated these events. At a Gibbs discussion I moderated at the New School upon the publication of *Backward Ran Sentences,* my fellow panelists Kurt Andersen and Mark Singer quite outclassed me. Although James Wolcott could not participate in that forum, he has long inspired this book. So have Tim Page, David Lehman, Robert Boynton, Whit Stillman, Craig Lambert, Jack Heidenry, and Harlan Ellison.

Some final and personal embraces:

To Sam Roe, Michael Bologna, Theresa Braine, Michael Cannell,

ACKNOWLEDGMENTS

Darryl McGrath, Pamela LiCalzi O'Connell, John Jeter, Glen Craney, and other cherished classmates from the Columbia University Graduate School of Journalism;

    To Mary Reilly;

    To my brothers, Raymond and Billy;

    To my mother, Aurora;

    And to the memory of my father, William.

$\wedge$

NOTES

$\vee\vee\vee\vee\vee\vee\vee\vee\vee\vee\vee\vee\vee\vee\vee\vee\vee\vee\vee\vee$

ABBREVIATIONS:

EBW: E. B. White
HWR: Harold Wallace Ross
JOH: John O'Hara
JT: James Thurber
KSW: Katharine Sergeant White
NYPL: New York Public Library
StCM: St. Clair McKelway
TNY: *The New Yorker*
WG: Wolcott Gibbs
WS: William Shawn

INTRODUCTION: "EITHER COMPETENT OR HORRIBLE"

2 "I guess I really like it here": WG, "Dark Cloud in the Sky," *TNY*, June 22, 1946.

3 "It is the kind of play": WG, "More in Sorrow," *TNY*, September 19, 1942.

4 "If you don't know anything": WG, "Death in the Rumble Seat," *TNY*, October 8, 1942.

4 "His face, on the whole," etc.: WG, "St. George and the Dragnet," *TNY*, May 25, 1940.

4 "Timen have come to bulge," etc.: WG, "Time . . . Fortune . . . Life . . . Luce," *TNY*, November 28, 1936.

4 That Luce issue had set: HWR to WG, memo, March 1, 1937.

5 "Everyone who read this parody": Bernard DeVoto, "The Easy Chair: Distempers of the Press," *Harper's*, March 1937.

5 He had recently sworn off: Constantine Karvonides, interview by author, September 29, 2013.

5 "a competently executed trick": WG, "Notes and Comment," *TNY*, February 12, 1949.

5 "no references to juvenile": WG, *More in Sorrow*, p. viii.

6 "It occurs to me that writers": Ibid., p. vii.

6 "He took up so much room": WG, "Robert Benchley: In Memoriam," *New York Times*, December 16, 1945.

7 "I wish to Christ": Kinney, *Thurber Life and Times*, p. 914.

7 "semblance of unbaked cookies": Dorothy Parker, introduction to *The Seal in the Bedroom and Other Predicaments*, quoted in Holmes, ed., *Thurber Critical Essays*, p. 57.

7 "cretonnes for the soup": JT, "What Do You Mean It *Was* Brillig?," *TNY*, January 7, 1939.

8 "It would not be unfair to say": Ralph McAllister Ingersoll, "The New Yorker," *Fortune*, July 1934.

8 "some of the most moral": Herbert Mitgang, "E. B. White, Essayist and Stylist, Dies," *New York Times*, October 2, 1985.

8 "I think of White": KSW to S. N. Behrman, October 12, 1965.

9 "The town was strangely quiet": E. B. White, "Notes and Comment," *TNY*, March 11, 1933.

9 "White's prose had almost nothing": WG, "E. B. White," *Book-of-the-Month Club News*, January 1949.

9 "The Russians, we understand": EBW, "Notes and Comment," *TNY*, October 26, 1957.

10 out of "panic": KSW to William Maxwell, n.d., "April."

10 "the party was over": Bruccoli, *O'Hara Concern*, p. 181.

10 "Helen Morgan's singing belonged": WG, "Notes and Comment," *TNY*, October 18, 1941.

11 "*The New Yorker*, like New York itself": Joseph Epstein, "There at the *New Yorker*," *Weekly Standard*, December 12, 2011.

11 "geniuses": Charles Morton, "A Try for *The New Yorker*," *Atlantic Monthly*, April 1963; Morton, "Brief Interlude at *The New Yorker*," *Atlantic Monthly*, May 1963; Kunkel, *Genius in Disguise*, p. 186.

11 "I've just been to dinner": Allen Churchill, "Harold Ross: Editor of The New Yorker," *Hearst's International Combined with Cosmopolitan*, May 1948.

11 "trio about whom": JT, *Years with Ross*, p. 18.

12 "I can't imagine": EBW, interview by George Plimpton and Frank H. Crowther, "The Art of the Essay No. 1," *Paris Review*, Fall 1969.

NOTES

CHAPTER 1: "A LUDICROUS PASTIME"

13 "There were so many different Rosses": JT, *Years with Ross*, p. 13.

13 "warm and personal": Ibid., p. 221.

13 "a general tenor": Wilson, *Sixties: Last Journal*, p. 499.

13 "a kind person": Geoffrey T. Hellman, talk at Grolier Club, May 14, 1975.

13 "found it hard": Liebling, *Most of Liebling*, p. 321.

13 "a vitally intelligent man": Grant, *Ross, New Yorker, and Me*, p. 10.

13 "the most uncompromising lout": Cort, *Social Astonishments*, p. 196.

13 "I am frequently": HWR to JOH, September 24, 1947.

14 *"The New Yorker* is pure accident": HWR to George Jean Nathan, December 27, 1949.

14 "God damn it": Ingersoll, *Point of Departure*, p. 191.

15 "annoying or comic": Edmund Wilson to JT, March 22, 1958.

15 "Ross had an unquenchable": Kahn, *Sentimental Journal*, p. 59.

15 "If I stayed anywhere": Charles Morton, "A Try for *The New Yorker*," *Atlantic Monthly*, April 1963.

15 "I have never been": Gill, *Here at* New Yorker, pp. 191–92.

16 "liked the idea": Kramer, *Ross and* New Yorker, p. 29.

17 "more *in contempt*": EBW, notes, n.d., courtesy Cornell University; emphasis in the original.

18 Initially convinced: Kramer, *Ross and* New Yorker, p. 55.

18 Fleischmann would over the first three years: Kunkel, *Genius in Disguise*, p. 211.

18 Reportedly, within just a couple of years: Gill, *Here at* New Yorker, p. 186.

19 "undeniable respectability": WG, "J'Accuse Les États-Unis," *TNY*, February 1, 1947.

19 "The Gibbses were always boys": WG to Nancy Hale, n.d., ca. 1931–32, mentioned in connection with Mosher rejection of Hale's short story "Imagination."

20 "I spent considerable segments": Gibbs, *More in Sorrow*, p. viii.

20 "went bad": Tony Gibbs, interview by author, June 29, 2007.

20 a city so heavy with industry: Sarah Smith, interview by author, August 3, 2007.

21 "cut too close": Gelb, *City Room*, p. 441.

21 "not industrious" and "erratic": J. D. Warnock, Hill School report card, December 13, 1916.

21 17½ out of a possible: WG, jacket copy for WG, *Bird Life at the Pole*.

21 "It proved substantially impossible": WG, *More in Sorrow*, p. ix

21 "His particular activities": Headmaster Dwight Meigs (probable author) to George Gibbs, June 26, 1919.

21 "beyond question": WG, "The Diamond Gardenia" (Part I), *TNY*, November 20, 1937.

22 "I got fed up": Richard B. Gehman, "The Great Dissenter," *Theatre Arts*, March 1949.

22 "morosely designing": WG, *Bird Life at the Pole*, jacket copy.

23 "a pretty comic kind of railroad": WG, stage description from his unproduced play *Sarasota Special*.

23 "utterly wasted": "There Was No Other," *Newsweek*, August 25, 1958.

23 "It seemed to her," etc.: WG, "How I Became a Writer," *Fire Islander*, July 13, 1956.

23 seventy dollars a week: Richard B. Gehman, "The Great Dissenter," *Theatre Arts*, March 1949.

23 "dedicated to the social activities": WG, "The Huntress," *TNY*, August 3, 1935.

24 "A week in bed": WG, "A Little Murder Now and Then," *North Hempstead Record*, January 12, 1927.

25 "one of America's most distinguished": WG (anon.), "Head of New Yorker Ran Country Paper," *North Hempstead Record*, August 17, 1927.

25 a huge Ku Klux Klan rally: WG (anon.), "Blazing Cross, Fiery Talk, at Freeport," *Nassau Daily Star*, August 22, 1927.

25 "told Ross he better hire me": WG to EBW, n.d.

26 "I don't give a damn": WG, *Season and Other Pleasures*, p. vii.

26 "lousy the first year or two": John R. Wiggins, "E. B. White Boxes His Compass," *Ellsworth American*, October 26, 1966.

26 "You don't want to read that stuff": Dan Pinck, "Paging Mr. Ross: Old Days at 'The New Yorker,'" *Encounter*, June 1987.

27 "great path-finder": HWR to KSW, early 1940s.

27 "If an unhappy childhood": EBW, *Letters*, rev. ed., p. 1.

28 "wrote for the sake of writing": Elledge, *White: A Biography*, p. 55.

28 "Strunk's *parvum opus*": EBW, "Letter from the East," *TNY*, July 27, 1957.

29 "When three or more facts": EBW to HWR, May 2, 1946.

29 "Writing is a secret vice": EBW to KSW, May 31, 1937.

29 "Success seems to be imminent": EBW to Alice Burchfield, August 25, 1922.

29 "Capturing a thought": EBW, "Personal Column," *Seattle Times*, March 31, 1923.

30 "Mrs. Vander Regibilt": EBW, "The Vernal Account," *TNY*, April 18, 1925.

30 "Here is one commuter": EBW, "Defense of the Bronx River," *TNY*, May 9, 1925.

30 "In Which the Author": EBW, "Child's Play," *TNY*, December 26, 1925.

30 "I discovered a long time ago": EBW to Stanley White, January 1929.

31 "More than any other editor": William Shawn, "Katharine Sergeant White," *TNY*, August 1, 1977.

31 "Ross, though something of a genius": EBW, interview by George Plimpton and Frank H. Crowther, "The Art of the Essay No. 1," *Paris Review*, Fall 1969.

32 "the rich men's town," etc.: Davis, *Onward and Upward*, various pages.

32 "I was the youngest": KSW, "Books: Children's Books: Between the Dark and the Daylight," *TNY*, December 7, 1946.

33 "I have and always have had": Davis, *Onward and Upward*, p. 49.

34 "GENT's laundry taken home": EBW, Newsbreak, *TNY*, September 21, 1929.

34 "Quite well aware": EBW, "Notes and Comment," *TNY*, February 26, 1927.

34 "struck the shining note": JT, "E.B.W.," *Saturday Review*, October 15, 1938.

34 "Until I learned": JT to Frank Gibney, October 31, 1956.

34 "the size of a hall bedroom," etc.: EBW, "James Thurber," *TNY*, November 11, 1961.

35 "My father was not a machine man": JT, "Gentleman from Indiana," *TNY*, June 9, 1951.

35 "I owe practically everything": Henry Brandon, "Everybody Is Getting Serious," *New Republic*, May 26, 1958.

36 "a studious and sometimes": Bernstein, *Thurber: A Biography*, p. 29.

36 "I would put my eye" and "You are the main trouble": JT, "My Life and Hard Times—VII," *TNY*, September 23, 1933.

36 "City of Light and occasional Darkness": JT, "The First Time I Saw Paris," *Holiday*, April 1957.

37 "My anxiety dreams": Robert Vincent, "Always a Newspaper Man," *Columbus Dispatch Magazine*, December 14, 1959.

37 "By the way": JT to John Scott Mabon, March 16, 1946.

37 "I stopped off for a minute": JT, interview by Joseph Mitchell, *New York World-Telegram*, 1934, cited in Kinney, *Thurber Life and Times*, p. 310.

38 "must have a rejection machine": Thurber, *Years With Ross*, p. 33.

38 about a nondescript man: JT, "An American Romance," *TNY*, March 5, 1927.

38 "I knew Ross was looking": Bernstein, *Thurber: A Biography*, p. 159.

38 "You've been writing": JT, *Years with Ross*, pp. 16–17.

38 "visceral abhorrence": Yagoda, *About Town*, p. 53.

CHAPTER 2: "INFATUATION WITH PINHEADS"

39 "Ross gave us all a curious sense": EBW in *Newsweek*, ca. February 1960.

39 "was by no means": JT, *Years with Ross*, p. 71.

39 "The cast of characters": EBW, *Letters*, rev. ed., p. 71.

40 "an absolute infatuation": WG to JT, August 12, 1957.

40 Ross's first: Kramer, *Ross and* New Yorker, p. 75.

40 "I won't be back": WG to JT, "Monday," summer of 1957 or 1958.

40 "You can't fire me": Ibid.

40 "I am firing you": Hoopes, *Ingersoll: A Biography,* p. 149.

40 "I got a sad letter": Pemberton, *Portrait of Murdock,* pp. 28–29.

40 Pemberton said: Pemberton, *Portrait of Murdock,* p. 29.

40 "the worst copy we get": KSW memo to James M. Cain, n.d., 1933.

40 "[H]e used to write": WG to JT, "Monday," summer of 1957 or 1958.

41 "Comma King": Jon Michaud, "Who Was Hobie Weekes?" TheNew Yorker.com, May 3, 2012.

41 "an incandescent liberal": Brendan Gill, "Hobart G. Weekes," *TNY,* February 29, 1978.

41 rubicund: Brendan Gill, "Hobart G. Weekes: An Appreciation," *Princeton University Library Chronicle,* Autumn 1988.

41 jolly-faced: Frank Modell, interview by author, July 22, 2006.

41 a surprised *O*: Garrison Keillor, "Notes and Comment," *TNY,* March 11, 1991.

41 Actually, it was generally understood: Nathaniel Benchley to author, September 24, 2009.

41 that rose almost to his armpits: Keillor, "Notes and Comment."

41 "like a cross": Rogers E. M. Whitaker obituary, *New York Times,* May 12, 1981.

41 "a rolling sneeze" and "a little slice of selfishness": Landon Y. Jones, "Alumni Profile: Rogers E. M. Whitaker '22," *Princeton Alumni Weekly,* December 8, 1975.

42 "gentle, venomous, red-eyed": Gill, *Here at* New Yorker, p. 120.

42 "If you don't like us": Keillor, "Notes and Comment."

42 "One Easter": Parton, *Journey Through a Lighted Room,* p. 59.

42 "a beef-eating Englishman": Allen Churchill, "Harold Ross: Editor of The New Yorker," *Hearst's International Combined with Cosmopolitan,* May 1948.

42 "Facts were sacred": Brendan Gill, "Frederick Packard," *TNY,* November 25, 1974.

42 "The Penna Wine Company": Frederick Packard and Geoffrey Hellman, "Incidental Intelligence," *TNY,* November 24, 1951.

42 "Solar pawnbrokers": Packard, "Incidental Intelligence," *TNY,* June 5, 1954.

42 "If for any reason": Packard, "Incidental Intelligence," *TNY,* August 4, 1956.

43 "The *pavés*": Packard, "I Left My Haine in Arcachon Beside La Mer," *TNY,* June 23, 1956.

43 "He wasn't funny at all": Frank Modell, interview by author, July 22, 2006.

43 "delightful deviant": Murphy, Palleau-Papin, and Thacker, eds., *Cather: Writer's Worlds,* p. 334.

43 "Newspaper man," etc.: John Mosher entry in Charles W. Lester, ed., *Williams 1914,* courtesy Williams College.

44 "an editor whose prejudices" and "I must get back": JT, *Years with Ross,* p. 33.

44 "working in complete silence": Charles Morton, "Brief Interlude at *The New Yorker,*" *Atlantic Monthly,* May 1963.

44 "Jesus, what a review": Howard Dietz to John Mosher, May 22, 1940.

45 "that God damned old woman": HWR to Robert Benchley, August 24, 1937.

45 "in which he explained": WG to JT, "Monday," summer of 1957 or 1958.

45 "Mr. Ross usually showed up": Dan Pinck, "Paging Mr. Ross: Old Days at 'The New Yorker,'" *Encounter,* June 1987.

46 "piercing blue eyes," etc.: Groth, *Receptionist,* p. 2.; Daise Terry obituary, *New York Times,* August 23, 1973; Bakewell, *American Red Cross in Italy,* p. 244.

46 "short, fierce, dignified" and "Never say hello": James Stevenson, "The New Yorker Confidential," *New York Times,* January 4, 2011.

46 "She was not popular": KSW notes, courtesy Bryn Mawr College.

47 sixty to seventy-five hours: KSW to HWR and Hawley Truax, December 29, 1944.

47 "maid-of-all-work": EBW to Cass Canfield, November 14, 1938.

47 "I have asked": EBW to Daise Terry, n.d., 1939.

47 "God only knows": JT to Terry, n.d., 1936.

47 "Please lose this": WG to Terry, October 3, 1935.

47 "Miss Terry perhaps": WG to KSW, ca. 1937.

47 she once divested: WG to JT August 12, 1957.

48 "Petition to Miss Terry": staff memo to Daise Terry, 1934

48 "dehumanized figure": JT, *Years with Ross,* pp. 7–8.

48 "It was I who invented": Ralph Ingersoll to JT, August 1, 1959.

49 "Ingersoll was a great man": WG, "A Very Active Type Man" (Part I), *TNY,* May 2, 1942.

49 "I was the mother": Hoopes, *Ingersoll: A Biography,* p. 68.

49 "Jesus emeritus": Ibid., p. 74.

49 "manifold, peculiar, and perhaps," etc.: WG, "James Thurber," *Book-of-the-Month Club News,* February 1945.

49 "Every evening": WG to JT, "Monday," summer of 1957 or 1958.

50 "It was a lively, stormy time": KSW notes, courtesy Bryn Mawr College.

50 "In this otherwise courteous man," etc.: Hoopes, *Cain,* pp. 203 and 213–14.

51 "You seem to be under": James M. Cain to Geoffrey T. Hellman, April 21, 1931.

51 "To sum up this whole": Hellman to Cain, April 22, 1931.

51 "Let us get this thing": Cain to Hellman, April 23, 1931.

52 poison pen correspondence: Hellman to Cain, April 24, 1931.

52 "On the whole": Cain to WG, August 13, 1934.

52 "Honest to Jesus": Joel Sayre to KSW, n.d., 1933.

53 "exactly as it should," etc.: StCM to JT, April 2, 1958.

53 "He was Mr. Congeniality": Botsford, *Life of Privilege, Mostly*, p. 225.

53 "An awful lot": Edward Newhouse, interview by Christina Carver Pratt, January 14, 1997.

54 "rankly paradoxical,'" etc.: McKelway's background can be found in StCM, "The Cockatoo," *TNY*, October 19, 1957; StCM, "Sam Rosen and the Presbyterians," *TNY*, September 23, 1963; StCM, "Child Labor and the Presbyterians," *TNY*, October 12, 1963; and StCM, "The Presbyterian Captives," *TNY*, April 12, 1969.

55 was paid his salary in gold: StCM, "Quong," *TNY*, May 5, 1962.

55 "graceful muckraking": Sinclair, *Will the Real Sinclair Please Sit Down*, p. 54.

56 "Not a single measure," etc.: Waugh, *Bangkok*, pp. 160–73.

56 "valued gorilla," etc.: Walker, *City Editor*, pp. 278–80.

57 "In a very short time": StCM to JT, April 2, 1958.

CHAPTER 3: "BOY, DO I LIKE TO HANDLE AUTHORS!"

58 "What is the purpose": Merritt Nelson to *TNY*, December 19, 1932.

58 "We haven't any purpose": Anonymous to Nelson, n.d.

58 "In the minds of Harold": *The New Yorker: An Outline of its History* (company publication), 1946, p. 1.

59 "An awful lot": John Crosby, *New York Herald Tribune*, December 12, 1951.

59 "I can't remember": Ingersoll, *Point of Departure*, p. 203.

59 "silver and crystal": JT, "E.B.W.," *Saturday Review*, October 15, 1938.

59 "We notice that the minute": EBW, "Notes and Comment," *TNY*, June 24, 1933.

60 "each as guilty": Dale Kramer and George R. Clark, "Harold Ross and *The New Yorker*: A Landscape with Figures," *Harper's*, April 1943.

60 "since his mind worked": Kinney, *Thurber Life and Times*, pp. 417–18.

60 "I'm sure that Andy": Robert M. Coates, "*New Yorker* Days," *Authors Guild Bulletin*, December 1961.

61 " 'It's a form of escape' ": JT, "A Box to Hide In," *TNY*, January 24, 1931.

61 "brought mail in": Joel Sayre, "John O'Hara Early On," notes in Joel Sayre Papers, NYPL.

61 "the foibles": *New Yorker: Outline of Its History*, p. 2.

61 "a small red man": WG, "Mars," *TNY*, June 23, 1934.

61 fiendish cigarette consumption: WG, "Wit's End," *TNY*, October 21, 1933.

61 "touch is so light": *The New Yorker: Editorial Policy and Purpose* (company publication), 1946, p. 9.

62 "Ross is usually": Dale Kramer and George R. Clark, "Ross and *New Yorker:* A Landscape with Figures," *Harper's,* April 1943.

62 "a prejudice against writing": KSW to Will Cuppy, March 3, 1933.

63 "Sorry, this isn't": Harriet Walden *New Yorker* Papers, NYPL.

63 "One of the most": JT to EBW, April 16, 1956.

63 "just to catch": KSW to Harrison Kinney, March 23, 1973.

63 "lunatic," etc.: WG to StCM, n.d.

64 "Bad writing was an affront": Botsford, *Life of Privilege, Mostly,* pp. 174–75.

64 Gibbs even corrected: Elizabeth "Tish" Collins, interview by author, June 9, 2007.

64 He would revise his own: Tony Gibbs, interview by author, November 22, 2005.

64 "An average Profile-writer": Harriman, *Take Them Up Tenderly,* pp. xii–xiii.

64 there were 147 numbered queries: Dale Kramer and George R. Clark, "Ross and *New Yorker:* A Landscape with Figures," *Harper's,* April 1943.

65 "Good enough subject": WG to HWR, n.d., 1935.

66 If a piece was particularly: Gelb, *City Room,* p. 195.

66 "Being slow in paying": WG to W. E. Farbstein, March 10, 1930.

66 "not beautiful in the classic sense": Harriman, *Blessed Are the Debonair,* pp. 212–14.

67 "Mr. Ross says": Louis Forster to Frederick Packard, July 16, 1946.

67 "Executive Assistant," etc.: T. D. Quinn to Packard, April 10, 1942.

67 "I regret that we cannot": Lillie Jones to Packard, November 1941.

67 "Dear Mrs. Jones": Packard to Jones, November 14, 1941.

67 "Joe Lewis": Allen Churchill, "Harold Ross: Editor of The New Yorker," *Hearst's International Combined with Cosmopolitan,* May 1948.

67 "Ross has two gods": JT in McNulty, *World of McNulty,* p. 15.

67 "Commas in *The New Yorker*": EBW, interview by George Plimpton and Frank H. Crowther, "The Art of the Essay No. 1," *Paris Review,* Fall 1969.

68 "Wolcott ('Comma') Gibbs": Richard B. Gehman, "The Great Dissenter," *Theatre Arts,* March 1949.

68 "[I]f youse guys": JT to HWR, n.d.

68 "Did you know": EBW to JT, January 1936.

68 "blacklisted": Ik Shuman, memo, March 2, 1938.

68 "It seems that all refrigerators": WG to EBW, July 18, 1935.

68 "The editors I had": Irwin Shaw, interview by George Plimpton and John Phillips, "The Art of Fiction No. 4," *Paris Review,* Spring 1979.

68 "I wish editors were always": Clarence Day to KSW, July 8, 1935.

69 "Since I never write": JT to HWR, n.d.

69 "I wish you and your": WG to HWR, January 26, 1942.

69 "The average contributor": "Theory and Practice of Editing New Yorker Articles" was first published in JT, *Years with Ross,* but had been widely circulated within the magazine's office for years.

71 "I rather think," etc.: KSW to HWR, November 4, 1947.

71 "'Maternal' is the word": Maxwell, *Outermost Dream,* p. 167.

72 a five-and-one-half-page letter: KSW to Jean Stafford, August 16, 1957.

72 "I believe in all of us expressing": KSW to William Maxwell, n.d., ca. 1951.

72 "without one smile," etc.: KSW to HWR, n.d., 1935.

72 "She can write English": KSW to StCM, January 5, 1937.

72 "the most ravishing creature": Nancy Hale to Linda Davis, December 18, 1977.

72 "I was intimidated": William Walden, interview by author, July 27, 2006.

72 "the terrible Katharine White": Gordon Cotler, interview by author, July 15, 2006.

72 "a cold-blooded proposition": Danton Walker, *Danton's Inferno,* p. 263.

72 "I always had a feeling": Kinney, *Thurber Life and Times,* p. 570.

73 "I regard Mrs. White as essential": HWR to Raoul Fleischmann, December 11, 1933.

73 "He didn't want anyone": Sullivan, *Reminiscences.*

73 "a velvet hand": Davis, *Onward and Upward,* p. 144.

73 "sainted": Frank Sullivan to EBW, various correspondence.

73 "way beyond the call": Nancy Hale to Linda Davis, December 18, 1977.

73 "If you are too cross": KSW to Clarence Day, October 22, 1935.

73 "It is many ages": KSW to Will Cuppy, October 30, 1934.

73 "I'll surely try something": Cuppy to KSW, November 1934.

73 "I think the 'Hate Cuppy Movement'": KSW to Cuppy, November 14, 1934.

74 "There is abroad": Weidman, *Father Sits in the Dark,* pp. xvi–xvii.

75 "Once a writer has finished": Weidman, *Praying for Rain,* pp. 77–78.

75 "elliptical": Bruccoli, *O'Hara Concern,* p. 57.

75 "finger exercises": WG, preface to JOH, *Pipe Night,* p. x.

75 "He carried O'Hara along": KSW to Bruccoli, May 17, 1971.

75 "The particular virtue": WG, preface to JOH, *Pipe Night,* p. xi.

76 "rigid economy": WG in Woods, ed., *I Wish I'd Written That,* p. 278 .

76 J. D. Salinger, among many others: J. D. Salinger to WG, January 20, 1944.

76 "No matter how bad things were": Joel Sayre, review of Finis Farr, *O'Hara: A Biography,* n.d., *New Yorker* Records, NYPL.

76 "At his best he is": HWR, memo, November 13, 1934.

76 "How the hell is O'Hara": JOH, introduction to *Five Plays,* p. x.

77 "The ending must be clear" and "a very earnest attempt": WG to JOH, April 3, 1936.

77 "On the whole," "unfailingly polite," "mostly because": KSW to Bruccoli, May 17, 1971.

77 "starlet": WG to JOH, July 1, 1948.

77 "with some of the accumulating": WG, "Watch Out for Mr. O'Hara," *Saturday Review of Literature,* February 19, 1938.

78 "Gibbs, you're *fucking* my story!": Kunkel, *Genius in Disguise,* p. 263.

78 "I have decided to reject": JOH to HWR, January 1939.

78 "I am very discontented": JOH to WG, n.d., 1936.

78 "These pieces, and a slice": JOH to William Maxwell, early 1939.

78 "My pieces don't run second": JOH to KSW, ca. October 1947.

78 "a lovable man," "the greatest egotist": KSW to Bruccoli, May 17, 1971.

78 "Somebody told me": WG to C. A. Pearce, October 26, 1937.

78 "He started out with many": KSW to Bruccoli, May 17, 1971.

79 "My little pieces": JOH to Thomas O'Hara, October 23, 1933.

79 "You probably won't sell many": JOH to Thomas O'Hara, January 17, 1932.

79 "silly, vulgar drawings," etc.: WG to HWR, n.d., August 1937.

80 "advanced and intellectual verse": KSW to Louise Bogan, September 3, 1937.

80 "I guess there's no question": WG to HWR, August 23, 1937.

80 "I meant what I said": Bogan to WG, August 20, 1937.

81 "Writers are uterine": Janet Flanner to WS, June 10, 1954.

81 "[Y]ou probably use grammar": Louise Bogan to WG, March 28, 1933.

CHAPTER 4: "MOST INSANELY MISCAST"

82 "Everybody talks": HWR to Hugh Wiley, October 15, 1925.

82 "The one thing Ross had demanded": Philip Wylie to JT, January 3, 1958.

83 as many as a thousand: Ralph McAllister Ingersoll, "The New Yorker," *Fortune,* July 1934.

83 up to 2,500: HWR to Arnot Sheppard, January 19, 1948.

83 "Conceived in the spirit": Craven, *Cartoon Cavalcade,* p. 103.

84 "[B]efore *the New Yorker*": HWR to Alice Harvey, n.d.

84 Irvin wore a fedora: KSW note, "Re New York Times obit on Rea Irvin," April 1973.

85 "At the very beginning": Ibid.

85 "The invaluable Irvin" and "Wylie would hold up": JT, *Years with Ross,* p. 42.

86 "Where am I in this picture?": Kramer, *Ross and New Yorker,* pp. 127–29.

86 "Goddam awful": Grant, *Ross, New Yorker and Me,* p. 12.

86 "better dust": JT, *Years with Ross,* p. 48.

86 During World War II: Dale Kramer and George R. Clark, "Ross and *New Yorker:* A Landscape with Figures," *Harper's,* April 1943.

86 It took him a long time: Gill, *Here at* New Yorker, p. 15.

86 "too many goddam clubs": Dan Pinck, "Paging Mr. Ross: Old Days at 'The New Yorker,'" *Encounter*, June 1987.

87 "Drawings of sheep": Louis Forster to HWR, July 18, 1947; HWR to Hobart Weekes, September 8, 1947.

87 "Why, Henry Whipple": JT, *Years with Ross*, p. 49.

88 "I wouldn't have bought it": HWR to JOH, September 24, 1947.

88 "Not a bad idea": Carl Rose, "Harold Ross, Impatient, Irascible, Was Fighting 'an Innate Kindness,'" *Boston Globe*, December 8, 1951.

88 "The strain of looking": Ibid.

90 He had a good aesthetic sense: Tony Gibbs, interview by author, June 30, 2007.

91 Consistent with his peculiar ideas: KSW Note, April 1973.

91 "A great deal of what": William Maxwell, interview by John Seabrook, "The Art of Fiction No. 71," *Paris Review*, Fall 1982.

91 "always seemed uncomfortable": Syd Hoff, www.sacreddoodles.com, 1987.

91 "would make you redraw": Groth, *Road to New York*, p. 249.

92 "Arno: There's so much here": WG to Peter Arno, n.d., 1936.

93 Reportedly, only two artists: Carl Rose, "Harold Ross, Impatient, Irascible, Was Fighting 'an Innate Kindness,'" *Boston Globe*, December 8, 1951.

93 "Want me to run up": WG to HWR, n.d.

93 "For years I had been": JT, *Years with Ross*, p. 54.

93 "as a hell of a way": WG, "James Thurber," *Book-of-the-Month Club News*, February 1945.

94 "It was White who got": JT, *Years with Ross*, p. 55.

94 "I don't remember just when": WG to JT, "Monday," n.d., summer of 1957 or 1958.

94 "These, I take it, are": EBW and JT, *Is Sex Necessary?* (1950 ed.), p. 6.

94 "[I]t was I who, during": Ibid. (1929 ed.), p. 195.

95 fifty thousand copies: Bernstein, *Thurber: A Biography*, p. 186.

95 "How the hell did you": JT, *Years with Ross*, p. 57.

95 "would in all probability": JT, "Dogs I Have Scratched," *Harper's Bazaar*, January 1933.

96 "He hated their goddam guts!": Kinney, *Thurber Life and Times*, p. 534.

97 "My drawing?": Eddie Gilmore, "'Call Me Jim': James Thurber Speaking," *Columbus Sunday Dispatch*, August 3, 1958.

97 "I very much resent": JT to Daise Terry, n.d., 1937.

97 "most insanely miscast": WG, "Fresh Flowers," in *Seventh New Yorker Album*.

98 "a little too pure for my taste," "tainted with dust," etc.: Lewis Mumford, "The Undertaker's Garland," ibid.

98 "perplexing lot," etc.: WG, "Fresh Flowers," in *Seventh New Yorker Album*.

98 "one of the most alarming": WG, foreword to George Price, *Who's In Charge Here?* (New York: Farrar and Rinehart, 1943).

98 "economy of means": WG, preface to Alan Dunn, *Should It Gurgle?: A Cartoon Portfolio, 1946–1956* (New York: Simon and Schuster, 1956).

98 "intensely emotional atmosphere": WG, foreword to William Steig, *The Lonely Ones* (New York: Duell, Sloan and Pearce, 1942), p. 8.

99 "the best caricatures": WG to Al Frueh, November 30, 1950.

99 "I can only report": WG, foreword to Charles Addams, *Addams and Evil: An Album of Cartoons* (New York: Random House, 1947).

99 "He had a sweetness": Davis, *Charles Addams*, p. 161.

100 "That's really not the sort of thing": Ibid., pp. 91–92.

100 But his midtown Manhattan apartment: Ibid., p. 13.

100 like the black rubber spider: Saul Pett, "Grim, Repressed Violence Comes to Charles Addams the Diabolical Cartoonist," Charleston (S.C.) *News and Courier*, October 11, 1953.

100 "Charley is this kind of a guy" and "I don't think much about why": Ibid.

101 "dominant strain": WG, foreword to *Addams and Evil*.

101 "Will you take it with you": HWR to Margaret Case Harriman, April 10, 1950.

101 "[S]omething really ought to be done": WG to Charles Addams, n.d., 1947.

102 "six cases of weed killer": "The Christmas Caller" manuscript can be found in Box 1649 of *New Yorker* Records, NYPL.

102 "I ended up feeling": Addams to HWR, February 25, 1948.

102 "I'm convinced": HWR to WG, n.d., 1948.

103 One of eleven children: Sarah Herndon, interview by author, August 3, 2013.

104 "Make them funny": Herbert Valen, "Funny Came First at The New Yorker," *New York Times*, June 11, 1997.

104 "Make it beautiful": Dana Fradon, interview by Michael Maslin, November 14, 2013, Michaelmaslin.com.

104 "Nothing, Geraghty" and "Gibbs was delighted": James L. Geraghty, Box 11, James Geraghty Papers, NYPL.

104 "I got very sick": WG to JT, August 12, 1957.

CHAPTER 5: "SOME VERY FUNNY PEOPLE"

105 "We thought nothing": Davenport, *Too Strong for Fantasy*, p. 119.

106 "There was always the little": Lois Long, "Tables for Two: One Hundred Years with 'The New Yorker,'" *TNY*, February 19, 1927.

106 "she used the doorknob": Kramer, *Ross and New Yorker*, p. 83.

106 As for the crap games: Don Mankiewicz, interview by author, August 21, 2012.

106 "The single-spaced stuff," etc.: Altman, *Laughter's Gentle Soul*, pp. 272–73.

106 "[She] would tell me," etc.: WG to JT, "Monday," n.d., summer of 1957 or 1958.

107 SWELL JAM I'M IN: WG to Dorothy Parker, telegram, March 26, 1928.

107 "held very clumsily," etc.: HWR to Raoul Fleischmann, April 9, 1935.

107 "I saw some very funny people": WG to JT, "Monday," n.d., summer of 1957 or 1958.

108 "a cesspool of loyalties": JT to HWR, August 15, 1947.

108 "Pest": Bennett Cerf, "Try and Stop Me" column, *Kentucky New Era*, February 1, 1949.

108 "*The New Yorker* did not begin": JT, *Years with Ross*, p. 229.

108 "a ribbon clerk's salary": Ibid., p. 231.

108 As late as 1934: Raoul Fleischmann, memo, September 19, 1934.

109 Two years later Gibbs: Anonymous *TNY* memo, April 16, 1936.

109 "There is only one White": HWR to EBW, July 1, 1942.

109 "Harold's relationship with Andy": KSW to S. N. Behrman, October 12, 1965.

109 "White's customary practice": JT, "E.B.W.," *Saturday Review*, October 15, 1938.

109 "We got on fine": Elledge, *White: A Biography*, p. 132.

109 "[O]ne of the persons": Ibid., p. 130.

110 At the end of his life: A photograph of the sculpture, taken after White's death is with other personal photos in Boxes 220A and 220B of the E. B. White Papers at Cornell University.

110 "To know Thurber": EBW to Lillian Hellman, n.d., 1975.

110 "With Thurber, the scene": Kinney, *Thurber Life and Times*, p. 547.

110 "We Whites were in such": KSW cover note re: letter from Maxwell, April 8, 1974.

110 "a talent": William Maxwell to KSW, April 8, 1974.

110 "I've never known": Kinney, *Thurber Life and Times*, p. 389.

110 "discussing his bowels": EBW to KSW, July 21, 1930.

110 "He had the semi-hangdog air": Jim Munves, interview by author, July 15, 2006.

110 "I can almost hear": Frank Modell, interview by author, July 22, 2006.

110 "glided past like": Edmund Wilson to JT, March 22, 1958.

110 "sourpuss": Brinnin, *Truman Capote*, p. 35.

110 "I never saw him smile": Frank Modell, interview by author, July 22, 2006.

110 "The few times I saw him": William Walden, interview by author, July 27, 2006.

110 "high spirits are those": EBW to JT, January 8, 1938.

110 "When you were with him": WG, "Robert Benchley: In Memoriam," *New York Times*, December 16, 1945.

111 "Gilbert Seldes hanging": Davis, *Charles Addams*, p. 66.

111 "was a really dependable": Tony Gibbs, interview by author, July 1, 2007.

112 "They were not pals": KSW to Harrison Kinney, March 23, 1973.

112 "You think you can be": Kinney, *Thurber Life and Times*, p. 547.

112 "Don't think I am": JOH, "Vox, Possibly, Humana," *Newsweek*, August 25, 1941.

112 he once compared: WG, introduction to JOH, *Pipe Night*.

112 "If...he can contrive": WG, "Watch Out for Mr. O'Hara," *Saturday Review of Literature*, February 19, 1938.

112 "a kindly man whose days": JOH, "All Packed?" *Newsweek*, May 12, 1941.

112 "The conversation was animated": JOH, *Sweet and Sour*, p. 94.

113 He once sent Gibbs: Roger Angell, interview by author, September 20, 2007.

113 "Gibbs and John": KSW to Bruccoli, May 17, 1971.

113 "I have no arguments": Kriendler, "*21*," pp. 108–11.

113 "putting wrestling holds," etc.: MacShane, *Life of O'Hara*, p. 85.

113 "I know him better than anybody": WG to KSW, ca. October 1934.

114 about a hapless fellow: Russell Maloney, "Inflexible Logic", *TNY*, February 3, 1940.

114 "something like 2,600": Russell Maloney obituary, *New York Times*, September 5, 1948.

114 "a cranky genius": James L. Geraghty, notes, Box 11, James Geraghty Papers, NYPL.

114 "very bad reporters" and "Perfection": Russell Maloney, "Tilley the Toiler: A Profile of the *New Yorker* Magazine," *Saturday Review of Literature*, August 30, 1947.

114 "totally incompetent," etc.: HWR to JOH, September 24, 1947.

114 "psychosis" and "mostly by abusing us": KSW to HWR, November 4, 1947.

114 Growing up in Newton Centre: Much of this information on Maloney's background comes from Amelia Hard to author, personal statements, February and March, 2013.

115 he was only about nine: Amelia Hard, interview by author, February 10, 2013.

115 "went stomping in": Russell Maloney to family, October 30, 1943.

115 "As far as I can tell": Maloney, *It's Still Maloney*, p. 10.

115 During the first half: Maloney to family, January 1, 1944.

115 "filled by a Greek": HWR to Ik Shuman, n.d., 1939.

115 "no evidence": I. Schwartz to *TNY*, May 15, 1939.

116 "He was frustrated": HWR to JOH, September 24, 1947.

116 "no trace of imagination": Russell Maloney, "The Wizard of Hollywood," *TNY*, August 19, 1939.

116 "The Giants have come": James L. Geraghty, notes, Box 11, James Geraghty Papers, NYPL.

116 "in his gas mask": EBW to StCM, December 7, 1953.

116 "a bonus of twice": Russell Maloney to family, January 1, 1944.

116 "a definite offer": Maloney to family, October 30, 1943.

116 "the current Eustace": Maloney to EBW and KSW, October 3, 1943.

116 "mistaken kindness" and "One night": WG to JT, "Monday," n.d., summer of 1957 or 1958.

117 "was out to do away," etc.: Russell Maloney to "Famlet, dear," December 12, 1942.

118 "getting out a weekly": WG, *Season and Other Pleasures*, p. xii.

118 ostensibly because: Russell Maloney obituary, *New York Times*, September 5, 1948.

118 "to broaden my scope," etc.: Maloney, personal statement., ca. 1947, courtesy of Amelia Hard.

118 his last *New Yorker* casual: Russell Maloney, "Frankly . . . The Memoirs of a Bankrupt," *TNY* of February 12, 1944.

118 "pretty," "melodious" and "dull": WG, "George Washington Slipped Here," *TNY*, June 12, 1948.

119 Many years later: Details of Miriam's appeal can be found in her correspondence with KSW, and Leo Hofeller, dated February 26, and March 1, 4, 11, and 14, 1963, in Box 1323 of *New Yorker* Records, NYPL.

119 "Ah, here's Mac" and "You ungainly creature, you": Kinney, *Thurber Life and Times*, pp. 568–69.

119 "He thought if the magazine had its own speakeasy": Ibid., p. 380.

120 "I've always rebelled," etc.: Peter Arno obituary, *New York Times*, February 23, 1968.

120 "Occasionally she would come into": Marcia Davenport to Thomas Kunkel, April 14, 1992.

120 "was busy buying": Lois Long to Morris Ernst, "In re former-husband trouble," n.d., 1938.

121 singing as he drew: James L. Geraghty, notes, Box 11, James Geraghty Papers, NYPL.

121 He paid the artist: Arthur Getz to HWR, November 1940.

121 when two of his cartoon captions: Peter Arno to HWR, n.d., 1949.

121 Cornelius Vanderbilt, Jr.: Dilberto, *Debutante*, pp. 143–44.

121 gave her a shiner: Ibid.

121 "Jim, congratulate me," "quite an armament," and "seething reclusivity": James L. Geraghty, notes, Box 11, James Geraghty Papers, NYPL.

121 "Have we completely lost our mind?": Charles McGrath, "Omit Needless Rules," *New York Times Book Review*, October 19, 2014.

122 "a much older woman": Davis, *Onward and Upward*, p. 232.

122 "I went to Reno": KSW to Caroline Angell, Christmas 1976.

123 "I do want to see *you*" and "This attractive thing": KSW to EBW, May 31, 1929.

123 "This marriage is a terrible challenge": EBW to KSW, late November 1929.

124 "She is the one": HWR to Lloyd Paul Stryker, October 29, 1945.

124 "beautiful and mysterious": Kunkel, *Genius in Disguise*, p. 205.

124 "was the deadly": JT, *Years with Ross*, p. 182.

125 "grabber": Tony Gibbs, interview by author, July 1, 2007.

125 "She was the domineering type": Bernstein, *Thurber: A Biography*, p. 117.

125 "When we finally found each other": Ibid., p. 247.

125 shades of pea green: Elizabeth "Tish" Collins, interview by author, June 9, 2007.

125 "That was a good piece": Kinney, *Thurber Life and Times*, pp. 371–72.

125 "Helen Stark": Susan Shapiro, "A Librarian with Great Stories in Her Files," *Newsday*, March 3, 1992.

126 "You were in love!": Edward Newhouse, interview by Cynthia Carver Pratt, January 14, 1997.

126 "I'd been thwarted": Kinney, *Thurber Life and Times*, pp. 371–72.

126 "He always carried a torch": Bernstein, *Thurber: A Biography*, p. 175.

126 "Our love . . . never ripened": JT to EBW, December 22, 1952.

126 "Miss Honeyclutch": WG to Nancy Hale, n.d., ca. 1931.

126 IN BED A BROKEN MAN: WG to Ann Honeycutt, telegram, n.d.

126 a bout between Primo Carnera: WG to Hale, June 28, 1933.

126 third of the owner-management: Leonard Lyons, "The Lyons Den," syndicated column, March 7, 1941.

127 Poems to two of his: WG, "Paula" and "Babette," *North Hempstead Record*, December 22 and 29, 1926.

128 Helen Marguerite Galpin: Most of the information about Helen's background comes from Peter Powers, interview by author, October 6, 2009. A copy of the marriage certificate was provided by the Nassau County (N.Y.) Clerk's Office.

128 "a respectable girl": WG, "Love, Love, Love," *TNY*, July 20, 1946.

129 dangerous harpy named "Hilda": WG, "Hilda Has Her Little Joke," *North Hempstead Record*, February 2, 1927.

129 a native of Detroit: Elizabeth's Detroit background was established by the 1910 and 1920 U.S. Censuses.

129 a sojourn in Bermuda: Ship's manifest, *S.S. Bermuda*, September 10, 1929.

129 Elizabeth committed suicide: Conflicting stories of the suicide can be found in Hoopes, *Ingersoll: A Biography*, p. 78; Gill, *Here at New Yorker*, p. 118; and KSW to Geoffrey T. Hellman, October 3, 1975. Newspaper accounts include the April 1, 1930, editions of *New York Times*, *New York World*, *Daily News*, and *New York Herald Tribune*.

130 "Could you come right over" etc.: KSW to Hellman, October 3, 1975.

130 So concerned was O'Hara: MacShane, *Life of O'Hara*, p. 52.

131 "Miss Dirty Dishes": WG to Nancy Hale, n.d., ca. 1931.

131 "orange and green seraglio": WG to Hale, September 3, 1931.

131 "When I got back": Sillman, *Here Lies Leonard*, pp. 139–40.

132 "new girl," "Hats," etc.: WG, "Shall We Pan the Ladies?," *North American Review*, April 1931.

132 "It seems very likely": WG to Hale, n.d., ca. 1931–32.

132 "I love you because": WG to Hale, March 11, 1931.

132 "I miss you terribly": WG to Hale, August 22, 1931.

133 "Christ, a year ago": WG to Hale, September 10, 1931.

133 "When you're away: WG to Hale, November 22, 1931.

133 "Darling, I've spent two days": WG to Hale, "Mother's Day by jesus," n.d., ca. 1933.

134 "in trade": Collins, interview.

134 "honorable intentions" and "unsatisfactorily entangled": Waugh, *Best Wine Last*, p. 43.

135 "A love story, to be typical": Waugh to Elinor Mead Sherwin, Christmas 1931, courtesy Tish Collins.

135 "my great-uncle Alec": Alexander Waugh to author, July 27, 2007.

136 "Yes, the little darlings": Tony Stern, interview by author, June 13, 2009.

136 "Don't hand her to me": Sarah Smith, interview by author, October 23, 2008.

136 Susan Douglas: Tony Gibbs, interview by author, July 1, 2007.

136 that Elinor was the mistress: JOH to John Hayward, March 22, 1960.

136 When Benchley died: Gibbs interview, July 1, 2007.

136 "They lived in the same house": Linda Kramer, interview by author, December 11, 2005.

136 "quite strange": Arthur Gelb, interview by author, December 1, 2007.

137 "I think I've done everything": WG to Elinor Gibbs, n.d., 1935.

CHAPTER 6: "AN OFFENSE TO THE EAR"

138 "which I strongly suspect": WG, "Well, I Give Up," *TNY*, May 3, 1941.

138 Wilson got an office: Dabney, *Edmund Wilson*, pp. 311–12.

139 "as arbitrary": Edmund Wilson, "Ambushing a Best-Seller: 'The Turquoise,'" *TNY*, February 16, 1946.

139 "It has happened to me," etc.: Edmund Wilson, "Somerset Maugham and an Antidote," *TNY*, June 8, 1946.

139 "nothing but rose water," etc.: Lois Long to HWR, June 1, 1931; Long to HWR, April 15, 1931; James R. Hayes to HWR, April 5, 1934; EBW, "Notes and Comment," *TNY*, April 7, 1934.

139 "Your emotions must not destroy": HWR to Lois Long, April 17, 1931.

140 "Leon Fraser is one of New York's": Matthew Josephson, "The Hat on the Roll-Top Desk," parts 1 and 2, *TNY,* February 14 and 21, 1942.

140 "We seldom make idols": Anonynous to Elizabeth Brackett, March 28, 1939.

141 "I think I may": Frank Sullivan to EBW, ca. 1942.

141 "I had an unexpectedly": StCM to John Bainbridge, November 1, 1939.

142 "The statement 'Ethel Merman'": Ethel Merman to Bainbridge, June 7, 1940.

142 "The statement of which": Leopold Stokowski to Bainbridge, June 5, 1940.

142 "the item regarding separation": Cliff Lewis to Bainbridge, June 11, 1940.

142 "completely inaccurate and groundless": Kenichiro Yoshida to Bainbridge, May 28, 1940.

143 "This is a good place": StCM to HWR, March 22, 1940.

143 "There's no use taking": WS to HWR, May 5, 1940.

143 "My instinct is for blood": HWR to WS, n.d.

144 This was such explosive stuff: "Books and Authors," *New York Times,* September 29, 1940.

144 did not wear undershorts: Kunkel, *Genius in Disguise,* p. 282.

145 "my best to take": HWR to *TNY* staff, September 6, 1940.

145 "[U]nder the compulsion" etc.: HWR to Mark Woods, July 1, 1942.

146 "Woollcott could be": KSW, "Further Notes by KSW on Woollcott and *The New Yorker* and 'Shouts and Murmurs,'" p. 10.

146 "Woollcott was, above all": Walker, *Danton's Inferno,* p. 247.

146 "America's most interesting woman," "on the plane," and "the best achievement": Adams, *Woollcott: Life and World,* p. 253.

146 "was so capricious": Ibid., pp. 373–74.

146 "By some miracle": Ibid., p. 219.

146 "write literately and fairly well": Ibid., p. 161.

146 "At a dinner party": Walker, *Danton's Inferno,* p. 263.

147 "That was, of course, Woollcott's": HWR to Raoul Fleischmann, December 24, 1934.

147 "forever the deadly enemy": KSW (?) to Frank Sullivan, December 23, 1936.

147 "an attentive": WG, "Doyle & Burke," *North Hempstead Record,* February 9, 1927.

148 "To return, however, to": WG, "Primo, My Puss", *TNY,* January 5, 1935.

148 "He took on this weekly chore": KSW to Howard Teichmann, September 17, 1975.

148 "sculptured from the very best Jello" and "terrible detriment": WG, unpublished notes on Woollcott, n.d., courtesy of Tony Gibbs.

148 "As other men fear": WG, "Big Nemo," *TNY,* April 1, 1939.

148 "the flavor": JT, *Years with Ross,* pp. 288–89.

148 "I was up there once": Sullivan, *Reminiscences.*

148 REGRET CANT GET: WG to Alexander Woollcott, telegram, March 1, 1939.

149 "High spot of the evening": Frank Sullivan to EBW, December 26, 1938.

149 a thorough dissection: WG, "Big Nemo," *TNY*, April 1, 1939, March 18, 1939, and March 25, 1939.

150 YOU HAVE MADE ME: Woollcott to WG, telegram, probably March 2, 1939.

151 "I have on my conscience": Woollcott to WG, ca. March 1939.

151 Alfred Lunt and Lynn Fontanne: Behrman, *People in a Diary*, p. 130.

151 "I've tried by tender": Woollcott to HWR, April 18, 1942.

151 "lying, cruelty and treachery": Woollcott to HWR, September 28, 1942.

151 "For how much of this": Woollcott to HWR, April 29, 1942.

151 "I would be glad": HWR to Woollcott, October 6, 1942.

152 "To me you are no longer": Woollcott to HWR, October 10, 1942.

152 "and asked him to leave": Frank Sullivan to EBW, May 16, 1939.

152 "All the time Alec wrote for us": HWR to Samuel Hopkins Adams, February 4, 1943.

152 "a particularly monstrous lounging sofa": Arnold Schulman to HWR, September 16, 1947.

152 "We don't want any additional": Louis Forster to Arnold Schulman, September 22, 1947.

153 "*Time*'s inaccuracies": Elson, *Time Inc.*, p. 92.

154 "one of the great literary comedies": WG, "Senora Cyclops," *TNY*, December 3, 1949.

154 "undressing them": Elson, *Time Inc.*, p. 85.

154 "Hadden had not set out": Wilner, *Man Time Forgot*, p. 131.

154 "Naturally . . . knifed each other": Cort, *Social Astonishments*, p. 196.

155 "Damn it, the old lady," etc.: Elson, *Time Inc.*, p. 88.

155 "I wish you would do something": Wilner, *Man Time Forgot*, p. 184.

156 "Hadn't you better show it": HWR to Ralph Ingersoll, November 7, 1933.

156 "every wise guy": HWR to Ingersoll, August 9, 1934.

156 "kicked up all sorts": HWR to Gluyas Williams, August 7, 1934.

156 "I do not make": StCM to JT, May 25, 1958.

156 "Gossip Note": EBW, "Notes and Comment," *TNY*, August 18, 1934.

156 "Please stick with us": HWR to Williams, August 7, 1934.

156 The project was initially assigned: Talmey's initial role can be found in letters among HWR, StCM, and Ralph Ingersoll, dated April 12, 15, 22, and 26, 1935.

156 "Thanks for your note": Ralph Ingersoll to HWR, April 15, 1935.

157 "because nobody but business executives" and "such an antic job": These quotes, and much of the account of the *Time–New Yorker* dust-up, come from Frazier, *It's About Time.*

157 "after giving him a cocktail": Margaret Case Harriman, "The Candor Kid—II," *TNY*, January 11, 1941.

157 "Write that down": James Munves, memo recounting conversation with WG, ca. 1950–51.

158 "The fewer facts you give them": Hoopes, *Ralph Ingersoll*, p. 149.

158 "They hate you": Kramer, *Ross and* New Yorker, p. 249.

158 "It became an office project," "deadpan manner," etc.: StCM to JT, May 25, 1958.

158 "Look, this is too damned obvious" and "So sly": Frazier, *It's About Time*, pp. 143, 149.

159 "One scholarly study": Chen, *English Inversion*, p. 258.

161 "I thought that was the funniest footnote": William Walden, interview by author, July 27, 2006.

162 "Hearst tactics!": StCM to JT, May 25, 1958.

162 "Time-Life was in an uproar": William Maxwell, interview by John Seabrook, "The Art of Fiction No. 71," *Paris Review*, Fall 1982.

162 Drawing out the drama: StCM to JT, May 25, 1958.

162 "Bulls like to fight": Kramer, *Ross and* New Yorker, p. 250.

162 "Oh, that terrible night": Brinkley, *Publisher: Henry Luce*, p. 200.

162 "[He] lost his nerve": Hoopes, *Ingersoll: A Biography*, p. 149.

162 "a man of weak character": James Munves, memo recounting conversation with WG, ca. 1950–51.

162 "on the grounds that": Frazier, *It's About Time*, p. 144.

162 "Luce came straight across": StcM to JT, May 25, 1958.

162 Luce stammered, etc.: Frazier, *It's About Time*; Hoopes, *Ralph Ingersoll*, pp. 149–50; Kunkel, *Genius in Disguise*, p. 290.

164 "The article went to your office," etc.: HWR to Henry Luce, November 23, 1936.

167 "Thank you for your letter": Luce to HWR, November 24, 1936.

167 "a gem of the purest ray": Frank Crowninshield to HWR, March 7, 1946.

168 "the most creditable thing": Alexander Woollcott to WG, December 3, 1936.

168 "the most distinguished public": Bernard DeVoto, "The Easy Chair: Distempers of the Press," *Harper's*, March 1937.

168 Winchell reported a rumor: Walter Winchell column, November 30, 1936.

168 "one of the best pieces ever run": HWR to Frank Crowninshield, February 25, 1946.

168 "There is no doubt the Luce piece": HWR to WG, March 1, 1937.

168 note that effectively accused: "Funny Coincidence Department," *TNY*, December 12, 1936.

168 "I find it hard to dissociate": Eric Hodgins to Ralph Ingersoll, December 10, 1936.

168 "The river looks very": Ingersoll to HWR, December 22, 1936.

169 "to be partially set": "Department of Correction, Amplification, and Abuse," *TNY*, January 2, 1937.

169 Ingersoll mischievously added: Elson, *Time Inc.*, p. 267.

169 DOES THE PRESENT MRS LUCE: Frederick Packard (ostensibly) to Eric Hodgins, telegram, March 18, 1940.

169 "Once upon a time": Margaret Case Harriman, "The Candor Kid," January 4 and 11, 1941.

169 "As for Harriman's bitchy tone": WS to HWR, November 27, 1940.

169 "fulfilled its mission of laughter": Clare Boothe Luce to HWR, October 25, 1951.

170 "Exalted Supreme": Charles Morton, "Time Marches Up!" *TNY*, August 4, 1945.

170 "probably the third heaviest": WG, "Notes and Comment," *TNY*, July 16, 1938.

170 "They merely photographed a life": WG and EBW, "Notes and Comment," *TNY*, March 2, 1940.

170 "I don't *know!*": WG, "Notes and Comment," *TNY*, April 5, 1944.

170 "very beautiful and strange": WG, "Beauty and Gutzon Borglum," *TNY*, September 10, 1938.

170 "*Time* is terrifying": HWR to Martha Gellhorn, February 15, 1943.

170 "If either of the Luces": HWR to Gellhorn, March 8, 1943.

171 "I saw it in *Life*": HWR to staff, ca. 1947.

171 "And what do you suppose": Elson, *Time Inc.*, p. 268.

171 evoking at least one complaint: HWR to WG, July 8, 1946.

171 "This brings me to money": WG to Robert Coughlan, February 6, 1948.

172 "I wanted to change": JT, *Years with Ross*, pp. 217–18.

172 "It seemed to me at first": WG, *More in Sorrow*, pp. vii–viii.

CHAPTER 7: "PRETTY GUMMY AT BEST"

173 "Ross had no valid relationship": Cort, *Social Astonishments*, p. 196.

174 a retrospective look: JT's "Where Are They Now?" articles about Ederle, O'Hanlon, and Sidis ran in *TNY*, April 18 and December 19, 1936, and August 14, 1937.

174 "go away somewhere": Bernstein, *Thurber: A Biography*, p. 262.

175 "You're throwing away ideas on *PM*": JT, *Years with Ross*, p. 121.

175 "MLLE: If you had been": JT, "He Said and She Said," *Mademoiselle*, March 1942.

176 At one point Thurber tripped: Kinney, *Thurber Life and Times*, p. 745.

176 "an unfunny Thurber drawing" and "didn't think it": Terry to KSW, January (?) 1940.

177 "We Ask the New Yorker": Katharine Strong to *TNY*, January 1939.

178 "about the difficulty people are": EBW to JT, September 1, 1942.

178 "I see him roaming": EBW in *New York Herald Tribune*, January 4, 1936.

178 "about the only thing": Gluyas Williams to KSW, January 10, 1935.

178 "almost impossible to write anything": EBW to Gus Lobrano, October (?) 1934.

178 "Speaking for the writer": EBW to HWR, April 18, 1935.

179 "among the best stuff": HWR to EBW, September 4, 1935.

179 "Your page is stronger": HWR to EBW, May 7, 1935.

179 "The suggestion has often been made": Robert van Gelder, "Books of the Times," *New York Times,* October 6, 1934.

179 "Never has there been": JT to EBW, January 20, 1938.

179 "I never said any such": Lillian Hellman to EBW, March 31, 1975.

180 "gentle complacency": Ralph Ingersoll to EBW, March 17, 1937.

181 "I want to see what it feels like": EBW to Stanley Hart White, March 13, 1937.

181 "I want time to think about many": EBW, "Notes and Comment," *TNY,* August 7, 1937.

181 "In the main" and "places where my spoor": EBW to KSW, May 31, 1937.

181 "I don't think I ever": KSW to EBW, September 1937.

181 "Enjoyed working in your shop": EBW to HWR, n.d., 1937.

181 "He just sails around": WG to EBW, September 1937.

182 "an unholy mess": EBW to JT, January 8, 1938.

182 "on a theme which engrosses me": EBW to KSW, May 31, 1937.

182 "listening to the beat": EBW to JT, January 8, 1938.

182 were among her happiest: Davis, *Onward and Upward,* p. 128.

182 "My life here is fantastic": KSW to Ruth McKenney, August 29, 1938.

183 "If you haven't seduced her," etc.: Dorothy Lobrano Guth, interview by author, March 10, 2013.

183 Lobrano easily passed: KSW to Gus Lobrano, n.d., ca. 1937.

184 "a tall, diffident man," etc.: Wechsberg, *First Time Around,* pp. 159–60.

184 "pure rubbish": Edmund Wilson, "Kay Boyle and the *Saturday Evening Post*," *TNY,* January 15, 1944.

184 "Miss Boyle had exactly": Gus Lobrano to HWR, March 22, 1944.

184 "Something must be left": Gustave Lobrano obituary, *New York Journal American,* March 2, 1954.

184 "He did not enter lightly": EBW, "G. S. Lobrano," *TNY,* March 10, 1956.

184 organized a children's Sunday: Guth interview, March 10, 2013; Guth to author, August 15, 2014.

185 So high was the regard of S. J. Perelman: S. J. Perelman, interview by William Cole and George Plimpton, "The Art of Fiction No. 31," *Paris Review,* Summer–Fall 1963.

185 "I have been with the NYer": Gus Lobrano to EBW, September 1938.

185 "catching mackerel": KSW to Eileen McKenney, August 29, 1938.

185 "Gibbsy": EBW to WG, n.d., 1934.

185 the three hundred dollars he would earn: Elledge, *White: A Biography,* p. 211.

185 "spare the reading public": Ibid., p. 216.

186 "I began to sustain the illusion": EBW, "Once More to the Lake," *Harper's,* October 1941.

186 "I wish I could believe": Russell Maloney to EBW and KSW, October 3, 1941.

186 "steadily laying shingles": EBW, "Clear Days," *Harper's,* December 1938.

186 "I think that 'One Man's Meat'": Roger Angell, introduction to EBW, *One Man's Meat* (1997 ed.).

187 poignant short stories: WG, "Another Such Victory—," *Harper's Bazaar,* May 1932; WG, "November Afternoon," *Harper's Bazaar,* November 1933.

187 Therefore, in the living room: Tony Gibbs, interview by author, June 29, 2007.

187 "Injun Joe": Tony Gibbs, interview by author, June 30, 2007.

187 "strangled vines": WG, "Notes and Comment," *TNY,* November 5, 1938.

187 using his hose to squirt: Elizabeth "Tish" Collins, interview by author, June 9, 2007.

188 the subtle maneuverings: WG, "To Sublet, Furnished," *TNY,* September 29, 1934.

188 feign sickness at boring: WG, "Be Still, My Heart," *TNY,* December 29, 1934.

188 "a perfect example": WG to EBW, n.d., ca. summer 1940.

188 "a port in the storm" and "He so dramatically": Alec Wilkinson, interview by John Thorne, "Relationships of Invention," *Atlantic Unbound,* May 15, 2002.

188 "One day Wolcott Gibbs asked me": William Maxwell, interview by John Seabrook, "The Art of Fiction No. 71," *Paris Review,* Fall 1982.

189 "was always able to fix up": JT, *Years with Ross,* p. 129.

189 "permitting the suit": WG, "Boo, Beau!" *TNY,* November 8, 1930.

189 whose eponymous scribe: WG, "Edward Damper," *TNY,* November 26, 1932.

189 "You're damn right there is": WG, "To a Little Girl at Christmas," *TNY,* December 24, 1949.

190 "The city of Grand Revenant": WG, "Shad Ampersand," *TNY,* October 27, 1945.

190 "during a period of considerable stress": WG, "Future Conditional," *TNY,* May 8, 1937.

190 "This play is a masterpiece": WG, "Shakespeare, Here's Your Hat," *TNY,* January 13, 1940.

190 "The parodies are, I guess": WG, *Season and Other Pleasures,* p. x.

191 "His friends call him Buzz," etc.: WG, "Up from Amherst," *TNY,* April 3, 1937.

191 "whimsical evaluation": Meredith, *So Far, So Good*, p. 8.

191 "surprisingly gentle": Hoopes, *Ingersoll: A Biography*, p. 258.

191 "in general he has an air": WG, "A Very Active Type Man," *TNY*, May 9, 1942.

191 "Backward go the sentences": Meredith, *So Far, So Good*, p. 179.

192 "So help me God," etc.: Ralph Ingersoll to WG, April 28, 1942.

192 "I think I was offended": Ingersoll to WG, n.d.

192 "to make the jurors feel they": WG and John Bainbridge, "St. George and the Dragnet," *TNY*, May 25, 1940.

193 Suspecting that the Democrats: Kinney, *Thurber Life and Times*, pp. 373–74.

193 "a beautiful operation": Westbrook Pegler, "Fair Enough," *New York World Telegram*, June 17, 1940.

193 "We spent an hour in the library": WG, "Notes and Comment," *TNY*, April 29, 1939.

194 "entirely on one note": WG, "Notes and Comment," *TNY*, July 1, 1939.

194 perverse pride: WG to KSW, n.d., 1939.

194 "I asked Gibbs": Jonathan Schwartz to author, September 27, 2013.

195 "[They] will now think continuously": WG, "Notes and Comment," *TNY*, September 9, 1939.

195 "The trouble with Gibbs' stuff": HWR to EBW, n.d., 1931.

195 "We all try very hard": WG to EBW, n.d., ca. summer 1940.

195 "a member of the rabble," etc.: WG, "In Defense of Captain Queeq," *TNY*, January 30, 1954.

195 stabbed Harold Guinzberg: WG, "King Spider," *TNY*, April 3, 1943.

196 "I want you to be a little": WG, "Ring Out, Wild Bells," *TNY*, April 4, 1936.

196 "Gibbs wrote a perfect opening scene" and "was the only publishable thing": StCM, "On Wolcott Gibbs," *New York Herald Tribune*, September 24, 1950.

196 "virtuous brakeman," etc.: WG, *Sarasota Special*. Tony Gibbs provided the manuscript along with accompanying notes, correspondence, and outline.

197 "just the bunk": Richard B. Gehman, "The Great Dissenter," *Theatre Arts*, March 1949.

197 "It did not get uproarious": John P. Shanley, "Art Carney Finishes Season in Comedy," *New York Times*, May 7, 1960.

CHAPTER 8: "A SILLY OCCUPATION FOR A GROWN MAN"

198 "There is nothing": Louis Sobol, "Rhapsody in Boo," *Hearst's International Combined with Cosmopolitan*, February 1945.

199 "in the manner": Wolcott Gibbs obitiuary, *New York Herald Tribune*, August 17, 1958.

199 "standards so high": Nat Benson, "The Critics," *Saturday Night: The Canadian Illustrated Weekly* 62, no. 45 (July 12, 1947), p. 23.

199 *"The Man with Blond Hair,"* etc.: The reviews ran, respectively, in *TNY* November 15, 1941; September 12, 1942; September 22, 1945; November 8, 1939; and May 22, 1937.

200 "God, he's brilliant": Kramer, *Ross and* New Yorker, p. 164.

200 "as deft": WG, "Resurrection Man," *TNY*, November 15, 1941.

200 "I don't think": WG, "Bouquets, Brickbats, and Obituaries," *TNY*, January 8, 1949.

200 "the quality of his work": WG, "Well Worth Waiting For," *TNY*, February 19, 1949.

200 "Critics in New York": Shaw, *Assassin*, pp. xix–xx.

201 "godawful, sentimental": Tish Dace, "Henry Hewes: 'Always Right Is No Excuse,'" in Jenkins, ed., *Under the Copper Beech*, pp. 59–60.

201 "I've always felt": Arthur Gelb, "Critic in the Spotlight," *New York Times*, October 15, 1950.

201 "detaching herself suddenly," etc.: WG, "Little Nemo and the Cardboard Lion," *TNY*, May 25, 1935.

202 "one of the most insanely complicated": WG, "Robert Benchley: In Memoriam," *New York Times*, December 16, 1945.

202 "Once, shortly after Robert": Benchley, *Benchley: A Biography*, p. 197.

202 "obviously better," etc.: Benchley to HWR, October 30, 1938.

202 And so it was that Gibbs: Tony Gibbs, interview by author, June 30, 2007.

202 "I had not the foggiest notion": Ibid.

203 "[T]here are seldom any cabs," etc.: WG, "Stuff and Nonsense, Mr. C.," *New York Herald Tribune*, May 20, 1951.

204 "Lanchstr get face stuck": WG, "What Every Boy Should Know," *TNY*, March 29, 1941.

205 "What are all these people": Ari Hogenboom, interview by author, June 23, 2006.

205 "There was said to be": WG, "Strange But Wonderful," *TNY*, November 11, 1944.

205 "massacre": WG, "Such a Pretty Face," *TNY*, December 1, 1945.

205 "He was always right": Frank Modell, interview by author, July 22, 2006.

205 "unique and indispensable": Vernon Young, "New Books in Review," *Yale Review*, June 1956.

205 "sick critical viewpoint": Charles Cooke to HWR, February 21, 1947.

205 "You don't suck me": HWR to Cooke, March 18, 1947.

205 "I read the Gibbs review": Dashiell Hammett to Lillian Hellman, May 16, 1944.

206 "Dear Mr. Gibbs": Dalton Trumbo to WG, April 11, 1949.

206 "I'd avoid it": WG, "Dolls Aren't Enough," *TNY*, May 26, 1951.

206 "the most stupid thing": James B. Allen et al. to Raoul Fleischmann, May 24, 1951.

206 "egregious": Eric Bentley, "The 'Old Vic,' the Old Critics and the New Generation," *View*, Fall 1946.

206 "The fact that Gibbs": Raymond Chandler to Charles Morton, June 14, 1946.

207 "Dear Sir": Kunkel, *Genius in Disguise*, pp. 389–90.

207 "I have no idea": WG, "Triple-Threat Man," *TNY*, January 4, 1958.

207 "Mr. Gibbs, why": Scott Simon, "Mel Brooks Blazes Wacky Trail," National Public Radio, May 24, 2008.

207 "When youth and beauty": Collier, *Fancies and Goodnights*, p. 394.

207 "Every now and then": Joel Raphaelson, "Off the Cuff," *Harvard Crimson*, October 1, 1948.

207 "We decided to call Gibbs": Silverman, *Michener and Me*, p. 42.

207 "continual carping": James Reilly to HWR, December 17, 1948.

208 "Mr. Reilly's is funniest": HWR to WG, WS, and Botsford, December 22, 1948.

208 the producer, Jed Harris: "Today's Fight Card: Gibbs vs. Harris," *Billboard*, November 2, 1946.

208 "On the whole": WG, "Out of the Library," *TNY*, October 26, 1946.

208 Congressman Emanuel Celler: *Billboard*, February 18, 1950.

208 "It was quite exciting": Linda Kramer, interview by author, December 11, 2005.

208 "a completely enchanting performance": WG, "With Thanks," *TNY*, April 10, 1943.

208 "I want to congratulate you": de Mille, *Dance to the Piper*, p. 333.

208 "I put on a one-woman": Bankhead, *Tallulah: Autobiography*, pp. 234–35.

209 Mike Todd once commissioned: "Sign Men Love Art in a Great Big Way," *New York Times*, March 29, 1949.

209 "First Nighters": Atkin and Adler, *Interiors Book of Restaurants*, pp. 116–17.

209 "[F]rom time to time": WG to John Mason Brown, August 30, 1946.

209 "pretty bleak and strange": WG to Catherine Brown, December 5, 1942.

209 "the best parodist," etc.: Stevens, *Speak for Yourself*, p. 243.

210 "Mr. Nathan can be": Nathan, *Theatre Book of the Year, 1950–1951*, p. 47.

210 "George Jean Nathan probably will": Russel Crouse, "Arsenic and Old Lace," *Life*, April 3, 1944.

210 "Burton's Anatomy of Rascoe": WG, "Don't Look Now, But I Think They're Gone," *TNY*, October 9, 1943.

210 "I'm sure Mr. Rascoe": WG to John Mason Brown, December 5, 1942.

210 "the New Yorker's tired young man," etc.: Burton Rascoe, "In Which the Critic Comments on a Critic," *New York World-Telegram*, April 5, 1943.

210 "I have done many terrible things": Max. J. Herzberg and the staff of the

Thomas Y. Crowell Co., *The Reader's Encyclopedia of American Literature* (New York: Thomas Y. Crowell Co. (1962 ed.), pp. 383–84.

211 "The curtain goes up": WG, "The Jukes Family Revisited," *TNY*, April 9, 1949.

211 "correct and literate": WG, "My Neck Is Out," *TNY*, April 13, 1946.

211 "While having an altogether": Kronenberger, *No Whippings*, p. 91.

212 "worst play in nearly": Ward Morehouse, "Talking of the Theater—," *New York Sun*, March 12, 1946.

212 "the worst play I have seen": "Café Brawl," *Time*, March 11, 1946.

212 "group of men": Advertisement in *New York Times*, March 1, 1946.

212 "I'd say offhand": *Time*, March 11, 1946.

212 A rather more serious incident: Sam Zolotow, "4 Critics Quit Circle; Feud Seen as Cause;" "Rascoe Quits Circle; Asked its Dissolution;" "Kaufman to Direct Rose's New Revue," *New York Times*, October 12 and 13, 1943, and February 14, 1944; and Ward Morehouse, "Drama Critics Circle Doomed—Good Riddance," *New York Sun*, October 12, 1943.

213 "Aside from his immediate relatives": Russell Maloney, "These Things Are Fated," *TNY*, April 7, 1945.

213 a dozen or so specific queries: Packard's casuals were "A Casket of Amontillado" and "A Hogshead of Soup," *TNY*, July 17, 1948, and April 30, 1949.

213 "Many farmers in recent years": StCM, "The Mare's Nest," *TNY*, November 1, 1941.

213 "sporty, cosmopolitan": WG, untitled "First Treatment," ca. 1943.

213 "I can sum up": Israel, *Kilgallen*, p. 154.

214 "I am Professor Tweedy," etc.: WG, "The Diamond Gardenia," *TNY*, November 20–27, 1937.

214 "a pretty toy": WG, "One with Ninevah," *TNY*, March 24, 1956.

214 "probably the most disastrous": Sheldon, *Other Side of Me*, pp. 147–48.

214 "not of good taste": WG, "Catnap with Kollmar," *TNY*, May 27, 1944.

215 "a fiend in human form": Lucius Beebe, "This New York" column, *New York Herald Tribune*, October 10, 1942.

215 "the most prosperous gnome," etc.: WG, "The Customer Is Always Wrong," *TNY*, October 11, 1941.

215 "spout Elizabathenisms": Jack Gould, "R. Maney, Man and Legend," *New York Times*, February 3, 1941.

215 "Press agentry is no business": Richard Maney obituary, *New York Times*, July 2, 1968.

216 "You *actor*, you!": Wilson, *Gazing into My 8-Ball*, p. 40.

216 "All female stars": WG, "The Customer Is Always Wrong," *TNY*, October 11, 1941.

216 "My most hair-raising moment": Richard Maney, "About the Guest Expert," *New York Times*, September 17, 1944.

216 "a perfectionist, a stickler," etc.: Richard Maney, "Notes and Comment on Wolcott Gibbs," *New York Times,* August 24, 1958.

CHAPTER 9: "I AM A CHILD OF THE SUN"

217 when the likes of Edmund Wilson: Frank, *Louise Bogan,* p. 143.

217 "O those wonderful summer": Louise Bogan to "Diomedes-Heathcliff" (Morton Dauwen Zabel), July 29, 1939.

218 "When we all trooped": Midgley, *How Many Words Do You Want?,* p. 46.

218 "virtually none of the manic": Kunkel, *Genius in Disguise,* p. 227.

218 "I'm going to Colorado": HWR to KSW, n.d., 1939 or 1940.

218 "Hollywood got some of them": WG, "Big Nemo," *TNY,* April 1, 1939.

219 "I carry dry shavings": EBW to Charles G. Muller, January 18, 1940.

219 "The missus": EBW to WG, n.d., 1934.

219 The Whites had to contend: Davis, *Onward and Upward,* p. 128.

220 "Maine suddenly seems too remote": EBW to Harry Lyford, December 28, 1941.

221 "another one of those Adventures": EBW to Eugene Saxton, January 28, 1942.

221 "should surprise nobody," etc.: EBW and KSW, *Subtreasury of American Humor,* pp. xvi–xviii.

221 "[G]et right after it": Davis, *Onward and Upward,* p. 139.

221 "our finest essayist": Irwin Edman, *New York Herald Tribune,* June 14, 1942.

221 "Everybody thinks it is" and "The O'Hara omission": WG to EBW and KSW, n.d., 1941.

222 "I am an older man": JT to EBW, September 1938.

222 "the intermittent fall": JT to Herman and Dorothy Miller, September 22, 1931.

222 "He could *feel*": Bernstein, *Thurber: A Biography,* p. 268.

222 "worn and a little depressed": JT to EBW, September 1938.

222 "It is nice to be back": JT to EBW, October 1938.

222 "[H]e cannot go out alone": Helen Thurber to Ronald and Jane Williams, July 1941.

223 "A blind man benefits": Maurice Dolbier, "A Sunday Afternoon with Mr. Thurber," *New York Herald Tribune Book Review,* November 2, 1957.

223 the hapless husband escapes: JT, "The Secret Life of Walter Mitty," *TNY,* March 18, 1939.

224 "In your way you are just": Bernstein, *Thurber: A Biography,* p. 312.

224 "As much as anything else": Gibbs, *More in Sorrow,* pp. ix–x.

224 For such a physically slight man: WG, response to Fireside Theatre questionnaire, 1950.

224 "As you will note": WG to Alec Waugh, June 6, 1950.

224 "He kept on rooting": Tony Gibbs, interview by author, June 30, 2007.

225 "he sleep-walked" and "really seedy, smelly pigpen": Tony Gibbs, interview by author, June 29, 2007.

225 "next to a man": Kronenberger, *No Whippings*, pp. 282–83.

225 "There is still a hollow place": WG to Nancy Hale, ca. 1932.

226 a place he had occasionally: Phoebe Frackman, interview by author, August 1, 2007.

226 "stretched out like a basking": Fowler, *Second Handshake*, p. 29.

226 three short stories about it: Mosher's stories—"Beachcombers," "Built upon the Sand," and "Out in the Sun"—ran in *TNY* on May 27, June 24, and September 16, 1939.

226 "party animals and old-fashioned families": Elizabeth Hawes, "Castles in the Sand," *New York Times Magazine*, July 11, 1993.

226 "Most people these days": WG, *Season in the Sun*, p. 23.

226 "I am a child of the sun": WG to Nancy Hale, n.d., ca. fall 1933.

227 "It could do three miles": WG, "Notes and Comment," *TNY*, January 22, 1949.

227 "she told him solemnly": Smith, *Life and Legend of Fowler*, p. 201.

227 "stuffy or Victorian," etc.: Manley, *Long Island Discovery*, pp. 203–5.

228 "Everyone's absolutely": Adler, *House Is a Home*, pp. 351–52.

228 "my caravansary": Goldie Hawkins, "How a Piano Affects Star," *New York Journal-American*, June 8, 1955.

228 "demon": WG, "Just Some Little Thing," *TNY*, October 16, 1943.

228 "a man with a face like Punch": WG, "Mr. Jermyn's Lovely Night," *TNY*, November 10, 1943.

229 Following a major hurricane: Tony Gibbs, interview by author, July 1, 2007.

229 "an island booby hatch," etc.: Smith, *Life and Legend of Fowler*, p. 201.

229 "They are a very strange people": WG, "Notes and Comment," *TNY*, June 3, 1939.

229 "At one point—there were": Arthur Gelb, interview by author, December 1, 2007.

230 "It's the children, darling": The Addams cartoon ran in *TNY*, August 30, 1947.

230 "My then-wife": Charles Addams on *Dick Cavett Show*, March 29, 1978.

230 With simultaneous awe: Gelb, *City Room*, p. 195.

230 "Every time he passed": Alfred Bester, "My Affair with Science Fiction" in Aldriss and Harrison, eds., *Hell's Cartographers*, p. 63.

230 an obese Liebling: Susan Cookson, interview by author, May 27, 2009.

230 "He would say something": David Behrman, interview by author, December 21, 2008.

230 "I especially remember him": Cookson to author, June 24, 2010.

231 "He started getting mean": Tony Stern, interview by author, June 13, 2009.

231 hot grapefruit: Betty Rollin, interview by author, September 13, 2007.

231 "smaller than a grain of rice": Joanna Simon, interview by author, September 14, 2007.

231 arranged for a cherry picker: Isabel Konecky, interview by author, September 14, 2007.

231 Born in Brooklyn, etc.: Walt Brevig, "Fire Island Loses One of Its Old Friends," *Newsday*, n.d., probably October 9, 1964.

231 He joined the Coast Guard: Gibbs interview, July 1, 2007.

232 "he had an almost" and "He was good," etc.: Ibid.

232 "He had one ": WG, "Love, Love, Love," *TNY*, July 20, 1946.

233 a droll, meandering sketch: WG, "Song at Twilight," *TNY*, July 6, 1946.

233 little boy who is rebuked: WG, "The Foreign Population," *TNY*, August 17, 1946.

233 a woman's moccasins: WG, "Crusoe's Footprint," *TNY*, September 14, 1946.

233 out-and-out comedy: WG, "Cat on the Roof," *TNY*, August 24, 1946.

233 "extremely disreputable" and "What happened": WG to S. N. Behrman, n.d., 1946.

233 solid wooden railing: David Behrman, interview by author, December 21, 2008.

233 "We ourself would like": WG, "Notes and Comment," *TNY*, June 15, 1940.

233 In contrast to his dapper: Tony Gibbs interview, July 1, 2007.

234 "A man with an impressive": WG, "In Defense of Dermathermy," *Hearst's International Combined with Cosmopolitan,* July 1949.

234 he went out daily with Richard Adler: Adler, *You Gotta Have Art*, p. 65.

234 "had locked himself": Gelb, *City Room*, p. 195.

CHAPTER 10: "ALWAYS POISON"

235 "Every drink was an adventure": Waugh, *Year to Remember*, p. 21.

235 one hundred thousand speakeasies: Peretti, *Nightclub City*, p. 11.

235 a memorable portrait: Niven Busch, "Speakeasy Nights," *TNY*, May 7, 1927.

235 "to spend the afternoon": WG, "Ah, Youth!" *North Hempstead Record*, January 12, 1927.

236 "The liquor . . . is not very good": WG, "Another Speakeasy Night," *TNY*, January 5, 1929.

236 "You went out": Lois Long, "That Was New York—and Those Were Tables for Two," *TNY*, February 17, 1940.

236 "Preciousness almost engulfed us": Angell, *Let Me Finish*, p. 161.

236 "And then I thought": HWR to Frank Sullivan, October 19, 1933.

237 "He once said to me 'Eighty'": JT to WG, n.d., ca. spring 1936.

237 "Everyone seemed to drink": Susan Shapiro, "A Librarian with Great Stories in Her Files," *Newsday*, March 3, 1992.

237 "I never could figure out": Kinney, *Thurber Life and Times*, p. 544.

237 "He ordered a martini": Walter Bernstein, interview by author, December 15, 2012.

237 "Bat's mo": Amelia Hard, interview by author, February 10, 2013.

237 "A man can do": EBW to Gerald Nachman, March 15, 1980.

238 a devotee of the English language: Kinney, *Thurber Life and Times*, p. 668.

238 its food was often terrible: Gill, *Here at* New Yorker, p. 309.

238 "a long narrow shoebox of a space": Ibid., p. 304.

238 In one often-retold story: Bruccoli, *O'Hara Concern*, p. 172.

239 "some of the best arguments": Charles McCabe, "Saloon Arguifiers: Beer to Birchard," *Toledo Blade*, April 30, 1983.

240 "prepared to talk and sing until dawn": Kinney, *Thurber Life and Times*, p. 668.

240 "when the presses rolled": Information about Bleeck's came from Zinsser, *Writing About Your Life*, p. 44; Kluger, *Paper: Life and Death*, pp. 264–68; Maney to StCM, August 9, 1963; Maney, "Life Goes to Bleeck's," *Life*, November 26, 1945; Midgley, *How Many Words*, pp. 40–48; Nunnally Johnson to Gene Fowler, March 17, 1955; "The Place Downstairs," *Time*, May 3, 1963; Westbrook Pegler column, "The Hangout," May 5, 1958; Bellows, *Last Editor*, p. 124; Joel Sayre Papers, interview, December 19, 1973, in NYPL; JT to EBW, January 20, 1938; and John Bleeck obituary, *New York Herald Tribune*, April 24, 1963.

240 However, a patron: Bernstein, *Thurber: A Biography*, p. 240.

244 when Packard was cat sitting: Amelia Hard, interview by author, February 10, 2013.

244 once, when his steak slipped: Duncan Kinkead, interview by author, June 3, 2007.

244 "Hey, Wolcott!": Wilson, *Gazing into My 8-Ball*, p. 40.

244 "Their talk was keen": Bernstein, *Inside Out*, pp. 132–33.

245 "embraced the flower," etc.: Richard Maney to StCM, August 9, 1963.

245 the charismatic writer had a habit: Edward Newhouse, interview by Christina Carver Pratt, January 9, 1997.

245 "an ugly drunk": Lawrenson, *Stranger at Party*, pp. 84–85.

245 a suicide: Botsford, *Life of Privilege, Mostly*, p. 173.

246 "a hell of a way for booze to treat me": MacShane, *Life of O'Hara*, p. 158.

246 never took another drink: Ibid., pp. 158–59, and Farr, *O'Hara*, pp. 216–17.

246 "I think he wrote better": Davis, *Onward and Upward*, p. 233.

246 "There is no such thing": Nan Robertson, "Life Without Katharine: E. B. White and His Sense of Loss," *New York Times*, April 8, 1980.

246 "He actually did fall": Edith Iglauer Daly to author, May 25, 2007.

247 "He faded into the couch": Susan Cookson, interview by author, May 27, 2009.

247 "At a party Gibbs": Cort, *Sin of Henry Luce*, p. 59.

247 to nearly immolate himself: Beebe, *Snoot If You Must*, p. 268.

247 "Occasionally he would burn": Tony Gibbs, interview by author, July 1, 2007.

247 "Most of the time I lie": WG to Nancy Hale, February 10, 1931.

247 "[t]he gift of repartee": WG, "A Man May Be Down", *TNY*, September 23, 1933.

247 "Gibbs would quite often come": Tish Dace, "Henry Hewes: 'Always Right Is No Excuse,'" in Jenkins, ed., *Under the Copper Beech*, pp. 59–60.

247 "I'd say, 'Oh my God'": Jane Hewes, interview by author, May 28, 2007.

248 "he had to be carried" and "He can't possibly": Gottfried, *Arthur Miller*, p. 219.

248 ON BEHALF OF A NUMBER: League of New York Theatres to HWR, November 27, 1946.

248 "I concur in your opinion": HWR to Richard Rodgers, December 10, 1946.

248 "wanted to depose and eat": HWR to Russel Crouse and Howard Lindsay, January 8, 1947.

248 "Serious critics should treat": Lillian Hellman to WG, December 30, 1946.

249 "Why don't that dame": Richard Maney to StCM, August 9, 1963.

249 "was seen being held up": Cheryl Crawford to HWR, May 22, 1951.

249 "The cat has a headache": Linda Hall, interview by author, January 21, 2012.

249 "On Fire Island": Gibbs interview, July 1, 2007.

250 Elinor Gibbs and . . . Hazel: Edie Lieber, interview by author, September 8, 1997.

250 "He looked old and shriveled": Bel Kaufman, interviews by author, March 13 and 21, 2012.

250 "Alcohol is one": StCM, private journal, ca. 1954, in Box 130 of *New Yorker* Records, NYPL.

250 "John McCarten, our old": Susan Shapiro, "A Librarian with Great Stories in Her Files," *Newsday*, March 3, 1992.

251 Ross went to Riggs: HWR to Horace K. Richardson, February 8, 1940.

251 ARRIVED AT THE MINES: WG to Elinor Gibbs, telegram, May 31, 1934.

251 "I have had a talk with McKelway": HWR to Richardson, February 8, 1940.

251 $800 for two months: StCM, notes, n.d., 1940.

251 This figure did not: StCM to Ik Shuman, ca. March 1940.

252 "Thurber shouting and waving bottles": Daise Terry to KSW, January 1941.

252 "I'm not going to any god-damn": WG, "Eden, With Serpents", *TNY*, April 20, 1935.

252 "It's nice here," "The food is excellent" and "not strict or rigorous": JT to Ann Honeycutt, three undated letters, spring of 1935.

253 "So nice not to wake up" and all WG's subsequent observations about Foord's: WG to Elinor Gibbs, hand- and typewritten letters in the mid- and late 1930s, courtesy Tony Gibbs.

253 "Among his sources of satisfaction": Horace K. Richardson to HWR, March 25, 1940.

254 "Ross just made one bench": StCM to HWR, February 22 (1940?).

254 "I have just been hosed and pummeled": WG to Ann Honeycutt, ca. March 1935.

255 "His ideas about what was best": Carol Hazlehurst, interview by author, February 5, 2012.

255 "Drinking did kill him in the end": EBW to Gerald Nachman, March 15, 1980.

255 "Gibbs hasn't had a drink": HWR to KSW, August 24, 1937.

255 "Gibbs hasn't had any jitters": HWR to EBW, September 1938.

255 "[H]ere is a nervous": WG to S. N. Behrman, February 26, 1948.

256 "They challenge each other": Page, ed., Diaries of Dawn Powell, p. 209.

CHAPTER 11: "FLYING HIGH AND FAST"

257 "War came to us": WG, "Notes and Comment," TNY, December 13, 1941.

258 "Internationally, there is no question," etc.: HWR to EBW, May 1941.

259 "depressed and shaken": Bernstein, Thurber: A Biography, pp. 318–21.

260 "It is a fearsome picture": EBW, "Thurber's Decline of the West," Scribner's, January 1940.

260 "The fascist ideal": EBW, "The Wave of the Future," Harper's, December 1940.

261 "My wife was getting": EBW, "Intimations," Harper's, December 1941.

261 "The Japs got me": HWR to WG, December 9, 1941.

261 "the day before the bombers flew": Russell Maloney and Philip Hamburger, "S-s-s-s-s!," TNY, December 13, 1941.

262 "We're sure that a lot," etc.: All contents ran in TNY, December 20, 1941.

263 "The clear sky pricked": WG, "Some of the Nicest Guys You Ever Saw," TNY, January 3, 1942.

263 "by telling McKelway": Sokolov, Wayward Reporter, p. 126.

264 "By now there were perceptible": A. J. Liebling, "A Reporter at Large: Paris Postscript—II," TNY, August 10, 1940.

264 "Liebling treated war as if": Sokolov, Wayward Reporter, p. 152.

264 "Then on Xmas Eve": A. J. Liebling to WS, December 31, 1944.

265 "John was naturally brave": A. J. Liebling, "John Lardner," TNY, April 2, 1960.

265 URGENT GET THIS: Liebling to WS, telegram, October 21, 1944.

266 "a remarkably able": WG, "David Lardner," *TNY*, October 28, 1944.

266 "more bloodless": JT to Gus Lobrano, July 10, 1951.

266 A dozen years after Lardner's: JT to WS, July 31, 1956.

266 more than thirty writers: *Conflict* (*New Yorker* internal newsletter), May 21, 1943.

266 "I don't know what will become": HWR to EBW, June 25, 1942.

266 "The office is quite literally": Russell Maloney in *Conflict*, January 18, 1943.

266 His death followed a tumultuous year: Maloney to EBW and KSW, September 12, 1942.

266 "I always had the feeling": HWR to KSW, September 1942.

266 "I don't remember ever being": WG to JT, "Monday," n.d., summer of 1957 or 1958.

266 "witty, perceptive": WG, "John Mosher," *TNY*, September 12, 1942.

266 "I wouldn't be surprised if he": WG to Charles Jackson, November 26, 1945.

267 "sober, tactful": HWR to director of naval officer procurement, November 12, 1942.

267 "I'll bet you're the only": Dorothy Lobrano Guth, interview by author, March 10, 2013.

267 "I am still shaking down": Rogers E. M. Whitaker to WS, 1944.

268 "He considered that I was": StCM to JT, April 2, 1958.

268 "Pvt. Ross please note": StCM to WS, July 14, 1943.

268 Arthur Kober mistook: Kober to Gus Lobrano, August 31, 1944.

268 "If you were a great big": StCM, untitled, 1919, courtesy Christina Carver Pratt.

269 McKelway saw duty: StCM, "A Reporter with the B-29s," *TNY*, June 9, 16, 23, and 30, 1945.

270 "I have the answer": Edward Newhouse, interview by Christina Pratt, January 14, 1997.

270 "twelve separate and distinct," etc.: WS, "St. Clair McKelway," *TNY*, January 28, 1980.

270 "on the whole, fairly level-headed" etc.: StCM to S. N. Behrman, n.d., "November 26."

271 McKelway's internal mental battle: StCM, "The Blowing of the Top of Peter Roger Oboe," *TNY*, June 14, 1958.

271 "compulsive practice" and "Kill the s.o.b.!": Edward Newhouse, interview by Christina Carver Pratt, January 9, 1997.

272 "As you doubtless know, we had": Russell Maloney to EBW and KSW, September 12, 1942.

273 "little 4f's": Maloney, in *Conflict*, January 18, 1943.

273 "a dozen or more": Terry to KSW, n.d.

273 "I practically live": Terry to EBW, September 23, 1943.

273 "About 7 o'clock": Terry to KSW, n.d.

273 "Things move in such": Terry to KSW, n.d., 1944.

274 He earned minor sums: Don Wharton to WS, memos, late 1933.

274 "shepherd of the fact stuff": HWR to Morris Markey, December 1, 1939.

274 "Shawn is now highly eligible": HWR to EBW, n.d., 1942.

274 "Gibbs is the perfect": Charles Cooke to Ross, February 20, 1947.

275 "too many children" and "in squalor": WG to Joseph Hergesheimer, December 15, 1944.

275 "the last movie piece": WG to WS, September 1945.

275 "It is my indignant opinion," etc.: WG, "The Kingdom of the Blind," *Saturday Review of Literature,* November 17, 1945.

276 "It probably doesn't sound": WG to Hergesheimer, January 15, 1945.

276 "Last week I reviewed no less": WG to Hergesheimer, January 31, 1945.

276 "Unlike White I am capable": WG to WS, n.d., 1941.

277 "The last time I looked": WG to EBW, n.d., ca. 1943.

277 "fidgety," etc.: HWR to KSW, n.d., 1939 or 1940.

277 "Don't be discouraged": EBW to Alice Burchfield, June 18, 1923.

278 "He has gone to Maine": HWR to Robert Benchley, July 3, 1942.

278 "Morning comes and bed": EBW, "Cold Weather," *Harper's,* January 1943.

278 "Hitler and I are about": EBW, "First World War," *Harper's,* October 1939.

278 "The true shape of man": EBW, "Control," *Harper's,* February 1943.

279 "I found it distinctly painful": WS to HWR, February 5, 1943.

279 Limited Editions Club's Gold Medal: Elledge, *White: A Biography,* p. 249.

279 "Although some one might accuse": Roger Angell to EBW, January 6, 1945.

279 "Running a column": EBW to Frederick Lewis Allen, March 20, 1943.

279 "Well, I am, of course, greatly": HWR to EBW, early 1943.

280 "whom Katharine was not": Slawenski, *Salinger,* p. 167.

280 "Now, of course, promptness": KSW to Gus Lobrano, June 20, 1938.

281 "dear friend" and "Andy's oldest": KSW to "Mrs. Detwold," March 3, 1956.

281 "Everybody thought she": Dorothy Lobrano Guth, interview by author, March 10, 2013.

281 "a difficult, sticky situation" and "many, many happy times": Davis, *Onward and Upward,* p. 142.

282 "unique cycle of apprehension": JT to "Dr. Jorden," December 3, 1958.

282 "books which are full": EBW, "Notes and Comment," *TNY,* July 1, 1944.

CHAPTER 12: "THE MORAL CLIMATE IS AGAINST IT"

283 "The young men": WG, "The Theatre," in Goodman, ed., *While You Were Gone,* p. 487.

284 "the most famous": Hendrik Hertzberg, "John Hersey," *TNY,* April 5, 1993.

284 pretty much enshrined: John Hersey, "Survival," *TNY*, June 17, 1944.

284 The idea for the piece: Much of this background comes from Kunkel, *Genius in Disguise*, pp. 369–74.

285 "one of the most remarkable": HR to Rebecca West, August 27, 1946.

285 "I've just read that long": Kramer, *Ross and* New Yorker, p. 292.

286 "Build the museum": EBW, "Alamogordo," *Holiday*, November 1946.

287 "I have given up planning": EBW, "Compost," *Harper's*, June 1940.

287 By one estimate: Elledge, *White: A Biography*, p. 240.

287 "Science is universal": EBW to HWR, October 21, 1944.

287 "I just went on down": EBW, "Beautiful upon a Hill," *TNY*, May 12, 1945.

288 "Neither the Russian people": EBW, "Notes and Comment," *TNY*, July 20, 1946.

288 "I say dismiss any fear": HWR to EBW, October 1944.

288 "has good will and intelligence": Robert Warshow, "Melancholy to the End," *Partisan Review,* January–February 1947.

288 "eating some of the words": EBW to Harland W. Hoisington, Jr., December 15, 1950.

288 "a little uninformed" and "had no conception": Roderick Nordell, "The Writer as a Private Man," *Christian Science Monitor*, October 31, 1962.

289 "The Civil Defense Organization": Tom Gorman to *TNY* staff, interoffice memo, February 1951.

289 "rather foolish to hold": Harvey Breit, "Talk with James Thurber,"*New York Times Book Review,* June 29, 1952.

289 "genteel, hand-wringing style": Editorial, Springfield, Ohio, *Sun*, December 11, 1947.

289 "I am a party": EBW to *New York Herald Tribune*, November 29, 1947.

290 Even Gibbs, whose politics: Hobson, *Laura Z*, pp. 470–71.

290 "No one has come along": John Ferris, "Thurber Has His Own Brand of Humor," *Columbus Citizen*, November 8, 1953.

290 "not one": HWR to Ogden Nash, November 14, 1949.

291 "editor of an adult comic book," etc.: "Mr. Parsont," reporter of New York State Public Service Commission, transcript, December 22, 1949.

292 "practically incoherent": HWR to EBW, December 27, 1949.

292 spectator pastimes: EBW, "Preposterous Parables," *TNY*, October 25, 1947.

292 "Your sports parable": WG to EBW, late October 1947.

292 "nervous crack-up," etc.: EBW to Harry Lyford, October 28, 1943.

292 "decided to go to a doctor": EBW to Stanley Hart White, March 2, 1944.

293 "mice in the subconscious": EBW to Stanley Hart White, January 1945.

293 Katharine underwent: Davis, *Onward and Upward*, p. 141.

293 So foul: Kunkel, *Genius in Disguise*, p. 251.

293 For much of the first half: Tony Gibbs, interview by author, July 1, 2007.

293 "I'll close now": WG to Gus Lobrano, spring 1947.

293 "The spot was the size": WG to HWR, spring 1947.

293 "Do not bother your": HWR to WG, April 10, 1947.

293 "I've still got a little": WG, "Where Was I?," *TNY*, April 12, 1947.

293 "That was white of him": Liebling, *Most of Liebling*, p. 320.

294 "*Dear* Daddy!": WG, "Mewow, Mewow, Mewow," *TNY*, June 21, 1947.

294 "The damned things": StCM to Gus Lobrano, August 19, 1946.

294 "He was the least *blind*": KSW to Harrison Kinney, March 23, 1973.

294 "He had a manuscript": Frank Modell, interview by author, July 22, 2006.

295 Walter Bernstein found himself: Walter Bernstein, interview by author, December 15, 2012.

295 "so goddam sensitive": JT, "The Cane in the Corridor," *TNY*, January 2, 1943. The revenge background is described in Fensch, *Man Who Was Mitty*, p. 233.

295 "The surprise comes from": JT to HWR, October 10, 1949.

295 "tampering with my books": JT to Hamish Hamilton, April 7, 1952.

295 "Ordinarily Ronnie and Jim": Kinney, *Thurber Life and Times*, p. 956.

296 "Is that you, Thurber?": Bernstein interview, December 15, 2012.

296 "The doctor would have them": Melvin Hershkowitz to author, August 13, 2013.

296 HOPE YOU GET: WS to StCM, August 18, 1945.

296 "more like carpentry," etc.: StCM to KSW, March 1, 1946.

296 "like a continuation": StCM to JT, April 2, 1958.

296 "consisted largely of spicing up," "I wound up after two weeks," "transmuted into a shapely girl dancer," "Production was frequently halted," and "reasonably fabulous": StCM, "Literary Adventures of a Hollywood Novice," *New York Herald Tribune*, March 21, 1948.

297 "I am in my usual shape": StCM to KSW, March 1, 1946.

297 "Melville once said" and "the illusory comforts": StCM to HWR, June 25, 1948.

297 brief but unhappy stint: StCM to JT, April 2, 1958.

297 He also flirted: StCM to HWR, n.d., "April 13."

298 "scheming not writing" and "ambitious beach-comber": HWR, notes on telephone talk with StCM, October 27, 1949.

298 "He was a personable": StCM, "Mister 880," *TNY*, August 27, September 3 and 10, 1949.

299 "I felt that": JOH to HWR, November 5, 1934.

299 "an intensely shy": C.D.B. Bryan, "My John O'Hara," *Esquire*, July 1985.

299 "a catastrophe": Brendan Gill, "The O'Hara Report and the Wit of Miss McCarthy," *TNY*, August 20, 1949.

299 "had called me the master": Jack Keating, "John O'Hara's World of Yale, Society and Sex," *Cosmopolitan*, September 1960.

299 "I went down to Princeton": WG to Gus Lobrano, ca. 1954–55.

300 "the most important author": JOH, "The Author's Name Is Hemingway,"*New York Times Book Review,* September 10, 1950.

300 "All the people": Arthur Kober to Gus Lobrano, September 28, 1950.

300 "I have lived an extremely": JOH, "Appointment with O'Hara," *Collier's,* March 2, 1956.

301 "made me jump": WG to JT, n.d., spring 1956.

301 "a new version of the old": JT to Herman and Dorothy Miller, December 9, 1944.

301 "escapism and self-indulgence": JT, *13 Clocks,* pp. 11–12.

302 "a wondrous tale," etc.: EBW to JT, June 6, 1950.

302 "disappointed that you didn't develop": EBW, "The Librarian Said it Was Bad for Children," *New York Times,* March 6, 1966.

303 "non-affirmative, inconclusive": Ibid.

303 "So far. . . *Charlotte's Web*": EBW to Ursula Nordstrom, October 22, 1952.

303 "New York lay stretched": EBW, "The Hotel of the Total Stranger," *Harper's,* September 1941.

304 "money, disappointment in love": The screen treatment is dated May 23, 1952.

304 "I vacillate between thinking," etc.: EBW to StCM, December 7, 1953.

304 "New York is to the nation": EBW, "Here Is New York," *Holiday,* April 1949.

305 "I regard you as I do": Jack Arbolino to EBW, March 25, 1949.

305 He got nowhere: Gibbs wrote to Hergesheimer regarding *Balisand* on December 15, 1944, and January 15, 1945. His involvement with *Zuleika Dobson* is referenced in Behrman, *Portrait of Max,* p. 19, and Mix, *Max and Americans,* p. 166. The *Belle of New York* venture is mentioned in *New York Times,* April 9, 1944.

305 he imagines himself effortlessly: WG, "The Secret Life of Myself," *TNY,* January 19, 1946.

305 Thurber later wrote a spoof: JT, "The Theory and Practice of Criticizing the Criticism of the Editing of *New Yorker* Articles," written May 18, 1959, was published thirty years later in Rosen, *Collecting Himself.*

306 While recovering: WG, response to Fireside Theatre questionnaire, 1950.

306 "[A] time is apt to come," etc.: WG, précis of *Season in the Sun,* addressed to S. N. Behrman, ca. 1946.

307 "He tottered between": Meredith, *So Far, So Good,* p. 179.

307 "whose invariable modest boast": Gill, *Here at* New Yorker, p. 132.

307 But Gibbs specifically stated: WG told Moss Hart that the Colgate character "will resemble my friend John O'Hara," letter ca. 1948–49.

308 "She spent a lot of time": Joan Castle Sitwell, interview by author, October 28, 2008.

308 "Almost everybody connected" and "[t]hey had to let him go": George Ives, interview by author, May 19, 2006.

308 "Dicky was drinking" and "Joan was amazing": Meredith, *So Far, So Good,* p. 181.

309 some even picketed: Edie Lieber, interview by author, August 15, 2007.

309 "He holds a colorless martini": Arthur Gelb, "Drama Critic Gives Fire Island a Problem," *New York Times,* August 27, 1950.

310 "During rehearsal you discover": WG, "Thurber Advises Gibbs," *New York Times,* September 24, 1950.

310 "Cut out any sentence" and "How do they manage": Marjory Adams, "Principals of 'Season in the Sun' Eat Well Before Premiere Verdict,"*Boston Globe,* November 12, 1950.

310 "When we opened": George Ives, interview by author, May 19, 2006.

310 "He told me it was a funny": WG to JT, August 12, 1957.

311 "sharp, witty dialogue," etc.: Elinor Hughes, "Critic Writes a Play, and Fine Actress Comes to Town," *Boston Herald,* September 17, 1950.

311 "I thought my colleagues": Arthur Gelb, "Critic in the Spotlight," *New York Times,* October 15, 1950.

311 "I don't think I spoke": Leonard McCombe, interview by author, January 30, 2006.

311 "The opening night": George Ives, interview by author, May 19, 2006.

312 "The photographer kept telling me": Gelb, "Critic in the Spotlight."

312 "vastly amusing": Brooks Atkinson, "At the Theatre,"*New York Times,* September 29, 1950.

312 "a sophisticated uproar": William Hawkins, "'Season in the Sun' Is Laugh-Getter," *New York World-Telegram and Sun,* September 29, 1950.

312 "a glittering comedy of manners": Howard Barnes, "The Theaters," *New York Herald Tribune,* September 29, 1950.

312 "I nearly busted myself": John Chapman, "'Season in the Sun' Is Humor at Its Best, and Beautifully Acted," *Daily News,* September 29, 1950.

312 In the final photo: The McCombe spread ran in *Life,* October 9, 1950.

312 "I suppose you're going," etc.: Gelb, "Critic in the Spotlight."

312 "gaily, sharply and constantly satirical": John Lardner, "By Slow Stages to a Sandbar," *TNY,* October 7, 1950.

312 "a turkey": Claudia Cassidy, "Turkey 'Season' at the Selwyn Where Cast Makes Bad Play Worse," *Chicago Tribune,* December 11, 1951.

312 "Rivers swirled," etc.: Botsford, *Life of Privilege, Mostly,* pp. 175–76.

313 there wasn't a single laugh: William Walden, interview by author, July 27, 2006.

313 "It was not a great play": Mary D. Kierstead, interview by author, August 1, 2006.

313 "Office very happy": Janet Flanner to Natalia Danesi Murray, November 15, 1950.

313 The play brought Gibbs: Gelb, "Critic in the Spotlight."

313 "To think that I wrote": Lawrence Perry in *Pittsburgh Press*, July 22, 1951.

313 slightly sozzled: "Walter Matthau to Host Tony Awards," *Sarasota Herald Tribune,* April 18, 1970.

313 Dressed only in a towel: Jada Rowland, interview by author, May 27, 2006.

313 Less than a year before: William Walden, interview by author, July 27, 2006.

314 There was talk: Tony Gibbs, interview by author, June 29, 2007.

314 "a bunch of vaudeville routines": WG to Bill Birmingham, February 15, 1954.

314 He even bet: Lewis Funke, "News and Gossip Gathered Along the Rialto," *New York Times,* July 8, 1951.

314 "Now that I've found": Gelb, "Critic in the Spotlight."

CHAPTER 13: "A LOT OF SUICIDAL ENTERPRISES"

315 "It ran until about 4": Gus Lobrano to Arthur Kober, March 24, 1950.

315 "I'm sorry I didn't": HWR to L. L. Winship, March 28, 1950.

315 "I never got pulled": HWR to Jay Hormel, March 21, 1950.

315 "That party proved one thing": John Cheever to Polly and Milton C. Winternitz, March 6, 1950.

316 "I write as a duodenum-scarred": HWR, introduction to Sara M. Jordan and Sheila Hibben, *Good Food for Bad Stomachs,* p. 6.

316 At a preliminary diagnosis: Kunkel, *Genius in Disguise,* pp. 421–23.

316 "Runners keep telling me": Ann Honeycutt to HWR, received May 31, 1951.

316 "I have taken back": HWR to Rebecca West, October 11, 1951.

317 "I'm half under the anesthetic": JT, *Years with Ross,* p. 304.

317 "Ross won't leave my thoughts": Frank Sullivan to Gus Lobrano, "Friday," December 1951.

317 "disemboweled": EBW to Stanley Hart White, December 11, 1951.

317 "Andy!": Kunkel, *Genius in Disguise,* p. 432.

317 "Ross always knew when," etc.: EBW, "H. W. Ross," *TNY,* December 15, 1951.

317 "I started reading": Carol Mendelson Valensi to EBW, December 13, 1951.

317 "You know, these days": Carl Rose to KSW, December 15, 1951.

318 "No, Ross wouldn't have liked it": EBW to Marion Tourt, December 17, 1951.

318 "Reverend Harold Ross": *TNY* to Elmer Davis, telegram, December 10, 1951.

318 "about four hundred": EBW to Howard Cushman, December 17, 1951.

318 "My job was to be": Frank Modell, interview by author, July 22, 2006.

318 "afraid Ariane would take it": JT to KSW and EBW, June 2, 1958.

318 "I cannot bear to think": Ariane Ross to EBW and KSW, December 18, 1951.

319 "a third of the money": Kunkel, *Genius in Disguise*, p. 435.

319 "The same thing that happened to analysis": JT, *Years with Ross*, p. 308.

319 "as different from Ross" and "I like to do": "The Press: The New Yorker's Choice," *Time*, February 24, 1952.

319 "I'm beginning to worry": JT to Peter De Vries, October 16, 1952.

320 "a particularly bullish charge": Cheever, *Home Before Dark*, p. 91.

320 Suggestions to the contrary: Dorothy Lobrano Guth, interview by author, March 10, 2013.

320 "a trail of friendship": EBW, "G. S. Lobrano," *TNY*, March 10, 1956.

320 "A great part of my pleasure": John Collier to KSW, March 3, 1956.

320 "the most remarkable summing up": KSW to William Maxwell, March 11, 1956.

321 Katharine scrupulously divided: Katharine Sergeant White Papers, Bryn Mawr College.

321 "No one was used to a party": Betsy Flagler, interview by author, July 17, 2006. She is also the source for the clothing homages and the feather boa.

321 Lillian Ross met Peter Arno: Lillian Ross, interview by author, September 29, 2007.

321 "Charlie Addams, you're a pig!" etc.: Davis, *Charles Addams*, p. 110. Davis also described Shawn playing the piano.

321 In private life: Botsford, *Life of Privilege, Mostly*, p. 212.

321 "because the other states": WG to Bill Birmingham, February 15, 1954.

321 "execrable" and "I was gonna": Edward Newhouse, interview by Christina Carver Pratt, January 14, 1997.

321 the free-spirited Eileen: Meade, *Lonelyhearts*, pp. 210–13.

322 the actress Natalie Schafer: Dorothy Kilgallen column, October 28, 1948.

322 "It may not have been": William Maxwell, introduction to Brennan, *Springs of Affection*, p. 4.

322 "like two children": Bourke, *Maeve Brennan*, p. 181.

322 "My objectives in life": StCM, diary.

322 Brennan would publish half a dozen: The stories, as they ran in *TNY*, were "The View from the Kitchen," November 14, 1953; "The Anachronism," January 30, 1994; "The Stone Hot-Water Bottle," November 27, 1954; "The Servant's Dance," May 22, 1954; "The Gentleman in the Pink-and-White Striped Shirt," May 7, 1955; and "The Divine Fireplace," April 21, 1956.

322 In 1981 Maeve camped out: Bourke, *Maeve Brennan*, p. 271.

323 "Are geniuses aware": The clipping is in Box 130 of *New Yorker* Records, NYPL. In an accompanying note, StCM wrote, "Maeve sent me this just before Christmas, 1959, after we had decided to live apart."

323 "Since he draws and writes": StCM to KSW, June 9, 1949.

323 Stationed in France: Details of St. Clair McKelway, Jr.'s death can be found in *Cornell Daily Sun*, June 14, 1954; *Cornell Alumni News*, April 15, 1957; *New York Times*, June 5, 1954; and the 2011 report of the alumni historian of the Cornell chapter of Delta Kappa Epsilon.

323 coded messages via automobile: Christina Carver Pratt, interview by author, December 26, 2012.

323 "to mention a few," etc.: StCM, "The Edinburgh Caper," *TNY*, October 13, 1962.

324 "a miraculously skillful": WS to WG, memo, June 2, 1941.

324 "I remember Bill Shawn": Lillian Ross, interview by author, September 15, 2007.

324 "adored": Wallace Shawn to Craig Lambert, June 13, 2011.

324 "I've been worried": S. N. Behrman to StCM, April 17, 1952.

324 "slim, dapper, jaunty-looking": Ross, *Here But Not Here*, p. 65.

325 "He hadn't been seen," etc.: Murray, *Janet, My Mother, and Me*, pp. 239–40.

325 Its status was so sacrosanct: KSW to WS, memo, November 12, 1956.

325 had an extramarital affair: Sarah Smith, interview by author, October 23, 2008.

325 "She was a fine girl": WG to S. N. Behrman, January 15, 1955.

325 a domestic comedy called *Diana*: Eric Gibbs provided a copy of *Diana*; *The New York Times* reported its pending production on January 22, 1954.

325 his failure to deliver: *Publishers Weekly*, November 28, 1953, and note in Box 1311 of *New Yorker* records, NYPL

325 Random sued him: "Random House Seeks Recovery of Advance," *Publishers Weekly*, November 28, 1953, and information in Box 1311 of *New Yorker* Records, NYPL.

325 "I owe so much": WG to HWR, November 14, 1950.

325 "That was my mother's": Tony Gibbs, interview by author, July 1, 2007, and Elizabeth "Tish" Collins, interview by author, June 9, 2007.

326 "My own secret feeling": WG to JT, n.d., spring 1956.

326 "I figure there are seven people": JT, "A Note in Conclusion," unused portion of JT, *Years with Ross*, courtesy Yale University.

326 "I think, Mr. Brooks": Linda Hall, interview by author, March 16, 2012.

327 "the exposure of unlisted private telephone numbers": Hirschfeld, *Show Business Is No Business*, p. 52.

327 "The parties are incessant": George Spelvin, "Feudin' an' Fightin'," *Theatre Arts*, November 1954.

327 "written in something": "Critic on the Beach," *Newsweek*, July 19, 1954.

327 "We worked once on a Long Island": WG, "Some Initial Comments About This Paper," *Fire Islander*, May 28, 1954.

328 "one half of a desk": Tony Gibbs, interview by author, July 1, 2007.

328 "as dim as Miss Bush League": WG to Bill Birmingham, "Sunday," spring 1954.

328 "Jesus Christ, this job," etc.: Constantine Karvonides, interview by author, April 11, 2013.

329 "totally incompetent": Gibbs interview, June 29, 2007.

329 "I could just find": Gibbs interview, July 1, 2007.

329 As the deadline approached: Karvonides interview, April 11, 2013.

330 "have been shot by a firing squad": Roger Hall obituary, *New York Times*, July 28, 2008.

330 "I don't like kids": "Critic on the Beach," *Newsweek*, July 19, 1954.

330 "as abundant out here": Sam Zolotow, "Gibbs Will Cover Fire Island Beat," *New York Times*, May 12, 1954.

330 "I'm sure this is": WG to George Price, May 17, 1954.

330 "I've never been to Fire Island": WG to JT, May 13, 1954.

330 "hell's own imposition": WG to EBW, n.d., probably July 5, 1954.

331 He even paid *The New Yorker*: WG to Bill Birmingham, "Thursday," spring 1954.

331 "mr gibbs promised": Fred Allen to Herman Wouk, August 13, 1954.

332 "We simulated a publication meeting": Constantine Karvonides, interview by author, September 29, 2013.

332 "Contrary to persistent rumors": WG, "Wolcott Gibbs and The Fire Islander," *Fire Islander*, July 3, 1956.

332 "thousands of good words": Bruccoli, *O'Hara Concern*, p. 241.

333 "in an ever-rising" and "none of the rest of us": Irwin Shaw to Charles Addams, November 23, 1957.

333 a take-off on Hemingway: EBW, "Across the Street and into the Grill," *TNY*, October 14, 1950.

333 among the funniest things: KSW and EBW exchange, October 1950.

333 "At Wormwood": EBW, "Letter from the East," *TNY*, December 24, 1955.

333 Jack Case, an editor at Macmillan: Elledge, *White: A Biography*, p. 325.

334 "My single purpose": EBW to Jack Case, December 17, 1958.

334 "She is a better grammarian": EBW to Case, November 3, 1958.

335 "Mrs. White has a lawn" and "sheer insolence": Cort, *Glossy Rats*, p. 162.

335 "I am very sad": John Updike to KSW, December 27, 1959.

335 "wonderful and perfect": JT to Rosemary Thurber Sauers, February 19, 1953.

336 "that terrible institution" and "I wish the entire": JT to Lester Getzloe, October 26, 1951.

336 "approval or as indifference": JT to Howard L. Bevis, December 6, 1951.

336 watch Mexican jumping beans: Bernstein, *Thurber: A Biography*, p. 453.

336 "I have been much worse": JT to Ronald and Jane Williams, October 15, 1952.

336 "I feel better than I ever": JT to KSW and EBW, October 7, 1953.

336 "no violent pencil," "[A] letter of mine," etc.: JT, "A Note in Conclusion," unused portion of *Years with Ross,* courtesy Yale University.

336 "one of the great figures": Nizer, *Jury Returns,* p. 411.

337 "I fear that where my fancy": JT to John McNulty, n.d.

337 "rather painful": WG, "Twenty-Two Characters in Search of Pirandello," *TNY,* December 24, 1955.

337 "a very sad and confusing situation": WG, "Enough Is Enough Is Enough," *TNY,* May 5, 1956.

337 "an exceptionally cheerful offering": WG, "Triple-Threat Man," *TNY,* January 4, 1958.

338 "With the passing years": WG, "Broadway: The Season Just Past; The Season to Come," *Playboy,* December 19, 1956.

338 "They couldn't live with each other": Gibbs interview, July 1, 2007.

338 "That was shocking," "Gibbs used to complain," and "I think I'm going": Karvonides interview, April 11, 2013.

338 "By his standards" and "I think they just": Elizabeth "Tish" Collins, interview by author, June 9, 2007.

339 "He found the prospect": Ross, *Here But Not Here,* p. 65.

339 "They were so continuously unpleasant": Gibbs interview, July 1, 2007.

339 "a complete 180": Collins interview, June 9, 2007.

339 seeing a psychoanalyst: Karvonides interview, September 29, 2013.

339 "I am just about the only member": WG, "Witch Doctor Bewitched," *TNY,* January 2, 1954.

339 "It was a letter typical": JT, *Years with Ross,* p. viii.

339 "should serve always" and "Because of a late-blooming": Gibbs, *More in Sorrow,* p. x.

CHAPTER 14: "WHOSE DAYS, IN ANY CASE, WERE NUMBERED"

341 "I'll be here": WG to Nancy Hale, n.d.

341 "the last of the fashionable": WG, "A Fellow of Infinite Jest," *TNY,* April 13, 1957.

341 "masterly": KSW to WG, February 26, 1957.

341 "Mrs. Wolcott Gibbs was": Walter Winchell column, September 8, 1958.

342 "Gibbs was upstairs": Botsford, *Life of Privilege, Mostly,* p. 181.

342 "My understanding," etc.: Tony Gibbs, interview by author, July 1, 2007.

343 "Congestion and Cyanosis of Lungs": The death certificate was signed by P. J. Laviano on August 17, 1958.

343 Elinor suspected: Ari Hoogbenboom, Gibbs entry in *Dictionary of American Biography, Supplement Six, 1956–1960,* p. 237.

343 "She would sweep through": Tony Gibbs, interview by author, June 30, 2007

343 "He seemed rather, for him": Elizabeth "Tish" Collins, interview by author, June 9, 2007.

344 DEEPLY SHOCKED: JT to WS, telegram, August 18, 1958.

344 "drenched in grief": Tom Gorman to KSW, August 18, 1958.

344 When word reached O'Hara: Bruccoli, *O'Hara Concern*, p. 278.

344 "I had hoped": JOH to Joseph W. Outerbridge, late August 1958.

344 "We can't bear it": Cassie and John Mason Brown to Elinor Gibbs, August 19, 1958.

344 "He wasn't about to": Tony Gibbs, interview by author, July 1, 2007.

344 Gibbs's brothers in theatrical: "Rites for Gibbs Conducted Here," *New York Times*, August 21, 1958.

344 "Just can't": S. N. Behrman diary, entry for August 21, 1958.

345 "Often the editor": EBW, "Wolcott Gibbs," *TNY*, August 30, 1958.

345 "Terrible that it had to be": JT to EBW, September 20, 1958.

345 "He literally jumped" and "He was a born actor": Bernstein, *Thurber: A Biography*, p. 477.

345 "Memorized!": Kinney, *Thurber Life and Times*, p. 1063.

346 "My old relationship really died": JT to Milton Greenstein, April 26, 1961.

346 "Thurber's copy often came in": Kinney, *Thurber Life and Times*, p. 1042.

346 "God bless . . . goddam": Charles S. Holmes, *The Clocks of Columbus: The Literary Career of James Thurber*, p. 329.

346 "I am one of the lucky": EBW, "James Thurber," *TNY*, November 11, 1961.

347 "about an impostor" and "study of imposture": StCM, application to Yaddo, ca. early 1963.

347 Yaddo canceled: Elizabeth Ames to StCM, July 29, 1963.

347 "I did not know": Cheever to Polly Winternitz, June 30, 1963.

347 a self-obsessed account: StCM, "A Reporter at Large: A Journalist in Bellevue," killed in 1970, can be found in Box 1542 of *New Yorker* Records, NYPL.

347 "amazed that creditors": HWR, notes on telephone conversation with StCM, October 27, 1949.

347 he was in hock: New York State Tax Commission statement, June 28, 1954.

347 his creditors included: HWR notes of October 27, 1949, and various bills and correspondence in Box 1321 of *New Yorker* Records, NYPL.

347 doodle on the walls: Deirdre Carmody, "There at The New Yorker, with Thurber," *New York Times*, February 19, 1991.

347 "dotty": Craig Seligman, "The Talk of the (Seedy) Side of Town," *New York Times Book Review*, March 7, 2010.

348 in 1963 his income tax payment alone: Bruccoli, *O'Hara Concern*, p. 315.

348 "I maintain that much of": JOH to Graham Watson, July 20, 1964.

348 "toughness and grittiness": Charles McGrath, introduction to JOH, *Appointment in Samarra* (2013 ed.), p. xvii.

349 "one of the half-dozen": MacShane, *Life of O'Hara*, p. 238.

349 "I don't think we want to": Davis, *Charles Addams*, p. 200.

349 more than thirteen hundred illustrations: Roger Angell, "Charles Addams," *TNY*, October 17, 1988.

349 he made $141,276: Davis, *Charles Addams*, p. 200.

350 "She may be the moodiest": Ibid., p. 202.

350 Ignobly, he seems: Ruth O'Hara, interview by author, August 1, 2006.

350 "It's my favorite place": Carey Winfrey, "Cartoonist Weds Dog Fancier at Private Cemetery for Pets," *New York Times*, June 1, 1980.

350 "an American landmark": John Russell, "Art: Monumental Lichtenstein Works," *New York Times*, November 2, 1974.

351 "muffed" and "I really had not intended": EBW to Robert and Helen Strider, May 30, 1964.

351 "I dislike cameras": EBW to Andy Rooney, January 1978.

351 "died of exposure": EBW, "Notes and Comment," *TNY*, November 30, 1963.

351 "Like every great river": EBW, "Notes and Comment," *TNY*, July 26, 1969.

352 "White wrote back": Louis Menand, "A Friend Writes: Life Catches Up with *The New Yorker*," *New Republic*, February 26, 1990.

352 "a feather in Shawn's cap": KSW to S. N. Behrman, October 12, 1965.

352 "a bent and horrible" and "a burden to myself": Davis, *Onward and Upward*, p. 229.

352 "dull and feeble": Ibid., p. 251.

353 "Saint Valentine and I": KSW to EBW, 1955.

353 "This place doesn't fit me": Nan Robertson, "Life Without Katharine: E. B. White and His Sense of Loss," *New York Times*, April 8, 1980.

353 "I was reduced alternately": EBW to Scott Elledge, February 10, 1984.

354 "A vulnerable, intensely private man": Linda Davis, "The Man on the Swing," *TNY*, December 27, 1993.

SELECTED BIBLIOGRAPHY

Adams, Samuel Hopkins. *A. Woollcott: His Life and His World*. New York: Reynal and Hitchcock, 1945.

Addams, Charles. *Addams and Evil*. New York: Random House, 1947.

Adler, Polly. *A House Is Not a Home*. New York: Rinehart, 1950.

Adler, Richard, with Lee Davis. *You Gotta Have Art: An Autobiography*. New York: Donald I. Fine, 1991.

Aldriss, Brian W., and Harry Harrison, eds. *Hell's Cartographers: Some Personal Histories of Science Fiction Writers*. New York: Harper and Row, 1975.

Altman, Billy. *Laughter's Gentle Soul: The Life of Robert Benchley*. New York: W. W. Norton, 1997.

Angell, Roger. *Let Me Finish*. New York: Harcourt, 2006.

Atkin, William Wilson, and Joan Adler. *Interiors Book of Restaurants*. New York: Whitney Library of Design, 1960.

Bailey, Blake. *Cheever: A Life*. New York: Alfred A. Knopf, 2009.

Bakewell, Charles M. *The Story of the American Red Cross in Italy*. New York: Macmillan, 1920.

Bankhead, Tallulah. *Tallulah: My Autobiography*. New York: Harper and Brothers, 1952.

Barzun, Jacques. *The Energies of Art: Studies of Authors Classic and Modern*. New York: Harper and Brothers, 1956.

Beebe, Lucius. *Snoot If You Must*. New York: D. Appleton-Century, 1943.

Behrman, S. N. *Portrait of Max: An Intimate Memoir of Sir Max Beerbohm*. New York: Random House, 1960.

———. *The Suspended Drawing Room*. New York: Stein and Day, 1965.

————. *People in a Diary: A Memoir.* Boston: Little, Brown, 1972.

Bellows, James G. *The Last Editor: How I Saved* The New York Times, The Washington Post *and the* Los Angeles Times. Kansas City: Andrews McMeel, 2002.

Benchley, Nathaniel. *Robert Benchley: A Biography.* New York: McGraw-Hill, 1955.

Bernstein, Burton. *Thurber: A Biography.* New York: Dodd, Mead, 1975.

Bernstein, Walter. *Inside Out: A Memoir of the Blacklist.* New York: Alfred A. Knopf, 1996.

Berry, Faith. *Langston Hughes: Before and Beyond Harlem.* Westport, Conn.: Lawrence Hill, 1983.

Bloom, Gilbert Leigh. *An Analysis of the Criticism of Wolcott Gibbs as It Appeared in* The New Yorker. Ph.D. diss., University of Iowa, 1971.

Botsford, Gardner. *A Life of Privilege, Mostly: A Memoir.* New York: St. Martin's, 2003.

Bourke, Angela. *Maeve Brennan: Homesick at* The New Yorker: *An Irish Writer in Exile.* New York: Counterpoint, 2004.

Brennan, Maeve. *The Springs of Affection: Stories of Dublin.* New York: Houghton Mifflin, 1998.

Brinkley, Alan. *The Publisher: Henry Luce and His American Century.* New York: Alfred A. Knopf, 2010.

Brinnin, John Malcolm. *Truman Capote: Dear Heart, Old Buddy.* New York: Delacorte, 1986.

Bruccoli, Matthew. *The O'Hara Concern: A Biography of John O'Hara.* New York: Random House, 1975.

Bruccoli, Matthew, ed. *As Ever, Scott Fitz—: Letters Between F. Scott Fitzgerald and His Literary Agent, Harold Ober, 1919–1940.* New York: Lippincott, 1972.

————, ed. *Selected Letters of John O'Hara.* New York: Random House, 1978.

Burkhardt, Barbara. *William Maxwell: A Literary Life.* Urbana: University of Illinois Press, 2005.

Burnett, Whit, ed. *This Is My Best: America's 93 Greatest Living Authors Present Over 150 Self-Chosen and Complete Masterpieces, Together with Their Reasons for Their Selections.* New York: Dial Press, 1942.

Case, Frank. *Tales of a Wayward Inn.* New York: Frederick A. Stokes, 1938.

Chancellor, Paul. *The History of the Hill School, 1851–1976.* Pottstown, Penn.: Hill School, 1976.

Cheever, Susan. *Home Before Dark: A Personal Memoir of John Cheever by His Daughter.* Boston: Hougton Mifflin, 1984.

Chen, Rong. *English Inversion: A Ground-Before-Figure Construction.* Berlin: Walter de Gruyter, 2003.

Collier, John. *Fancies and Goodnights: Tales Unlike Other Tales.* Garden City, N.Y.: Doubleday, 1951.

Cort, David. *Is There an American in the House?* New York: Macmillan, 1950.

———. *Social Astonishments.* New York: Macmillan, 1963.

———. *The Glossy Rats.* New York: Grosset and Dunlap, 1967.

———. *The Sin of Henry R. Luce.* Secaucus, N.J.: Lyle Stuart, 1974.

Craven, Thomas, Florence Weiss, and Sidney Weiss, eds. *Cartoon Cavalcade: A Collection of the Best American Humorous Cartoons from the Turn of the Century to the Present.* New York: Simon and Schuster, 1943.

Cuthbertson, Ken. *Nobody Said Not to Go: The Life, Loves and Adventures of Emily Hahn.* London: Faber and Faber, 1998.

Dabney, Lewis M. *Edmund Wilson: A Life in Literature.* New York: Farrar, Straus and Giroux, 2005.

Davis, Linda H. *Onward and Upward: A Biography of Katharine S. White.* New York: Harper and Row, 1987.

———. *Charles Addams: A Cartoonist's Life.* New York: Random House, 2006.

Davenport, Marcia. *Too Strong For Fantasy.* New York: Charles Scribner's Sons, 1967.

Day, Clarence. *The Best of Clarence Day.* New York: Alfred A. Knopf, 1948.

de Mille, Agnes. *Dance to the Piper.* Boston: Little, Brown, 1952.

Denham, Robert P., ed. *Northrop Frye on Literature and Society, 1936–1989: Unpublished Papers.* Toronto: University of Toronto Press, 2002.

Dilberto, Gioia. *Debutante: The Story of Brenda Frazier.* New York: Alfred A. Knopf, 1987.

Dolzani, Michael, ed. *Northrop Frye's Notebooks on Renaissance Literature.* Toronto: University of Toronto Press, 2006.

Donaldson, Frances. *Yours, Plum: The Letters of P. G. Wodehouse.* London: Hutchinson, 1990.

Donnelly, Liza. *Funny Ladies: The New Yorker's Greatest Women Cartoonists and Their Cartoons.* Amherst, Mass.: Prometheus, 2005.

Douglas, Ann. *Terrible Honesty: Mongrel Manhattan in the 1920s.* New York: Farrar, Straus and Giroux, 1995.

Dunn, Alan. *Should It Gurgle? A Cartoon Portfolio, 1946–1956.* New York: Simon and Schuster, 1956.

Elledge, Scott. *E. B. White: A Biography.* New York: W. W. Norton, 1984.

Elson, Robert T. *Time Inc.: The Intimate History of a Publishing Enterprise 1923–1941.* New York: Atheneum, 1968.

Erskine, John. *The Memory of Certain Persons.* Philadelphia: Lippincott, 1947.

———. *My Life as a Teacher.* Philadelphia: Lippincott, 1948.

Farr, Finis. *O'Hara: A Biography.* Boston and Toronto: Little, Brown, 1973.

Fensch, Thomas, ed. *Conversations with James Thurber.* Jackson: University Press of Mississippi, 1989.

———. *The Man Who Was Walter Mitty: The Life and Work of James Thurber.* The Woodlands, Tex.: New Century Books, 2000.

Fishlove, Howard Irwin. *O. Wolcott Gibbs: Dramatic Criticism and Reviewing, 1933–1958.* Master's thesis, University of Wisconsin, 1960.

Flagg, Thomas R. *New York Harbor Railroads in Color.* Scotch Plains, N.J.: Morning Sun Books, 2003.

Flanner, Janet. *Darlinghissima: Letters to a Friend.* New York: Random House, 1985.

Ford, Corey. *The Time of Laughter.* Boston: Little, Brown, 1967.

Fowler, Will. *The Second Handshake.* Secaucus, N.J.: Lyle Stuart, 1980.

Frank, Elizabeth. *Louise Bogan: A Portrait.* New York: Alfred A. Knopf, 1985.

Frazier, George. *It's About Time.* Unpublished manuscript, 1967.

Garraty, John A., ed. *Dictionary of American Biography: Supplement Six, 1956–1960.* New York: Scribners, 1980.

Gelb, Arthur. *City Room.* New York: G. P. Putnam's Sons, 2003.

Gibbs, George. *The Gibbs Family of Rhode Island and Some Related Families.* New York: private printing, 1933.

Gibbs, Wolcott. *Bird Life at the Pole.* New York: William Morrow, 1931.

———. *Bed of Neuroses.* New York: Dodd, Mead, 1937.

———. *Season in the Sun and Other Pleasures.* New York: Random House, 1946.

———. *Season in the Sun.* New York: Random House, 1951.

———. *More in Sorrow.* New York: Henry Holt, 1958.

Gill, Brendan. *Here at* The New Yorker. New York: Random House, 1975.

———. *A New York Life: Of Friends and Others.* New York: Poseidon, 1990.

Goodman, Jack, ed. *While You Were Gone: A Report on Wartime Life in the United States.* New York: Simon and Schuster, 1946.

Gottfried, Martin. *Arthur Miller: His Life and Work.* New York: Da Capo Press, 2003.

Grant, Jane. *Ross,* The New Yorker *and Me.* New York: Reynal, 1968.

Griscom, Lloyd C. *Diplomatically Speaking.* New York: Literary Guild of America, 1940.

Groth, Janet. *The Receptionist: An Education at The New Yorker.* Chapel Hill: Algonquin Books of Chapel Hill, 2012.

Groth, Michael. *The Road to New York: The Emigration of Berlin Journalists, 1933–1945.* Munich: Minerva-Fachserie, 1984.

Guth, Dorothy Lobrano, and Martha White, eds. *Letters of E. B. White,* rev. ed. New York: HarperCollins, 2006.

Hall, Roger. *You're Stepping on My Cloak and Dagger.* Annapolis, Md.: Naval Institute Press, 1957.

Harbage, Alfred. *Theatre for Shakespeare.* Toronto: University of Toronto Press, 1955.

Harriman, Margaret Case. *Take Them Up Tenderly: A Collection of Profiles.* New York: Alfred A. Knopf, 1944.

———. *The Vicious Circle: The Story of the Algonquin Round Table.* New York: Rinehart, 1951.

———. *Blessed Are the Debonair.* New York: Rinehart, 1956.

Harrison, Richard J. *Long Island Rail Road Memories: The Making of a Steam Engineer*. New York: Quadrant, 1981.

Hirschfeld, Al. *Show Business Is No Business*. New York: Simon and Schuster, 1951.

Hobson, Laura Z. *Laura Z: The Early Years and Years of Fulfillment*. New York: Donald I. Fine, 1986.

Hodgins, Eric. *Trolley to the Moon: An Autobiography*. New York: Simon and Schuster, 1973.

Holmes, Charles, ed. *The Clocks of Columbus: The Literary Career of James Thurber*. London: Secker and Warburg, 1972.

———. *Thurber: A Collection of Critical Essays*. Englewood Cliffs, N.J.: Prentice-Hall, 1974.

Hoopes, Roy. *Ralph Ingersoll: A Biography*. New York: Atheneum, 1985.

———. *Cain: The Biography of James M. Cain*. New York: Holt, Rinehart and Winston, 1987.

Hough, Henry Beetle, ed. *Vineyard Gazette Reader*. New York: Harcourt, Brace and World, 1967.

Hughes, Glenn. *A History of the American Theatre, 1700–1950*. New York: Samuel French, 1951.

Ingersoll, Ralph. *Point of Departure: An Adventure in Autobiography*. New York: Harcourt, Brace and World, 1961.

Israel, Lee. *Kilgallen*. New York: Dell, 1980.

Jenkins, Jeffrey Eric, ed. *Under the Copper Beech: Conversations with American Theater Critics*. Foundation of the American Theatre Critics Association, 2004.

Johnson, Doris, and Ellen Leventhal, eds. *The Letters of Nunnally Johnson*. New York: Alfred A. Knopf, 1981.

Jordan, Sara M., and Sheila Hibben. *Good Food for Bad Stomachs*. Garden City, N.Y.: Doubleday, 1951.

Kahn, E . J., Jr. *About* The New Yorker *and Me: A Sentimental Journal*. New York: G. P. Putnam's Sons, 1979.

Kaufman, Beatrice, and Joseph Hennessey, eds. *The Letters of Alexander Woollcott*. New York: Viking, 1945.

Kazin, Alfred. *Contemporaries: From the 19th Century to the Present*. Boston: Atlantic Monthly Press, 1982.

Kernan, Alvin B., ed. *The Modern American Theater: A Collection of Critical Essays*. Englewood Cliffs, N.J.: Prentice-Hall, 1967.

Kinney, Harrison. *James Thurber: His Life and Times*. New York: Henry Holt, 1995.

Kinney, Harrison, and Rosemary Thurber, eds. *The Thurber Letters*. New York: Simon and Schuster, 2002.

Kluger, Richard. *The Paper: The Life and Death of the* New York Herald Tribune. New York: Alfred A. Knopf, 1986.

Kramer, Dale. *Ross and* The New Yorker. Garden City, N.Y.: Doubleday, 1951.

Kriendler, Peter, with H. Paul. Jeffers. *"21": Every Day Was New Year's Eve: Memoirs of a Saloon Keeper.* Boulder, Colo.: Taylor, 1999.

Kronenberger, Louis. *No Whippings, No Gold Watches: The Story of a Writer and His Job.* Boston: Atlantic Monthly Press, 1970.

Kunkel, Thomas. *Genius in Disguise: Harold Ross of* The New Yorker. New York: Random House, 1995.

———. *Man in Profile: Joseph Mitchell of* The New Yorker. New York: Random House, 2015.

Kunkel, Thomas, ed. *Letters from the Editor:* The New Yorker's *Harold Ross.* New York: Modern Library, 2000.

Lancaster, Marie-Jaqueline, ed. *Brian Howard: Portrait of a Failure.* London: Anthony Blond, 1968.

Lant, Antonia, with Ingrid Periz, eds. *Red Velvet Seat: Women's Writing on the First Fifty Years of Cinema.* London and New York: Verso, 2006.

Lawrenson, Helen. *Stranger at the Party.* New York: Random House, 1974.

Layman, Richard, and Julie M. Rivett, eds. *Selected Letters of Dashiell Hammett, 1921–1960.* Washington, D.C.: Counterpoint, 2001.

Lee, Judith Yaross. *Defining* New Yorker *Humor.* Jackson: University Press of Mississippi, 2000.

Lerner, Michael. *Dry Manhattan: Prohibition in New York City.* Cambridge, Mass.: Harvard University Press, 2007.

Lester, Charles W., ed. *Williams 1914: Ten Year Book.* Williamstown, Mass.: Williams College, 1924.

Liebling, A. J. *The Most of A. J. Liebling.* New York: Simon and Schuster, 1963.

Limmer, Ruth, ed. *What the Woman Lived: Selected Letters of Louise Bogan, 1920–1970.* New York: Harcourt Brace Jovanovich, 1973.

MacShane, Frank. *The Life of John O'Hara.* New York: E. P. Dutton, 1980.

MacShane, Frank, ed. *Selected Letters of Raymond Chandler.* New York: Columbia University Press, 1981.

McCarthy, Joe, ed. *Fred Allen's Letters.* Garden City, N.Y.: Doubleday, 1965.

McNulty, John. *The World of John McNulty.* Garden City, N.Y.: Doubleday, 1957.

Maloney, Russell. *It's Still Maloney, or Ten Years in the Big City.* New York: Dial, 1945.

Maney, Richard. *Fanfare: Confessions of a Press Agent.* New York: Harper and Brothers, 1957.

Manfull, Helen. *Additional Dialogue: Letters of Dalton Trumbo, 1942–1962.* New York: M. Evans, 1972.

Manley, Sean. *Long Island Discovery: An Adventure into the History, Manners, and Mores of America's Front Porch.* Garden City, N.Y.: Doubleday, 1966.

Martin, Jay. *Nathanael West: The Art of His Life.* New York: Farrar, Straus and Giroux, 1970.

Marx, Harpo. *Harpo Speaks!*. New York: Bernard Geis, 1961.

Maxwell, William. *The Outermost Dream: Literary Sketches*. New York: Alfred A. Knopf, 1989.

Mayes, Herbert R. *The Magazine Maze: A Prejudiced Perspective*. Garden City, N.Y.: Doubleday, 1980.

Meade, Marion. *Bobbed Hair and Bathtub Gin: Writers Running Wild in the Twenties*. New York: Nan A. Talese–Doubleday, 2004.

———. *Lonelyhearts: The Screwball World of Nathanael West and Eileen McKenney*. Boston: Houghton Mifflin, 2010.

Meredith, Burgess. *So Far, So Good: A Memoir*. Boston: Little, Brown, 1994.

Midgley, Leslie. *How Many Words Do You Want? An Insider's Story of Print and Television Journalism*. New York: Birch Lane–Carol Publishing Group, 1989.

Mix, Katherine Lyon. *Max and the Americans*. Brattleboro, Vt.: Stephen Greene, 1974.

Mom, Gijs. *The Electric Vehicle: Technology and Expectations in the Automobile Age*. Baltimore, Md.: Johns Hopkins University Press, 2004.

Mordden, Ethan. *The Guest List: How Manhattan Defined American Sophistication—From the Algonquin Round Table to Truman Capote's Ball*. New York: St. Martin's, 2010.

Morehouse, Ward. *Forty-Five Minutes Past Eight*. New York: Dial Press, 1939.

Murphy, John J., Françoise Palleau-Papin, and Robert Thacker, eds. *Willa Cather: A Writer's Worlds*. Lincoln: University of Nebraska Press, 2010.

Murray, William. *Janet, My Mother, and Me: A Memoir of Growing Up with Janet Flanner and Natalia Danesi Murray*. New York: Simon and Schuster, 2000.

Nathan, George Jean. *The Theatre Book of the Year*. New York: Alfred A. Knopf, 1945, 1951.

Newton, Esther. *Cherry Grove, Fire Island: Sixty Years in America's First Gay and Lesbian Town*. Boston: Beacon Press, 1993.

Nizer, Louis. *The Jury Returns*. Garden City, N.Y.: Doubleday, 1966.

O'Hara, John. *Appointment in Samarra*. 1934; reprint New York: Penguin, 2013.

———. *Pipe Night*. New York: Duell, Sloan and Pearce, 1945.

———. *Sweet and Sour*. New York: Random House, 1954.

———. *Five Plays*. New York: Random House, 1961.

———. *My Turn*. New York: Random House, 1966.

Page, Tim. *Dawn Powell: A Biography*. New York: Henry Holt, 1998.

Page, Tim, ed. *The Diaries of Dawn Powell, 1931–1965*. South Royalton, Vt.: Steerforth, 1995.

———, ed. *Selected Letters of Dawn Powell, 1913–1965*. New York: Henry Holt, 1999.

Parker, Douglas M. *Ogden Nash: The Life and Work of America's Laureate of Light Verse*. Chicago: Ivan R. Dee, 2005.

Parton, Margaret. *Journey Through a Lighted Room*. New York: Viking, 1973.

Pemberton, Sally. *Portrait of Murdock Pemberton*. Minneapolis: Picture Book Press, 2011.

Peretti, Burton W. *Nightclub City: Politics and Amusement in Manhattan*. Philadelphia: University of Pennsylvania Press, 2007.

Plimpton, George. *Truman Capote: In Which Various Friends, Enemies, Acquaintances, and Detractors Recall His Turbulent Career*. New York: Nan A. Talese–Doubleday, 1997.

Price, George. *Who's In Charge Here?*. New York: Farrar and Rinehart, 1943.

Root, Robert L., Jr., ed. *Critical Essays on E. B. White*. New York: G. K. Hall, 1994.

Rosen, Michael J. *Collecting Himself: James Thurber on Writing and Writers, Humor and Himself*. New York: Harper and Row, 1989.

Rosmond, Babette. *Robert Benchley: His Life and Good Times*. Garden City, N.Y.: Doubleday, 1970.

Ross, Lillian. *Here But Not Here: My Life With William Shawn and* The New Yorker. Washington, D.C.: Counterpoint, 2001.

Rovere, Richard. *Arrivals and Departures: A Journalist's Memoir*. New York: Macmillan, 1976.

Russell, Isabel. *Katharine and E. B. White: An Affectionate Memoir*. New York: W. W. Norton, 1990.

Scheaffer, Louis. *Reminiscences of Marc Connelly*, oral history conducted October 15, 1979, and November 9, 1979, Columbia University.

Schickel, Richard. *Elia Kazan: A Biography*. New York: HarperCollins, 2005.

Schulian, John, ed. *The John Lardner Reader: A Press Box Legend's Classic Sportswriting*. Lincoln: University of Nebraska Press, 2010.

The Seventh New York Album. New York: Random House, 1935.

Shaw, Irwin. *The Assassin: A Play in Three Acts*. New York: Random House, 1946.

Sheldon, Sidney. *The Other Side of Me*. New York: HarperCollins, 2005.

Sillman, Leonard. *Here Lies Leonard Sillman, Straightened Out at Last: An Autobiography*. New York: Citadel, 1959.

Silverman, Herman. *Michener and Me: A Memoir*. Philadelphia: Running Press, 1999.

Sims, Michael. *The Story of Charlotte's Web: E. B. White's Eccentric Life in Nature and the Birth of an American Classic*. New York: Walker, 2011.

Sinclair, Gordon. *Will the Real Gordon Sinclair Please Sit Down*. Toronto: McClelland and Stewart, 1975.

Slawenski, Kenneth. *J. D. Salinger: A Life*. New York: Random House, 2011.

Smith, H. Allen. *To Hell in a Handbasket: The Education of a Humorist*. Garden City, N.Y.: Doubleday, 1962.

———. *The Life and Legend of Gene Fowler*. New York: William Morrow, 1977.

Sobel, Bernard. *Broadway Heartbeat: Memoirs of a Press Agent*. New York: Hermitage House, 1953.

Sokolov, Raymond. *Wayward Reporter: The Life of A. J. Liebling*. New York: Harper and Row, 1980.

Spinzia, Raymond E., and Judith A. Spinzia. *Long Island's Prominent North Shore Families: Their Estates and Country Homes*. VirtualBookworm.com, 2006.

Steig, William. *The Lonely Ones*. New York: Duell, Sloan and Pearce, 1942.

Steinman, Michael, ed. *The Element of Lavishness: Letters of Sylvia Townsend Warner and William Maxwell, 1938–1978*. Washington, D.C.: Counterpoint, 1994.

Stevens, George. *Speak for Yourself, John. The Life of John Mason Brown, with Some of His Letters and Many Opinions*. New York: Viking, 1974.

Sullivan, Frank. *Reminiscences of Frank Sullivan*. Oral history conducted by James Gaines, July 21, 1974, Columbia University.

Swanberg, W. A. *Luce and His Empire*. New York: Charles Scribner's Sons, 1972.

Tebbel, John, and Mary Ellen Zuckerman. *The Magazine in America, 1741–1990*. New York: Oxford University Press, 1991.

Thurber, James. *The Seal in the Bedroom and Other Predicaments*. New York: Harper and Row, 1932.

———. *My Life and Hard Times*. New York: Harper and Brothers, 1933.

———. *The 13 Clocks*. New York: Simon and Schuster, 1950.

———. *The Years with Ross*. Boston: Little, Brown, 1959.

Traynor, Carol A., and Robert B. Mackay, eds. *Long Island Country Houses and Their Architects, 1860–1940*. New York: W. W. Norton, 1997.

Walker, Danton. *Danton's Inferno: The Story of a Columnist and How He Grew*. New York: Hastings House, 1955.

Walker, Stanley. *City Editor*. New York: Frederick Stokes, 1934.

Wallis-Tayler, A. J. *Motor Vehicles for Business Purposes*. London: Crosby Lockwood and Son, 1905.

Waugh, Alec. *Bangkok: The Story of a City*. Boston: Little, Brown, 1971.

———. *The Fatal Gift*. New York: Farrar, Straus Giroux, 1973.

———. *A Year to Remember: A Reminiscence of 1931*. London: W. H. Allen, 1975.

———. *The Best Wine Last: An Autobiography Through the Years 1932–1969*. London: W. H. Allen, 1978.

Weales, Gerard. *American Drama Since World War II*. New York: Harcourt, Brace and World, 1962.

Wechsberg, Joseph. *The First Time Around: Some Irreverent Recollections*. Boston: Little, Brown, 1970.

Weidman, Jerome. *My Father Sits in the Dark, and Other Selected Stories*. New York: Random House, 1961.

———. *Praying for Rain*. New York: Harper and Row, 1986.

Wenzel, Paul, and Maurice Krakow. *American Country Houses of To-Day*. New York: Architectural Book Company, 1915.

Whitaker, Jan. *Tea at the Blue Lantern Inn: A Social History of the Tea Room Craze in America*. New York: St. Martin's, 2002.

White, E. B. *One Man's Meat*. New York: Harper and Brothers, 1942.

————. *The Second Tree from the Corner*. New York: Harper and Brothers, 1954.

————. *Letters of E. B. White*. Edited by Dorothy Guth. Revised and updated by Martha White. New York: HarperCollins, 2006.

White, E. B., and James Thurber. *Is Sex Necessary? or Why You Feel the Way You Do*. New York: Harper and Brothers, 1929, 1950.

White, E. B., and Katharine White, eds. *A Subtreasury of American Humor*. New York: Coward-McCann, 1941.

Wilkinson, Alec. *A Young Man's Friendship with William Maxwell*. Boston: Houghton Mifflin, 2002.

Wilner, Isaiah. *The Man Time Forgot: A Tale of Genius, Betrayal, and the Creation of* Time *Magazine*. New York: HarperCollins, 2006.

Wilson, Earl. *I Am Gazing Into My 8-Ball*. Garden City, N.Y.: Doubleday, Doran, 1945.

Wilson, Edmund. *The Sixties: The Last Journal, 1960–1972*. Edited by Lewis Dabney. New York: Farrar Straus and Giroux, 1993.

Wodehouse, P. G. *America, I Like You*. New York: Simon and Schuster, 1956.

Wodehouse, P.G., and Scott Meredith, eds. *The Best of Modern Humor*. New York: Medill McBride, 1951.

Woods, Eugene J., ed. *I Wish I'd Written That: Selections Chosen by Favorite American Authors*. New York: Whittlesey, 1946.

Yagoda, Ben. *About Town: The New Yorker and the World It Made*. New York: Scribner, 2000.

Zinsser, William. *Writing About Your Life: A Journey into the Past*. New York: Marlowe, 2004.

CREDITS

IMAGE CREDITS

1. Hilde Hubbuck, by permission of Tony Gibbs and Susan Ward Roncalli.
2. Courtesy of the Carl A. Kroch Library, Cornell University; by permission of White LLC, Rosemary Thurber and Sara Sauers.
3. © Nickolas Muray Photo Archives; courtesy of Carl A. Kroch Library, Cornell University; by permission of Martha White and Roger Angell.
4. © Pach Brothers / Corbis.
5. Photographer unknown, courtesy of Allen Shawn.
6. Consuelo Kanaga, courtesy of Brookie Maxwell.
7. Courtesy of Elmira College.
8. Courtesy of Vassar College; by permission of Patricia Arno.
9. Courtesy of the Sophia Smith Collection, Smith College.
10. Courtesy of Christina Carver Pratt.
11. Courtesy of Amelia Hard.
12. © Fabian Bachrach, courtesy of Williams College.
13. Courtesy of Hamilton College.
14. Photograph of John O'Hara reproduced from Volume I of two scrapbooks assembled by Sister O'Hara for reviews of *From the Terrace,* 1958. From the John O'Hara Study, Eberly Family Special Collections Library, Pennsylvania State University Libraries.
15. Paramount Pictures, courtesy of Nat Benchley.
16. From the collection of the Tee and Charles Addams Foundation.
17. Anita Carr, courtesy of Sarah Herndon.
18. With permission of the Peter Arno estate.

19. The Granger Collection, New York.
20. Courtesy of Penelope Lord.
21. Ray Shorr for Mademoiselle © Condé Nast, 1952, © Condé Nast Publications, Inc., (1980); courtesy of Dorothy Lobrano Guth.
22. From the collection of the Tee and Charles Addams Foundation.
23. Valentine Sherry; courtesy of Bryn Mawr College; by permission of Tony Gibbs and Susan Ward Roncalli.

TEXT CREDITS

Credit is gratefully acknowledged for permission to reprint the following works:

"A Christmas Greeting to The New Yorkers" by Phyllis McGinley, courtesy of Patsy Blake.

All content from *The New Yorker* © Condé Nast.

All material by Wolcott Gibbs copyright 2015 by the estate of Wolcott Gibbs.

All works by E. B. White copyright by E. B. White. Used by permission. All rights reserved. Courtesy of White Literary LLC.

Excerpts from *Letters of E. B. White, Revised Edition,* originally edited by Dorothy Lobrano Guth and revised and updated by Martha White © 2006 by E. B. White, by permission of HarperCollins Publishers.

Excerpts from *Onward and Upward: A Biography of Katharine S. White,* copyright © 1987 by Linda H. Davis, by permission of HarperCollins Publishers.

The quotes on pages 186, 260, 261, and 278 from "Once More to the Lake," "Clear Days," "The Wave of the Future," "Intimations," "Cold Weather," "First World War," "Control," and "Compost," respectively, in *One Man's Meat,* text copyright © 1941 by E. B. White. Copyright renewed. Reprinted by permission of Tilbury House Publishers, Thomaston, Maine.

Correspondence from and work by James Thurber reprinted by arrangement with Rosemary A. Thurber and the Barbara Hogenson Agency, Inc. All rights reserved.

Excerpts from "University Days" by James Thurber from *My Life and Hard Times,* copyright © 1933.

Excerpts from "A Box to Hide In" by James Thurber from *The Middle-Aged Man on the Flying Trapeze,* copyright © 1935.

Excerpts from "What Do You Mean It 'Was' Brillig?" by James Thurber from *My World—and Welcome to It,* copyright © 1942.

Excerpts from "The Cane in the Corridor" by James Thurber from *The Thurber Carnival,* copyright © 1945.

Excerpts from "Gentleman From Indiana" by James Thurber from *The Thurber Album,* copyright © 1952.

Excerpts from "The First Time I Saw Paris" by James Thurber from *Alarms and Diversions,* copyright © 1957.

INDEX

INDEX

INDEX